LIBRARY OF NEW TESTAMENT STUDIES

665

Formerly Journal for the Study of the New Testament Supplement Series

Editor
Chris Keith

Editorial Board
Dale C. Allison, Lynn H. Cohick, R. Alan Culpepper, Craig A. Evans,
Jennifer Eyl, Robert Fowler, Simon J. Gathercole, Juan Hernández Jr., John S.
Kloppenborg, Michael Labahn, Matthew V. Novenson, Love L. Sechrest, Robert
Wall, Catrin H. Williams, Brittany E. Wilson

THE PAULINE BOOK AND THE DILEMMA OF EPHESIANS

Benjamin J. Petroelje

t&tclark
LONDON · NEW YORK · OXFORD · NEW DELHI · SYDNEY

T&T CLARK

Bloomsbury Publishing Plc

50 Bedford Square, London, WC1B 3DP, UK
1385 Broadway, New York, NY 10018, USA
29 Earlsfort Terrace, Dublin 2, Ireland

BLOOMSBURY, T&T CLARK and the T&T Clark logo
are trademarks of Bloomsbury Publishing Plc

First published in Great Britain 2023
Paperback edition published 2024

Copyright © Benjamin J. Petroelje, 2023, 2024

Benjamin J. Petroelje has asserted his right under the Copyright, Designs and Patents Act, 1988, to be identified as Author of this work.

For legal purposes the Acknowledgments on p. xiii constitute an extension of this copyright page.

All rights reserved. No part of this publication may be reproduced or transmitted in any form or by any means, electronic or mechanical, including photocopying, recording, or any information storage or retrieval system, without prior permission in writing from the publishers.

Bloomsbury Publishing Plc does not have any control over, or responsibility for, any third-party websites referred to or in this book. All internet addresses given in this book were correct at the time of going to press. The author and publisher regret any inconvenience caused if addresses have changed or sites have ceased to exist, but can accept no responsibility for any such changes.

A catalogue record for this book is available from the British Library.

Library of Congress Cataloging-in-Publication Data:

Names: Petroelje, Benjamin J., author.
Title: The Pauline book and the dilemma of Ephesians / Benjamin J. Petroelje.
Description: London ; New York : T&T Clark, 2022. | Series: The library of New Testament studies, 2513-8790 ; 665 | Includes bibliographical references and index. | Summary: "This book scrutinizes the Ephesians-as-Pauline development thesis of modern scholarship, arguing instead that Ephesians is well-positioned to function as the substance of the corpus Paulinum"-- Provided by publisher.
Identifiers: LCCN 2022000362 (print) | LCCN 2022000363 (ebook)
| ISBN 9780567703729 (hardback) | ISBN 9780567703750 (paperback)
| ISBN 9780567703736 (pdf) | ISBN 9780567703767 (epub)
Subjects: LCSH: Bible. Ephesians--Criticism, interpretation, etc.
Classification: LCC BS2695.52 .P48 2022 (print) | LCC BS2695.52 (ebook)
| DDC 227/.506--dc23/eng/20220317
LC record available at https://lccn.loc.gov/2022000362
LC ebook record available at https://lccn.loc.gov/2022000363

ISBN:	HB:	978-0-5677-0372-9
	PB:	978-0-5677-0375-0
	ePDF:	978-0-5677-0373-6
	ePUB:	978-0-5677-0376-7

Series: Library of New Testament Studies, volume 665
ISSN 2513-8790

Typeset by: Trans.form.ed SAS

To find out more about our authors and books visit www.bloomsbury.com and sign up for our newsletters.

For Amy

The problem of Ephesians is inextricably intertwined with that of the Pauline corpus;
it cannot be dealt with apart from it.
—Edgar J. Goodspeed, *The Meaning of Ephesians*

Ephesians [is] that epistle of the apostle which stands in the middle in concepts
as well as order. Now I say middle not because it comes after the first epistles
and is longer than the final ones, but in the sense that the heart of an animal is
in its mid-section, so that you might understand from this the magnitude of the
difficulties and the profundity of the questions it contains.
—Jerome/Origen, *The Commentaries of Origen and Jerome
on St. Paul's Epistle to the Ephesians*

CONTENTS

List of Tables	xi
Acknowledgments	xiii
Abbreviations	xv

INTRODUCTION	1
The Pauline Book	1
The Dilemma of Ephesians	2
Outline and Proposal	4
Methodology and Approach	6
Ephesians, Authorship, and Paul	8

Part 1
READING PAUL AND EPHESIANS IN MODERN CRITICISM

Chapter 1

DISMEMBERING PAUL	17
Restoring the 'Natural Order'	18
F. C. Baur and the Revolution in the Study of Paul	24
The Genres of the Revolution	31
Putting the Revolution to Use: Paul and 'Paul'	35
Conclusion	42

Chapter 2

DISPLACING EPHESIANS	44
The Enigma of the Consensus	45
The Quest for the Historical Ephesians	47
The Parting of the Ways	56
The Quest's Fragility and Failure	63
An Alternative Not Followed	67
Conclusion	71

Part 2
READING PAUL AND EPHESIANS IN LATE ANTIQUITY

Chapter 3
ASSEMBLING PAUL   75
   Reading Ancient Corpora   76
   Reading Paul in Late-Antique Editions   82
   When Paul Was a Book   93
   Conclusion   102

Chapter 4
PLACING EPHESIANS   104
   Textual Origins and Ephesians   104
   Ephesians in Late-Antique Editions of Paul   107
   Ephesians in Late-Antique Commentaries on Paul   113
   Conclusion   130

Part 3
READING EPHESIANS AMONG THE PAULINES

Chapter 5
IMAGING PAUL IN EPHESIANS   135
   Paul, the Apostle of the Church?   136
   The Image of Paul in Ephesians:
      Reading Ephesians 3.1–13 among the Paulines   138
   Conclusion   161

CONCLUSION   163

Bibliography   172
Index of References   198
Index of Authors   207

TABLES

Table 1
The Chronological Rearrangement of Ancient Letter Collections   22

Table 2
Ἀνακεφαλαίωσις τῶν Ἀναγνώσεων [PG 85:716b–720b]   85

Table 3a
Ἀνακεφαλαίωσις Θείων Μαρτυριῶν (SHORT LIST) [PG 85:720d–724c]   85

Table 3b
Ἀνακεφαλαίωσις Θείων Μαρτυριῶν (LONG LIST) [PG 85:725d–745d]   86

Table 4
Priscillian's Canon 15   91

Table 5
Priscillian's Use of Pauline *Testimonia* in his Canons   109

Table 6
Number of *Testimonia* that Reach Certain Citation Thresholds
in the Canons   110

ACKNOWLEDGMENTS

The long process of which this book is the culmination calls to mind my teachers, and I hope it is not poor form to suggest that I have had the best. I first met the Greek text of Paul in the classroom of Bill Heth at Taylor University. Unsurprisingly, the text was Ephesians, and I was hooked. Much has changed since then, but the quality of my teachers has not. For a semester in the Greek of Romans that more or less launched this path for me, I have David Seemuth to thank. At Regent College, where do I stop?—Hans Boersma, Mariam Kamell, Don Lewis, Phil Long, Iain Provan, Sarah Williams, and Rikk Watts all deserve mention. The School of Divinity (New College) at the University of Edinburgh provided a wonderful research environment, which shaped this book in ways I could not have anticipated when I began. My thanks to Helen Bond, Paul Foster, Timothy Lim, and the late Larry Hurtado for important conversations along the way. This project itself, though, bears in ways large and small the marks of my three most important teachers: Hans Boersma, Iain Provan, and now Matthew Novenson. All three have been looking over my shoulder as I write, and to the degree that this project is compelling, it is largely because I have been given the great gift of learning from them. As a revision of my University of Edinburgh dissertation, pride of place, however, belongs to the last, my exceptional doctoral supervisor Matthew Novenson. Given our mutual appreciation for the work of Nils Dahl, I find it fitting to say to Matt what Jacob Jervell and Wayne Meeks say to Dahl in his Festschrift: 'Your devotion to your students has won their dedication, but you have expected from them no conformity, no academic orthodoxy, but the best work they could do on projects they chose'. For this, I am deeply grateful.

Other conversation partners impacted this project significantly along the way, some directly and others indirectly. I am grateful to John Barclay for a conversation early in the life of this project that ended up shaping it considerably, and to T. J. Lang, who I am never quite sure where his research interests end and mine begin. His consistently prescient bibliographical directions and his interest at every stage was always an encouragement. My colleagues at Edinburgh have been first-rate, and the Novenson cohort a joy to walk through a PhD with: my sincere thanks to J. Thomas Hewitt, Bernardo Cho, Daniel Jackson, Sydney Tooth, Brian Bunnell, Patrick McMurray, Sofanit Abebe, Ryan Collman, and Matthew Sharp. My thanks also to Simeon Burke, Joshua Bruce, Jesse Nickel, Ryan Tafilowski, and Nomi Pritz-Bennett—all friends first, but with whom I also enjoyed countless conversations about our projects. In the final stages, I benefited greatly from the valuable feedback of my dissertation examiners, Larry Hurtado and Francis Watson, as well as from the anonymous reviewer from

Bloomsbury T&T Clark, who generously spared me a number of errors. This project is better, in ways large and small, for their insightful criticisms, and whatever deficiencies remain are, of course, my responsibility alone. My thanks also to Helen Westra, who read the entire work with her keen editorial eye; to Anna Christians, who provided help with the bibliography; and to Chris Keith and the entire team at Bloomsbury T&T Clark (LNTS), specifically Sarah Blake, for all their work in bringing this book to print.

The process toward a PhD, and so the one that resulted in this book, inevitably involves upheaval—not least for our family in two significant moves, first to Vancouver, then to Edinburgh. For our family, though, it has enriched our lives more. The church communities at St. John's Vancouver, Chalmers (Edinburgh), and in the final stages, 14th St. CRC (Holland, MI) have been a gift to us. The best part of it all has been the friendships along the way. To the Miller, DePriest, Chase, Nickel, Tafilowski and Pritz-Bennett crews, you have been our lifelines over the past decade, our families-away-from-family, and thank you seems wildly inadequate. To the family we were away from during this time, both the Petroelje and Larson sides, your love and support have sustained us. To my parents, Rob and Sally Petroelje, it is a woeful understatement to say we could not have done this without you. Thank you is in no way enough. But thank you.

If I said above that the process that led to this book makes me think of my teachers, what is more true is that it makes me think of my family. We moved to Edinburgh a family of three, left a family of five, and now are a family of six. To our four children, you have made life a joy, always putting this project in its place, and pointing the way toward more important things. To my wife, Amy, the same—only a million times over. These have been hard years, but good years. And I could not have done them, nor written this book, with anyone else, which is why I dedicate it to you, with love.

The Commentaries of Origen and Jerome on St. Paul's Epistle to the Ephesians © 2002, Ronald Heine, Oxford University Press, Oxford. Used by permission of Oxford Publishing Limited. All rights reserved.

ABBREVIATIONS

For ancient primary sources and modern secondary literature, I follow the abbreviation system prescribed in *The SBL Handbook of Style: For Biblical Studies and Related Disciplines*, ed. Billie Jean Collins, Bob Buller, and John F. Kutsko, 2nd ed. (Atlanta: SBL, 2014), with modifications to fit Bloomsbury/T&T Clark house style. For sources not listed there, I follow, for Greek and Roman sources, the system of *The Oxford Classical Dictionary*, ed. Simon Hornblower, Antony Spawforth, and Esther Eidinow, 4th ed. (Oxford: Oxford University Press, 2012), and for patristic sources, that of *A Patristic Greek Lexicon*, ed. G. W. H. Lampe (Oxford: Clarendon, 1961).

INTRODUCTION

The Pauline Book

Sometime in the fourth century CE, a Paulinist composed a series of fourteen letters that set Paul, apostle to the gentiles, in an imagined first-century epistolary dialogue with Seneca, famous Roman Stoic and tutor to Nero.[1] In *Ep.* 1, Seneca reports that when a few Paulinists happened to join him in the Roman gardens of Sallust, they took the opportunity together to read something from the 'little book' (*libellus*) of Paul.[2] Seneca apparently found the experience invigorating, for in *Ep.* 3 he writes to Paul of his intention to read the letters to Nero, noting his own modest editorial work in passing: 'I have put the rolls [*volumina*] in order and set them in place by their divisions'. In the context of the fiction, Seneca's reference to Pauline *volumina* is an attempt at verisimilitude—a description of the physical artefact (the roll) on which Paul's letters were sent. Seneca arranges them as he sees fit, and now, as he writes at the close of *Ep.* 3, he awaits Paul's arrival to check his work before showing it to Nero.[3] The reference to Paul's *libellus* in *Ep.* 1, however, is a telling slip, reflecting the material form in which the pseudepigrapher (but not 'Seneca') would have known them. Paul's letters, which in the first century comprise a series of *volumina*, have become by the fourth a *libellus*, a little Pauline book.[4]

---

[1] The critical edition is C. W. Barlow, *Epistolae Senecae ad Paulum et Pauli ad Senecam <Quae Vocantur>* (Rome: American Academy in Rome, 1938), 122–38, with Eng. trans. at 139–49. See also the introduction and translation of Cornelia Römer, 'The Correspondence of Paul and Seneca', in *New Testament Apocrypha*, ed. Wilhelm Schneemelcher, trans. R. McL. Wilson, 2 vols. (Cambridge: James Clarke, 1991–92), 2:46–53. For discussion, see Ilaria L. E. Ramelli, 'The Pseudepigraphical Correspondence Between Seneca and Paul: A Reassessment', in *Paul and Pseudepigraphy*, ed. Stanley E. Porter and Gregory P. Fewster, Pauline Studies 8 (Leiden: Brill, 2013), 319–36, who thinks the core of the correspondence goes back to somewhere between the late first and late third century (334–6). Translations are my own unless noted.

[2] *Libellus* can refer to a single letter (thus Barlow's 'treatise'), but here it almost certainly depicts something more substantial (thus, Römer's 'little book'), given that Seneca goes on immediately to reference the *litteras* it contains. See Ramelli, 'Seneca and Paul', 333. Compare Lewis and Short, s.v. *libellus* II and II.B.6.

[3] *Pace* Barlow, *Epistolae Senecae ad Paulum*, 140–1 (cf. 37–8), Seneca's editorial work is not on his *own* writings but on Paul's. Only Paul's have been mentioned to this point in the correspondence, and after Seneca complains of Paul's absence (*Ep.* 5), Seneca shows Nero Galatians, 1 Corinthians, and 'Achaeans'—presumably the collection he references working on in *Ep.* 3.

[4] On references to Paul's collection as a 'book' (βίβλιον/*liber*) in the fourth/fifth centuries, see my Chapter 3.

The Dilemma of Ephesians

But what does this move, from *volumina* to *liber*, mean for one of the letters within that newly constituted book, namely Ephesians? Or to use the language of our title, what does the Pauline book have to do with the dilemma of Ephesians? In the typical way of conceiving the problem, the answer is nothing at all. The Pauline book (i.e. collection) is elided, eclipsed by focused attention on the individual letters and their own particularity. The dilemma, in other words, is with *Ephesians*—its idiosyncratic vocabulary, style, literary relationships, and theology—and the debate proceeds largely along the standard lines of an analysis of these critical prolegomena. A number of works written between 1925 and 1975 that consider the authorship question, not to mention virtually every modern commentary, do just this, but succeed only in showing that the decision is largely reducible to the individual scholars' tolerance for difference within the corpus—that is, how maximal their Paul is.[5]

How much difference a scholar will tolerate, however, assumes a prior knowledge of where Paul may be found. Since roughly the 1980s, the critically acceptable answer to that question has been the seven so-called undisputed letters—Romans, 1 and 2 Corinthians, Galatians, Philippians, 1 Thessalonians, and Philemon. The modern approach to Paul thus not only reverses the process of collection, it also replaces it with a new seven-letter collection—the 'real Paul'.[6] The dilemma of Ephesians, now, is a dilemma of *this* letter's fit with *this* Paul.

Over 175 years, and progressively from German to American to British scholarship, the consensus on Ephesians has hardened, such that there is no dilemma any longer. The non-Pauline authorship of Ephesians is simply a critical a priori, cemented at the institutional level of our discipline (Society of Biblical Literature) and taken for granted across the wide range of genres that comprise Pauline scholarship today.[7] Even for those who think Paul did write Ephesians, the near-universal assumption is that it reflects a later period of Paul's apostolic career. In other words, it is just axiomatic that Ephesians is development of or away from the 'real Paul' of the seven letters.

It is here, rather than in the authorship question per se, that my interest piques, for it is the ubiquity of this development thesis, *whatever one's view of authorship*, that I find strange, and for three reasons. First, as the great German *Neutestamentler* Adolf Jülicher predicted one hundred years ago, the setting of Ephesians remains an 'unsolved riddle' (*rätselhaft*), with proposed solutions spanning the century

---

[5] See, e.g., Josef Schmid, *Der Epheserbrief des Apostels Paulus: Seine Adresse, Sprache und literarischen Beziehungen* (Freiburg: Herder, 1928); Ernst Percy, *Die Probleme der Kolosser- und Epheserbriefe* (Lund: Gleerup, 1946); C. L. Mitton, *The Epistle to the Ephesians: Its Authorship, Origin, and Purpose* (Oxford: Clarendon, 1951); and A. van Roon, *The Authenticity of Ephesians*, NovTSup 39 (Leiden: Brill, 1974).

[6] For a trenchant critique of the 'real Paul' discourse of modern Pauline studies, see Benjamin L. White, *Remembering Paul: Ancient and Modern Contests Over the Image of the Apostle* (New York: Oxford University Press, 2014), 1–7, 21–7.

[7] See my sections 'Putting the Revolution to Use: Paul and "Paul"', and 'The Parting of the Ways' in Chapters 1 and 2 below.

from Paul (50 CE) to Marcion (150 CE).⁸ This is unsurprising, since Ephesians lacks precisely the sort of hard data by which it might be confidently located—even, in the earliest manuscripts, an address. Yet if, on the one hand, Ephesians floats historically severed from a setting, on the other, it appears connected to nearly every possible setting. As Nils Dahl writes,

> It is possible to adduce more or less relevant parallels to Ephesians from the Qumran texts, from synagogue prayers, from rabbinic exegesis, and Hekaloth mysticism, from Philo, from Middle Platonism and from the Hermetic writings and other sources. The very diversity of the materials makes it impossible to give a precise description of the setting of Ephesians by means of a comparative history of religions approach.⁹

Here one is tempted to go further and suggest that in Ephesians we meet the limits of historical criticism itself, insofar as such interpretation depends on a precise historical setting. How, in other words, if Ephesians appears historically connected both to nothing and to everything, do we know that it is late and developed, either within Paul's lifetime or well after his death? What stands behind this judgment?

The second conundrum has to do with Ephesians and the history of Pauline scholarship. Put directly, the Paulinism that generated the consensus on Ephesians in the nineteenth century is very different from the Paulinism on offer today.¹⁰ If a Lutheran Paulinism helped displace Ephesians on account of its 'Jewishness', then the growing movement to read Paul *within* Judaism requires the reassessment of a letter displaced on those very grounds. This is not to say, of course, that all scholars read Paul within Judaism, but that is all the more to the point. There is no single Paulinism today, only a variety of Pauline portraits, with both similarities and fundamental differences.¹¹ As in Paulinism, so also in Paul—'the Christian Proteus', as one notable Pauline scholar calls him, not without warrant (1 Cor 9.19-23).¹² If such variety exists both in Paul and the study of Paul, then why do such a wide array of scholarly Paulinists, with divergent if not diametrically opposed Pauls, themselves studying a protean figure, nevertheless all agree that Ephesians is late, and therefore developed? What stands behind these judgments?

⁸ Adolf Jülicher, *Einleitung in das Neue Testament*, 7th ed. (Tübingen: Mohr Siebeck, 1931 [1894]), 142. See my sections 'The Quest for the Historical Ephesians' and 'The Quest's Fragility and Failure' in Chapter 2 below.
⁹ Nils A. Dahl, 'The Letter to the Ephesians: Its Fictional and Real Setting', in *Studies in Ephesians: Introductory Questions, Text- & Edition-Critical Issues, Interpretation of Texts and Themes*, ed. David Hellholm, Vemund Blomkvist, and Tord Fornberg, WUNT 131 (Tübingen: Mohr Siebeck, 2000), 456.
¹⁰ For cogent discussion of the term Paulinism, see Robert Morgan, 'The Significance of Paulinism', in *Paul and Paulinism: Essays in Honour of C. K. Barrett*, ed. Morna D. Hooker and Stephen G. Wilson (London: SPCK, 1982), 320-38.
¹¹ The language of Pauline 'portraiture' is that of Margaret M. Mitchell, *The Heavenly Trumpet: John Chrysostom and the Art of Pauline Interpretation* (Louisville: Westminster John Knox, 2002), passim, but especially 381-9.
¹² Wayne A. Meeks, 'Epilogue: The Christian Proteus', in *The Writings of St. Paul: Annotated Text, Reception and Criticism*, ed. W. A. Meeks and J. T. Fitzgerald, Norton Critical Edition (London: Norton, 2007), 689-94.

The third conundrum arises from the position of Ephesians within historical reconstructions of Christian origins—a corollary to the second problem above. As we will see, the specters of Ferdinand Christian Baur's and Ernst Käsemann's accounts of early Christianity loom large here. For both, Ephesians plays a central, transitional role in their historical narratives of decline, whether as the hinge in the descent of the radical gentile Paulinism of early Christianity to the modified Jewish Paulinism of the Catholic synthesis (Baur), or by denuding Paul's own eschatological fervor, characterized by the imminent expectation of the parousia, thus paving the way for the 'settling down' of Paulinism into early catholicism (Käsemann). Over the past few decades, these grand narratives of trajectories through early Christianity have rightly been criticized, but the results they generated endure. It is precisely in this period of major shifts in the study of Paul and early Christianity (the 1980s to the present) that the consensus on Ephesians hardens. The theological and historical scaffolding which held Ephesians in the late first century has come down, but Ephesians remains suspended there as confidently as ever.[13] What accounts for this?

It is the above state of affairs—the solidity of the development thesis despite a scholarly milieu marked by (1) historical ambivalence vis-à-vis setting; (2) theological fragmentation vis-à-vis Paulinism; and (3) historiographical dissolution vis-à-vis Christian origins—that constitutes what I call the enigma of Ephesians in modern research, and the dilemma to which I address myself in this book.[14] This is not a study of the authorship question, at least directly, nor is that my primary interest. Rather, what intrigues me is how to read Ephesians vis-à-vis Paul and the other letters of the collection, whether Paul wrote it or not. Edgar Goodspeed is right, 'It is no solution of Ephesians to say that it is the work of a Paulinist in the eighties'—nor, frankly, of Paul in Rome in the 60s.[15] Why, then, are these settings, and the judgments of development that arise from them, the working assumption of virtually all contemporary Pauline and Ephesians scholarship? Or again, if neither history, nor Paulinism, nor historiography is firstly responsible for dislodging Ephesians, and if scholarly shifts in the above do not relocate it, what *does* displace Ephesians and generate the development thesis? What, in fact, causes the dilemma of Ephesians?

Outline and Proposal

What causes it, I suggest, is how one reads the Pauline book. To show this, I turn back to the first-order evidence that we have for Paul—the letter collection—and ask fundamental questions about how to read it.[16] Applying the seminal insights of Mary

---

[13] For a prescient critique of the overconfidence of many reconstructions of Christian origins, see Samuel Sandmel, *The First Christian Century in Judaism and Christianity: Certainties and Uncertainties* (Oxford: Oxford University Press, 1969), 7–8, and for an emerging alternative, Larry Hurtado, 'Interactive Diversity: A Proposed Model of Christian Origins', *JTS* 64 (2013): 445–62.

[14] The allusion, here and in my title, is to Henry J. Cadbury, 'The Dilemma of Ephesians', *NTS* 5 (1959): 91–102—still a helpful essay on the ambivalence of scholarship's relationship to Ephesians.

[15] Edgar Goodspeed, 'The Place of Ephesians in the First Pauline Collection', *AThR* 12 (1930): 211.

[16] This first-order evidence is, to be sure, a second-stage phenomenon. The individual letters were dispatched and circulated prior to, and independent of, their later presence in the collection. But our primary *access* to those letters, and so to Paul, is now mediated via a subsequently editorialized

Beard and Roy Gibson in classical epistolography for the first time to the study of the *corpus Paulinum*,[17] in Part 1 I demonstrate that the widespread modern turn toward disaggregating and chronologically rearranging Paul's letter collection for the sake of narrating Pauline biography and early Christianity (Chapter 1) has a profound effect on how modern scholars read Ephesians (Chapter 2). For all the real insight that such a hermeneutic affords the reading of Paul, I argue that it fundamentally distorts Ephesians, since Ephesians does not offer the sort of historical and chronological anchors on which such a reading strategy depends. That is to say, the modern consensus on Ephesians is a construct of modern criticism. Development is neither intrinsic to nor an obvious feature of Ephesians, but a function of an implied reading order. A modern chronological way of reading the collection, that is, creates development in Ephesians. And this explains the ubiquity of these judgments in defenders of pseudepigraphy and authenticity alike, for real differences aside, everyone reads the collection this way. It is basic to our modern reading *culture*.

In Part 2, I turn to late antiquity to ask how Paul's late-ancient tradents read his letter collection (Chapter 3), so as to ascertain what impact this has on how a series of fourth- and fifth-century commentators read Ephesians (Chapter 4). For these readers of Paul, the collection as such is central. Beginning in the fourth century, Paul's letters are collectively called a book (βιβλίον/*liber*), which does not efface the integrity of the letters, but which does take hermeneutical priority. This means different things for the various commentators surveyed, but it consistently results in a relatively central place for Ephesians in late-ancient portraits of Paul. A hermeneutic that privileges the collectivity of the letters—what the corpus says in its entirety—finds the most general letter in the collection useful for its purposes. How one reads the Pauline book, in other words, either creates or obviates the dilemma of Ephesians, as my Chapters 2 and 4 will show, and as Edgar Goodspeed's epigraph to this book highlights so summarily.

What, then, if we were to return to the collection as our primary set of comparative data for reading Ephesians (so, in view of the insight of Part 2), but without privileging a late first-century setting or an implied (chronological) order of reading (so, in view of the criticism of Part 1)? This is the task of Part 3, in which I turn to Eph 3.1–13, a text widely judged by modern scholars to evince a developed image of Paul, to test this reading strategy (Chapter 5). After fifty years of being read pervasively alongside Colossians, the Pastorals, and Acts, I argue that a far more redolent set of co-texts for Eph 3.1–13 sits (ironically) in the *Hauptbriefe*. Moreover, far from developed,

---

collection. Every attempt to get at Paul, then, has to reckon with this collection as our primary source for Paul. This is what I mean, here and throughout, when I refer to the collection itself, rather than the letters, as our first-order evidence. It is a statement about the nature of the data and our access to Paul, not a claim about the collection's temporal priority.

[17] The seminal work here is Mary Beard, 'Ciceronian Correspondences: Making a Book Out of Letters', in *Classics in Progress: Essays on Ancient Greece and Rome*, ed. T. P. Wiseman (Oxford: Oxford University Press, 2002), 103–44, followed on by Roy Gibson in 'On the Nature of Ancient Letter Collections', *JRS* 102 (2012): 56–78; and idem, 'Letters into Autobiography: The Generic Mobility of the Ancient Letter Collection', in *Generic Interfaces in Latin Literature: Encounters, Interactions and Transformations*, ed. Theodore D. Papanghelis, Stephen J. Harrison, and Stavros Frangoulidis, Trends in Classics—Supplementary Volumes 20 (Berlin: de Gruyter, 2013), 387–416. See my Chapters 1 and 3 for discussion.

Eph 3.1–13 helps balance one-sided portraits of Paul that arise from a one-sided reading of these letters.[18] Ephesians 3.1–13, that is, holds together tensions between the *Hauptbriefe* themselves, and while undoubtedly general, offers us the 'gist' of Paul's image in these letters.[19]

Methodology and Approach

My methodology is implicit in the large-scale structure of the book, but it is worth being explicit about it here. Try as we may, critical scholarship's quest for a fierce readerly independence, under the guise of a neutral approach to texts, proves an impossible task. As William Johnson argues in *Readers and Reading Culture in the High Roman Empire*, reading cultures—their assumptions, conventions, and practices—are socially constructed; reading is inescapably a sociological phenomenon.[20] Taking this as my starting point, Parts 1 and 2 explore and purposefully juxtapose two such reading cultures—modern and late-antique, specifically how each reads a letter collection.

For the sake of clarity, it will be useful here to detail why I do this, and what I am suggesting (and as importantly what I am not) in structuring the argument this way. To say it plainly, I do not do this because I am concerned, firstly, with how to read a letter collection,[21] nor am I suggesting a return to reading the *arrangement* of Paul's collection as hermeneutically meaningful in itself,[22] nor am I rejecting wholesale modern, historical ways of reading Paul's collection. Each of these is important to say clearly and up front. What follows is not a canonical argument (in the sense of the *theological* priority of the canon), nor a privileging of canonical over historical readings of Paul—something I consider largely a false choice regardless.[23] In Part 1,

---

[18] On this, I agree with the potential of Ephesians noted in Markus Barth, *Ephesians: Introduction, Translation and Commentary*, 2 vols., AB 34-34A (Garden City: Doubleday, 1974), 1:48: 'Ephesians may force extreme Paulinists of all times to revise their prejudices'.

[19] On the language of 'gist', see White, *Remembering Paul*, 176–7 and 181, and the opening of my Chapter 5.

[20] William A. Johnson, *Readers and Reading Culture in the High Roman Empire: A Study of Elite Communities*, Classical Culture and Society (New York: Oxford University Press, 2010), 3–16, and particularly his five propositions on reading at 11–12, drawn from idem, 'Toward a Sociology of Reading in Classical Antiquity', *AJP* 121 (2000): 593–627 (602–3).

[21] This question, posed to Paul's collection, is fascinating in its own right, and worth further study since all Pauline scholars are, in the end, students of a late-antique letter collection. My Chapters 1 and 3 should prove useful here, as they apply the insights of Beard and Gibson to the study of the *corpus Paulinum*. I could not have written these chapters without the impetus of their work and their probing criticisms of the modern transformation of ancient editorial arrangements.

[22] This is central to Beard and Gibson's project, and while I find their readings of the arrangements of the ancient letter collections they study compelling, I am less sanguine that the *corpus Paulinum* has anything substantive to offer in this regard. That said, as we will see in Chapter 3, this did not stop Paul's late-ancient tradents from *making* something of this order. For (very different) recent attempts along these lines, see David Trobisch, *Die Entstehung der Paulusbriefsammlung: Studien zu den Änfangen christlicher Publizistik*, NTOA 10 (Göttingen: Vandenhoeck & Ruprecht, 1989), 84–104; cf. Trobisch, *Paul's Letter Collection: Tracing the Origins* (Minneapolis: Fortress, 1994); and Brevard S. Childs, *The Church's Guide for Reading Paul* (Grand Rapids: Eerdmans, 2008).

[23] Because both the 'historical Paul' and the 'canonical Paul' are editorial constructions grounded in prior images of Paul (White, *Remembering Paul*), modern scholarly discourse has no claim on a neutral, disinterested (i.e. 'historical') vantage point vis-à-vis the collection. Moreover, to urge a

I do not seek to dismiss historical criticism and its interpretive project vis-à-vis the collection—a project which, in principle, is valid and has borne enormous interpretive fruit. When in Chapter 1 I narrate the major shifts in how to read the *corpus Paulinum* attendent in the historicist revolution, I regard this work as largely descriptive of the phenomenon rather than a normative critique of it, even if I do want to trouble along the way any sense that historicism involves a more 'natural' approach to a corpus than other possibilities. My criticism, then, is not of the historical project in principle, but of the utility of this project for Ephesians, and the interpretive effect it has had on this letter.

Put more positively, I structure the argument of this book as I do because my central concern is, in the end, a quite traditional one: the question of whether and how to read Ephesians vis-à-vis Paul and Paul's other letters. I did not begin with an interest in letter collections per se, but in Paul and Ephesians. In the course of research, it became clear that the genesis of the consensus on Ephesians is inextricably bound up with attendant shifts in how to read Paul's letter collection—still more, that it *depends* on these shifts. My turn to study the hermeneutics of how to read a letter collection, then, was a pragmatic response to the problem of Ephesians in modern research on Paul as I saw it.

The turn to *late antiquity*, though, and its way of reading a letter collection, was a conscious choice—a way of trying to deal with Gadamer's hermeneutical insight that all interpretation is historically effected (*Wirkungsgeschichte*).[24] Asking Paul's late-antique readers the same questions I was asking of Paul's modern ones, and allowing them to answer differently, seemed to me the best way to answer the question I was asking about the problem I saw in modern criticism: why is it so obvious to everyone, and to scholars of very different stripes, that Ephesians is development?

The turn to late antiquity in Part 2, then, to say it again, is not reception-historical in the sense that I think late antiquity somehow gets us closer to Paul or to Ephesians, or ought to be privileged. Part 2, and especially Chapter 4, is manifestly not intended to be a catalogue of reception that represents 'better' interpretation of Ephesians than the modern work I detail in Chapter 2. Nor do I consider ancient arrangements of the collection (Chapter 3) superior to their modern counterparts (Chapter 1). The turn to late antiquity, rather, is an attempt to self-consciously appropriate Gadamer's insight about *Wirkungsgeschichte* and Johnson's insight about the social nature of reading, and to apply this to the specific question of the modern consensus on Ephesians. How do we know what we know? Why do we think we know it? It seems to me that these questions are most important precisely when what we think we know seems most obvious.

---

return to the collection (i.e. 'canonical') is itself a *historical* claim rooted in the nature of the available evidence.

[24] Hans-Georg Gadamer, *Truth and Method*, trans. Joel Weinsheimer and Donald G. Marshall, 2nd rev. ed. (New York: Crossroad, 1991), 300–307. My understanding of what *Wirkungsgeschichte* is (and as importantly, is not) in Gadamer is indebted to the discussion in Robert Evans, *Reception History, Tradition, and Biblical Interpretation: Gadamer and Jauss in Current Practice*, LNTS 510 (London: Bloomsbury, 2014), 2–9.

In many respects, then, my Part 3 is quite traditional. I come back to the text of Ephesians, not with a new method, but with a new set of comparative data, which turns out to be an old set—the collection, our first-order evidence for Paul. To Eph 3.1–13 and its Pauline co-texts I put the traditional historical, philological, and literary tools of our discipline. The purpose and aim is to clarify how we ought to read this text vis-à-vis Paul and the other letters. I envision this as the first step toward doing this for Ephesians more broadly, since other texts in Ephesians have similarly borne the brunt of modern ways of reading. My hope in this study is to make Pauline scholars more self-critical about the issues at play in their judgments about Ephesians—that by examining the constructed nature of how we read the Pauline book, we might see how *we* have constructed the dilemma of Ephesians. More still, I hope this work plays some part in deconstructing the present chasm between Pauline and Ephesians scholarship. Success may well be marked by the indices of future works on Paul, if the Ephesians sections therein start to grow, signaling that scholars are beginning to read Ephesians with Paul again, whether they think he wrote it or not.

Ephesians, Authorship, and Paul

This last point is vital to stress: agreement with my basic thesis is possible whatever one's view of authorship. What follows is not a subtle argument for or against Pauline authorship, nor a more sophisticated way of doing an authorship study. To be sure, it would be fruitless to feign neutrality,[25] and insofar as this book successfully shows the fragility of modern judgments about Ephesians, as well as the surprising overlap of Ephesians with the *Hauptbriefe* in particular, I do regard my work as having significant implications for the authorship question. Some readers, then, may understandably feel as if that question haunts these pages, and desire clarity from the beginning with respect to my view on authorship. For reasons deeply tied to the overall rhetoric and shape of my argument, I save fuller discussion of my judgment for the conclusion, where I think it belongs.[26] To signal this in advance, however, for the curious reader, I have been unable to convince myself of both the critical consensus (a Paulinist writing in the 80s/90s CE) *and* the traditional consensus (Paul writing from Rome in the early 60s CE). For reasons internal to the letter, as well as what I regard as the

---

[25] More specifically, it would be fruitless to pretend that my initial impressions of authorship, forged over long engagement with this letter in particular contexts, do not shape my reading of the history of scholarship on the question of Paul and Ephesians that I detail in Chapters 1 and 2. Such impressions form the basis for all academic inquiry—every attempt at gaining knowledge—and are epistemologically basic. In and of themselves, they are neither positive nor negative, and must be chastened by evidence. Their utility, in the end, is proven (or not) by their fruit—whether in this instance, they have led me to insight on the question of Paul and Ephesians, and on the history of the modern study of this question, that other Pauline scholars find persuasive.

[26] See my quotation of Kenneth Dover in Chapter 1 about the 'starting point' of historical inquiry, and what it is for historiography to 'take things in the right order'. By delaying fuller discussion of the letter's setting until the Conclusion, I attempt rhetorically to press home this historiographical point. With respect to a text like Ephesians, this is all the more important. Any suggestion on the letter's setting should come after the interpretive process has run its course, rather than shaping it from the beginning.

basic weakness of the history of secondary arguments for both locations, I tentatively regard 'Ephesians' as Paul's letter to Laodicea mentioned in Col 4.16, written from an unknown imprisonment (2 Cor 6.5; 11.23), likely prior to his Corinthian, Galatian, and Roman correspondence.[27] I will say more about the exegetical potential of this setting in the conclusion. For now, if this setting strikes the reader as speculative, such is the nature of Ephesians scholarship. When it comes to a setting, I suspect a tentative suggestion is as good as we can do, and it enjoys the virtue of being honest about the nature of the available evidence.

It bears repeating, however: whether or not scholars end up agreeing with my conclusion on authorship is of marginal interest to me, for I am not arguing that Paul wrote Ephesians, only that scholars should begin using Ephesians again as a vital source for Paul, whether they think he wrote it or not.[28] It follows, then, that I do not criticize a soft view of pseudonymity (where it exists), in which scholars think Paul did not write Ephesians but nevertheless continue to read it critically and openly alongside the other letters, using it where it offers continuity with, insight into, or potentially a challenge to certain ways of reading the other letters.[29] I do criticize, however, the hard view of pseudonymity that prevails, in practice if not in theory, in Pauline scholarship today. While many scholars may not have settled convictions about Ephesians, they work within a field that does, and one of the rules of that field is not to regard Ephesians, in any sense, as a source for Paul. On this view, as soon as a text is deemed pseudonymous, it is set aside and considered unusable. Any and all differences are highlighted, read as development, and allowed to elide continuity, which only deepens the separation, making it appear increasingly self-evident. This explains the tendency in Pauline scholarship to simply ignore Ephesians, or to transmit now-traditional refrains and judgments about the letter without substantively engaging the text of Ephesians itself. This view of pseudonymity is suspect in its own right, but is particularly so with respect to Ephesians,

---

[27] The identification with Laodiceans is hardly new, although the chronological position may surprise. Informed readers will sense my indebtedness to Douglas Campbell for this provenance (*Framing Paul: An Epistolary Biography* [Grand Rapids: Eerdmans, 2014]), which ultimately goes back, in basic shape at least, to Theodore of Mopsuestia. While I would quibble with some of Campbell's particulars, I find his setting pregnant with exegetical potential, although none of my conclusions in this study depend on it.

[28] Scholars trained in the historical method, rightly concerned to draw a distinction between primary and secondary sources, have long acted as if these are one and the same question, but they are not. There is no reason, in principle, that a text not written by Paul himself, but written in his name within a generation or two of his death (to grant, for the moment, the view of the consensus), could not provide vital access to Paul. The somewhat odd truth is that many Pauline scholars would seem to consider the historical and theological synthesis of a leading (Protestant) Pauline scholar, some 2,000 years removed from the object of study himself—say, e.g., E. P. Sanders's *Paul*—a more useful source for understanding Paul than a text written by a Jewish Paulinist, quite possibly from Paul's circle, within a few decades of his death. In a scholarly milieu rightly attuned to Paul's Jewishness, this is surely a strange irony.

[29] See, rightly, along these lines, Daniel Boyarin, *A Radical Jew: Paul and the Politics of Identity* (Berkley: University of California Press, 1994), 310 n. 25. In practice, this is how both Lloyd Gaston and now Matthew Thiessen use Ephesians (see discussion on p. 63 n. 112 below), as well as the helpful article of Paul Foster, 'The First Contribution to the πίστις Χριστοῦ Debate: A Study of Ephesians 3.12', *JSNT* 85 (2002): 75–96.

since it is difficult to square with a curiously enduring, albeit admittedly minority, strand of scholarship that sees in Ephesians something like the 'quintessence' of Paulinism.[30] Whether one agrees with this judgment or not, it is strange that a text that could even *conceivably* be considered Paul's 'quintessence' (no one has ever said that about 1 Timothy or 2 Thessalonians) could also be reckoned unusable in Pauline scholarship today.

In Chapter 2, I narrate this growing unusability as a story of historical and theological judgments about Ephesians that arises from a distinctly modern way of reading the collection. A word is in order here, however, about two critical issues to which scholars frequently appeal to separate Ephesians from Paul, but which I do not address in the chapters that follow: stylistic differences and Ephesians' relationship to Colossians. To state the question directly, how do matters of critical prolegomena bear on my primary question—whether and how to read Ephesians vis-à-vis Paul and the other letters? To be sure, such questions bear obviously on the *authorship* question, but their utility for my question is less immediately obvious. This last sentence may surprise, given that we tend to think about what sources we use as strictly based on decisions about authorship, and given that authorship decisions tend to be reduced to compiling verdicts on various aspects of critical prolegomena. In principle, however, Ephesians could be the most stylistically variant letter in the collection *and* dependent on Colossians, and still be judged a vital source for Paul. The latter judgment can only result from comparative exegesis.

That said, the critical questions are not nearly so settled as scholars like to imagine. The confidence of judgments about style and dependence is frequently overstated, and the conclusions drawn from these judgments misplaced.[31] That Ephesians is stylistically different than Galatians is obvious; the significance of that difference is not. And it is telling that in at least one major stylometric study of Paul's corpus, Ephesians sits closer to the norm than both 1 Corinthians and Philemon, and 2 Timothy sits closer still.[32] Stylometry does not support, at least not yet, a hard divide between Ephesians and the seven allegedly authentic letters. A similar ambivalence obtains on the question of the relationship of Ephesians and Colossians. That there is a close relationship between Ephesians and Colossians is, again, self-evident; the nature, direction, and significance of that relationship is not.

---

[30] I discuss this strand further in Chapter 2 in the section titled, 'Excursus: The [Alternative] Quest in British Scholarship: From Lightfoot to Bruce.'

[31] Campbell, *Framing Paul*, has an excellent discussion of these matters (style: 286–92, 334–6; dependence: 283–6, 321–6) in both Colossians and Ephesians.

[32] Anthony Kenny, *A Stylometric Study of the New Testament* (Oxford: Clarendon, 1986), 80–100 (here 98). Nor does Kenneth J. Neumann, *The Authenticity of the Pauline Epistles in the Light of Stylostatistical Analysis*, SBLDS 120 (Atlanta: Scholars Press, 1990) find the differences in Ephesians meaningful for authorship. David L. Mealand, 'Positional Stylometry Reassessed: Testing a Seven Epistle Theory of Pauline Authorship', *NTS* 35 (1989): 266–86; idem, 'The Extent of the Pauline Corpus: A Multivariate Approach', *JSNT* 59 (1995): 61–92; and Gerard Ledger, 'An Exploration of Differences in the Pauline Epistles Using Multivariate Statistical Analysis', *Literary and Linguistic Computing* 10 (1995): 85–97 are less sanguine, and find the differences more significant, although largely only in the material of Eph 1–3.

The history of the study of this question, along with its potential solutions, is well-told elsewhere and need not detain us here.[33] While a few scholars have argued in major synoptic studies that the relationship is literary/textual (i.e. one text consciously adapting the other) and that Colossians enjoys priority,[34] others have argued for Ephesians' priority,[35] while others have suggested mutual dependence.[36] Still others, more recently, have questioned whether the relationship is, properly speaking, literary at all: in a well-known 1997 article, Ernest Best opts for two Paulinists making independent use of Pauline and traditional material to address new situations in Paul's name,[37] while in his 2014 *Framing Paul* Douglas Campbell argues that the dynamics of oral/aural composition and the exigencies of the letters' compositional setting help explain the unique relationship of two texts authored by Paul himself.[38] The array of options is dizzying, and the matter clearly less decided than scholars like to think.

Turning to the texts themselves, the only extensive verbal parallels occur at the letters' beginning and end (Eph 1.1-2//Col 1.1-2; Eph 6.21-22//Col 4.7-8), but the direction of alleged dependence here is far from obvious. Which is more likely: Eph 6.21 muddying the clear grammatical water of Col 4.7, or Col 4.7 clarifying the muddy and redundant water of Eph 6.21?[39] Or perhaps the parallel simply reflects the final stage of editing two letters intended to be dispatched and read together (Col 4.16)—a way of weaving them into a 'single extended epistolary event'.[40] Or perhaps this is just a cunning pseudepigrapher, exploiting a hole in the corpus to insert his clever fiction at just this point.[41] What eludes us here is not just certainty, but even probability.

---

[33] George H. van Kooten, *Cosmic Christology in Paul and the Pauline School: Colossians and Ephesians in the Context of Graeco-Roman Cosmology, with a New Synopsis of the Greek Texts*, WUNT 2/171 (Tübingen: Mohr Siebeck, 2003), 215-22; Ernest Best, 'Who Used Whom? The Relationship of Ephesians and Colossians', NTS 43 (1997): 72-4.

[34] Edgar J. Goodspeed, *The Meaning of Ephesians* (Chicago: University of Chicago Press, 1933), 82-165; Mitton, *Epistle to the Ephesians*, 279-315; and van Kooten, *Cosmic Christology*, 239-90.

[35] E. T. Mayerhoff, *Der Brief an die Kolosser, mit vornehmlicher Berücksichtigung der drei Pastoralbriefe* (Berlin: Schultze, 1838); John Coutts, 'The Relationship of Ephesians and Colossians', NTS 4 (1958): 201-207.

[36] Heinrich J. Holtzmann, *Kritik der Epheser- und Kolosserbriefe: auf Grund einer Analyse ihres Verwandschaftsverhältnisses* (Leipzig: Wilhelm Engelmann, 1872), 35-87; W. Munro, 'Col.iii.18-iv.1 and Eph.v.21-vi.9: Evidence of a Late Literary Stratum?', NTS 18 (1972): 434-47.

[37] Best, 'Who Used Whom', 72-96 (directly at 93-4, 96).

[38] Campbell, *Framing Paul*, 321-5.

[39] Compare the two texts below, with the words unique to both underlined. See discussion in Best, 'Who Used Whom', 77-9.

> Eph 6.21-22: "Ἵνα δὲ εἰδῆτε καὶ ὑμεῖς τὰ κατ' ἐμέ, τί πράσσω, πάντα γνωρίσει ὑμῖν Τύχικος ὁ ἀγαπητὸς ἀδελφὸς καὶ πιστὸς διάκονος ἐν κυρίῳ, ὃν ἔπεμψα πρὸς ὑμᾶς εἰς αὐτὸ τοῦτο, ἵνα γνῶτε τὰ περὶ ἡμῶν καὶ παρακαλέσῃ τὰς καρδίας ὑμῶν.

> Col 4.7-8: Τὰ κατ' ἐμὲ πάντα γνωρίσει ὑμῖν Τύχικος ὁ ἀγαπητὸς ἀδελφὸς καὶ πιστὸς διάκονος καὶ σύνδουλος ἐν κυρίῳ, ὃν ἔπεμψα πρὸς ὑμᾶς εἰς αὐτὸ τοῦτο, ἵνα γνῶτε τὰ περὶ ἡμῶν καὶ παρακαλέσῃ τὰς καρδίας ὑμῶν.

[40] Campbell, *Framing Paul*, 319.

[41] van Kooten, *Cosmic Christology*, 193-203.

Widening the frame, between the letters' formally parallel opening and closing lies a macrostructure that also runs largely parallel, as George van Kooten perceptively recognizes.[42] This, of course, raises the obvious question: which depends on which? Is Colossians prior, and Ephesians nothing short of a 'full-scale critical commentary' on Colossians, taking over its structure in order to revise its theology in a more Pauline direction (van Kooten)?[43] Or is Ephesians prior, and Colossians a hastily written abridgment of that more thoughtful and drawn-out letter, written in the face of the arrival (via Onesimus) of word of the threatening 'Colossian philosophy', eliciting a rather urgent epistolary response, which Paul provides from a nearby imprisonment (Campbell)?[44] Both lead to sophisticated ways of reading Ephesians, but they arise from diametrically opposed visions of the letters' relationship to one another. Which one a reader finds persuasive, it seems to me, cannot be decided by appeals to literary dependence, but only to interpretation: which one makes better sense of the texts themselves? That decision may well lie in the eye of the beholder.

The trouble goes deeper, however, for what is certainly true of the letters' relationship at the macro-level—largely parallel structures that must be in some relationship of dependence—is virtually impossible to show at the micro-level. Over nineteen painstaking pages, in which he reviews all the passages Leslie Mitton used to argue for Ephesian dependence, Best shows how difficult it is to be confident of, much less prove, the direction in which alleged verbal dependence runs.[45] To take just one of many possible examples, is Eph 1.7 (Ἐν ᾧ ἔχομεν τὴν ἀπολύτρωσιν διὰ τοῦ αἵματος αὐτοῦ, τὴν ἄφεσιν τῶν παραπτωμάτων) a conflation of Col 1.14 and 20, or did the latter drop the reference to blood in v. 14 (ἐν ᾧ ἔχομεν τὴν ἀπολύτρωσιν, τὴν ἄφεσιν τῶν ἁμαρτιῶν), only for it to reappear in v. 20 (εἰρηνοποιήσας διὰ τοῦ αἵματος τοῦ σταυροῦ αὐτοῦ)? Or are such subtle divergences simply what happens in oral composition when an author rehearses a previously made argument, and should we stop casting ancient authors in the image of modern source critics?[46] In any case, after reviewing all of Mitton's parallels, Best's judgment is worth quoting in full:

> On the whole if we commence from the hypothesis that one author knew the other's letter and used it, it would be possible to force the evidence to produce a result in conformity with either the use of Colossians by A/Eph or of Ephesians by A/Col. Evidence should never be forced to fit a preconceived theory.[47]

Best himself goes further, however. At the granular level of a synoptic study, it is not just impossible to prove the direction but the *fact* of dependence as well, which explains why he resorts repeatedly to the independent use of traditional material by

---

[42] van Kooten, *Cosmic Christology*, 223–4.
[43] van Kooten, *Cosmic Christology*, 202.
[44] Campbell, *Framing Paul*, 318–20.
[45] Best, 'Who Used Whom', 75–93; cf. Mitton, *Epistle to the Ephesians*, 279–315.
[46] Campbell, *Framing Paul*, 322–3, appealing here to the seminal work of Walter J. Ong, *Orality and Literacy: The Technologizing of the Word*, 2nd 30th anniversary ed. (New York: Routledge, 2012).
[47] Best, 'Who Used Whom', 92.

two Paulinists to explain the evidence.[48] The similarities, while real, are simply too random to be confidently labeled *literary* dependence.[49] As soon as this is admitted, however, the choice between two authors working independently with Pauline material (Best) and one author working over Pauline material for two different settings (Campbell) is just that, a choice—and one that lies largely in the eye of the beholder. And Best recognizes this. At the close of his 1997 article, Best sets out what he regards as the two most plausible scenarios for the letters' relationship: his own two-author scenario, and one remarkably similar in general outline to what Campbell reconstructs twenty years later in characteristically more colorful detail.[50] In three major recent studies on the question of Ephesians and Colossians, then, three distinct positions emerge: (1) a strong view of literary dependence, with Colossian priority (van Kooten); (2) a rejection of literary dependence in favor of two independent compositions (Best); and (3) a rejection of literary dependence in favor of a single author, with Ephesian priority (Campbell). From those who have studied the question most closely, this is hardly a consensus.

I have ventured into the question of literary dependence in some detail above because it is the most frequently asserted 'objective' criteria to separate Paul and Ephesians, and so it creates the impression of answering my question before we even begin. In light of the above, I regard any high degree of confidence in this criteria (much less a scholarly consensus) misplaced. But here is the vital point: even if there *was* a consensus—if it could be proven that Ephesians used Colossians—that may well answer the authorship question, but it still has no bearing on the question to which I address myself in this book.[51] It tells us very little, that is, about how Ephesians sits

---

[48] Best, 'Who Used Whom', 92: 'If we look back over the way we have come...we see that in almost every case it is impossible to say with any certainty that A/Eph used Colossians or that A/Col used Ephesians. In many instances the similarity exists simply because both were indebted to tradition. There are no passages where it is possible to come down firmly and say with certainty that either author used the other.' See also his final judgment on pp. 93-4, 96.

[49] While committed to Colossian priority, even Mitton agrees, rejecting 'rigid or mechanical' notions of dependence that suggest 'a writer who has a document open in front of him as he writes and laboriously incorporates sections from it into his work'. Instead, Mitton envisions an author who was 'thoroughly familiar with Colossians, so that his mind could move easily along the lines of developing argument in that epistle' (*Epistle to the Ephesians*, 57). Reverse the direction of 'familiarity' (i.e. dependence), and this is essentially how Campbell envisions the letters' relationship (*Framing Paul*, 318-25).

[50] Best, 'Who Used Whom', 93-5.

[51] I tend to agree with Campbell that if Colossian priority could be proven it would be best to regard Ephesians as a pseudepigraphon (*Framing Paul*, 321), but the latter does not necessarily follow from the former. For a previous era of Pauline scholarship, most influentially in F. C. Baur and Ernst Käsemann, there was a strong myth of originality that surrounded Paul. See directly at F. C. Baur, *Paul the Apostle of Jesus Christ: His Life and Works, His Epistles and His Doctrine*, trans. Eduard Zeller, 2 vols., Theological Translation Fund 1 (London: Williams & Norgate, 1873-75), 2:106-8, and Ernst Käsemann, 'Paul and Early Catholicism', in *New Testament Questions of Today*, NTL (London: SCM, 1969 [1963]), 249-50; idem, 'Ephesians and Acts', in *Studies in Luke-Acts: Essays Presented in Honor of Paul Schubert*, ed. L. E. Keck and J. L. Martyn (Nashville: Abingdon, 1966), 288-90. In other words, Paul would never reduce himself to shuffling around the pieces of an argument he had already made (Baur), nor was he dependent on or beholden to tradition (Käsemann). Paul was novel and always original. But in view of recent work on ancient letter writing, it is almost certain that Paul kept copies of his letters, which would allow him to rework an earlier letter in a subsequent composition. See E. Randolph Richards, *Paul and First-Century Letter Writing: Secretaries, Composition and Collection* (Downers Grove: InterVarsity, 2004), 156-70.

vis-à-vis Colossians and the other letters with respect to *Paul*. It could mean that Ephesians straightforwardly develops the Pauline tradition beyond Colossians, as many scholars assume, but it could also mean that Ephesians 'corrects' the subsequent tradition back *towards* Paul (as van Kooten's own argument shows), in which case a chronologically later Ephesians would be a *more* useful source for Paul. The only way to determine an answer to the question of how to read Ephesians vis-à-vis Paul, then, is not by making an authorship decision, nor by settling the vexed question of literary dependence, nor by uncritically accepting critical tradition, but rather by doing comparative exegesis with all the pieces on the table. This is what I attempt to do in Chapter 5.

Finally, as in any study of Ephesians, we face the question of nomenclature: how to refer to the author of the letter? In some ways, this is decided by my own tentative judgment on authorship shared above. But since authorship is not the focus of my argument, should I resort to a more neutral term for the author? Best famously uses 'AE' in his commentary to signal 'the author of Ephesians', and most others opt for the seemingly neutral language of 'the author'. This is true insofar as it goes, but no Pauline scholar refers neutrally to 'the author' of Romans, or 'AR'. When it comes to reading Ephesians vis-à-vis Paul and the other letters, then, the language of 'the author' is not neutral, but a prejudicial choice that linguistically deepens the divide between Paul and Ephesians. Given that one of the central arguments of this book is that this space is largely constructed space and needs closing down, the nomenclature I use for the author is a relatively easy decision: I refer to the author as Paul throughout, including in my own constructive work on Eph 3.1–13 in Chapter 5. I recognize that this decision is itself prejudicial in the opposite direction, and my use of 'Paul' should not be taken as a rigorous claim about authorship per se, nor as an attempt to subtly harmonize Ephesians with the other letters. But it is also not purely a matter of convenience. It *is* a claim—a way of resisting a linguistic commonplace that looks neutral but in fact perpetuates and deepens a divide I find artificial. If using 'Paul' vis-à-vis Ephesians linguistically supports my attempt, argued on other grounds, to close down that now-175-year-old space, I take that as a step in the right direction, and make no apology for it.

Part 1

READING PAUL AND EPHESIANS
IN MODERN CRITICISM

Chapter 1

DISMEMBERING PAUL

Sometime near the turn of the third century CE, a scribe sat down to copy, in relatively bare form, ten letters of the apostle Paul. He or she placed them within a single codex, arranged by decreasing length: Romans, Hebrews, 1 and 2 Corinthians, Ephesians, Galatians, Philippians, Colossians, and 1 and 2 Thessalonians. The result, as we know it, is the antiseptically titled Papyrus 46.[1] Roughly 150 years later, another scribe (or series of scribes) took on a more arduous task, copying the entire Greek Bible—Old and New Testaments alike and the Apocrypha, save Maccabees. The result, Codex Vaticanus, is a forerunner of the modern Bible, but unlike its modern counterparts, Paul's letters appear after Acts *and* the Catholic Epistles. Like modern Bibles, Vaticanus divides the letters into chapters, but the numbers run consecutively across epistolary boundaries, treating the letters as a collective. Some 600 years after Vaticanus, a tenth-century minuscule (1739) opts for the middle ground, issuing an apostles' edition—Acts, Catholic Epistles, then Paul—the latter of which is mediated via marginalia drawn from a veritable who's who of patristic authors (Irenaeus, Clement, et al.). Before any of the above manuscripts witness to something else, then (i.e. an 'original text'), each is its own textual artefact—an ancient letter collection, or a collection within a collection: a ten-letter Paul on his own; a fourteen-letter Paul in a Bible; and a fourteen-letter Paul among the Jerusalem pillars (Gal 2.9), introduced by the alleged work of his travelling companion (Luke).[2] These are three very different manuscripts, and three very different experiences of reading Paul.

The historical critic's experience reading Paul, as we will see, is quite different, with Paul variously configured as a zero-, four-, and now ubiquitously seven-letter

---

[1] On 𝔓46 and the other manuscripts below, see Bruce M. Metzger, *The Text of the New Testament: Its Transmission, Corruption, and Restoration*, 2nd ed. (Oxford: Clarendon, 1968), 37–8, 47–8 and 65.

[2] This turn toward the study of manuscripts as evidence of the literary culture of early Christianity itself is well represented by Harry Y. Gamble, *Books and Readers in the Early Church: A History of Early Christian Texts* (New Haven: Yale University Press, 1995), and Larry W. Hurtado, *The Earliest Christian Artifacts: Manuscripts and Christian Origins* (Grand Rapids: Eerdmans, 2006). Gamble, in fact, argues that the early Christian preference for the codex owes to an early edition of a Pauline collection (*Books and Readers*, 58–65; cf. Hurtado, *Earliest Christian Artifacts*, 73–4, 80) published in this form. Neither Gamble nor Hurtado, however, makes much of these manuscripts belonging to the wider literary genre of the letter collection (see briefly Gamble, *Books and Readers*, 95–101, and Hurtado, *Earliest Christian Artifacts*, 38–9). Here, see Trobisch, *Entstehung der Paulusbriefsammlung*, 84–104; cf. Trobisch, *Paul's Letter Collection*.

figure, chronologically arranged.³ And yet, no such Paul exists except as a scholarly construct—a useful and powerful one, but a construct still. This was Kenneth Dover's relentless point in his 1966/1967 Sather Classical Lectures on the collection of thirty-four speeches assigned to the classical Athenian orator Lysias. He writes, 'The starting point of my enquiry is a twelfth-century manuscript, and the end of the inquiry will necessarily involve us in assessing some aspects of Athenian society. This, in my view, is to take things in the right order. Objects which we can see and touch and smell are the data of history: all else is construction.'⁴ Turning back to Paul, the above manuscripts are all that remain of him—the first-order data we can see, touch, and smell—and so are where the historical study of Paul begins.

It would seem significant, then, that for the typical historical critic, this is *not* where it begins, but rather with an already-interpreted critical edition,⁵ or still more, with only half of that edition, and that half rearranged. The historical analysis of the modern study of Paul, then, rightly begins with how it treats this most basic object of its study—the letter collection. Any judgment about any Pauline letter, it turns out, is not firstly a claim about Paul, but about how to read the *corpus Paulinum*—an attempt, that is, to unravel a collection that goes back, as far as we can tell, as early as 100 CE.⁶ This chapter interrogates that hermeneutic and its result, narrating how modern criticism, in order to know Paul and history, dismembers the only Pauls we have.

Restoring the 'Natural Order'

Not surprisingly, the story begins with Ferdinand Christian Baur, whose 1845 *Paulus der Apostel Jesu Christi* launches the modern critical study of Paul. By 1845, however, Baur's *Paulus* is, vis-à-vis an ancient letter collection, methodologically conventional, eschewing secondary biography (Acts) for the biographical potential of a rearranged letter collection—a trend two centuries old when Baur writes. Before turning to Baur,

---

³ Bruno Bauer, *Kritik der paulinischen Briefe*, 3 vols. (Berlin: Hempel, 1850–52), famously argues that all of the letters transmitted under Paul's name are products of the second century. The Paul of the (four-letter) *Hauptbriefe* is, of course, that of Baur, *Paul the Apostle*. On the seven-letter Paul, see below.
⁴ Kenneth J. Dover, *Lysias and the Corpus Lysiacum*, Sather Classical Lectures 39 (Berkeley: University of California Press, 1968), 1.
⁵ So rightly, Stanley K. Stowers, 'Text as Interpretation: Paul and Ancient Readings of Paul', in *Judaic and Christian Interpretation of Texts: Contents and Contexts*, ed. Jacob Neusner and Ernest S. Frerichs, vol. 3 of *New Perspectives on Ancient Judaism*, Studies in Judaism (Lanham, MD: University Press of America, 1987), 17–27.
⁶ The theories are numerous and secondary literature extensive, but relatively widespread agreement exists that the earliest form(s) of the collection go(es) back, at least, to the turn of the second century CE. The seminal study is Günther Zuntz, *The Text of the Epistles: A Disquisition Upon the Corpus Paulinum*, Schweich Lectures 1946 (Oxford: Oxford University Press, 1953), with proposed dating at page 279. Since the late nineteenth century, substantial proposals have been made by Zahn, Harnack, Goodspeed, Zuntz, Schmithals, Schenke, Dahl, Trobisch, and Gamble. For overview and bibliography, see Stanley E. Porter, 'When and How was the Pauline Canon Compiled? An Assessment of Theories', in *The Pauline Canon*, ed. Stanley E. Porter, Pauline Studies 1 (Leiden: Brill, 2004), 95–128; E. H. Lovering, 'The Collection, Redaction, and Early Circulation of the Corpus Paulinum' (PhD diss., Southern Methodist University, 1988); and the taxonomy of Robert M. Price, 'The Evolution of the Pauline Canon', *HvTSt* 53 (1997): 36–67.

then, I outline this broader shift in how to read an ancient collection in which he should be situated.

I begin, however, with an influence closer to home—Friedrich Schleiermacher (1768–1834), and his project of reading a still more famous set of ancient works, the Dialogues of Plato. The three-volume result, Schleiermacher's celebrated *Platons Werke* (1804–28), is a German translation of the dialogues, with critical introduction to each and a general introduction prefixed to the whole.[7] Reading the latter anticipates, with remarkable congruity, Baur's introduction to his *Paulus* a few decades later, and it was Schleiermacher, moreover, who first applied (in 1807) the sort of critical tools to the *corpus Paulinum* that Baur himself would pick up.[8]

What drives Schleiermacher's project is a historical and philological criticism that can free Plato from the subsequent tradition attached to his name and recover the man himself.[9] Most frequently, this tradition turns out to be the ancient editions themselves—Thrasyllus's tetralogies and Aristophanes's trilogies in particular—which obscure more than they reveal.[10] At its most basic level, then, criticism involves adjudicating authenticity: 'Now, if the natural order of the Platonic works is to be restored out of the disarrangement in which they at present are, it would seem necessary to determine first what pieces are really Plato's and what are not. For otherwise…how can even what is genuine fail to appear quite in a false light, if violence be used to place what is ungenuine in connection with it?'[11] The inclusion of spurious dialogues in editions of Plato is an act of editorial violence that obscures Plato, and so a truly 'searching criticism' can never 'rest upon those authorities'.[12] To get Plato, the *corpus Platonicum* needs critical sifting.

It also needs to be rearranged, and this, for Schleiermacher, was the real *novum* of his *Platons Werke*.[13] His criticism of earlier Plato studies, in fact, trains relentlessly on their acquiescing to a 'confused' reading order inherited from Thrasyllus and Aristophanes. Against the 'disarrangement' of previous attempts, Schleiermacher's project offers a return to their 'natural order'.[14] As he writes, 'The restoration…of this natural order is, as every one sees, an object very far distinct from all attempts hitherto made at an arrangement of the works of Plato, inasmuch as these attempts in part terminate in nothing but vain and extravagant trifling…without having anything like a whole in view'.[15] What Thrasyllus's tetralogies and Aristophanes's trilogies reveal, in

---

[7] Julia A. Lamm, 'Schleiermacher as Plato Scholar', *JR* 80 (2000): 206–39, provides a thorough discussion of Schleiermacher's 'General Introduction', situating it within Plato scholarship of the late eigteenth and early nineteenth centuries.

[8] Friedrich D. E. Schleiermacher, *Über den sogenannten ersten Brief des Paulos an den Timotheos: Ein kritisches Sendschreiben an J. C. Gass* (Berlin: Realschulbuchhandlung, 1807).

[9] This tradition may be ancient (Neoplatonism) or modern (the Kantian re-reading of Plato published in 1792 by Wilhelm Gottlieb Tennemann, *System der platonischen Philosophie* [Leipzig: J. A. Barth]). See Lamm, 'Schleiermacher as Plato Scholar', 219–20.

[10] See Friedrich D. E. Schleiermacher, 'General Introduction', in *Introductions to the Dialogues of Plato*, trans. William Dobson (London: J. W. Parker, 1836), 1–2, 19–22, 26–8. I treat Thrasyllus and Aristophanes's arrangements in Chapter 3.

[11] Schleiermacher, 'General Introduction', 26.

[12] Schleiermacher, 'General Introduction', 27 and 29.

[13] Lamm, 'Schleiermacher as Plato Scholar', 218.

[14] Schleiermacher, 'General Introduction', 20–1; cf. 14.

[15] Schleiermacher, 'General Introduction', 19–20.

fact, is 'how soon the true arrangement of the Platonic works was lost'.[16] What, then, *is* the 'natural order' and 'true arrangement'?

For Schleiermacher, it is chronological—a task that lay at the heart of the project from the beginning.[17] Only via this arrangement can one understand not only the individual dialogue (by its position within the whole), but Plato himself in his entirety—the philosopher par excellence. Thus, Schleiermacher's purpose is to 'restore them to the connection in which, as expositions continuously more complete as they advance, they gradually developed the ideas of the writer, so that while every dialogue is taken not only as a whole in itself, but also in its connection with the rest, [Plato] may himself be at last understood as a Philosopher and a perfect Artist'.[18] The right dialogues in the right order—this is the promise of Schleiermacher's *Platons Werke*. Ancient editions, with their own reading strategies, are left behind—dismembered for the sake of philosophical narration and biography: 'Plato may *himself* be at last understood'. One act of editorial violence is traded for another, all under the rhetoric of the retrieval of Plato's 'natural order'. The primitive biographies that head Plato's ancient editions, in fact, are no longer necessary, for Schleiermacher's rightly arranged corpus stands in for biography—a way to know the *Mensch* 'from the works themselves'.[19]

Plato's dialogues, of course, are not letters. But the watershed he represents in Plato studies vis-à-vis ancient editions is, by 1804, well afoot in the parallel project among classicists of chronologically rearranging ancient letter collections.[20] At the same time that Schleiermacher is busy salvaging Plato, C. M. Wieland (1808–21) and C. G. Schütz (1809–12) are doing the same for Cicero's letters.[21] As early as 1611, Adamus Theodorus Siberus set out to chronologically revise Cicero's *ad Familiares*, a sixteen-book, 435-letter collection arranged predominantly by addressee and theme. The purpose, as Siberus writes, was to assemble 'the whole of the *Epistulae Familiares*

---

[16] Schleiermacher, 'General Introduction', 21.
[17] The *Platons Werke* originated as a joint work with Friedrich Schlegel, with whom Lamm locates the original chronological impulse ('Schleiermacher as Plato Scholar', 210 and 213). Be that as it may, after Schlegel dropped out, the final arrangement is clearly Schleiermacher's ('General Introduction', 26, 40, 46). Tennemann's 1792 *System* arranged the dialogues chronologically—an attempt Schleiermacher calls 'critical in its principle' and worthy of a 'historical investigator' (Schleiermacher, 'General Introduction', 24). Lamm, 'Schleiermacher as Plato Scholar', 218–22 and 228–32, helpfully clarifies Schleiermacher's chronological method vis-à-vis Tennemann's.
[18] 'General Introduction', 14.
[19] Schleiermacher, 'General Introduction', 1.
[20] The seminal essay detailing the chronological turn in editions of Cicero's letters is Beard, 'Ciceronian Correspondences'. Beard urges a return to a 'radically old fashioned' way of reading Cicero's correspondence—that is, according to the original book divisions of each collection, an arrangement with its own 'aims, assumptions, and priorities' (115). This project has now been significantly advanced by Gibson in 'Ancient Letter Collections', and idem, 'Letters into Autobiography'. See also, now, the indispensable guide of Cristiana Sogno, Bradley K. Storin, and Edward J. Watts, eds., *Late Antique Letter Collections: A Critical Introduction and Reference Guide* (Oakland, CA: University of California Press, 2017). The discussion below is deeply indebted, in particular, to Gibson, and the relevant essays in *Late Antique Letter Collections* (hereafter *LALC*). See further my Chapter 3.
[21] C. M. Wieland, *M. Tullius Cicero's sämmtliche Briefe* (Zurich: Gessner, 1808–21); C. G. Schütz, *M. T. Ciceronis Epistolae ad Atticum ad Quintum Fratrem et quae vulgo ad Familiares dicuntur temporis ordine dispositae* (Halae: Hemmerdeana, 1809–11).

into their true and original order'—i.e. chronological—so as to restore a 'continuous history'.[22] The letter collection, rather than a literary artefact in its own right, becomes an archaeological site—excavated for (unmediated) access to the past, and rearranged to reveal it.[23]

In this respect, Cicero's corpus of 900+ letters, spread across four collections (*ad Familiares* [16 books, 435 letters], *ad Atticum* [16 books, 426 letters], *ad Quintum Fratrem* [1 book, 27 letters], and *ad Brutum* [1 book, 25 letters]), and covering the period 68–43 BCE, proves too suggestive. First Wieland (German), then Schütz (Latin), then Tyrrell and Purser (English) collate and chronologically arrange Cicero's *entire* epistolary corpus. The titles of their works tell the story: *M. T. Cicero's Sämmtliche Briefe* (Wieland); *M. T. Ciceronis Epistolae ... temporis ordine dispositae* (Schütz); and *The Correspondence of M. Tullius Cicero, arranged according to its chronological order...* (Tyrrell and Purser).[24] One could easily miss, in fact, if one picked up Tyrrell and Purser, that Cicero's letters ever existed in collections, much less were divided into discrete books. All one meets is Letter #1, Letter #2, Letter #3, and so forth, up to Letter #931.[25] Ancient editions are discarded to reveal the Cicero of history, just as they were for Schleiermacher.

Cicero's letters are hardly unique in being subjected to such 'editorial violence'—or more generously put, 'creative energy'.[26] Of the eleven collections Roy Gibson surveys in his 2012 essay, 'On the Nature of Ancient Letter Collections', modern editors have chronologically rearranged eight—a history Gibson probes further in his 2013 'Letters into Autobiography'. What Wieland, Schütz, and Tyrrell and Purser do to Cicero's corpus, then, is hardly idiosyncratic (see Table 1), but reflects a pervasive turn toward using letter collections—more specifically, the letters therein—as the raw data with which to write history and biography.[27]

---

[22] *M. Tullii Ciceronis Epistolarum Familiarum nova editio* (1611); cited in, and translation from, Gibson, 'Letters into Autobiography', 399.

[23] Beard, 'Ciceronian Correspondences', 123-4 and 143-4; Gibson, 'Letters into Autobiography', 394-400. The same is true of F. X. Schönberger's 1813-14 edition (*M. T. Ciceronis Epistolae ... temporis ordine dispositae*) of Cicero's letters. In the preface, he writes, 'I thought that this edition of Cicero's letters should be arranged as to lay out before the reader the entire corpus in the form of a "chronicle" of highly significant times' (trans. Gibson, 'Letters into Autobiography', 393).

[24] Robert Yelverton Tyrrell and Louis Claude Purser, eds., *The Correspondence of M. Tullius Cicero, Arranged According to its Chronological Order*, 2nd ed., 7 vols. (London: Longmans, Green & Co., 1879-1933). On the history of this project, see Beard, 'Ciceronian Correspondences', 106-16. The editions of D. R. Shackleton Bailey retain the integrity of the collections but arrange each chronologically. D. R. Shackleton Bailey, *Cicero: Letters to Atticus*, 5 vols. (Cambridge: Cambridge University Press, 1965-66); idem, *Cicero: Epistulae ad Familiares*, 2 vols. (1977); and idem, *Cicero: Epistulae ad Quintum Fratrem et M. Brutum* (1980).

[25] Beard, 'Ciceronian Correspondences', 109. The only hint of the original arrangement is the parenthesis on the title line of each letter with the traditional reference.

[26] Beard, 'Ciceronian Correspondences', 123; Gibson, 'Letters into Autobiography', 390; and Sogno, Storin, and Watts, 'Introduction: Greek and Latin Epistolography and Epistolary Collections in Late Antiquity', in *LALC*, 2, all use the phrase 'editorial violence' or one like it. The juxtaposition of 'editorial violence' and 'creative energy' is in Gibson 'Letters into Autobiography', 390.

[27] So, the thesis of Gibson, 'Letters into Autobiography', at 389.

Table 1. The Chronological Rearrangement of Ancient Letter Collections

Ancient Letter Collection	Modern Chronological Editions (Author, Date, Series)
Cicero, *ad Fam.*; *ad Att.*; *ad Brut.*; *ad Q. Fratr.*	Siberius (*ad Fam.*, 1611); Wieland (1808–21); Schütz (1809–12); Tyrrell and Purser (1879–1933); Bailey (1965–80)
Fronto	Haines (1919–20, Loeb)
Julian	Bidez and Cumont (1922)
Basil of Caesarea	Garnier and Maran (1721–30); Migne (1886, PG 32); Deferrari (1926–34, Loeb); Courtonne (1957–66 [2003])
Gregory of Nazianzus	du Friche, Louvard, Maran, and Clemencet (1778, 1840); Migne (1862, PG 37); Gallay (1964, 1967, 1969); Storin (2012)
John Chrysostom	Malingrey [17 letters to Olympias] (1947 [1968], SC)
Synesius of Cyrene	Druon (1878)
Jerome	Martianay (1693–1706); Vallarsi (1734–42); Migne (1845, PL 22)
Augustine	Blampin (1679–1700); Migne (1865, PL 33); Goldbacher (1895, CSEL); Daur (2004–, CCSL)
Paulinus of Nola	le Brun des Marettes (1685); Muratori (1736); Migne (1861, PL 61); Hartel (1894, CSEL)
Sidonius Apollinarus	Baret (1879)

a. The information in Table 1 is collated from Gibson, 'Letters into Autobiography', and the relevant essays in *LALC*.

By the early twentieth century, both Fronto's 348 letters and the emperor Julian's 284 are rearranged by date in modern editions—again, on appeal to the historical payoff of such an editorial move.[28] More striking, though, is the project initiated some three centuries earlier by the Benedictines of St. Maur—a reform-minded group of

[28] Fronto, *Correspondence*, 2 vols., LCL 112 (Cambridge, MA: Harvard University Press, 1919–20); Joseph Bidez and Franz Cumont, eds., *Iuliani imperatoris epistulae, leges, poematia, fragmenta varia* (Paris: Société d'Édition 'Les Belles Lettres', 1922). For discussion of Fronto, see Gibson, 'Letters into Autobiography', 408–9; and of Julian, see Susanna Elm, 'The Letter Collection of the Emperor Julian', in *LALC*, 54–68 (here 55–7).

French Catholic monks who copiously published new editions of the Greek and Latin fathers in the period 1660–1750.[29] In their hands, the letter collections of Augustine (1679–1700), Paulinus of Nola (1685), Ambrose (1686–90), Jerome (1693–1706), Basil of Caesarea (1721–30), and Gregory of Nazianzus (1778, 1840) are all issued in new, chronological order.[30] From the nineteenth century forward, editors have done the same for the collections (or portions thereof) of Synesius of Cyrene (1878), Sidonius Apollinarus (1879), and John Chrysostom (1947).[31] Names, dates, and titles change, but the hermeneutical act remains the same.

This Maurist turn maps well on to another shift, detailed by Janet Altman, toward using contemporary (or posthumously published) letter collections for the sake of narrative biography in late seventeenth- and early eighteenth-century French literary circles.[32] Altman writes:

> The presentation and organization of Bussy's and Sévigné's letters in the early eighteenth-century editions likewise reveals a profound shift toward historical narrativity as a primary value. The letters are carefully dated and organized chronologically to tell as complete a story as possible; … newly discovered letters are chronologically melded with previous ones in subsequent editions. The author's personal history has become the organizing principle for the letter collection.[33]

The letter book, that is—be it ancient and editorially rearranged, or modern and authorially constructed—gets put to use to narrate a life. Reflecting on the work of Prudentius Maran, the Maurist editor of Basil's collection, Abbé Marius Bessières makes this connection explicit: 'Dom Maran fixa l'ordre des lettres qui est l'ordre chronologique, et ceci constituait une revolution dans l'histoire des éditions basiliennes. Une fois la chronologie établie, on pouvait enfin songer à écrire une vie de S. Basile sur dés documents de premiére main.'[34] It is little surprise, then, that Maran himself went on to write Basil's first modern biography.[35] Suitably disaggregated and

---

[29] On the Maurists, see Daniel-Odon Hurel, 'The Benedictines of the Congregation of St. Maur and the Church Fathers', in *The Reception of the Church Fathers in the West: From the Carolingians to the Maurists*, ed. Irena Backus, vol. 2 (Leiden: Brill, 1997), 1009–38.

[30] Full bibliography of Maurist editions is at Hurel, 'The Congregation of St. Maur', 1031–4. For secondary discussion, with varying detail, see the relevant essays in Sogno, Storin, and Watts, *LALC*, and Gibson, 'Letters into Autobiography', 400–405. The lasting influence of Maurist arrangements owes to their reprinting by J. P. Migne in his *Patrologia Graecae* (Basil, Gregory) and *Patrologia Latina* (Jerome, Augustine, Paulinus), which themselves form the basis for the recent editions in Loeb (Basil), CSEL (Augustine, Paulinus), and CCSL (Augustine).

[31] See, again, the essays in *LALC*.

[32] Janet Gurkin Altman, 'The Letter Book as a Literary Institution 1539–1789: Toward a Cultural History of Published Correspondences in France', *Yale French Studies* 71 (1986): 17–62, here especially 49–61. Gibson discusses the contemporary phenomenon in 'Letters into Autobiography', 410–14.

[33] Altman, 'Letter Book as a Literary Institution', 52.

[34] Marius Bessiéres, 'La tradition manuscrite de la correspondance de Saint Basile, Chapitre I', *JTS* 21 (1919): 18; cited in Andrew Radde-Gallwitz, 'The Letter Collection of Basil of Caesarea', in *LALC*, 69.

[35] Radde-Gallwitz, 'Letter Collection of Basil of Caesarea', 69.

rearranged, the collection reveals (great) men and their times—the ineluctable result of being read in its 'natural order'. So too, it turns out, with antiquity's most well-read letter collection—the fourteen letters that comprise the *corpus Paulinum*.

F. C. Baur and the Revolution in the Study of Paul

Given the above, if there is a surprising feature of Pauline scholarship of the nineteenth century, it is that no critical edition of the *corpus Paulinum* has arranged the letters chronologically.[36] The collection's apparent priority here, however, is a chimera. The idiosyncrasy of editions aside, the revolution detailed above happens simultaneously in the study of Paul. To begin near the end, take Adolf Deissmann's programmatic definition of Paul's correspondence as 'real letters' in his 1908 *Licht vom Osten*.[37] For Deissmann, the payoff is massive and, in light of the above, familiar: 'Their [i.e. Paul's letters] non-literary characteristics as letters are a guarantee of their reliability, their positively documentary value for the history of the apostolic period of our religion, particularly the history of St. Paul himself and his great mission. His letters are the remains (unfortunately but scanty) of the records of that mission.'[38] Here there is no mention of the collection, nor of the form in which we meet said letters, just discrete letters, first-order windows into 'the history of St. Paul himself'—history, that is, and biography.

The seminal work that depicts this shift is Baur's *Paulus*, and it is worth outlining his project with a particular view to what he does vis-à-vis the sort of textual artefacts adumbrated above.[39] On this, Baur is admirably direct: 'Only the crudest empiricism

---

[36] The only exception that I am aware of is the Norton Critical Edition edited by John T. Fitzgerald and Wayne A. Meeks, *The Writings of St. Paul: Annotated Text, Reception and Criticism*, 2nd ed. (New York: W. W. Norton, 2007).

[37] Adolf Deissmann, *Licht vom Osten: Das Neue Testament und die neuentdeckten Texte der hellenistisch-römischen Welt*, 4th ed. (Tübingen: Mohr Siebeck, 1923); Eng. trans. *Light from the Ancient East: The New Testament Illustrated by Recently Discovered Texts of the Graeco-Roman World*, trans. Lionel R. M. Strachan (New York: Harper & Brothers, 1922), 228–30, 234–41 (directly at 234 and 240).

[38] *Light from the Ancient East*, 241. So also William Wrede, *Paul*, trans. Edward Lummis (London: Green, 1907), for whom the letters offer Paul's 'own voice, unmuffled and free from any distracting sound' (xii).

[39] Baur's project—its historiographical and philosophical foundations, its historical and theological (de)merits, and its ongoing significance—is well summarized elsewhere, and need not detain us here. See, most recently, the wide and diverse engagement in Martin Bauspiess, Cristof Landmesser, and David Lincicum, eds., *Ferdinand Christian Baur und die Geschichte des frühen Christentums*, WUNT 333 (Tübingen: Mohr Siebeck, 2014). Anglophone interest in Baur was revived through the work of Peter C. Hodgson, *The Formation of Historical Theology: A Study of Ferdinand Christian Baur*, Makers of Modern Theology (New York: Harper & Row, 1966). Although overly polemical, Horton Harris, *The Tübingen School: A Historical and Theological Investigation of the School of F. C. Baur* (Leicester: Apollos, 1990), is still useful for Baur in the context of his *Schule*. On Baur's historical method, see Werner Georg Kümmel, *The New Testament: The History of the Investigation of its Problems*, trans. S. McLean Gilmour and Howard Clark Kee (London: SCM, 1973), 126–43; Hans Rollman, 'From Baur to Wrede: The Quest for a Historical Method', *SR* 17 (1988): 443–54; and now Johannes Zachhuber, *Theology as Science in Nineteenth Century Germany: From F. C. Baur to Ernst Troeltsch*, Changing Paradigms in Historical and Systematic Theology (Oxford: Oxford University Press, 2013); cf. the distillation of his argument on Baur in 'The Absoluteness of Christianity and the Relativity of All History: Two Strands in Ferdinand Christian Baur's Thought', in *Baur und*

can believe that one simply surrenders oneself to things, that the objects of historical investigation can only be taken directly as they lie before us.'[40] To get at Paul, the sources need critical sifting (*Kritik*). The first object of Baur's criticism, therefore, is Acts, comprising Part 1 of his *Paulus*.[41] His programmatic point, now commonplace, is the absolute priority of the letters: 'The foregoing inquiry [Part 1] shows what a false picture of the personality of the Apostle Paul we should form if the Acts of the Apostles were the only source we had to draw from. The Epistles of the Apostle are thus the only authentic documents for the history of his apostolic labours.'[42] Baur conveniently omits that the collection itself results from a process of selection, arrangement, and editing not unlike Acts. But to the degree that his conclusion seems obvious today, it reveals the depth of our tacit agreement with him—of the hermeneutical triumph of history and biography as the natural way to read a letter collection.

But not the entire collection—thus Part 2, Baur's sifting of the corpus itself. The Acts impulse, in fact, cuts through the collection, and so needs to be cut out:

> The deeper we go in the study of the Epistles the richer and the more peculiar do we find that life to be which the Pauline spirit developed. Yet on this ground also we find that double of the Apostle making his appearance at his side, who in the Acts completely supplanted him. That all these thirteen Pauline Epistles, which Christian antiquity unanimously recognised, and handed down as the Epistles of the Apostle, cannot make equal claim to authenticity, and that several of them labour under an overwhelming suspicion of authenticity, is a result of recent criticism.[43]

We return below to the emphasis on personal biography (the 'rich' and 'peculiar' Pauline spirit). Here, note Baur's scepticism of Acts (Paul's 'double') leveraged on the textual artefact that mediates Paul. Claiming the right of criticism to 'deny and destroy', Baur divides the collection in three—the *Homologoumena* (Romans–Galatians), *Antilegomena* (Ephesians–2 Thessalonians), and *Notha* (Pastorals)—and returns to Paul what rightfully belongs to him, and only that: Romans, 1–2 Corinthians, and Galatians.[44]

---

   die Geschichte, 313–31. For incisive discussion of Baur's *Paulus*, both critical and appreciative, see Robert Morgan, 'Biblical Classics II. F. C. Baur: Paul', *ExpTim* 90 (1978): 4–10.
[40] Baur writes here in 1847 in the preface to his *Lehrbuch der christlichen Dogmengeschichte*, 2nd ed. (Tübingen: Fues), vii; Eng. trans. *History of Christian Dogma*, trans. Peter C. Hodgson and Robert F. Brown (Oxford: Oxford University Press, 2014), 43. His reading of Paul, however, reflects unequivocally the principle here stated.
[41] Baur, *Paul*, 1:15–241. Baur's rhetoric of *Kritik* (or *historischen Kritik*), directed particularly against Acts, appears regularly in his introduction (1–14) and serves to vindicate Paul, who is otherwise obscured by the 'subjective aims' of Acts (4–5).
[42] *Paul*, 1:245.
[43] Baur, *Paul*, 1:245.
[44] Baur's categories (*Paul*, 1:246) are, of course, those of Eusebius (*Hist. eccl.* 3.25). Baur's source reduction is summarized at *Paul*, 1:245–9. Interestingly, Baur defends his tripartite division of the collection, in part, by appeal to Marcion's edition, which he thinks merged two chronological collections (Galatians → Romans; 1 Thessalonians → Philemon), with the Pastorals added later as an appendix (*Paul*, 1:247–9).

In light of the above, Baur's next move is typical. Using his famous positive criticism, Baur excavates textual origins and rearranges the collection chronologically.[45] Thus, the purpose and shape of Part 2: 'To divide the Epistles standing in the Canon, under the name of the Apostle, into authentic and unauthentic, Pauline and pseudo-Pauline, and to arrange the later ones according to their probable chronological order'.[46] Not just the later ones, though, but the *Hauptbriefe* as well, so that Baur's Part 2 is, at bottom, a chronological reading of the *corpus Paulinum*. The payoff of this chronological arrangement is massive—it is the sine qua non of Baur's project. Moreover, given his division of the corpus, Part 2 is less a chronology of Paul, and more the seeds of a chronology of Christian origins—seeds that would flower, some eight years later, in his *Kirchengeschichte der drei ersten Jahrhunderte*.[47] Disaggregating the collection, it turns out, has powerful potential for narrating early Christianity:

> The Epistles which thus carry us beyond the age of the apostle, and…to a later set of circumstances, come under the same category with the legends of the apostle's last fortunes. They belong, *not to the biography of the apostle himself, but to the history of the party which used his name*, and to their party circumstances. How Paulinism was developed, what modifications it admitted, with what antagonisms it had to contend, what influence it exerted in moulding the features of the time, from the varied elements of which the unity of the Christian church was to emerge, this is what we find in these Epistles.[48]

The history of the study of Paul's disputed letters is, more or less, a series of footnotes to Baur at this point. One letter collection becomes two, and the latter (the 'disputed Paul') becomes, generically, a species of history.

The former, for Baur, is less history and more (theological) biography. To be sure, Part 2 of Baur's *Paulus* rearranges the *Hauptbriefe*, and treats them in chronological order. These letters evince an obvious 'historical connection' (i.e. are native to their time) and, most famously, the conflict that drives his reconstruction of Christian origins—Paul v. Peter, and gentile v. Jewish Christianity—is most palpable therein.[49] But the real payoff of this scope (*Hauptbriefe*) and order (chronological) is biographical. It offers Baur the raw data for *Paul*. Parts 1 and 2, that is, uncover the 'true historical basis of his *personality*',[50] and set the stage for Part 3, Baur's discussion of Pauline *Lehrbegriffe*, a theological biography written strictly on the basis of the *Hauptbriefe*. Duly delimited and rearranged, Paul—and Paul's genius—appears from

---

[45] On the importance of textual origins for Baur, see *Paul*, 2:108–9.
[46] Baur, *Paul*, 1:249 n. 1.
[47] Tübingen: Fues, 1863, but first published in 1853 as *Das Christenthum und die christliche Kirche der drei ersten Jahrhunderte* (Tübingen: Fues); Eng. trans. *The Church History of the First Three Centuries*, trans. Allan Menzies, 2 vols., 3rd ed. (London: Williams & Norgate, 1878).
[48] Baur, *Paul*, 2:111.
[49] Baur, *Paul*, 2:108.
[50] Baur, *Paul*, 2:115. Emphasis mine.

the mist of the collection.⁵¹ Not Romans → Titus, though, but Galatians → Romans, full stop. Arranged thus, the *Hauptbriefe* all exhibit a 'true organic development'; they 'proceed from one root idea' and are 'founded in one creative thought'—one with 'such inherent force' so as to 'originate all the stages of its development'.⁵² Baur's Idealism is here wedded to Pauline biography in the service of Christian origins: to Paul belongs the idea ('the principle of Christian consciousness') that drives the particulars of history.⁵³ My point here, however, is rather more simple. Baur can only arrive at this conclusion (his 'Paul', Part 3) by reading a new textual artefact—let us call it Papyrus Hauptbriefe (chronologically arranged)—or rather, by not reading the ones we have.

Baur would agree. The collection gives not 'the natural truth of history' but a 'confused web of artificial combinations'.⁵⁴ His *Paulus*, then, aims to restore history's 'natural truth'—and the Paulinism of Paul—by ignoring the collection as such. Scholars ever since have agreed, and the result has been nothing short of a revolution. To return to Dover's point, however, Baur's Paul, like the original act of collection itself, is a construct—just one that now purports to offer history and biography.⁵⁵ The power of the editor to (mis)shape Paul, however, remains the same.

From Baur's 1845 *Paulus* to another famous editorializing of the Pauline collection—the Englishman William Paley's 1790 *Horae Paulinae*.⁵⁶ At first blush, collocating Baur's *Paulus* and Paley's *Horae* may seem strange: Paley is sanguine on Acts, thinks all thirteen letters authentic, and treats them in their canonical order. 'Crude empiricism', Baur might call it, and not without reason. Paley's project is an apologia for the reliability of Acts and Paul, and the truth of the history they narrate.⁵⁷ Despite very different aims and widely divergent results, however, Paley and Baur converge just here—in their effacement of the collection to reveal history. Paley writes,

> If it be true that we are in possession of the very letters which St. Paul wrote, let us consider what confirmation they afford to the Christian history. In my opinion they substantiate the whole transaction. The great object of modern research is to come at the epistolary correspondence of the times. Amidst the obscurities, the silence, or the contradictions of history, if a letter can

---

⁵¹ So, Baur, *Paul*, 1:257: 'The ideas which appear in the Epistle to the Romans as a complete system of Pauline doctrine, worked out in all its particulars, appear in the Galatian Epistle in their outlines, yet distinctly and clearly traced. We can thus start from [Galatians] to trace the development of the Pauline doctrinal system through the various stages at which we meet it in the four great Epistles'.
⁵² Baur, *Paul*, 2:107.
⁵³ Baur discusses this principle, at length, in the opening of Part 3 on Pauline *Lehrbegriffe* (*Paul*, 2:123-33).
⁵⁴ Baur, *Paul*, 2:111.
⁵⁵ David Lincicum, 'Ferdinand Christian Baur and the Theological Task of New Testament Introduction', in *Baur und die Geschichte*, 100-101, makes the same point about Baur's reorganization of the canon.
⁵⁶ *Horae Paulinae; or the Truth of the Scripture History of St. Paul Evinced, by a Comparison of the Epistles Which Bear His Name, with the Acts of the Apostles, and with One Another* (London: SPCK, 1855 [1790]). For overview of Paley and his *Horae*, see David M. Thompson, *Cambridge Theology in the Nineteenth Century: Enquiry, Controversy and Truth* (New York: Routledge, 2016), 25-30.
⁵⁷ Paley's *Horae* copiously compares Acts and Paul's letters in search of 'undesigned coincidences' (i.e. not explained by dependence) that would mutually corroborate the history to which they attest. For Paley's description of the project, see *Horae*, 1-12.

be found, we regard it as the discovery of a land-mark; as that by which we can correct, adjust, or supply the imperfection and uncertainties of other accounts.[58]

If this be so, the letters need not 'be read together', but vis-à-vis the historical particularity of Paul's life—thus Paley's ubiquitous collocation of the letters with Acts.[59] Paley thus rejects the collection, and refuses it hermeneutical significance; the 'very letters' take priority, although still discussed in canonical order.

It is precisely this last aspect of Paley's *Horae*, however, that gets 'corrected' by Anglophone scholars working in his wake. For the English clergyman James Tate, writing fifty years later, Paley had missed his work's true genius and potential.[60] If all of the letters contain suggestive links to Acts, they should be inscribed therein, resulting in a 'continuous history' of Paul—the story of Paul in Acts buttressed by a chronologically restored *corpus Paulinum*. As of 1840, Tate considers this a 'great desideratum', and so this is what he does.[61] Through the 'correct and clear arrangement' of the corpus, Tate turns the 'great beginnings of the Horae Paulinae into something like a regular narration'.[62] What is left is Paul's 'personal narrative'.[63]

All of this flowers, in 1852, in that seminal Victorian biography of Paul—W. J. Conybeare and J. S. Howson's *The Life and Epistles of St. Paul*.[64] 'The purpose of this work', write Conybeare and Howson in the book's opening line, 'is to give a living picture of St. Paul'.[65] This picture follows the narrative of Acts, and gains its color from the wealth of historical, archaeological, and geographical data it deploys, but the letters—inserted chronologically within Acts—remain the most vivid source for Pauline biography. A collage of quotations makes this clear:

> If [Paul's] letters had never come down to us, we should have known indeed what he did and suffered, but we should have had very little idea of *what he was*.... We must listen to his words, if we would learn *to know him*. If fancy

---

[58] *Horae Paulinae*, 250. This is a perfect instance of the hermeneutical impulse described by Sogno, Storin, and Watts, 'Introduction', in *LALC*, 1.

[59] Compare here Paley, *Horae Paulinae*, 11 and 249.

[60] James Tate, *The Horae Paulinae of William Paley, D.D., Carried out and Illustrated in a Continuous History of the Apostolic Labours and Writings of St. Paul, on the Basis of the Acts, with Intercalary Matter of Sacred Narrative Supplied from the Epistles* (London: Longman, Orme, Brown, Green & Longmans, 1840), v–vii.

[61] Tate, *Continuous History*, v. In the two hundred years prior to Tate, a few attempts were made along these lines—Ludovicus Cappellus (1632/1633), John Pearson (1688), George Benson (1756) and Nathaniel Lardner (1760)—but using only a few of the letters. See the bibliography in Tate, *Continuous History*, v; and Paley, *Horae*, 11–12.

[62] Tate, *Continuous History*, v–vi.

[63] Tate, *Continuous History*, viii. In 1849, T. R. Birks, *Horae Paulinae; ... by William Paley, D.D. with notes and a Supplementary Treatise entitled Horae Apostolicae by the Rev. T. R. Birks* (London: Religious Tract Society), appends his own *Horae Apostolicae* to an edition of Paley's *Horae*, with the letters now arranged chronologically. Strikingly, Birks nowhere acknowledges this change, other than to say that each letter now appears fixed in its 'true place' (189). The biographical potential of the simple act of rearrangement is now so obvious, it seems, as to require no justification.

[64] London: Longman, Brown, Green and Longmans, 1852.

[65] *Life and Epistles of St. Paul*, xv. Citations are from the unabridged edition of 1870 (New York: Scribner).

did her utmost, she could give us only his outward not his *inward life*.... Moreover an effort of imagination and memory is needed to recall the past, but in his Epistles *St. Paul is present with us*.... *His Epistles are to his inward life*, what the mountains and rivers of Asia and Greece and Italy are to his outward life,—the imperishable part which still remains to us, when all that time can ruin has passed away.... Here we have not treatises, or sermons, which may dwell in the general and abstract, but *real letters*, written to meet the actual wants of living men.... In his case it is not too much to say that *his letters are himself*—a portrait painted by his own hand.[66]

What impresses the authors is the immediacy of Paul's letters. There is no sense, here, that anything stands in the way—no sense of the collection that editorially bequeaths Paul. The collection concealed, Conybeare and Howson are free to trade its frame for that of Acts, and the first Anglophone historical biography of Paul is the result.

As of 1852, however, this turn had born little fruit, in the English-speaking world, in reading Paul's letters themselves. This would change with two rather more well-known figures in mid-nineteenth century British theological circles, Benjamin Jowett and Joseph Barber Lightfoot. In 1855, Jowett publishes commentaries on 1 and 2 Thessalonians, Galatians, and Romans, and the choice of letters is no accident.[67] The origins of Jowett's commentaries—which comprise a critical Greek text, English translation, notes, and appended dissertations—lay in an unfinished project by Thomas Arnold to produce a chronological edition of Paul.[68] Jowett thus handles four of Paul's six earliest letters, while A. P. Stanley wrote the volume on the Corinthian letters.[69] So Jowett's essay, 'On the Chronology of St. Paul's Life and Writings',[70] appended to his *Galatians*, is little surprise. Like Schleiermacher on Plato, Jowett thinks the evidence for a fixed chronology of Paul's letters too meager.[71] A relative chronology, however, is possible, and it is only this that is hermeneutically necessary.

> What we desire to know is reduced within narrow limits—the time and succession of the Apostle's journeys, during about fifteen years of his life, and their relation to his *Epistles*. The comparison will enable us to arrange the writings of the Apostle in a chronological order, and to trace the growth of his thoughts as the Church spread, as the Gentile world opened before him.[72]

---

[66] *Life and Epistles*, xix–xx. Emphasis mine.
[67] Benjamin Jowett, *The Epistles of St. Paul to the Thessalonians, Galatians, Romans, with Critical Notes and Dissertations*, 2 vols., 2nd ed. (London: John Murray, 1859 [1855]).
[68] See Geoffrey R. Treloar, *Lightfoot the Historian: The Nature and Role of History in the Life and Thought of J. B. Lightfoot (1828–1889) as Churchman and Scholar*, WUNT 2/103 (Tübingen: Mohr Siebeck, 1998), 308.
[69] A. P. Stanley, *The Epistles of St. Paul to the Corinthians*, 2 vols. (London: John Murray, 1855).
[70] In *Epistles of St. Paul*, 272–86, conveniently republished together with Jowett's other dissertations in *The Interpretation of Scripture, and Other Essays* (London: Routledge, 1907), 151–63. Page numbers below are from this latter volume.
[71] Jowett, 'Chronology', 151–2.
[72] Jowett, 'Chronology', 153.

Note, again, the method and the payoff: 'chronological order' so as 'to trace the growth of his thoughts'. With the help of Acts, Jowett reconstructs four temporally distinct groups within the collection: (1) 1 and 2 Thessalonians; (2) Galatians, 1 and 2 Corinthians, and Romans; (3) Ephesians, Colossians, Philemon, and Philippians; and (4) 1 and 2 Timothy, and Titus.⁷³ Jowett tends not to read the letters with a strong view to textual origins, but in one place at least, his new internal order pays a significant dividend: on the basis of 2 Cor 5.16—Paul's testimony of a time in which he knew Christ only κατὰ σάρκα—Jowett reckons 1 and 2 Thessalonians Jewish texts, evincing a Paul not fully extricated from Judaism.⁷⁴ As in Baur, Jowett's rearranged collection is a pregnant resource for theological biography.

Within five years, a young Joseph Lightfoot was busy at work on the same project. Lightfoot's *Galatians* is published in 1865, but already in 1859 he outlines the project in a letter to his friend and colleague Brooke Foss Westcott: 'To begin with a thin volume, or a portion of a volume[,] of introductory matter, explaining the history, doctrinal connexion & so forth, of the Epistles: & then to take the Epistles in chronological order, beginning therefore with the Thessalonians'.⁷⁵ Lightfoot, in fact, begins with Galatians, likely owing to Baur's influence,⁷⁶ but his purpose, as of 1865, remains chronological: 'The present work [i.e. his *Galatians*] is intended to form part of a complete edition of St Paul's Epistles which, if my plan is ever carried out, will be prefaced by a general introduction and arranged in chronological order'.⁷⁷ For the sake of biography—'to place the Epistles in connexion with his life'—Lightfoot had worked out that order in his 1863 'The Chronology of St. Paul's Life and Epistles',⁷⁸ delineating (like Jowett) four phases in the corpus, but now (contra Jowett) with dates attached: (1) 1 and 2 Thessalonians (52/53 CE); (2) Romans, 1 and 2 Corinthians, and Galatians (57/58); (3) Philippians, Ephesians, Colossians, and Philemon (62/63); and (4) 1 Timothy, Titus, and 2 Timothy (67/68). All of this does more work for Lightfoot, who mines each letter's origins—both within Paul's career, and the life of its recipients—for the sake of interpretation.⁷⁹ The rearranged corpus, though, is now useful to catalogue Pauline development: from the primitive expectation of the parousia (1 and 2 Thessalonians), to the core of his thought (Romans–Philemon), to his late concern for ecclesial organization (Pastorals).⁸⁰ Lightfoot's editorial rearrangement reveals not only history, then, but the center of Pauline theology as well.

---

[73] Jowett, 'Chronology', 158–63.
[74] See the discussion in Jowett, *Epistles of St. Paul*, 1:3–16, especially at 8–9, 14–15.
[75] Lightfoot to Westcott, 4 December 1859; cited in Treloar, *Lightfoot the Historian*, 312.
[76] Treloar, *Lightfoot the Historian*, 329; and James Carleton Paget, 'The Reception of Baur in Britain', in *Baur und die Geschichte*, 358–60.
[77] Joseph B. Lightfoot, *Saint Paul's Epistle to the Galatians: A Revised Text with Introduction, Notes, and Dissertations*, 9th ed. (London: Macmillan, 1887 [1865]), vii.
[78] Lightfoot wrote the essay in 1863, but it was only published (posthumously) in his *Biblical Essays*, 2nd ed. (London: Macmillan, 1904 [1893]), 215–33 (quotation at 215). For a concise summary of Lightfoot's chronology, see the table on 224.
[79] Lightfoot, 'Chronology', 227.
[80] Lightfoot, 'Chronology', 227–33. That said, in practice, Lightfoot tends to draw back from developmental explanations, appealing rather to the exigencies of Paul's recipients to explain difference (227).

Given where this section began, with Baur's *Paulus*, it is fitting that it close with Jowett and Lightfoot. Both are frequently read vis-à-vis Baur's legacy in Britain: either as his mediator (Jowett) or slayer (Lightfoot).[81] To my mind, though, the tacit assumption they all share is at least as interesting: that Paul's letter collection, in order to be hermeneutically meaningful, requires dismembering and rearranging. Their very real differences aside, then, by 1855 this revolution on the *how* and *why* of reading Paul's collection is in the ground water. To read Paul is to read him in his 'natural', which is to say chronological, order.

The Genres of the Revolution

Again, however, what makes this so intriguing is that this is precisely *not* how one will read Paul in the critical editions: not that of Lachmann (1831–50), nor Tischendorf (1869–72), nor Westcott-Hort (1881), nor Nestle (1898–1963), nor Weymouth (1902), nor the United Bible Society (1966–), nor Nestle-Aland (1979–).[82] None do for Paul what Wieland, Schütz, and Tyrrell and Purser do for Cicero, and the Maurists for the Fathers. How, then, did this way of reading Paul become 'natural'? In distinction from classical and patristic letter collections, the story of disaggregating and reordering Paul is best told not through a genealogy of critical editions, but through the rise of two disciplinary genres—the *Einleitung in das Neue Testament* and the *Geschichte des Urchristentums*—which dictate how Paul's letter collection comes to be read.[83]

First, then, the project of *Einleitung*, the roots of which go back to Johann Salomo Semler's 1771 *Abhandlung von freier Untersuchung des Canon*.[84] For Semler, the biblical canon, a collection of otherwise disparate texts, requires a 'free investigation' to determine the validity (i.e. authenticity) of its component parts.[85] Semler thus rightly recognizes the space between a text's origins and its presence in the canonical artefact, and invites the former to judge the latter. In 1844, Hermann Hupfeld states the task of *Einleitung* as a two-part question: 'Was waren die unter den Namen des Bibel vereinigten Schriften ursprünglich, und wie sind sie geworden was sie jetzt sind'?[86] The distinction is Semler's: *ursprünglich* denotes textual origins, *jetzt* the canonical artefact, and the *Einleitung* sets out to disentangle the two. So too, in 1850,

---

[81] A classic instance of the latter is Stephen Neill and Tom Wright, *The Interpretation of the New Testament, 1861–1986*, 2nd ed. (Oxford: Oxford University Press, 1988), 34. See also the collected essays in George R. Eden and Frederick C. Macdonald, eds., *Lightfoot of Durham: Memories and Appreciations* (Cambridge: Cambridge University Press, 1932). Paget, 'Reception of Baur', 347–8, discusses Jowett vis-à-vis Baur.

[82] For the history of each, save the last two, see Metzger, *Text of the New Testament*, ad loc.

[83] Many of the figures dealt with below are treated in Heinrich J. Holtzmann, *Lehrbuch der historisch-kritischen Einleitung in das Neue Testament* (Freiburg: Mohr, 1886), 1–20. James Moffatt, *An Introduction to the Literature of the New Testament*, 3rd ed. (Edinburgh: T. & T. Clark, 1918), 1–12, is an excellent overview of the issues.

[84] Halle: Hemmerde, 1771–75.

[85] For summary, see Kümmel, *History of the Investigation*, 62–69; William Baird, *From Deism to Tübingen*, vol. 1 of *History of New Testament Research* (Minneapolis: Augsburg Fortress, 1992–2013), 117–27.

[86] Hermann Hupfeld, *Über Begriff und Methode der sogennanten biblischen Einleitung* (Marburg: Elwert, 1844), 13.

Baur defines the task of *Einleitung* simply *as* 'Kritik des Kanons'. In fact, locating 'the origin [*Ursprung*] and original character [*ursprüngliche Beschaffenheit*] of the canonical writings' is the 'most vital and essential' part of the discipline.[87] And when, in 1911, James Moffatt argues that an Introduction should indicate 'the later processes of ecclesiastical rearrangement [Hupfeld's *jetzt*] by which often it was shifted from its original position [Hupfeld's *ursprünglich*] to a more or less alien place in the collection', he is simply translating Hupfeld for an Anglophone audience.[88] For Hupfeld, Baur, and Moffatt, the *Einleitung* runs history backwards, unravels the artefact, and, in so doing, recovers textual origins.

It is little surprise, then, that over the course of its history, a genre that begins as an Introduction to the *New Testament* (qua canon) becomes an Introduction to the *Writings* of the New Testament, with the typical divisions—general (on text/canon) and special (on individual texts)—waxing and waning accordingly.[89] This is simply, at the level of secondary New Testament scholarship, the same shift noted earlier in classical and patristic scholarship, and what would come to shape the study of Paul as well: trading the inherited form of a collection for its component parts. By 1975, the eclipse of the artefact is total in Werner Georg Kümmel's influential definition of *Einleitung*: 'The science of introduction is a strictly historical discipline which, by illuminating the historical circumstances of the origin of the individual writings, provides for exegesis the necessary presuppositions for understanding the writings in their historical uniqueness'.[90] If this is the project, it is also little surprise that such disaggregation turns quickly to chronological reaggregation—the dominant organizing principle of the *Einleitung* since the mid-nineteenth century—in an effort to reconstruct early Christianity.[91]

---

[87] F. C. Baur, 'Die Einleitung in das Neue Testament als theologische Wissenschaft. Ihr Begriff und ihre Aufgabe, ihr Entwicklungsgang und ihr innerer Organismus', *Theologische Jahrbücher* 9 (1850): 463–566 (here 483). For discussion, see Lincicum, 'Baur and the Theological Task', 96–8.

[88] Moffatt, *Introduction*, 8.

[89] The early *Einleitungen* of J. D. Michaelis, *Einleitung in die göttlichen Schriften des neuen Bundes*, 4th ed., 4 vols. (Göttingen: Vandenhoeck & Ruprecht, 1788); Eng. trans. *Introduction to the New Testament*, trans. Herbert Marsh (London: Rivington, 1823); W. M. L. de Wette, *Lehrbuch der historisch-kritischen Einleitung in die kanonischen Bücher des neuen Testaments*, 5th ed. (Berlin: Reimer, 1846 [1826]); Eng. trans. *An Historico-Critical Introduction to the Canonical Books of the New Testament*, trans. F. Frothingham (Boston: Crosby, Nichols, & Company, 1858); Holtzmann, *Einleitung* (1886); and Jülicher, *Einleitung*, all have substantial sections on text and/or canon. Moffatt, *Introduction*, omits general introduction, and sections on text/canon wane across the twentieth century, culminating in their near-total omission in Udo Schnelle, *Einleitung in das Neue Testament*, 8th ed. (Göttingen: Vandenhoeck & Ruprecht, 2013 [1994]), and Bart D. Ehrman, *The New Testament: A Historical Introduction to the Early Christian Writings*, 6th ed. (Oxford: Oxford University Press, 2015 [1997]).

[90] Kümmel, *Introduction*, 28.

[91] The first to do this comprehensively are Samuel Davidson, *An Introduction to the Study of the New Testament: Critical, Exegetical, and Theological*, 2nd rev. ed., 2 vols. (London: Longmans, Green andCo., 1882 [1868]) and Adolf Hilgenfeld, *Historisch-Kritische Einleitung in das Neue Testament* (Leipzig: Fues's Verlag, 1875). Subsequent *Einleitungen* tend to hold literary groups together, but work chronologically within and across these groups, as Edgar J. Goodspeed, 'A New Organization of New Testament Introduction', in *New Chapters in New Testament Study* (New York: Macmillan, 1937), 50–74, rightly observes. For Helmut Koester, excavating textual origins so as to map early Christianity is basic to the *Einleitung* ('New Testament Introduction: A Critique of a Discipline', in vol. 1 of *Christianity, Judaism and Other Greco-Roman Cults: Studies for Morton Smith at Sixty*, ed. J.

More narrowly, this chronological impulse goes back still further, vis-à-vis Paul's letters, to the earliest instance of the modern genre itself, J. D. Michaelis's 1788 *Einleitung*. Trying to make sense of its order, Michaelis suggests that Paul's collection is arranged by rank of city addressed, from Rome on down. Michaelis sets this traditional arrangement aside, however: 'I shall treat of St. Paul's Epistles not according to the order in which they are placed in the New Testament, but according to the time when they were written'.[92] In short order, the major *Einleitungen* of Hug (1808), Eichhorn (1812), de Wette (1826), Credner (1836), and Schleiermacher (1845) all follow suit, chronologically rearranging Paul's letters.[93] In 1845, then, when Baur turns his hand on Paul, he inherits a chronological revolution sixty years in the making, and one with a long shelf-life: since 1788, to meet Paul via a critical *Einleitung* is to meet not the Paul of the New Testament, but a Paul critically rearranged. Twenty major examples from 1788–2000 should suffice to make the point:

J. D. Michaelis (1788); J. G. Eichhorn (1812); W. M. L. de Wette (1826); S. Davidson (1868); A. Hilgenfeld (1875); H. Holtzmann (1886); F. Godet (1893–98); A. Jülicher (1894); T. Zahn (1897–99); B. W. Bacon (1900); J. Moffatt (1911); R. Knopf (1919); M. Goguel (1925); E. F. Scott (1932); G. Bornkamm (1971); W. G. Kümmel (1975); H. Koester (1980); U. Schnelle (1994); R. Brown (1997); B. Ehrman (1997).[94]

Each treats Paul's letters chronologically. To be sure, for many the letters remain together, if rearranged. But if the purpose is chronology of the *New Testament*, those

---

Neusner, 4 vols., SJLA 12 [Leiden: Brill, 1975], 1–20 [here 8 and 14]). Only thus does one overcome the canonical arrangement—what Eduard Reuss in 1842 calls 'accidental and capricious tradition' (*History of the Sacred Scriptures of the New Testament*, trans. E. L. Houghton [Boston: Houghton, Mifflin, 1884], 2) and Moffatt calls the 'problem of tradition' (*Introduction*, 4).

[92] Michaelis, *Introduction*, 4:2.

[93] Johann Leonhard Hug, *Einleitung in die Schriften des neuen Testaments*, 3rd ed., 2 vols. (Tübingen: Gotta, 1826); Johann Gottfried Eichhorn, *Einleitung in das neue Testament*, 5 vols. (Leipzig: Weidmann, 1804–27); de Wette, *Einleitung*; Karl August Credner, *Einleitung in das neue Testament* (Halle: Waisenhaus, 1836); Friedrich D. E. Schleiermacher, *Einleitung ins neue Testament*, pt. 1 vol. 8 of *Friedrich Schleiermacher's sämmtliche Werke*, ed. G. Wolde (Berlin: Reimer, 1845). Outside of this genre, see also Karl Georg Wieseler, *Chronologie des apostolischen Zeitalters, bis zum Tode der Apostel Paulus und Petrus* (Göttingen: Vandenhoeck & Ruprecht, 1848), who treats the thirteen letters in chronological order (232–478), but recognizes that this disrupts the arrangement (*Ordnung*) of the corpus, and so comments justifying his procedure (227–32).

[94] Only works not cited earlier are noted here: Frédéric Godet, *Introduction au Nouveau Testament*, 2 vols. (Paris: Librairie Fischbacher, 1894–99); Theodore Zahn, *Einleitung in das Neue Testament*, 3 vols. (Leipzig: A. Deichert, 1897–99); Benjamin W. Bacon, *An Introduction to the New Testament* (New York: Macmillan, 1900); Rudolf Knopf, *Einführung in das Neue Testament* (Giessen: Töpelmann, 1919); Maurice Goguel, *Introduction au Nouveau Testament*, 4 vols. (Paris: Ernest Leroux, 1922–26); Earnest Findlay Scott, *The Literature of the New Testament* (New York: Columbia University Press, 1932); Günther Bornkamm, *Bibel, das Neue Testament: Eine Einführung in seine Schriften im Rahmen der Geschichte des Urchristentums* (Stuttgart: Kreuz-Verlag, 1971); Werner Georg Kümmel, *Introduction to the New Testament*, trans. Howard Clark Kee (London: SCM, 1975); Helmut Koester, *Introduction to the New Testament*, 2nd ed., 2 vols. (Berlin: de Gruyter, 1995 [Germ. orig. 1980]); Raymond E. Brown, *An Introduction to the New Testament* (New York: Doubleday, 1997). The number of Introductions published since 2000 is extensive, and the data would be repetitive. A list of forty published in English alone since 2000 is in Lincicum, 'Baur and the Theological Task', 91–2 n. 1.

Introductions that physically separate Paul and pseudo-Paul, following the lead of Davidson (1868) and Hilgenfeld (1875), instantiate the vision with greater rigor. Moffatt is representative: when one opens his *Introduction*, one finds a nine-letter Paul on pages 64–176, but for the rest of the collection, one must turn to pages 373–420, where Moffatt treats Ephesians, 1 and 2 Timothy and Titus in a section entitled 'Homilies and Pastorals'. The effect on the *corpus Paulinum* is, quite literally, corrosive, rendering it irrelevant. Suitably divided, the Pauline *varia* enjoy a new set of co-texts—the collection dismembered and scattered across the New Testament to depict the growth of early Christianity. On this scheme, the seven-letter (eight-, nine-, etc.) Paul is prioritized, and the six-letter (five-, four-, etc.) pseudo-Paul displaced.

This divide, made haltingly in the *Einleitung*, is immortalized in the *Geschichte des Urchristentums*, a parallel genre that expands the source material. Various figures, beginning with Eduard Reuss in 1842 and culminating with Helmut Koester in 1982, argue that this expansion is the duty of the *Einleitung* itself, but their followers are few, and this larger historical work tends to fall to the *Urchristentum*.[95] Major works here proliferate from the middle of the nineteenth century on, largely within Baur's orbit.[96] Baur's own 1853 *Kirchengeschichte* and the second edition of Ritschl's *Die Entstehung der altkatolischen Kirche* (1857), similar in scope if not in results, both take the story up to Constantine.[97] Later works written in their wake fill in or correct Baur and Ritschl in detail: Karl Weizsäcker restricts his focus to texts of the apostolic age; Otto Pfleiderer to one strand (Paulinism) of early Christianity, and then to a comprehensive account up to the mid-second century; and similarly Johannes Weiss up to 130 CE.[98] Here the literary skeleton of the *Einleitung* becomes the enfleshed narrative, inclusive of all relevant texts, of early Christianity. To that end, New Testament texts matter, but not the New Testament qua artefact.

---

[95] See Reuss, *New Testament*, 12; Koester, 'Critique of a Discipline', 8; and idem, *Introduction*, xxiii. The key is the expansion of source material beyond the canon. After Reuss, see Knopf (1919) and Bornkamm (1971) for examples prior to Koester. Philipp Vielhauer's 1975 *Geschichte der urchristlichen Literatur: Einleitung in das Neue Testament, die Apokryphen und die apostolischen Väter* (Berlin: de Gruyter) sits between the *Einleitung* and *Urchristentum*.

[96] Baur opens his *Paul* by suggesting that, as of 1845, the literary reconstruction of primitive Christianity remains a desideratum (1). See, then, in quick order, Albert Schwegler, *Das nachapostolische Zeitalter in den Hauptmomenten seiner Entwicklung* (Tübingen: Fues, 1846); Karl Christian Planck, 'Judenthum und Urchristenthum', *Theologische Jahrbücher* 6 (1847): 258–93, 409–34, 448–506; Karl Reinhold Köstlin, 'Zur Geschichte des Urchristenthums', *Theologische Jahrbücher* 9 (1850): 1–62, 235–302. For Baur's influence on this genre, see Stefan Alkier, *Urchristentum: zur Geschichte und Theologie einer exegetischen Disziplin*, BHT 83 (Tübingen: Mohr Siebeck, 1993), 200–44, 253–4.

[97] Philip Hefner, 'Baur Versus Ritschl on Early Christianity', *CH* 31 (1962): 259–78, compares Baur and Ritschl's projects. On the French side, see Ernest Renan's seven-volume *Histoire des origins du christianisme* (Paris: Michel Lévy, 1863–83). Slightly later, Adolf von Harnack's *Geschichte der altchristlichen Litteratur bis Eusebius*, 4 vols. (Leipzig: J. C. Hinrichs, 1893–1904), also belongs here.

[98] Karl Weizsäcker, *Das apostolische Zeitalter der christlichen Kirche*, 2nd ed. (Tübingen: Mohr Siebeck, 1892); Otto Pfleiderer, *Der Paulinismus: ein Beitrag zur Geschichte der urchristlichen Theologie*, 2nd ed. (Leipzig: Riesland, 1890 [1873]); idem, *Das Urchristentum: seine Schriften und Lehren in geschichtlichen Zusammenhang*, 2nd ed. (Berlin: Reimer, 1902); Johannes Weiss, *Das Urchristentum* (Göttingen: Vandenhoeck & Ruprecht, 1917); Eng. trans. *The History of Primitive Christianity*, ed. Frederick C. Grant, trans. Four Friends, 2 vols. (London: Macmillan, 1937). See also, earlier, Adolf Hilgenfeld, *Das Urchristenthum in den Hauptwendepuncten seines Entwickelungsganges* (Jena: Friedrich Mauke, 1855).

The effect is only further to diffuse Paul's collection. As in the *Einleitung*, the first half is prioritized and the second half displaced, now with a still more robust set of co-texts. This is simply the fruit of a chronological hermeneutic combined with judgments about authenticity. As Weiss puts it, with admirable clarity, 'The history of primitive Christianity is usually written as the history of St. Paul'.[99] Quite so, given that Paul's letters remain our earliest Christian texts. It needs saying, however, that the Paul from which this *primitive* history is written is variably a four- (Baur), twelve- (Ritschl), seven- (Weizsäcker;), and nine-letter (Pfleiderer; Weiss) figure. The remaining letters do a different set of work, read with texts as diverse as John's Gospel, Acts, Hebrews, James, 1 Peter, 1–3 John, Revelation, the Apostolic Fathers and Justin Martyr to depict trajectories of development and competing interests within early Christianity. The *Urchristentum*, then, depends upon and further instantiates this rearranged and divided collection.

Together, the *Einleitung* and *Urchristentum* do what the critical edition does not, and ensconce in Paul the hermeneutic leveraged on classical and patristic collections. Here, then, are the genres of the revolution—the place in which this way of reading becomes natural. Rather than a corpus with its own integrity, the collection is thirteen data points to be plotted on a historical canvas. Two hundred years later, this has proven, for the study of Paul and Christian origins, a powerful and productive way to read the collection. The revolution, that is, has been put to use.

Putting the Revolution to Use: Paul and 'Paul'

From the 1950s onward, and across a host of scholarly genres, the rearranging and sundering of Paul's letter collection is pervasive, and contemporary depictions of Paul and Christian origins depend on it. The *corpus Paulinum* has been systematically dismembered, rearranged, and renarrated. A way of reading Paul that began as a criticism of tradition has become its own tradition, frequently appealed to and rarely argued for. Below, I show how thoroughly this is the case in order to argue that the modern project of knowing Paul depends, at bottom, on rendering his corpus in a particular, now traditional way.[100]

Pauline Life and Letters

Take, for instance, the *Life and Letters*—a staple genre that approximates, for the study of Paul, a critical *Einleitung*. Since 1970, the genre enjoys some of Pauline scholarship's most notable names: Bornkamm (1971); Roetzel (1974); Bruce (1977); Keck (1979); Barrett (1994); Cousar (1996); Harrill (2012); and now Sanders (2016).[101] This is the

---

[99] Weiss, *Primitive Christianity*, 1:1.
[100] While the bibliographical summaries below are inevitably brief, in each section I engage at greater length in the footnotes with one particularly noteworthy recent example from each genre to show that the issues at play are alive and well.
[101] Again, in chronological order of first publication: Günther Bornkamm, *Paul*, trans. D. M. G. Stalker (London: Hodder & Stoughton, 1971 [1969]); Calvin J. Roetzel, *The Letters of Paul: Conversations in Context*, 4th ed. (Louisville: Westminster John Knox, 1998 [1974]); F. F. Bruce, *Paul: Apostle of the Heart Set Free* (Grand Rapids: Eerdmans, 1977); Leander E. Keck, *Paul and His Letters*, 2nd rev. and

legacy of Conybeare and Howson, now less indebted to Acts—the life drawn mostly from the letters, although not all of them. The division of the collection is ubiquitous in these works, and they universally arrange the letters chronologically.[102] So, Leander Keck: 'Whoever wants to read the undisputed letters of Paul must extract this genuine corpus from the order in which the NT now has them.... Moreover, whoever wants to read the seven undisputed letters in the order in which Paul wrote them must rearrange the sequence.' Extraction and rearrangement gain access to Paul, and overcome the 'problem' (Keck's language) of the collection.[103]

This enjoys the side benefit of illuminating the period after Paul (à la Baur). The headings under which these works treat the disputed letters tell the story: 'The First Interpreters of Paul' (Roetzel); 'Pauline Theology: The Sequel' (Barrett); 'The Rest of the Story' (Cousar); and 'Competing Stories about Paul in Late Antiquity' (Harrill). One collection is now, functionally, two. More striking, however, is the *Life and Letters* that does not treat the disputed six at all (Bornkamm; Keck; Sanders), nor even mention them (A. N. Wilson), thus reducing Paul, without remainder, to his seven-letter form.[104] On the other hand, J. Albert Harrill's 2012 *Paul the Apostle* completely diffuses the letters, exploding the boundaries of the collection and incorporating all Pauline pseudepigrapha and Acts to offer the reader 'many different Pauls rather than "the" Paul'.[105] Whether the *Life and Letters* narrows, divides, or diffuses Paul, the one thing it never does is read the Pauls we have.

Pauline Chronology

Or take a *Chronology*—here, too, from 1950 on, a host of significant works litter the Pauline field: Knox (1950); Buck and Taylor (1969); Suhl (1975); Jewett (1979); Lüdemann (1980); Hyldahl (1986); Riesner (1994); Murphy-O'Connor (1997); Tatum

---

enl. ed. (Philadelphia: Fortress, 1988 [1979]); C. K. Barrett, *Paul: An Introduction to His Thought* (Louisville: Westminster John Knox, 1994); Charles B. Cousar, *The Letters of Paul*, Interpreting Biblical Texts (Nashville: Abingdon, 1996); J. Albert Harrill, *Paul the Apostle: His Life and Legacy in Their Roman Context* (Cambridge: Cambridge University Press, 2012); E. P. Sanders, *Paul: The Apostle's Life, Letters, and Thought* (Minneapolis: Fortress, 2016).

[102] See, e.g., the discussion in Sanders, *Paul*, 147–61, esp. 149–51 and 157–61. The recent volume edited by Oda Wischmeyer, ed., *Paul: Life, Setting, Work, Letters*, trans. Helen S. Heron, rev. Dieter T. Roth (London: T&T Clark, 2012), is a prominent example of the divide in a work that spans multiple authors. An exception, which narrates Paul's life from all thirteen letters, is Bruce, *Paul*.

[103] Keck, *Paul and His Letters*, 5–7. See here also Sanders's tables in *Paul*, 151.

[104] A. N. Wilson, *Paul: The Mind of the Apostle* (London: Sinclair-Stevenson, 1997).

[105] Harrill, *Paul the Apostle*, 3. Historiographically, Harrill's *Paul the Apostle* is a welcome advance in a relatively stale genre, although with respect to Paul's letter collection and our access to Paul, his work is at best ambivalent. Positively, he treats the collection as such and, recognizing that biography cannot repristinate its subject, Harrill's 'antibiography' (3, emphasis original) is at one level a study of Pauline traditions. On the other hand, Harrill's *Paul* is also deeply typical. Only the seven undisputed letters provide principal access to Paul, and give him occasion to speak of 'the *historical* Paul' (3; cf. 3–7, emphasis original). Harrill recognizes that all historiography is construction—his 'historical Paul' is not coterminous with the 'real Paul'—but his strong rhetorical distinction between Part 1 ('The Life'), based on the seven, and Part 2 ('The Legend'), based on Pauline traditions, suggests the opposite in practice of his theoretical declaration. Moreover, Harrill's treatment of the *corpus Paulinum* occurs in Part 2, despite the fact that it is unequivocally our *actual* primary source for Paul. There is thus a deep ambiguity in Harrill's *Paul*, which both diffuses and divides the letter collection for access to Paul, but largely ignores it as such as first-order evidence.

(2006); and now Campbell (2014).[106] In the nature of the case, these works reject the arrangement of the collection. Given the paucity of the letters' historical data, arguments over the aptness of a relative or fixed chronology and over the weight given Acts do not surprise. Earlier works depend heavily on Acts, but in his seminal *Chapters in a Life of Paul*, John Knox insists on the letters' priority, but again, not all of them.[107] Knox himself nearly grasped the nettle here: that the collection shapes our access to Paul and his letters, which are mediated via the editorial concerns of a collector in the late first/early second century.[108] But then Knox pulls back and works quite conventionally: he relies exclusively on nine letters, chronologically arranges them (without Acts), and thereby excavates Paul from the collection. His later chapters, which garner little attention, offer precisely this—a biography ('The Man') derived from his chronology.[109]

These three moves, post-Knox, are now ingrained in the genre, and the last—chronology *as* biography—means that the generic space between a *Chronology* and a *Life and Letters* is porous, and distinguishing them somewhat arbitrary.[110] The *Chronology* is just another way to write a *Life*—thus the subtitle of Douglas Campbell's *Framing Paul: An Epistolary Biography*, the most recent work in this genre.[111] Given the a priori winnowing of the collection, however, the *Chronology* begets a *Life* in

---

[106] John Knox, *Chapters in a Life of Paul*, rev. ed. (London: SCM, 1987 [1950]); Charles H. Buck and Greer Taylor, *Saint Paul: A Study of the Development of His Thought* (New York: Scribner, 1969); A. Suhl, *Paulus und seine Briefe: Ein Beitrag zur paulinischen Chronologie*, SNT 11 (Gütersloh: Mohn, 1975); Robert Jewett, *A Chronology of Paul's Life* (Philadelphia: Fortress, 1979); Gerd Lüdemann, *Paul, Apostle to the Gentiles: Studies in Chronology*, trans. F. Stanley Jones (Philadelphia: Fortress, 1984 [1980]); Niels Hyldahl, *Die paulinische Chronologie*, ATDan 19 (Leiden: Brill, 1986); Rainer Riesner, *Paul's Early Period: Chronology, Mission Strategy, Theology*, trans. Doug Stott (Grand Rapids: Eerdmans, 1998 [1991]); Jerome Murphy-O'Connor, *Paul: A Critical Life* (Oxford: Oxford University Press, 1997); Gregory Tatum, *New Chapters in the Life of Paul: The Relative Chronology of His Career*, CBQMS 41 (Washington, DC: Catholic Biblical Association of America, 2006); Campbell, *Framing Paul*. Riesner, *Paul's Early Period*, 3–28, has a valuable history of research.

[107] For his method, see Knox, *Chapters in a Life of Paul*, 3–28.

[108] Knox, *Chapters in a Life of Paul*, 5–7.

[109] Knox sets out his chronology in a mere twelve pages (31–42), while the largest—and largely ignored—portion of the book is Pauline biography (53–131). His reduction to nine letters is at pp. 8–9. Campbell, *Framing Paul*, 24–6, who otherwise follows Knox, is rightly critical of him at this point.

[110] Tom Wright's *Paul: A Biography* (London: SPCK, 2018), now sits in exactly this borderland.

[111] Of all works on Pauline chronology, Campbell's *Framing Paul* is to my mind the most methodologically important. Its central virtue is to reject the a priori reduction to seven letters pervasive in other chronologies. All literary-historical reconstruction is circular, but if one wants chronology—and from that biography and theology—one cannot use a presumed theology to dictate the sources for a chronology that bequeaths said theology. Campbell is right to call that 'vicious circularity' (13–15). Moreover, the scope (thirteen) and results (ten authentic, excluding the Pastorals) of Campbell's work may suggest a return to the collection's priority, since it coincides with Marcion's *Apostolikon*, the earliest attested collection (384–91; cf. 413). More fundamentally, though, *Framing Paul* is nothing if not an intensification of the hermeneutic described in this chapter. By treating each letter as if we have discrete access to it, Campbell builds a case from the ground up, eschewing the collection. In fact, knowing Paul depends on precisely this project: '*Any valid interpretation in any historical respect must begin with a workable account of the letters' circumstances in relation to one another*.... This is the sine qua non of all valid historical interpretation of Paul' (12, emphasis original). Chronology equals biography, and like his modern forebears, Campbell's 'new' (by now traditional) way of framing Paul is allied to the rhetoric of the retrieval of history. In its basic stance vis-à-vis Paul's collection, then, *Framing Paul* stands in a long tradition of textual excavation and chronological narration for the sake of biographical portrayal.

its own image; and given its order, it is a *Life* geared towards narrating theological development, of which Charles Buck and Greer Taylor's 1969 *St. Paul: A Study of the Development of His Thought* is simply the firstfruits.[112] In both a *Life and Letters* and a *Chronology*, then, to know Paul depends on disregarding the primary evidence for that knowledge. It depends, that is, on a fresh act of editorial construction.

Pauline Theology

What does a Pauline *Theology* do with the collection? The effect is less obvious here since a theology of Paul is, almost in the nature of the case, synthetic. Further, when Paul is read maximally (thirteen letters), and under the headings of dogmatic *loci* (anthropology, eschatology, etc.), the effect is actually to turn back the clock to a way of reading the collection more akin to Priscillian of Avila than, say, to Baur.[113] This is not, however, typical. How to arrange a Pauline *Theology* is precisely the question,[114] and chronology (and thus development) is felt less here than one might expect. No full-scale Pauline *Theology* makes development its organizing principle—Part 1 of Udo Schnelle's *Paulus: Leben und Denken* comes closest—although any that reads development within a specific strand of Paul's thought is reaping the harvest of the chronological turn.[115]

As a synthetic genre, though—a Pauline *Theology* does not end with the theology of individual letters but of *Paul*[116]—the question of sources is paramount, and

---

[112] For a critical appraisal, see Victor Paul Furnish, 'Development in Paul's Thought', *JAAR* 38 (1970): 289–303.

[113] I think here of works like Herman N. Ridderbos, *Paul, An Outline of His Theology* (London: SPCK, 1977 [1966]), and Thomas R. Schreiner, *Paul, Apostle of God's Glory in Christ: A Pauline Theology* (Downers Grove: InterVarsity, 2001), although it is also an apt description of that work—Leonhard Usteri's 1824 *Entwickelung des paulinischen Lehrbegriffes mit Hinsicht auf die übrigen Schriften des Neuen Testament* (Zurich: Orill, Füssli)—that Albert Schweitzer terms the 'starting-point of the purely historical study of Paulinism' (*Paul and His Interpreters: A Critical History* [London: Black, 1912], 9; see especially Usteri, *Entwickelung*, 5–9). See Chapter 3 for discussion of Priscillian.

[114] James D. G. Dunn, *The Theology of Paul the Apostle* (Grand Rapids: Eerdmans, 1998), 19–23.

[115] Udo Schnelle, *Apostle Paul: His Life and Theology*, trans. M. Eugene Boring (Grand Rapids: Baker Academic, 2005 [2003]). Schnelle's *Paulus* is a generic hybrid—a *Life and Letters* meets *Chronology* meets *Theology*—that perfectly represents modern hermeneutical judgments on the *corpus Paulinum*. Because '[Paul's] thought cannot be separated from his life' (41), a chronological approach to Paul's theology is crucial—thus Part 1, 'The Course of Paul's Life and the Development of His Thought'—yet one that respects the integrity of discrete letters, while not precluding a 'holistic interpretation of Pauline thought' (46)—thus Part 2, 'The Basic Structures of Pauline Thought'. Like the SBL group (see below), Schnelle regards the seven letters as self-evidently the sources for Paul's theology (32, 47–56), since in the others justification subsides, apocalyptic declines, and church order and ethics prevail (150). Vis-à-vis Paul and the collection, all the key elements are here—textual origins, chronology, biography, history, theology and a restricted corpus—as well as the ambiguities. For while Schnelle's *Paulus*, structurally, suggests that his Pauline theology (Part 2) is built on firm historical ground (Part 1), in fact, Part 2 is presupposed throughout Part 1—just as Baur's Parts 1 and 2 presupposed his Part 3. Strikingly, Schnelle does this despite his own historiographical reflections that would trouble this reduction and rearrangement. Noting that all historiography is constructed, Schnelle writes, 'History is thus available only as memory—mediated and formed by language' (28–29). And, more obviously still, by artefacts. Yet Schnelle disregards precisely the Pauline memorializations we do have for one we do not—a seven-letter Paul. His practice, that is, suggests access to history apart from memory that his theoretical discussion dismisses.

[116] See here Dunn, *Theology of Paul*, 13–19.

here the collection *is* set aside. Vis-à-vis sources, Pauline Theologies post-1950 are idiosyncratic: Paul can be synthesized from seven letters (Bultmann; Schnelle; Wolter), nine (Whiteley; Dunn), ten/eleven (Wright), and thirteen (Ridderbos; Schreiner).[117] It can also be, functionally, the theology of Romans (Bultmann; Dunn).[118] Institutionally, however, Pauline theology is a seven-letter discipline, as is clear from the four volumes that arose from the Society of Biblical Literature (SBL) Pauline Theology group (1986–95).[119] For all its hermeneutical sophistication,[120] the one question this group never asked was the basic one: which sources count?[121] By 1986, the collection's seven/six divide is inarguable and foundational. Even the task of writing a theology of the seven-letter Paul, however, lay beyond the group, whose output comprised four volumes of collected essays on different aspects of the theologies of the individual letters. The result surely disappoints vis-à-vis the group's title (*Pauline* Theology), but it is, in large part, the natural flowering of the critical project: the synthetic editorializing of the collection traded for the fragmentary editorializing of discrete letters, kept intentionally and explicitly separate.[122]

Pauline Monographs

What of a wider set of works related to Paul? Across very different works, with very different conclusions, the collection vanishes equally: the letters are 'genuine letters' (à la Deissmann),[123] and so provide direct access to the social,[124] apocalyptic,[125] and

---

[117] Rudolf Bultmann, *Theology of the New Testament*, trans. Kendrick Grobel, 2 vols. (Waco: Baylor University Press, 2007 [1951–55]), 2:190; Schnelle, *Apostle Paul*, 32, 47–56; Michael Wolter, *Paul: An Outline of His Theology*, trans. Robert L. Brawley (Waco: Baylor University Press, 2015 [2011]), 6; Dunn, *Theology of Paul*, 13; D. E. H. Whiteley, *The Theology of St. Paul*, 2nd ed. (Oxford: Blackwell, 1974), xix–xx; N. T. Wright, *Paul and the Faithfulness of God*, 2 vols., Christian Origins and the Question of God 4 (Minneapolis: Fortress, 2013), 56–63.

[118] Bultmann, *Theology*, 2:190; Dunn, *Theology of Paul*, 25–6.

[119] Jouette M. Bassler, David M. Hay, and E. Elizabeth Johnson, eds., *Pauline Theology*, 4 vols. (Minneapolis: Fortress, 1991–97). For initial engagement with the work of this group, see Childs, *Church's Guide for Reading Paul*, 1–3.

[120] Jouette M. Bassler, 'Paul's Theology: Whence and Whither?', in *Pauline Theology II*, 3–17, and Paul W. Meyer, 'Pauline Theology: A Proposal for a Pause in Its Pursuit', in *Pauline Theology IV*, 140–60, are both useful windows into the group's core questions and key debates. Dunn, *Theology of Paul*, 1–26, is also clearly wrestling with the questions that emerged there.

[121] See David M. Hay, 'Pauline Theology After Paul', in *Pauline Theology IV*, 181–95.

[122] The group was committed from the outset to assessing the theology of individual letters before attempting any synthesis, and chose to begin with the shorter letters so as to free them from the 'theological dominance that the *Hauptbriefe* usually exercise on the Pauline corpus' (Jouette M. Bassler, 'Preface', in *Pauline Theology I*, ix–x).

[123] To choose the most recent major example, Paula Fredriksen, *Paul: The Pagans' Apostle* (New Haven: Yale University Press, 2017), 62–4.

[124] Abraham J. Malherbe, *Social Aspects of Early Christianity*, 2nd enl. ed. (Minneapolis: Fortress, 1983 [1977]); Gerd Theissen, *The Social Setting of Pauline Christianity: Essays on Corinth*, ed. and trans. John H. Schütz (Edinburgh: T. & T. Clark, 1982); Wayne A. Meeks, *The First Urban Christians: The Social World of the Apostle Paul*, 2nd ed. (New Haven: Yale University Press, 2003 [1983]).

[125] J. Christiaan Beker, *Paul the Apostle: The Triumph of God in Life and Thought* (Edinburgh: T. & T. Clark, 1980); Martinus C. de Boer, *The Defeat of Death: Apocalyptic Eschatology in 1 Corinthians 15 and Romans 5*, JSNTSup 22 (Sheffield: JSOT Press, 1988); J. Louis Martyn, *Galatians: A New Translation, with Introduction and Commentary*, AB 33A (New York: Doubleday, 1997); Beverley R. Gaventa, *Our Mother Saint Paul* (Louisville: Westminster John Knox, 2007); and Douglas A.

ethnoreligious[126] matrix of Paul and his Christ-groups in the mid-first century. Moreover, the source-critical division of the collection is ubiquitous in monographs on Paul, and almost always via passing appeal to the consensus. The list that follows depicts this across diverse trends in Pauline scholarship, and in its most seminal works: Stendahl [1976]; Sanders [1977]; Beker [1980]; Meeks [1983]; Boyarin [1994]; and Fredriksen [2017] all appeal to this reduction. Other works do not even mention the reduction, but clearly work from it: Gaston [1987]; Hays [1989]; Gager [2000]; Engberg-Pedersen [2000]; Watson [2004; 2007]; and Barclay [2015].[127] On the other side, the disputed letters are treated in an epilogue, restricted to footnotes, or simply ignored. The indices of the above works vividly make the point: at the apex of the discipline, and across its varied schools, Paul is seven letters, and in reality, only two—Romans and Galatians.

This preference has a long pedigree, but in the last forty years it has grown increasingly conspicuous. A remarkable set of scholars—E. P. Sanders and James Dunn associated with the New Perspective; J. Christiaan Beker, Martinus de Boer, J. Louis Martyn, Douglas Campbell and Beverley Gaventa with apocalyptic; John Barclay and Francis Watson somewhere between or beyond these; and Lloyd Gaston, John Gager and Paula Fredriksen with Jewish readings of Paul—all pitch their exegetical battles almost exclusively on the turf of Romans and Galatians.[128] Vis-à-vis the sources, then, today's scholarly Paul, while far from univocal, *is* a dyad.[129] As the quality of the above

---

Campbell, *The Deliverance of God: An Apocalyptic Rereading of Justification in Paul* (Grand Rapids: Eerdmans, 2009).

[126] So first, Krister Stendahl, *Paul Among Jews and Gentiles, and Other Essays* (London: SCM, 1976); E. P. Sanders, *Paul and Palestinian Judaism: A Comparison of Patterns of Religion* (London: SCM, 1977); James D. G. Dunn, *Jesus, Paul, and the Law: Studies in Mark and Galatians* (Louisville: Westminster John Knox, 1990), which collects a series of articles from the early 1980s; idem, *The New Perspective on Paul*, rev. ed. (Grand Rapids: Eerdmans, 2008); and N. T. Wright, *The Climax of the Covenant: Christ and the Law in Pauline Theology* (Edinburgh: T. & T. Clark, 1991). Now, quite differently, Lloyd Gaston, *Paul and the Torah* (Vancouver: University of British Columbia Press, 1987), and John G. Gager, *Reinventing Paul* (Oxford: Oxford University Press, 2000), whose influence remains in Fredriksen, *Paul*, and the scholars whose work comes together in Mark D. Nanos and Magnus Zetterholm, eds., *Paul within Judaism: Restoring the First-Century Context to the Apostle* (Minneapolis: Fortress, 2015).

[127] The works not cited in notes immediately above are Boyarin, *A Radical Jew*; Troels Engberg-Pedersen, *Paul and the Stoics* (Louisville: Westminster John Knox, 2000); John M. G. Barclay, *Paul and the Gift* (Grand Rapids: Eerdmans, 2015); Richard B. Hays, *Echoes of Scripture in the Letters of Paul* (New Haven: Yale University Press, 1989); Francis Watson, *Paul, Judaism, and the Gentiles: Beyond the New Perspective*, rev. and exp. ed. (Grand Rapids: Eerdmans, 2007 [1986]); and idem, *Paul and the Hermeneutics of Faith* (London: T&T Clark International, 2004).

[128] Wright's *Climax of the Covenant* is a notable exception, ranging substantially across 1 and 2 Corinthians, Philippians, Colossians, and Philemon in addition to Romans and Galatians.

[129] This source-critical reduction comes into sharp relief in Paula Fredriksen's *Paul*—a brilliant book, genuinely novel, and also deeply typical. That is, Fredriksen is a remarkably astute reader of the Paul of Romans and Galatians. Index-counting will have to suffice: Fredriksen cites Romans 372×; 1 Corinthians 134×; 2 Corinthians 48×; Galatians 177×; Philippians 44×; 1 Thessalonians 29×; and Philemon 2×—her most important texts being Rom 1.3-4; 1.18-32; 9.4-5; 11.25-26; 15.8-12; Gal 1.13-14; 2.15; and 5.11 (cf. 1 Cor 15; Phil 3.5-6; 1 Thess 4.13-18). On the other side, she cites Ephesians 4×; Colossians 3×; 2 Thessalonians 2×; and 1 and 2 Timothy and Titus 1× each. In total, then, she cites the seven-letter Paul 806× and the six-letter (pseudo-)Paul 12×, and every time (save the two of Eph 6.12) to say that these latter citations get Paul wrong. Moreover, Fredriksen's reasons for rejecting the disputeds are thoroughly traditional, and rooted in perceived chronological development: fading eschatology, universalized ecclesiology, and creeping institutionalism (169). None,

works shows, this reduction is productive for knowledge of Paul, but also strange, for each claims to shift the study of Paul in substantial ways, but never invites a return to the very sources whose division was birthed by the now-vanquished reading. Fresh readings of Paul, that is, never drive Paul's modern readers back to the collection, and so never raise the fundamental hermeneutical question (i.e. what we read). The collection's divide is the sine qua non of the modern Pauline monograph.

Pauline Reception

Finally, what of the other side of the collection—the disputed letters cut away? If anything, the potential of modern ways of (not) reading the collection is greater here than even for Paul, for what Paul loses history gains. A period troublingly opaque (70–120 CE) receives six further points of illumination, and a series of works since the 1970s—most notably Barrett [1974], Schenke [1975], Lindemann [1979], Dassmann [1979], de Boer [1980], Beker [1991], Sterling [2007], Marguerat [2008], and now Pervo [2010]—have been quick to take up the task.[130] All of this, of course, goes back to Baur's perenially suggestive insight, that the disputeds 'belong, not to the biography of the apostle himself, but to the history of the party which used his name'—that is, with other 'legends' of Pauline reception.[131]

More than a century after Baur, C. K. Barrett finds in Ephesians, the Pastorals, Acts and 1 Clement an early 'hagiographical portrait of Paul' (or a 'positive Pauline legend') which fills in the otherwise strange silence vis-à-vis Paul up to Irenaeus.[132] So too in Hans-Martin Schenke's 1975 article: the disputeds reflect an early Paul-legend (*Paul-Sage*) that circulates prior to and independent of the earliest form of the collection (= 1 Corinthians; 2 Corinthians; Galatians; Philippians; 1 Thessalonians; Romans), and thus offer a window into the care of Paul's legacy in his *Schule*.[133] The

---

therefore, may speak for or illuminate Paul. The gospels, however, may: Fredriksen cites Matthew 26×; Mark 30×; Luke 18×; and John 6×. If citations tell a tale, Fredriksen finds the fourfold gospel roughly eight times more suggestive for knowing Paul than the six eponymous letters that on her view follow in his wake. Fredriksen's break in the corpus is thus not a little ironic, since the gospels and Acts, which she is happier to use, stem from the same period.

[130] C. K. Barrett, 'Pauline Controversies in the Post-Pauline Period', NTS 20 (1974): 229–45; H.-M. Schenke, 'Das Weiterwirken des Paulus und die Pflege seines Erbes durch die Paulus-Schule', NTS 21 (1975): 505–18; Andreas Lindemann, *Paulus im ältesten Christentum: Das Bild des Apostels und die Rezeption der paulinischen Theologie in der frühchristlichen Literatur bis Marcion*, BHT 58 (Tübingen: Mohr, 1979); Ernst Dassmann, *Der Stachel im Fleisch: Paulus in der frühchristlichen Literatur bis Irenäus* (Münster: Aschendorff, 1979); Martinus de Boer, 'Images of Paul in the Post-Apostolic Period', CBQ 42 (1980): 359–80; J. Christiaan Beker, *Heirs of Paul: Their Legacy in the New Testament and the Church Today* (Minneapolis: Augsburg Fortress, 1991; repr. Grand Rapids: Eerdmans, 1996); Gregory E. Sterling, 'From Apostle to the Gentiles to Apostle of the Church: Images of Paul at the End of the First Century', ZNW 99 (2007): 74–98; Daniel Marguerat, 'Paul après Paul: une histoire de réception', NTS 54 (2008): 317–37; Richard I. Pervo, *The Making of Paul: Constructions of the Apostle in Early Christianity* (Minneapolis: Fortress, 2010). On these works, see White, *Remembering Paul*, 42–9.

[131] Baur, *Paul*, 2:111.

[132] Barrett, 'Pauline Controversies', 235–41 (here 241). The language of 'legend' (243) is no accident; Barrett appeals to Baur's ongoing importance on the same page.

[133] Schenke, 'Das Weiterwirken des Paulus', 514. See here also Hans Conzelmann, 'Die Schule Des Paulus', in *Theologia Crucis—signum Crucis: Festschrift für E. Dinkler*, ed. C. Andresen and G. Klein (Tübingen: Mohr Siebeck, 1979), 85–96.

legend, of course, and the *Schule,* depend on Barrett and Schenke's inferred break in the collection—a break de Boer then exploits to depict six foci of this developing legend.[134] Critically, de Boer plots these images halfway along a trajectory from Paul to the second century, which thus indicates for him the late first-century origins of the letters in which they are inscribed.[135] Excised and relocated, these letters are then utilized by a series of monographs as the raw data for the varied ways in which Paul is put to work.[136] Variable though they are, however, they are still frequently read together, as if a mini-collective (thus, the *Schule*)—what Daniel Marguerat labels the 'doctoral' (i.e. theological *ressourcement*) pole of Pauline reception.[137] From the 1970s on, Baur's 'history of the party' gets written, but almost entirely via a sundered corpus. In larger-scale works, to be sure, this history does not depend entirely on the divide, and Andreas Lindemann and Richard Pervo rightly recognize the collection itself as an act of reception, which governs access to Paul.[138] From here, though, their work exhibits the same ambiguities as above, since both extract the generative layer of post-Pauline Paulinism from the disputed letters.[139] The key move, always and everywhere, is how to read the collection: its scope and order. The seven/six divide is productive on both sides.

Conclusion

How, then, does historical criticism read the only Pauls we have? The short answer is that it does not. 'Like a blow-lamp turned on a snowball', Robert Morgan writes, 'historical exegesis melts away layers of interpretation'—and, I would add, the

---

[134] de Boer, 'Images of Paul', passim, but nicely summarized on 370.
[135] de Boer, 'Images of Paul', 362.
[136] See, e.g., Margaret Y. MacDonald, *The Pauline Churches: A Socio-Historical Study of Institutionalization in the Pauline and Deutero-Pauline Writings*, SNTSMS 60 (Cambridge: Cambridge University Press, 1988); Anthony J. Blasi, *Making Charisma: The Social Construction of Paul's Public Image* (New Brunswick, NJ: Transaction Publishers, 1991); James W. Aageson, *Paul, the Pastoral Epistles and the Early Church* (Peabody, MA: Hendrickson, 2008).
[137] Marguerat, 'Paul après Paul', 322–3.
[138] Lindemann, *Paulus im ältesten Christentum*, 29–33; Pervo, *Making of Paul*, 23–61.
[139] Lindemann, *Paulus im ältesten Christentum*, 36–49; Pervo, *Making of Paul*, 63–118. As the subtitle suggests, Pervo's *The Making of Paul: Constructions of the Apostle in Early Christianity* is a study of the sundry ways Paul was put to use from the deutero-Paulines to Irenaeus. Chapter 1, neatly titled 'Paul Becomes a Book', admits that by the early second century, Paul's readers encounter him via a collection—the first making of Paul (23–61, here 61). Pervo's Paul, however, is made of quite different stuff—seven letters—and so his Chapter 2 ('The Pseudepigraphic Pauline Letters') describes, in part at least, still earlier instances of making Paul. Pervo's division, of course, presumes access to Paul apart from the collection, and this does a lot of argumentative work for him. Pervo uses the disputeds collectively to psychologize the collector, whose purpose is safely to transmit Paul for Catholic Christianity, and individually to depict the many and varied 'components of the developing Pauline legacy' by plotting them alongside non-canonical pseudepigrapha (6; cf. 63–118). With six more texts to hand, the early making of Paul is now considerably more robust—a welcome addition to Pervo's thesis, albeit one that depends entirely on dismembering Paul's collection. Without it, Pervo has neither the motivation for the collection, nor seventy-five years worth of material for Chapter 2. The first seventy-five years after Paul's death, in fact, see a veritable explosion in the making of Paul, so long as one can parse 'Paul' (the disputeds) from 'Paul' (the undisputeds) in the only Pauls (the collection) that we have.

collection itself, our primary source for Paul.[140] The project begun in Baur's 1845 *Paulus* runs apace. From the 1950s to the present, and across every genre of the study of Paul, that project accelerates and calcifies. The collection is thirteen discrete data points, grouped in two, with both halves chronologically rearranged; the former narrate Paul, and the latter the welter of his legacy. To pick up virtually any book on Paul today, creative though it may be in myriad ways, is to meet Paul dismembered. For a scholar like Leander Keck, this is a good thing:

> What does liberating Paul from the church involve? It means first of all emancipating him from the clutches of his friends in the [New Testament], namely from the consequences of reading Paul, insofar as we have him in the undisputed letters, through the lenses of the Pauline pseudepigrapha and of Acts.... By making him the house theologian of the institutional church, the radicality of Paul's gospel is blunted, for he now is made to speak for this church more than he is free to speak to it. Nowhere does this come through stronger than in Ephesians.[141]

Pace Keck, the 'consequences of reading Paul' are on display as acutely in the dissolution of the collection as they were in its construction. The now two-century old project of 'isolat[ing] the individual work of [Paul] within the body of work ascribed to him' is a legitimate project, but it is also a construct.[142] Undoing the manuscript, in principle valid, is deeply fragile—a task in which construction lies veiled beneath the ideological cloak of reconstruction. Such ideology is always as likely to misshape as to shape. To steal Keck's closing line, now for a different purpose, 'Nowhere does this come through stronger than in Ephesians'. That claim now requires a defense.

---

[140] Robert Morgan, 'Paul's Enduring Legacy', in *The Cambridge Companion to St. Paul*, ed. James D. G. Dunn (Cambridge: Cambridge University Press, 2003), 245.

[141] Leander Keck, 'What to Do with Paul', in *Christ's First Theologian: The Shape of Paul's Thought* (Waco: Baylor University Press, 2015), 269; cf. Barrett, 'Pauline Controversies', 244, and Victor P. Furnish, 'On Putting Paul in His Place', *JBL* 113 (1994): 3–17. Acknowledged or not, each is essentially a paraphrase of Käsemann, 'Paul and Early Catholicism', 249–50.

[142] The original quotation, *mutatis mutandis*, belongs to Kenneth Dover and refers to scholarship on Lysias, 'In attempting to isolate the individual work of Lysias within the body of work ascribed to him we are trying in the first instance to undo what was done in the fourth century' (*Lysias and the Corpus Lysiacum*, 26).

Chapter 2

DISPLACING EPHESIANS

In his famous 1963 article 'Paulus und der Frühkatholizismus', first given as a lecture in 1962 to the *Theologische Arbeitsgemeinschaft* in Tübingen, Ernst Käsemann closes with a panegyric to the 'real Paul':

> Alongside this [early catholic] image of Paul, to which the ecclesiastical future belonged, there is, however, the real Paul as well. This Paul remains confined in seven letters and for the most part unintelligible to posterity, not only to the ancient Church and the Middle Ages. However, whenever he is rediscovered…there issues from him explosive power which destroys as much as it opens up something new.[1]

What Paul's rediscovery destroys, it turns out, is early catholicism, but what it requires is the reading project I outline in Chapter 1: excavating the Paul 'confined in seven letters' and shrouded by *frühkatholische Briefe*. Enter Ephesians: 'In the New Testament', Käsemann writes elsewhere, 'it is Ephesians that most clearly marks the transition from the Pauline tradition to the perspectives of the early Catholic era'.[2]

While more muted rhetorically, Pauline and Ephesians scholarship since have largely agreed, and the effect on Ephesians is pervasive. Dislocated from Paul and relocated historically, Ephesians morphs into advanced, developed, conciliatory, catholicized, institutionalized Paulinism. Nothing in Ephesians itself, I argue, suggests (much less demands) these judgments. What is striking, though, is their ubiquity across very different works on Paul, and regardless of how one judges its authorship. This suggests that they derive from a prior set of convictions about the scope and, most importantly, order of Paul's letter collection. To put it directly, virtually all scholars read Ephesians as the genealogical heir of the *Hauptbriefe*, and so judgments about its alleged development prove remarkably stable. Chronology is king. It turns difference into historical distance, which then invites hermeneutical distance (i.e. development). Modern judgments about Ephesians are the product of modern ways of reading.

---

[1] Käsemann, 'Paul and Early Catholicism', 249–50, first published under its German title in *ZTK* 60 (1963): 75–89. One-hundred years earlier, Baur says much the same in his *Church History*, 1:113.
[2] Käsemann, 'Ephesians and Acts', 288; cf. 290.

The Enigma of the Consensus

In one sense, this is a simple matter of bibliography: the consensus on Ephesians is not a product of Ephesians scholarship, but of the *Einleitung* and *Urchristentum*, precisely those genres responsible for dissolving the collection. In Germany, this runs from the fourth edition of de Wette's *Einleitung*, in which the judgment is exceedingly tentative, to Baur's *Paulus* and *Kirchengeschichte* and on to Schwegler, Hilgenfeld, Weizsäcker and Pfleiderer—a series of works on Christian origins which draw Ephesians into the literary welter of post-Pauline Christianity, and then exploit this setting for maximal interpretive purchase.[3] It is telling that in his 1987 *Forschungsbericht* on Ephesians, Helmut Merkel focuses almost exclusively on these figures for this period: new judgments about Ephesians stem from its new place within Christian origins.[4] Moreover, all of this takes place while Ephesians scholarship proper—as seen in the commentaries of Gottlieb C. A. Harless (1834/1858), Hermann Olshausen (1840), and Heinrich Meyer (1843/1878)—remains firmly committed to its Pauline authorship.[5] From roughly 1845 to 1890, then, where the *Einleitung/Urchristentum* and *Kommentar* traditions stand at odds, the former prevails and the latter (eventually) follows suit.[6] A way of reading the collection precedes and generates a way of reading Ephesians.

The same is true, albeit less obviously so, in Anglophone scholarship. Here, too, the first substantial works to displace Ephesians are Introductions—Davidson (1868) and Moffatt (1911)—and again, against the full weight of the commentary tradition.[7]

---

[3] de Wette, *Introduction*, 274–85 decides largely on the basis of literary dependence, but he does not think that Ephesians actually shows *signs* of a later age (284–5). On the other figures mentioned, see below.

[4] Helmut Merkel, 'Der Epheserbrief in der neuren exegetischen Diskussion', *ANRW* 25.4:3156–246, here 3162–7. The major exception, at least in part, is Holtzmann, *Kritik der Epheser- und Kolosserbriefe*, who argues firstly from literary dependence.

[5] Gottlieb C. A. Harless, *Commentar über den Brief Pauli an die Ephesier*, 2nd ed. (Stuttgart: Liesching, 1858); Hermann Olshausen, *Biblical Commentary on St Paul's Epistles to the Galatians, Ephesians, Colossians, and Thessalonians*, trans. A Clergyman of the Church of England (Edinburgh: T. & T. Clark, 1851); Heinrich A. W. Meyer, *Kritisch-exegetisches Handbuch über den Brief an die Epheser*, 5th ed., KEK (Göttingen: Vandenhoeck & Ruprecht, 1878).

[6] Hermann von Soden, *Die Briefe an die Kolosser, Epheser, Philemon; die Pastoral Briefe*, 2nd ed., HKNT 3 (Freiburg: Mohr, 1893); Albert Klöpper, *Der Brief an die Epheser* (Göttingen: Vandenhoeck & Ruprecht, 1891); Martin Dibelius, *An die Kolosser, Epheser, an Philemon*, 3rd ed., HNT 12 (Tübingen: Mohr, 1953); Joachim Gnilka, *Der Epheserbrief*, 2nd ed., HThKNT 10 (Freiburg: Herder, 1982); Franz Mußner, *Der Brief an die Epheser*, ÖTK 10 (Gütersloh: Gütersloh Verlagshaus, 1982); Rudolf Schnackenburg, *Der Brief an die Epheser*, EKKNT 10 (Zurich: Benziger, 1982); Eng. trans. *Ephesians: A Commentary*, trans. Helen Heron (Edinburgh: T. & T. Clark, 1991); Petr Pokorný, *Der Brief des Paulus an die Epheser*, THKNT 10/2 (Leipzig: Evangelische Verlagsanstaldt, 1992); and now Gerhard Sellin, *Der Brief an die Epheser*, KEK 8 (Göttingen: Vandenhoeck & Ruprecht, 2008). The major exception is Heinrich Schlier, *Der Brief an die Epheser: Ein Kommentar* (Düsseldorf: Patmos, 1971).

[7] J. A. Eadie, *A Commentary on the Greek Text of the Epistle of Paul to the Ephesians*, 3rd ed. (Edinburgh: T. & T. Clark, 1883); C. J. Ellicott, *St. Paul's Epistle to the Ephesians: with a Critical and Grammatical Commentary, and a Revised Translation*, 5th ed. (London: Longmans, Green, 1884); T. K. Abbott, *A Critical and Exegetical Commentary on the Epistles to the Ephesians and to the Colossians*, ICC (Edinburgh: T. & T. Clark, 1897); J. A. Robinson, *St. Paul's Epistle to the Ephesians: A Revised Text and Translation with Exposition and Notes* (London: Macmillan, 1903); B. F. Westcott, *St. Paul's Epistle to the Ephesians* (London: Macmillan, 1906).

Moffatt gains few immediate followers, but two that he does gain are substantial: both Edgar Goodspeed (1930, et al.) and Leslie Mitton (1951) appeal to the force of Moffatt's analysis, and it is the latter that F. W. Beare thought had 'finally demolished the case for the tradition'.[8] Moffatt, Goodspeed, and Mitton argue largely from literary dependence, and so depend less on developmental theories of Christian origins than their German counterparts, but their judgments still arise from a distinctly modern (genealogical) way of reading the collection.[9]

It is worth saying, however, that these early Anglophone cracks do not prompt a consensus. The tradition, contra Beare, is more resilient than demolished after Mitton, who himself admits five years later that the question is still open.[10] The same is true of Henry Cadbury's 1958 SNTS presidential address—'The Dilemma of Ephesians'—which presupposes a scholarly stalemate. In 1960, the British patrist Henry Chadwick calls the authorship of Ephesians an 'unlösbaren Problem', and eight years later, Ralph Martin suggests it may never be 'resolved conclusively'.[11] Both turn, instead, to what they consider the more important question of the letter's purpose. To this scholarly agnosticism one may add the positive judgments of A. van Roon (1974) and Markus Barth (1974), the only full-scale Anglophone commentary (Barth) and the only monograph dedicated to the authorship question (van Roon) published in the twenty-five years after Mitton.[12] What we have in Anglophone Ephesians scholarship as of 1975, in other words, is not a consensus but a muddle.

So when, in 1984, Raymond Brown estimates that eighty percent of critical scholars think Ephesians pseudonymous, the number may surprise.[13] What happens in the twenty-five years between Cadbury's stalemate and Brown's consensus? The short answer is that Anglophone scholarship starts *using* Ephesians like its German counterparts, thanks in part to shifting conceptions of pseudepigraphy across the

---

[8] Goodspeed, 'Place of Ephesians', 189 n. 1; Mitton, *Epistle to the Ephesians*, 2; F. W. Beare, review of *Epistle to the Ephesians*, JBL 72 (1953): 70-2 (70).

[9] See here Henry J. Cadbury, in his review of *Epistle to the Ephesians* (JBR 20 [1952]: 210, 212): 'At some points I think Mitton's argument rests unconsciously on the supposed order of Paul's letters' (212).

[10] C. Leslie Mitton, 'Important Hypotheses Reconsidered: VII. The Authorship of the Epistle to the Ephesians', *ExpTim* 67 (1956): 195-8 (198). See, this same year, the edited volume of British scholarship on Ephesians, which opens with juxtaposed chapters on authorship, J. N. Sanders ('The Case for the Pauline Authorship', in *Studies in Ephesians*, ed. Frank Leslie Cross [London: Mowbray, 1956], 9-20) arguing for and Dennis Nineham against ('The Case Against the Pauline Authorship', 21-35).

[11] Henry Chadwick, 'Die Absicht des Epheserbriefes', *ZNW* 51 (1960): 145-53 (here 145); Ralph P. Martin, 'An Epistle in Search of a Life-Setting', *ExpTim* 79 (1968): 296-302 (here 297).

[12] van Roon, *Authenticity of Ephesians*; Barth, *Ephesians*. Aside from Mitton, the only major English-language monograph to argue against Pauline authorship during this period is John C. Kirby, *Ephesians, Baptism and Pentecost: An Inquiry into the Structure and Purpose of the Epistle to the Ephesians* (London: SPCK, 1968).

[13] Raymond Brown, *The Churches the Apostles Left Behind* (New York: Paulist, 1984), 47. In terms of scholars' positions in print, the number is surely inflated (see the tables in Harold W. Hoehner, *Ephesians: An Exegetical Commentary* [Grand Rapids: Baker, 2002], 6-20), but it tellingly reflects Brown's *impression* of critical scholarship as of 1984—different from Cadbury's in 1958, and even Barrett's ('Pauline Controversies', 239) in 1974. Pace Hoehner, more than a numbers game, a consensus is what a discipline allows to count at the institutional level (so, rightly, White, *Remembering Paul*, 183-9). In this respect, Brown's impressionistic judgment functions like an appeal to a scholarly magisterium, and reveals quite a lot about the status of Ephesians by 1984.

1970s that see these texts as literary *Fälschungen* (forgery).¹⁴ The upshot is an emphasis on literary disruption—seeking the particular purposes for which Paul is put to use. It is no accident, in other words, that this period sees the genesis of works on Pauline reception—Barrett (1974), Penny (1979), de Boer (1980), and Brown (1984)—that read the disputeds not vis-à-vis Paul but *each other* (and Acts, et al.) to reconstruct the warp and woof of Paul's legacy.¹⁵ Now (post-1975), and only now, is a consensus forged; and now, and only now, does Ephesians scholarship—the commentaries of Lincoln (1990), Kitchen (1994), Perkins (1997), Best (1998), MacDonald (2000), and Muddiman (2001)—follow suit.¹⁶ As in Germany, so also in Anglophone scholarship: dismembering the collection precedes, generates, and calcifies a certain way of reading Ephesians. The enigma of the consensus is that it is not firstly about Ephesians.

The Quest for the Historical Ephesians

It is, instead, about the historiographical shape of early Christianity, which itself depends on the way of reading a collection outlined in the last chapter. On this score, it is telling that the *Einleitung*, which begins this process, can only get one so far toward a negative judgment on Ephesians,¹⁷ but that the consensus takes root in the wake of those works that, following Baur, source-critically narrate early Christianity.

---

¹⁴ The bibliography here, since 1960, is expansive. The seminal works are those of Wolfgang Speyer (1971), Norbert Brox (1975), and now, on the English side, Bart D. Ehrman (2013). For concise history with bibliography, see David E. Aune, 'Reconceptualizing the Phenomenon of Ancient Pseudepigraphy', in *Pseudepigraphie und Verfasserfiktion in frühchristlichen Briefen*, ed. Jörg Frey et al., WUNT 246 (Tübingen: Mohr Siebeck, 2009), 789–824 (792–3); and also the indispensable annotated bibliography of Armin D. Baum, 'Authorship and Pseudepigraphy in Early Christian Literature: A Translation of the Most Important Source Texts and an Annotated Bibliography', in Stanley E. Porter and Gregory P. Fewster, eds., *Paul and Pseudepigraphy*, Pauline Studies 8 (Leiden: Brill, 2013), 11–63 (here 56–63).

¹⁵ See here, especially, Donald N. Penny, 'The Pseudo-Pauline Letters of the First Two Centuries', (PhD diss., Emory University, 1979), drawing on Speyer and Brox (Ephesians at 221–87). This legacy is increasingly cast in polemical terms, with the relevant texts involved in internecine dispute over Paul's legacy. For the impact on Ephesians, see van Kooten, *Cosmic Christology*; and Martin Hüneburg, 'Paulus versus Paulus: Der Epheserbrief als Korrektur des Colosserbriefes', in *Pseudepigraphie und Verfasserfiktion in frühchristlichen Briefen*, ed. Jörg Frey et al., WUNT 246 (Tübingen: Mohr Siebeck, 2009), 387–409, the latter of which is picked up by Bart D. Ehrman, *Forgery and Counterforgery: The Use of Literary Deceit in Early Christian Polemics* (New York: Oxford University Press), 189–90.

¹⁶ Andrew T. Lincoln, *Ephesians*, WBC 42 (Dallas: Word, 1990); Martin Kitchen, *Ephesians* (New York: Routledge, 1994); Pheme Perkins, *Ephesians*, ANTC (Nashville: Abingdon, 1997); Ernest Best, *A Critical and Exegetical Commentary on Ephesians*, ICC (Edinburgh: T. & T. Clark, 1998); Margaret Y. MacDonald, *Colossians and Ephesians*, SP 17 (Collegeville: Liturgical Press, 2000); and John Muddiman, *The Epistle to the Ephesians*, BNTC 10 (Peabody: Hendrickson, 2001), who regards the letter as largely that of a later Paulinist working with a core of authentic Pauline material. For defense of Pauline authorship, see Peter T. O'Brien, *The Letter to the Ephesians*, PNTC (Grand Rapids: Eerdmans, 1999); Harold W. Hoehner, *Ephesians: An Exegetical Commentary* (Grand Rapids: Baker Academic, 2002); Frank Thielman, *Ephesians*, BECNT (Grand Rapids: Baker Academic, 2010); Clinton E. Arnold, *Ephesians*, ZECNT (Grand Rapids: Zondervan, 2010); and now Lynn H. Cohick, *The Letter to the Ephesians*, NICNT (Grand Rapids: Eerdmans, 2020). Stephen E. Fowl, *Ephesians: A Commentary* (Louisville: Westminster John Knox, 2012), represents a return to the studied agnosticism of Cadbury.

¹⁷ As of 1842, *Einleitungen* offer only a positive valuation of Ephesians (Michaelis, Hug, Eichhorn, Credner, Schleiermacher) or a highly equivocal and tentative judgment against (de Wette).

To relocate Ephesians, in other words—*for there even to be a quest for the historical Ephesians*—one needs the larger story in which it fits. So it is little surprise that the nineteenth and twentieth centuries' most consequential and lasting judgments about Ephesians occur in the work of two scholars who do just this: F. C. Baur and Ernst Käsemann. This section, then, is largely taken up with Baur and Käsemann's readings of Ephesians in the context of their larger programs.

Baur's story of Christian origins is well known, and need not be described in detail. It proceeds in two basic stages: primitive Christianity, characterized by a factional conflict between a gentile (Pauline) and Jewish (Petrine) wing, slowly reconciles in the nascent Catholic church; this nascent Catholicism, then, faced with the dual threat of Gnosticism and Montanism, asserts its dogmatic and structural authority in the fully developed Catholicism of the late second century.[18] As we have seen, Baur's divided corpus helps narrate the Pauline side of this story, as Paul's followers develop and modify Paulinism in the face of its antagonists.

If his plot is well known, what may surprise is how equivocal Baur is about the *Antilegomena* when they are taken at face value, apart from his reconstruction. As he writes, 'There is not a single one against which, from the standpoint of the four chief Epistles, some objection or other cannot be raised. In their entire nature they are so essentially different from the four first Epistles, that even if they are considered as Pauline, they must form a second class of Epistles of the Apostle, as they must have been composed for the most part at a later period of his apostolic course.'[19] The surprise is not in the first sentence but the second, where Baur concedes their possible authenticity, albeit as the ebb of the Pauline tide. In the end, Baur decides otherwise, in part because of how he makes such a decision: 'A comprehensive historical theory… appeals to its broad general truth, to which details are subordinate, and on which they depend'.[20] The disputeds *could* be authentic, that is, if not for Baur's large-scale reconstruction (the 'general'), which makes sense of textual minutiae (the 'detail'), which then reinforce the solidity of the larger story—thus the circularity of Baur's positive criticism.[21] From the beginning, the quest for the historical Ephesians is bound up with the quest for the story of Christian origins.

Baur's reading of Ephesians reflects this. At the critical moments, he gains interpretive leverage by mirror-reading the letter at the nexus of his stages, depicting both a conciliatory *Tendenz* and the early rumblings of Gnosticism—all from the 'side of Paulinism'.[22] The latter judgment is largely linguistic—Baur reads πλήρωμα, σῶμα, μυστήριον, σοφία, γνῶσις, αἰών, κοσμοκράτωρ, φῶς and σκότος in Ephesians vis-à-vis

---

[18] Thus, the shape of Baur's *Kirchengeschichte*, Part 2 of which narrates the former, and Part 3 the latter. For concise summary, see Hefner, 'Baur Versus Ritschl', 259–63.
[19] Baur, *Paul*, 1:256.
[20] Baur, *Paul*, 1:vii; cf. Rollman, 'From Baur to Wrede', 447.
[21] To be sure, Baur's reconstruction is not a pure imposition (so rightly Morgan, 'F. C. Baur: Paul', 7), and he derives settings via exegesis. As early as 1831 Baur had located exegetically, via 1 Cor 1.12, the conflict that drives his history, which he then narrates source-critically across his oeuvre ('Die Christpartei in der korinthischen Gemeinde, der Gegensatz des petrinischen und paulinischen Christenthums in der ältesten Kirche, der Apostel Petrus in Rom', *Tübinger Zeitschrift für Theologie* 4 [1831]: 61–206). The point here is only that, given its generality, a text like Ephesians derives a good deal of its meaning from Baur's scheme itself.
[22] Baur, *Church History*, 1:122; cf. 1:127.

Valentinus (via Irenaeus)—and since Gnosticism, for Baur, is a purely second-century phenomenon, this linguistic overlap is enough to displace Ephesians.[23] Baur also derives a proto-gnostic setting from the letter's Christology, which has been transposed from the realm of soteriology (as in the *Hauptbriefe*) to ontology: Christ is now the 'absolute principle of all existence' and so the 'centre of the unity of all opposites'.[24]

This is not, however, Christology for Christology's sake, but rather a Christology forged to ground the unity of one particular set of opposites, Jewish and gentile Christianity.[25] And just here Baur's larger picture helps him locate Ephesians:

> All this carries us to that period when, not without the ferment and commotion of conflicting elements, the Christian church was coming to realize herself and to achieve her unity. *With all the authors of the immediately post-apostolic age whose writings have come down to us, the prominent interest of the time appears to have been the unity of the Church*, the necessity of which they recognised, and which they strove in various ways to usher in. We have thus before us *a state of affairs which lies beyond the stand-point of the apostle Paul*. His task was to lay the foundations of the Gentile Christian churches; but here we see the two parties fully formed, and confronting each other, and the great point is to bring them nearer to each other, and to bridge over the gulf which still divides them.[26]

On Baur's topography, a conciliatory *Tendenz* takes us beyond Paul, and this is what he finds in Ephesians: not Paul the evangelist of gentiles, but 'Paul' the ecumenist of the church. As with any ecumenist, this involves concessions—here to Jewish Christianity—that Baur thinks Paul would never allow.[27]

So, the Paulinist of Ephesians repurposes the death of Christ, from 'religious anthropology' (as in the *Hauptbriefe*) to the 'reconciliation of heathens and Jews' (i.e. ecclesiology).[28] He pairs faith and works in Eph 2.8–10, a catholicizing concession in the direction of James.[29] And he functionally reduces the law to circumcision (Eph 2.11–16).[30] But for Baur, the real problem, or, positively, the text that most illustrates this Jewish *Tendenz*, is Eph 2.11–22.

> [In it] the heathen have only received a share of what the Jews had before; and thus Christianity is not the absolute religion in which the negativeness

---

[23] Baur, *Paul*, 2:9–22; cf. *Church History*, 127. Baur rejects that this overlap may result from later gnostic use of Ephesians, or that gnostic antecedents pre-date the second century, to which Paul responds (*Paul*, 1:21). Gnosticism as exclusively a second-century mutation of Christianity, while understandable in Baur's day, is no longer tenable. See Michael Williams, *Rethinking Gnosticism* (Princeton: Princeton University Press, 1996); and Karen L. King, *What is Gnosticism* (Cambridge: Belknap, 2003).
[24] Baur treats the Christology of Ephesians and Colossians together. The above is stated most clearly in *Paul*, 2:6–9, but see also 35–7; cf. 39.
[25] See here Baur, *Paul*, 2:35–6.
[26] Baur, *Paul*, 2:38. Emphasis mine.
[27] Baur, *Paul*, 2:40.
[28] Baur, *Paul*, 2:41. More broadly, see 37–42, esp. 39.
[29] Baur, *Paul*, 2:39–40.
[30] Baur, *Paul*, 2:41.

of heathenism and that of Judaism come to an end together; on the contrary, the substantial contents of Christianity are just Judaism itself. Thus the universality of Christianity consists in this, that Judaism is extended to the heathen through the death of Christ.[31]

The central problem, it turns out, is that Ephesians fails to live up to Baur's pattern of the history of religion. Ephesians' Christianity is a relapse into Judaism, or simply Judaism writ large. And if anything characterizes Paul for Baur, it is his opposition to Judaism.[32]

To be sure, Baur identifies the above 'problems' via exegesis; Ephesians is not simply a palimpsest on which he works Hegelian mischief. But that these *are* problems, which necessitate Ephesians' displacement, is largely a function of Baur's Paulinism, together with his narration of Christian origins as the slow fall from a Lutheran Paul to the Roman church.[33] For this story, a rearranged *corpus Paulinum* is critical. But note the effect on Ephesians, and particularly the language of Baur's judgment. Catholicism blunts Paul's revolutionary idea by combining it with Jewish forms—'theocratic institutions', 'aristocratic forms', the episcopate, and a 'rule of life' in place of justification—and Ephesians is a stage on the way.[34] In seeking rapprochement with Jewish Christianity, the Paulinist of Ephesians concedes too much. It is too Jewish, and thus too Catholic, to be Pauline.

These dual judgments dominate in the generation after Baur.[35] For Adolf Hilgenfeld, the author is a 'Unionspauliner' who absorbs Paul within the broader apostolic ambit (2.20; 3.5–6), which betrays 'eine katholisirende Richtung'. The church in Ephesians is 'eine Einheit des Glaubens und der Verfassung' (4.5–6)—for Hilgenfeld, 'ein katholischer Zug'.[36] Heinrich Holtzmann condenses Baur's timeline, but largely retains his view of Ephesians, which reflects 'eine vereinigte Kirche der Juden und Griechen' that stands together in 'gefastigten Christianheit'—albeit closer to the 'jüdischen Standpunkte'.[37] Both, that is, see in Ephesians a universalized Jewish/Catholic ecclesiology foreign to Paul. So too in Karl Weizsäcker: Ephesians fails to defend 'das Recht der Heiden' as such, but merely enfolds them into the church. This Paulinist is, thus, a 'Vertreter der Gleich-berechtigung und der Einheit der Gemeinde im Prinzip', which makes him, unsurprisingly, a 'Vertreter des jüdischen Teiles der Christen' in 'einer dem geschichtlichen Paulus ganz fremden Weise'.[38] Otto Pfleiderer revises Baur's history and gives Ephesians a new setting—now in response to gentile 'Selbstüberhebung und Separationsgelüste'—but the interpretive upshot remains the same: 'Nicht mehr,

---

[31] Baur, *Paul*, 2:40; cf. *Church History*, 1:24–5.
[32] On the history-of-religions question, see e.g. *Church History*, 1:48; on Paul's rejection of Judaism, see most pointedly at *Paul*, 1:361–3 n. 1.
[33] Morgan, 'F. C. Baur: Paul', 6, but without reference to Ephesians.
[34] Compare Baur, *Church History*, 1:112–14 and 122–7.
[35] Thoroughgoing readings of Ephesians vis-à-vis Gnosticism do not appear until the 1930s with Heinrich Schlier and Ernst Käsemann in the wake of the *religionsgeschichtliche Schüle* (see below). For discussion, see Merkel, 'Epheserbrief', *ANRW* 25.4:3176–95.
[36] Hilgenfeld, *Einleitung*, 678.
[37] Holtzmann, *Kritik der Epheser- und Kolosserbriefe*, 304–5.
[38] Weizsäcker, *Apostolische Zeitalter*, 541.

wie zur Zeit des Paulus, um die Möglichkeit des Heidenchristenthums handelt es sich jetzt, sondern um die Herbeiführung der vollen Einheit desselben mit dem Judenchristenthum, also um die Verwirklichung der allgemeinen Kirche'. What follows is, by now, expected: 'Die Idee der Katholicität ist erstmals in unserm Brief zu dogmatischer Bestimmtheit und Alles beherrschender Bedeutung erhoben'.[39] In fact, it is just here, in its 'Idee der allgemeinen Kirche', that Ephesians betrays itself as a piece of 'werdenden Katholicismus'.[40]

I turn to the fragility of these conclusions below, but for now, a simple observation: the language of these judgments on Ephesians belongs not to Ephesians, but to its perceived place within the story of Christian origins. That is, Ephesians does not speak of Jewish and gentile Christianity (only gentiles and, in one instance, Israel), nor of a universal church (only an undefined Christ-assembly), and certainly not of Catholicism. But this language is ubiquitous, and bequeaths Ephesians a purpose via a conspicuous act of mirror-reading. So, Hilgenfeld: 'Den Übergang aus dem Urchristentum zu dem Katholicismus auf paulinischer Seite darzustellen, ist die eigentliche Bedeutung dieses Briefs'.[41] Or more evaluatively, Pfleiderer: 'Unter den Uebergangsformen des Paulinismus zum Katholicismus ist der Epheserbrief die entwickeltste und dogmatisch reifste'.[42] The quest for the historical Ephesians is inextricably intertwined with the quest for Christian origins. The interpretive poles are no longer Romans and 2 Timothy, but the historical Paul and Catholicism. Trading the corpus for history is profoundly productive; Ephesians now has a place—its *raison d'être*.

Many of these same judgments pervade the work of Ernst Käsemann, who returned to work on Ephesians repeatedly across the 1960s.[43] His earliest work, a 1933 Marburg dissertation written under Rudolf Bultmann, touches on the body/head motif in Ephesians in view of the then-popular gnostic redeemer myth.[44] But like Baur, Käsemann's Ephesians grows vastly in importance when fit within his reconstruction of early Christianity, a project he begins in the 1950s, but that by the early 1960s is pressing.[45] In his 1962 lecture with which this chapter began, Käsemann writes, 'The

---

[39] All of the above at Pfleiderer, *Paulinismus*, 435.
[40] *Paulinismus*, 464. The same judgment is in Hilgenfeld, *Urchristenthum*, 89 and 114.
[41] Hilgenfeld, *Einleitung*, 680.
[42] Pfleiderer, *Paulinismus*, 433.
[43] In chronological order, these works are 'Epheserbrief', in *RGG*³ 2:517–20 [1958]; 'Das Interpretationsproblem des Epheserbriefes', in *Exegetische Versuche und Besinnungen* 2, 3rd ed. (Göttingen: Vandenhoeck & Ruprecht, 1970 [1961]), 253–61; 'Paul and Early Catholicism' [1962]; 'Ephesians and Acts' [1966]; and 'The Theological Problem Presented by the Motif of the Body of Christ', in *Perspectives on Paul* (London: SCM, 1971 [1969]), 102–21.
[44] Ernst Käsemann, *Leib und Leib Christi: Eine Untersuchung zur paulinischen Begrifflichkeit* (Tübingen: Mohr, 1933). Bultmann had issued the challenge in 1926: 'Die religionsgeschichtliche Analyse der Briefe an die Kolosser und Epheser, wie sie sich unter dem Eindruck der neu erschlossenen Quellen (sc. der Manichaica und Mandaica) und der Forschungen Reitzensteins nahelegt' ('Urchristliche Religion [1915–1925]', *AR* 24 [1926]: 138–9; cited in Merkel, 'Epheserbrief', *ANRW* 25.4:3177). Heinrich Schlier's *Christus und die Kirche im Epheserbrief* (Tübingen: Mohr Siebeck, 1930), written also under Bultmann, is a response to the same.
[45] See here David V. Way, *The Lordship of Christ: Ernst Käsemann's Interpretation of Paul's Theology* (Oxford: Clarendon, 1991), 119–76 (directly at 122–5), who identifies the turn toward apocalyptic as the second stage of Käsemann's scholarship, away from his history-of-religions work pre-1950. The significant works here are 'An Apologia for Primitive Christian Eschatology', in *Essays on New*

traditional schemata are no longer usable. It is impossible to write a history of earliest Christianity on the basis of our present insights, unless a new schematization is first determined.'[46] By the 1950s, Baur's project had crumbled, and Käsemann's 'Paulus und der Frühkatholizismus' is the germ of a positive proposal.[47]

What, then, was this fresh schema? At the outset of the lecture, and in allusive contrast to Baur, Käsemann adumbrates his wedge which opens up Christian origins.

> Ever since the eschatological understanding of the New Testament replaced the idealistic interpretation,[48] we can and must determine the various phases of earliest Christian history by means of the original imminent expectation of the parousia, its modifications and its final extinction. Early catholicism means that transition from earliest Christianity to the so-called ancient Church, which is completed with the disappearance of the imminent expectation.[49]

Not 1 Cor 1.12 and internecine dispute, but eschatology—the gradual fading of the 'imminent expectation'—gives Käsemann his cartographical way forward. This raises a problem. How does one plot a text without an explicit eschatology? Käsemann is a subtle reader: an altered eschatological outlook shows itself in how texts conceive 'Spirit, Church, office, and tradition'. On this rubric, the New Testament attests diversity and development: 'The New Testament scholar has no right to regard earliest Christianity and the boundaries of the New Testament as coextensive'. And so Käsemann disassembles the canon to plot the story (note the poles) 'from earliest Christianity to the so-called ancient Church'—to narrate, that is, the eclipse of eschatology and the dawn of ecclesiasticism.[50]

Testament Themes (London: SCM, 1964 [1952]), 169-95; 'The Beginnings of Christian Theology', in *New Testament Questions* (1960), 82-107; and 'On the Subject of Primitive Christian Apocalyptic', in *New Testament Questions* (1962), 108-37.

[46] Käsemann, 'Paul and Early Catholicism', 236-37 n. 1.
[47] The timing is hardly an accident. A few months prior, Käsemann had written the 'Einführung' to volume 1 of Baur's *Ausgewählte Werke in Einzelausgaben*, ed. Klaus Scholder (Stuttgart: Frommann, 1963), viii–xxv, a collection of Baur's shorter essays on Christian origins, in which he praises Baur's impetus but acknowledges that the critical questions remain open. Käsemann's 'Einführung' is dated 'Ostern 1962' (xxv) while his lecture was given on 21 June 1962 ('Paul and Early Catholicism', 236*). For summary of Käsemann's introduction, see Peter C. Hodgson, 'The Rediscovery of Ferdinand Christian Baur: A Review of the First Two Volumes of His *Ausgewählte Werke*', *CH* 33 (1964): 208–9.
[48] Compare his 'Einführung': 'Es ist nun einmal höchst fragwürdig, ob und wie weit Geschichte logisch verläuft. Damit stehen wir jedoch vor dem wohl entscheidenden Problem der Methodik Baurs' (xiv).
[49] 'Paul and Early Catholicism', 236-7. For critique of Käsemann here, in large part by recognizing the plurality of Paul's eschatological language, see MacDonald, *Pauline Churches*, 153-4; cf. 79-80.
[50] All of the above at 'Paul and Early Catholicism', 236-7(n. 1). Käsemann's exegetical project here has a sharply polemical ecclesial edge, at the onset of the Second Vatican Council and in debate with his Tübingen colleague, the Catholic theologian Hans Küng. For Käsemann, to locate early catholicism in the New Testament—however historically justifiable it may have been—is to reject its ongoing significance for the German church of the mid-twentieth century ('Paul and Early Catholicism', 247-50; 'Theological Problem', 120-1). The religious necessity of Käsemann's project is highlighted most clearly in the final paragraph of his 'Paul and Early Catholicism', 250-1 n. 6; cf. Hans Küng,

What he wants, most pointedly though, is to know where Paul ends and Catholicism begins (thus, the search for *early* catholicism). In the *corpus Paulinum*, Käsemann finds this point in Ephesians, not in its eschatology per se but in its modified ecclesiology—a result of its (alleged) fading parousia-hope. The usual suspects are all here: the growing significance of the apostolate (2.20; 3.5); the appeal to the church as a rejoinder to heresy (4.5, 14–15); and the hardening of polity via Jewish-Christian forms that 'bind the Spirit to the office' (4.11–13).[51] But Käsemann's major piece of evidence, to put it directly, is that Ephesians *has* an ecclesiology. Of early catholicism, he writes, 'Its deepest theological significance…lay in the fact that it inseparably linked ecclesiology and christology together and thus made the Church an integral factor in the salvation event. Nowhere is this more apparent than in the letter to the Ephesians.'[52] But how does Käsemann know this?—by reading Ephesians genealogically against the *Hauptbriefe*.

Per Käsemann, the author of Ephesians modifies two of Paul's ecclesiological images—the body of Christ and the people of God—and unduly emphasizes the latter.[53] When Paul speaks of the σῶμα Χριστοῦ, Christ 'penetrate[s] the body pneumatically', and so the point is *Christ's* presence (via the Spirit), not the church's.[54] Just here, then, when Paul uses the body metaphor, 'christology and ecclesiology are not interchangeable'.[55] The situation is different in Ephesians, which makes Christ the head of the body (κεφαλή/σῶμα, Eph 4.15; 5.23). For Käsemann, this leads to the double-mistake of giving the church independence (it is the 'earthly deputy of the exalted one') and glory (it raises her 'into the heavenly places' [2.6]).[56] Through a subtle shift in a metaphor, Ephesians turns Christology into ecclesiology: the church is now 'the content of theology'; the 'exclusive place and means of salvation'; the 'eschatological phenomenon per se'; and an 'integral factor in the salvation event'.[57]

For Käsemann, a similar shift is at work in how Ephesians modifies and then emphasizes Paul's image of the people of God. This entails, as it did for Baur, an ecclesial move in the direction of Judaism, and the key text is Eph 2.11–22: 'There the conversion of the Gentile Christians is depicted as incorporation in the Jewish-Christian people of God, and the body of Christ is correspondingly interpreted as a union of Christians, both Jews and Gentiles, i.e., a union of two nations'.[58] Like Baur, only 115 years later, for Käsemann this is an unacceptable deviation from Paulinism:

Structures of the Church, trans. Salvator Attanasio (New York: Thomas Nelson, 1964), 152–69, and posing the problem directly at 156.

[51] Käsemann, 'Ephesians and Acts', 291–3; 'Paul and Early Catholicism', 247–8; cf. Bultmann, *Theology of the New Testament* 2:99. The winnowing of Spirit and hardening of office is a leitmotif in descriptions of early Christian development. See discussion at MacDonald, *Pauline Churches*, 4–6.

[52] Käsemann, 'Paul and Early Catholicism', 243.

[53] Bultmann, *Theology of the New Testament*, 151, calls Ephesians' modifications of these two images a 'strange mixture of cosmological and history-of-salvation terminology'.

[54] Käsemann, 'Ephesians and Acts', 290; cf. 'Theological Problem', 113 and 117.

[55] Käsemann, 'Paul and Early Catholicism', 245.

[56] Käsemann, 'Paul and Early Catholicism', 245; 'Theological Problem', 110; cf. 'Ephesians and Acts', 290. Käsemann's ecclesial politics—his insistence that the church has no independent authority in itself—are here read into Eph 2.6 as an exegetical wedge to separate Ephesians from Paul.

[57] The first three are at Käsemann, 'Ephesians and Acts', 290, and the latter in 'Paul and Early Catholicism', 243. See also 'Theological Problem', 120–1.

[58] Käsemann, 'Theological Problem', 109; cf. 'Ephesians and Acts', 291.

'The substantive distance from Paul can be recognized when one sees that here the theme of the people of God, the holy remnant and its proselytes, obscures the theme of the body of Christ and modifies it. Paul, likewise, speaks of a new people of God. But he does so polemically, in order to insist that the church, in contrast with Judaism, is the true Israel'.[59] Paul, that is, believes in a *verus Israel*, and Ephesians links gentiles to the old one. As a result, Käsemann displaces and relocates Ephesians. Right here, in its misapprehension of Paul's ecclesiological *novum*, the letter reveals its setting.

> What Paul mentioned hypothetically in Rom 11:17 ff. has happened here: Jewish Christianity is pushed aside and despised by the steadily growing Gentile Christianity. The author of Ephesians, doubtless a Jewish Christian, reminds the Gentile Christians of their roots and of the origin of the gospel. It is the indelible character of the church to be constituted out of Jews and Gentiles; by this means, spiritually understood, the Gentile Christians are proselytes.[60]

Suffice to say, this is not a compliment, nor a setting derived principally from history. Rather, the early catholicism Käsemann discovers in Ephesians depends on reading the collection genealogically, and then investing theological and historical significance in the most subtle of differences. I will return to the fragility of this conclusion below, but for now it is worth saying that the stories of Christian origins that this hermeneutic produces continue to shape conclusions about Ephesians—its concern for ecclesial unity (Baur) a product of the *longue durée* (Käsemann). While their organizing principles differ, at bottom Baur and Käsemann tell the same story: the devolution of Protestantism into Catholicism, with Ephesians the key witness. These Lutheran accounts of Christian origins trace Ephesians in the image of their present-day Catholic interlocutors. And from 1845 to the 1960s, the quest for the historical Ephesians changes very little.[61]

Excursus:
The (Alternative) Quest in British Scholarship:
From Lightfoot to Bruce

What of the situation in Britain during this time? As I argue in Chapter 1, the way of reading a letter collection is largely the same, and so the same issues are in play: a conception of Paul; a story of origins; and a reading order that supports both. In Britain, however, differences in the first two combined with agreement about the third leads to a different but parallel judgment: Ephesians not as degeneration *from* but rather the quintessence *of* Paul.

The early and critical figure is Lightfoot. While not ignoring primitive conflict, Lightfoot's 1865 'St Paul and the Three' is far more sanguine than Baur about Paul's relationship to Peter, James and John, and thus about the unity of the primitive church and the reliability

---

[59] 'Ephesians and Acts', 296.
[60] 'Ephesians and Acts', 291; cf. 'Theological Problem', 110.
[61] So rightly, Nils A. Dahl, 'Einleitungsfragen zum Epheserbrief', in *Studies in Ephesians*, 24: 'Die Forschung des 20. Jahrhunderts hat zum großen Teil die älteren Hypothesen variiert und mit neuen Beobachtungen unterbaut'. See the same judgment in Merkel, 'Epheserbrief', *ANRW* 25.4:3172.

of Acts.⁶² The upshot is that texts concerned with Jew/gentile unity are not displaced—a decision Lightfoot is aided in by a Paul who is far more amenable to Judaism than was Baur's.⁶³ A different portrait of Christian origins and of Paul make space for a more maximal *corpus Paulinum*. Lightfoot himself does not read development in Ephesians, but the setting he reconstructs for it—a circular to the churches of Asia Minor from a Roman imprisonment, to be identified with the Laodicean letter of Col 4.16—is a massive influence on subsequent British scholarship, and leads, in due course, to developmental readings.⁶⁴

This begins already in Lightfoot's colleague, Fenton J. A. Hort, and his 1895 *Prolegomena*, which deals exhaustively with the authorship question.⁶⁵ Hort hardly backs away from admitting difference: 'No one who carefully reads the Epistle to the Ephesians can doubt that its doctrinal contents do differ considerably from those of any one of St Paul's earlier epistles, or of all of them taken together'.⁶⁶ How, though, does he know Paul's other letters are earlier? He assumes it, only considering a late imprisonment in Caesarea or Rome.⁶⁷ So when Hort gets to his admission of difference, his answer is ready to hand: *development*. Over twenty-six pages, in fact, Hort repeatedly suggests that all the usual suspects of 'advanced Paulinism' either do not contradict, or are the natural outgrowth of, ideas nascent in the early letters.⁶⁸ And this, for Hort, just evidences the greatness of Paul's mind: 'A mind like his, in constant and living contact with truth, needing and receiving fresh enlightenment from day to day, for dealing with new and changing needs of the Churches, must assuredly have known growth'—not surprisingly, growth he finds in Ephesians.⁶⁹

Lightfoot and Hort are decisive for the next fifty years of British scholarship on Ephesians, particularly their judgment that Ephesians is a circular. T. K. Abbott's 1898 *Ephesians* (ICC) catalogues the same evidence as Lightfoot, arrives at a nearly identical conclusion, and patterns itself after Hort's *Prolegomena* throughout.⁷⁰ In his introduction to Brooke Foss Westcott's posthumously published 1906 commentary, J. M. Schulhof admits that he drew heavily from Lightfoot, Hort, and Abbott.⁷¹ In his 1903 commentary, J. Armitage Robinson confesses his debt on the letter's provenance to Lightfoot, Hort, and Westcott, and writes of Hort's *Prolegomena*, 'I have nothing to add to the discussion of the authorship of the epistle which these lectures contain'.⁷² Finally, C. H. Dodd adopts the encyclical hypothesis in his 1929 commentary, and lists Hort, Westcott, Abbott, and Robinson as recommended reading on the authorship question.⁷³ From 1873 (Lightfoot), then, until Mitton's 1951 *Ephesians*, the major British works on Ephesians are agreed: it is a Pauline encyclical from Rome, relatively late in his life.

---

⁶² Joseph B. Lightfoot, 'St Paul and the Three', in *Saint Paul's Epistle to the Galatians*, 295–311.
⁶³ Lightfoot, 'St Paul and the Three', 347–9.
⁶⁴ Lightfoot's detailed work here is in his 1873 'The Destination of the Epistle to the Ephesians', in *Biblical Essays*, 375–96.
⁶⁵ Fenton A. J. Hort, *Prolegomena to St Paul's Epistles to the Romans and the Ephesians* (London: Macmillan, 1895), 63–192.
⁶⁶ Hort, *Prolegomena*, 123.
⁶⁷ Hort, *Prolegomena*, 100. He also assumes, a priori, the authenticity of Ephesians, in order to use the data of Colossians and Philemon, before then going on to prove it (see 99).
⁶⁸ Hort, *Prolegomena*, 123–48.
⁶⁹ Hort, *Prolegomena*, 123–4.
⁷⁰ Abbott, *Ephesians*, i–xxxiv.
⁷¹ J. M. Schulhof, introduction to Westcott, *Ephesians*, vii–ix.
⁷² Robinson, *Ephesians*, vii.
⁷³ C. H. Dodd, 'Ephesians', in *The Abingdon Bible Commentary*, ed. F. C. Eiselen, E. Lewis and D. G. Downey (New York: Abingdon-Cokesbury, 1929), 1225.

Talk of development, then, is little surprise. So, Abbott writes of the letter's ecclesiology, 'These and other differences that have been pointed out are no doubt striking, but they involve no inconsistencies; they are only developments of ideas of which the germ is found in St. Paul's other writings'.[74] The stage is also set, however, for a still more famous thread through British work on Ephesians. If Ephesians is written by Paul to multiple churches, and late and developed, it is a small step to cast this judgment in a eulogistic hue. So, for Robinson, Ephesians is the 'crown of St Paul's writings'; for Dodd, it is the 'crown of Paulinism'; for G. B. Caird, it is a 'masterly summary of Paul's theology'; and for F. F. Bruce, it is the 'quintessence of Paulinism'.[75] In one sense, then, the results of the British and German quest for the historical Ephesians ca. 1850–1950 could not be more different. In another sense, however, very little separates them, for both regard it as late, developed, and somewhat removed from the pressing concerns of the *Hauptbriefe*. The only real difference, I suggest, between a judgment of development and quintessence is the preference of the reader.

• • •

The Parting of the Ways

Nor does this quest change a great deal to the present day. The study of Paul has changed vastly since the 1960s, and the study of Ephesians very little.[76] One might have thought this would raise the question of Paul and Ephesians again, and all the more since Krister Stendahl's classic 1963 essay 'Paul and the Introspective Conscience of the West', so influential still, reads like a criticism of Baur and Käsemann's Paul taken straight from the pages of Ephesians.[77] But the expected reassessment has not taken place. In fact, the last fifty years see only a widening of the gap—a bifurcation that continues to today in three relevant genres: works on Christian origins/Pauline reception, Ephesians, and Paul.[78] In the first chapter, I told this as the story of the collection's dismemberment; here, the corollary—what does Ephesians look like once displaced?

Christian Origins and Pauline Reception

First, Ephesians is an act of Pauline reception, which makes it, second, a data point for developing Christianity. Since the 1970s, major studies of Christian origins—Robinson/Koester [1971], Hultgren [1994], and now Dunn [2003–15; cf. 2006³]—do

---

[74] Abbott, *Ephesians*, xix–xx; cf. the same in Scott, *Ephesians*, 120.
[75] Robinson, *Ephesians*, vii; Dodd, 'Ephesians', 1224–5; G. B. Caird, *The Apostolic Age* (London: Duckworth, 1966), 133; Bruce, *Paul*, 424. See also the recent judgment of Wright, *Paul and the Faithfulness of God*, 2:1514–15.
[76] On this period, see N. T. Wright, *Paul and His Recent Interpreters: Some Contemporary Debates* (Minneapolis: Fortress, 2015).
[77] Easily accessible in Stendahl, *Paul Among Jews and Gentiles*, 78–96.
[78] As in Chapter 1, while my summaries of these areas of research are brief, I engage at greater length in the footnotes with important recent works in each genre to show the issues at play in detail.

comparatively little with Ephesians.[79] Dunn [2006] does the most, treating it with Luke-Acts, the Pastorals, 2 Peter and Jude, as a text depicting early catholicism.[80] Robinson and Koester largely follow Käsemann, but add to this the all-important language of trajectories. Theirs is an unflagging commitment to a genetic reading of early Christian texts, and vis-à-vis Paul their judgment is typical:

> One can trace a course…from Paul's theology to that of the gradually bifurcating Pauline school, with one stream moving via Ephesians to 1 Peter, Luke-Acts, the Pastorals and on to orthodoxy, the other via Colossians to Valentinus, Basilides, Marcion, and on to heresy; or from an 'unworldly' antiinstitutionalism rooted in the apocalyptic ideology of imminent expectation [i.e. Paul], toward a bifurcation into a relatively 'worldly' Christian establishment whose eschatological hope has lost its imminence or at least its existential urgency [i.e. Ephesians], and an 'otherworldly' disestablished Christianity, whose ideology has become gnostic rather than apocalyptic [i.e. Colossians].[81]

The language of trajectories has stuck, and locks Ephesians into the 80s/90s. Duly placed, a plethora of works on Pauline reception sketch a now-familiar picture: a late first-century Paulinist pens a vision of (1) a unified and universal church of Jews and gentiles, of which he makes (2) Paul '*the* apostle'—a way of (3) attenuating eschatology in the face of unexpected delay, and settling in for the *longue durée*. J. C. Beker, here, is representative:

> Indeed, Paul's portrait in Ephesians conforms to its vision of the church as the *una sancta catholica et apostolica ecclesia*. Paul is portrayed here as remembered by his pupils after his death; a figure whose authority and stature have increased enormously over time. He is now nostalgically transmitted to the churches of Asia Minor as the apostle of sacred memory whose struggles with Judaism and Judaizers have been forgotten and whose apocalyptic yearnings have been displaced by an ecclesiology of triumphant eschatological fulfillment.[82]

This judgment, almost without variation, is shared by Barrett [1974], Penny [1979], de Boer [1980], Keck [1989], Sterling [2007], Marguerat [2008], Pervo [2010], and now Marshall [2012].[83]

---

[79] James M. Robinson and Helmut Koester, *Trajectories through Early Christianity* (Philadelphia: Fortress, 1971); Arnold Hultgren, *The Rise of Normative Christianity* (Minneapolis: Fortress, 1994); James D. G. Dunn, *Unity and Diversity in the New Testament*, 3rd ed. (London: SCM, 2006 [1977]); and idem, *Christianity in the Making*, 3 vols. (Grand Rapids: Eerdmans, 2003–15).

[80] Dunn grows increasingly tentative about both the term 'early catholicism' and Ephesians as a source for it across his three editions. See the preface to his second (xlvii–xlix) and third (xxvi–xxvii) editions as well as his arguments about Ephesians in Chapter 14 of each.

[81] Robinson and Koester, *Trajectories*, 10; cf. 153–7. For incisive analysis, see Sanders, *Paul and Palestinian Judaism*, 21–2.

[82] Beker, *Heirs of Paul*, 72.

[83] See the opening of my Chapter 5.

How do they know this? The answer, in short, is that they are all telling Baur and Käsemann's story (the 'history of the party'), with the same poles and the same set of texts. And they all locate those texts via their perceived proximity to the poles—Paul and Catholicism. Following Barrett, de Boer is explicit about this: 'Second-century images of Paul may provide a useful methodological starting point for a determination of late first-century images of Paul since the latter are on a "trajectory" which finds its origins in the apostolic period and extends into the second century'.[84] It is little surprise, then, that de Boer finds in Ephesians an ecclesial Paul, and thus, a Catholic *Sitz im Leben*.[85] The force of the trajectory's telos is immense. Notice what it does to so careful a scholar as Barrett, describing the Paul of Ephesians:

> In particular, Paul is the apostle of the Gentiles, ὑπὲρ ὑμῶν τῶν ἐθνῶν (3.1); there is nothing strange in this, and it could be said to go no further than Gal 2.9. In practice, however, in the other epistles, and by no means least in Galatians, Paul appears as the apostle of particular Gentiles, whereas in Ephesians the stress is on the Gentiles as a body. As the apostle of the Gentile body Paul is the great architect of the unity of the church, for Ephesians looks back upon the gathering together in one of Jewish and Gentile Christians.[86]

Barrett is right. There *is* 'nothing strange' in 3.1, but because he knows Ephesians is late, he magnifies any perceived difference, tugged by the final pole of his trajectory. So, Paul is now '*the* apostle' (Ephesians never says this) of '*the* gentile body' (Paul himself claims this [Gal 2.9; Rom 1.5, 13–14; 11.13; 15.15–21])—the 'great architect of the unity of the church' (the latter term notably absent from Eph 2.11–3.13).[87] The same story could be told for all of the above figures: a new day; a universalized

---

[84] de Boer, 'Images of Paul', 362; cf. Marguerat, 'Paul après Paul', 329. Barrett never states this directly, but it is precisely the shape of his argument ('Pauline Controversies', 236).

[85] de Boer, 'Images of Paul', 364–5, 367, 378. From different angles, both James Dunn (*Unity and Diversity*) and Martinus de Boer ('Images of Paul') reveal how fragile a source Ephesians is for Pauline reception in the late first century. Take Dunn's early catholicism, characterized by (1) the 'fading of the parousia hope' (377–83); (2) 'increasing institutionalization' (384–92); and (3) the 'crystallization of the faith into set forms' (392–6). In Ephesians, Dunn really only finds (1) with any limited confidence, and himself suggests this shift may not postdate Paul (378). Vis-à-vis (2), Dunn thinks the 'universal Church' in Ephesians is a development, but notes that in terms of 'offices' (4.11–12), Ephesians may *resist* early catholicism rather than embody it (384). As for (3), Dunn finds nothing of the sort in Ephesians. On his own schema, then, and granting his interpretative work, Dunn finds little to suggest that Ephesians is early catholic, which he admits (397). The situation is similar in de Boer, who identifies six facets of the post-apostolic image of Paul in Colossians, Ephesians, Acts and the Pastorals: Paul, (1) the apostle (2) to the gentiles (363–6), who (3) evangelized the whole world and (4) suffered for it (366–70), and who was the (5) redeemed persecutor (370–8) and (6) authoritative teacher of the church (378–9). De Boer's evidence for (1) and (2) is exactly where, to my mind, Ephesians is not novel, and for (3) and (4) is non-existent. More seriously, his discussion of Eph 2.1–3.13 at (5) is beside the point, and of 4.20–22 at (6) is mistaken. Vis-à-vis Ephesians, though, this leaves de Boer without a case. Try as he might, Ephesians offers little that *might* attest a post-Pauline image, rather than just Paul's own self-image. Reading Dunn and de Boer, one gets the sense that Ephesians simply will not do the sort of work they want it to do, which may explain why, in his 2009 *Beginning from Jerusalem*, Dunn switches gears to suggest that Ephesians is a 'fitting tribute to Paul'—aptly labelled the 'quintessence of Paulinism' (1106, 1122).

[86] Barrett, 'Pauline Controversies', 239.

[87] Ἐκκλησία does occur in 3.10, where Paul's work is no longer the subject. See further my Chapter 5.

ecclesiology; an inflated Paulology—or so the story goes. This is how Ephesians is displaced.

Ephesians Scholarship

The story is largely the same in Ephesians scholarship. Methodologically, the study of Ephesians is not parochial. The same methods applied to the study of Paul also reach Ephesians, if later and with less frequency. Since the 1960s, the historical,[88] form-critical,[89] rhetorical,[90] literary,[91] sociological,[92] and theological[93] study of Ephesians

---

[88] Historical exegesis, of course, can take many forms. For readings that make use, specifically, of issues in Asia Minor in the first century, see, e.g., Clinton E. Arnold, *Ephesians: Power and Magic. The Concept of Power in Ephesians in Light of its Historical Setting*, SNTSMS 63 (Cambridge: Cambridge University Press, 1989); and Larry J. Kreitzer, *Hierapolis in the Heavens: Studies in the Letter to the Ephesians*, LNTS 368 (New York: T&T Clark, 2008). For works that read Ephesians against the backdrop of Gnosticism, see, e.g., Petr Pokorný, *Der Epheserbrief und die Gnosis: Die Bedeutung des Haupt-Glieder-Gedankens in der entstehenden Kirche* (Berlin: Evangelische Verlagsanstalt, 1965); and Andreas Lindemann, *Die Aufhebung der Zeit: Geschichtsverständnis und Eschatologie im Epheserbrief*, SNT 12 (Gütersloh: Gerd Mohn, 1975). Initial work on Ephesians and the texts of Qumran is in K. G. Kuhn, 'The Epistle to the Ephesians in the Light of the Qumran Texts', in *Paul and Qumran*, ed. Jerome Murphy-O'Connor OP (London: Geoffrey Chapman, 1968), 115–31; Franz Mussner, 'Contributions Made by Qumran to the Understanding of the Epistle to the Ephesians', in *Paul and Qumran*, 159–78; and N. A. Dahl, 'Ephesians and Qumran', in *Studies in Ephesians*, 107–44. Works emphasizing Ephesians as a piece of *Hellenistic* Judaism, or in view of Greco-Roman philosophy are, e.g., Carsten Colpe, 'Zur Leib-Christi-Vorstellung im Epheserbrief', in *Judentum, Urchristentum, Kirche: Festschrift für Joachim Jeremias*, ed. Walther Eltester, BZNW 26 (Berlin: Töpelmann, 1960), 172–87; Eberhard Faust, *Pax Christi et Pax Caesaris: Religionsgeschichtliche, traditionsgeschichtliche und sozialgeschichtliche Studien zum Epheserbrief*, NTOA 24 (Göttingen: Vandenhoeck & Ruprecht, 1993); and van Kooten, *Cosmic Christology*.

[89] See Kirby, *Ephesians, Baptism and Pentecost*; J. Paul Sampley, 'And the Two Shall Become One Flesh': *A Study of Traditions in Ephesians 5:21-33*, SNTSMS 16 (Cambridge: Cambridge University Press, 1971); and Markus Barth, 'Traditions in Ephesians', *NTS* 30 (1984): 3–25.

[90] Lincoln, *Ephesians*; John Paul Heil, *Ephesians: Empowerment to Walk in Love for the Unity of All in Christ*, StBibLit 13 (Atlanta: Society of Biblical Literature, 2007).

[91] I am thinking here primarily of intertextuality and Ephesians' use of the Old Testament in works like Andrew T. Lincoln, 'The Use of the OT in Ephesians', *JSNT* 14 (1982): 16–57; Thorsten Moritz, *A Profound Mystery: The Use of the Old Testament in Ephesians*, NovTSup 85 (Leiden: Brill, 1996); Mary E. Hinkle, 'Proclaiming Peace: The Use of Scripture in Ephesians' (PhD diss., Duke University, 1997); Thomas R. Yoder Neufeld, *'Put on the Armour of God': The Divine Warrior from Isaiah to Ephesians*, JSNTSup 140 (Sheffield: Sheffield Academic Press, 1997); Timothy G. Gombis, 'The Triumph of God in Christ: Divine Warfare in the Argument of Ephesians' (PhD diss., St. Andrews University, 2005); and Andrew M. Stirling, 'Transformation and Growth: The Davidic Temple Builder in Ephesians' (PhD diss., St. Andrews University, 2012).

[92] After the early work of Lincoln (*Ephesians*) and MacDonald (*Pauline Churches*), the last decade has seen a spate of studies in this vein: see Margaret Y. MacDonald, 'The Politics of Identity in Ephesians', *JSNT* 26 (2004): 419–44; Benjamin H. Dunning, 'Strangers and Aliens No Longer: Negotiating Identity and Difference in Ephesians 2', *HTR* 99 (2006): 1–16; Daniel K. Darko, *No Longer Living as the Gentiles: Differentiation and Shared Ethical Values in Ephesians 4:17–6:9*, LNTS 375 (London: T&T Clark, 2008); Minna Shkul, *Reading Ephesians: Exploring Social Entrepreneurship in the Text*, LNTS 408 (London: T&T Clark, 2009); Rikard Roitto, *Behaving as a Christ-Believer: A Cognitive Perspective on Identity and Behavior Norms in Ephesians*, ConBNT 46 (Winona Lake, IN: Eisenbrauns, 2011); Elna Mouton, 'Memory in Search of Dignity? Construction of Early Christian Identity Through Redescribed Traditional Material in the Letter to the Ephesians', *Annali di Storia dell'Esegesi* 29 (2012): 133–53; J. Albert Harrill, 'Ethnic Fluidity in Ephesians', *NTS* 60 (2014): 379–402; and Margaret Y. MacDonald, 'The Problem of Christian Identities in Ephesians', *ST* 70 (2016): 97–115.

[93] Fowl, *Ephesians*.

continues apace. But in the scope of the letter's co-texts—what Ephesians speaks with and for—Ephesians scholarship is increasingly parochial. Where Baur treats Ephesians in a work on Paul, the study of Ephesians today occurs largely in stand-alone articles/ monographs or works on Pauline reception. In large part, this attests the success of Baur's project. Pauline and Ephesians scholarship are now, in some ways, separate disciplines.

With the collection split, the genealogical reading of the second half serves as the de facto story of Paul's legacy. A teleological way of telling this story presses the letters into its mold. Margaret MacDonald's 1988 *The Pauline Churches* is a prime example: via a suitably divided and re-arranged collection, MacDonald traces the 'process of institutionalisation' of Paul's churches ca. 50–150.[94] Ephesians sheds light on MacDonald's middle stage ('community-stabilising institutionalisation') between the church's charismatic beginnings (i.e. Paul) and the 'tightly organised forms' of the Pastorals.[95] Other genetic readings narrow the sources to two, and make redaction-critical arguments on the basis of Ephesians' alleged dependence on Colossians. In his 2003 *Cosmic Christology in Paul and the Pauline School*, George van Kooten reads Ephesians as a 'full-scale critical commentary' on Colossians, taking over Colossians' structure in full, save three additions, in order to clarify that the ἐκκλησία (not the κόσμος) is at present the body of Christ.[96] For Martin Hüneberg, Ephesians corrects the over-realized soteriology of Colossians by wrapping it in a salvation-historical husk;[97] and the elevated *Paulusbild* Gregory Sterling discovers in Eph 3.1–13 results from subtle changes it makes to its source text, Col 1.24–29.[98] These are close readings of Ephesians, but for each the sine qua non of the work takes place off stage: the argument collapses if there is not, in fact, a genetic relationship that runs in this direction.[99]

Given the fragility of genetic readings as well as those that posit a narrow purpose, many works eschew such attempts and appeal to the broad consensus (a Paulinist of the 80s/90s) and get on with their work—a trend particularly evident in the recent spate of social-scientific work on Ephesians.[100] Skeptical of overly specific settings and not interested in theological development as such, the meta-level arguments of these works nevertheless remain speculative: the social groups they envision (via

---

[94] The project is only possible, that is, by appeal to varying historical layers in the corpus, and reading these layers chronologically, which means the entire project begins with a passing aside to the consensus on matters of critical introduction. See MacDonald, *Pauline Churches*, 1–4.
[95] MacDonald, *Pauline Churches*, 6–7, 235, and 237. On Ephesians, see pp. 85–158.
[96] van Kooten, *Cosmic Christology*, passim, but directly at 202. Methodologically, all that van Kooten's literary synopsis (239–90) uncovers is difference. What *displaces* Ephesians is his imputation of motive to that difference, precisely the thing so difficult to discern in a letter as general as Ephesians (so rightly, Fowl, *Ephesians*, 13–14).
[97] Hüneburg, 'Paulus versus Paulus'.
[98] Sterling, 'From Apostle to the Gentiles'.
[99] For discussion of the relationship of Ephesians and Colossians, see my Introduction ('Ephesians, Authorship, and Paul'). To be sure, the ability to appeal to a consensus is a convenient and necessary part of scholarship, since it forms the agreed-upon basis for subsequent work—in this case, redactional readings of Ephesians to hypothesize the letter's purpose. In this instance, I simply find that consensus not justified, and too fragile to hold the weight of redactional readings.
[100] The works of Margaret MacDonald cited above, which flesh out an increasingly specific social setting, are an exception to this rule.

conspicuous acts of mirror-reading) to which Ephesians responds are always fledgling Pauline communities in the generation after Paul's death, with Ephesians read accordingly.[101] In the commentaries, judgments about author and setting are rarely confident and typically couched in rhetorically tentative terms, and so at first sight appear hermeneutically benign.[102] In the end, however, they are anything but, since they bequeath a reading order and that most pliable of settings: the Pauline legacy. Development is thus baked in from the beginning. The conclusion of Ernest Best is both typical and telling:

> The purpose has been to meet a new situation and in meeting it the author who is a Paulinist will draw on his master. AE [=Author of Ephesians] did not begin by saying to himself, 'I must extend Paul's thought'; he began with a situation he saw needed addressing and because he was a Paulinist he dealt with it in Pauline terms and so extended Paul's theology. Of course if Paul is the author he will naturally be adapting and developing himself.[103]

Rather than stopping to ask if Ephesians *is* development, or why we are so sure it is, or on what assumptions this lies, the only question is whether this development takes place within Paul or not. This is the long legacy of the split corpus, and Baur and Käsemann on Christian origins.

Ironically, the modern way of reading a collection enjoys its greatest impact on Ephesians in a species of scholarship that treats it wholly apart from the question of Paul and Paul's other letters. The frequency of this move, particularly in doctoral dissertations, is striking.[104] To take just one example, Tet-Lim Yee's 2005 *Jews, Gentiles*

---

[101] To take one example, according to Minna Shkul (*Reading Ephesians*), Ephesians constructs, legitimates and shapes communal identity by reappropriating/altering a Jewish symbolic universe for a non-Israelite community—a task germane to 'emerging Christianness' in Paul's wake (240–5). Shkul rightly criticizes MacDonald (and Philip Esler) for using social-scientific tools to imagine greater access to the situation behind Ephesians than the text allows (6–9). Shkul's work, on the other hand, is text-centric—reading it as a 'vehicle for social influencing' which seeks 'to shape the world of [its] recipients' and provide a 'self-enhancing, legitimating discourse' (43). Why, though, does this project, or Shkul's thesis about Ephesians itself, require a post-Pauline setting? The answer is largely that it does not, except that Shkul has chosen to begin there. Much of Shkul's reading of how Ephesians constructs/shapes its readers' (social) identity is very good, but the setting of this formation is never argued—a setting that leads Shkul to read Eph 3.1–13, for instance, as a bit of Paulinist myth-making (of Paul; see 142–72). But did not Paul *himself* wish to forge gentile identity in the ways Shkul proposes? He did, and Shkul admits this: 'Naturally, a theoretical framework used in this study could be used from the traditional position, analysing how *Paul* shaped the community and his reputation through the letter to the Ephesians. Although I will adapt "wandering viewpoints" to test different reading positions in Chapter 3 below, I will not do so with regards the authorship' (3 n. 2). The consensus has done its work. If *Reading Ephesians* was truly text-centric, Shkul could make no claims about Ephesians' 'contribution to the development of early Christianities' (47). But that is precisely what she wants to do (47), so she begins her work with an appeal to the consensus, and an otherwise helpful study now reinforces the breach.

[102] For good examples, see Lincoln, *Ephesians*, lx; and Schnackenburg, *Ephesians*, 25.

[103] Best, *Ephesians*, 71.

[104] Tet-Lim N. Yee, *Jews, Gentiles and Ethnic Reconciliation: Paul's Jewish Identity and Ephesians*, SNTSMS 130 (Cambridge: Cambridge University Press, 2005), 33 n. 149. Besides Yee, see also Arnold, *Ephesians: Power and Magic*, 4 (although see 171); Gombis, 'Triumph of God', 7; Darko, *No Longer Living*, 25; and Stirling, 'Transformation and Growth', 6. While Sampley, *Traditions in*

and Ethnic Reconciliation reads Ephesians self-consciously towards a 'Paul' of recent scholarship (the New Perspective), but nevertheless confesses agnosticism on and avoids the authorship question. Whatever one makes of Yee's work, it is difficult to see how a consensus ever changes if Ephesians scholars who find it compatible with Paul never claim it for him. Surely such abstention is a loss for the broader enterprise of Pauline scholarship, only reinforcing the breach. Here the study of Paul and Ephesians truly part ways—the latter a parochial sub-discipline with one text at its disposal.

Pauline Monographs

What does the parting of the ways do to Ephesians in scholarship on Paul? In one sense, nothing, which is exactly the point. Over the last ten years (2009–18), the Pauline Epistles section of the Society of Biblical Literature has heard one paper on Ephesians—on post-Pauline Christian identity—as compared to thirty-nine on Romans, thirty-five on 1 Corinthians and twenty on Galatians.[105] The same selective sorting occurs in monographs as well, which tend either to ignore Ephesians completely (Hays [1989]; Engberg-Pedersen [2000]; Gager [2000]; Watson [2004; 2007]), or treat it exclusively in footnotes—either minimally (Sanders [1977]; Fredriksen [2017]) or somewhat more robustly (Meeks [1983]; Gaston [1987]; Barclay [2014]). Most typically, the latter highlight differences rather than commonalities, which only amplifies difference, widens the gap, and reinforces the initial decision. On this way of reading Paul, as E. P. Sanders suggests, to use Ephesians would lead to 'confusion and inaccuracies, to imprecisions which should be avoided'.[106]

There is a deep irony here, however, given the shifting sands of Pauline scholarship. For if Baur and Käsemann were right about Eph 2.11–22, it leads someway *toward* Sanders's Paul. So, post-1977, does this happen? Does a revised scholarly Paulinism lead to a rapprochement with Ephesians? On the contrary, the consensus hardens just here: at the same time that the Paul of contemporary scholarship becomes more Jewish, the Paul of Ephesians becomes more Christian. So, Richard Horsley: 'The inclusion of Ephesians [in the corpus] solidified Christian supersessionism over "Judaism"'.[107] Or Paula Fredriksen: 'The author of Ephesians trumpeted a new universal humanity, undoing the distinction between Israel and the nations upon which the historical Paul had staked so much (Eph 2.11–16)'.[108] Suffice to say, if Horsley and Fredriksen are right, Baur and Käsemann would never have excised Ephesians in the first place, and if the latter were right, a large swath of Pauline scholarship at present should like Ephesians. Instead, like ships passing in the night, a Christian apostle becomes a Jewish apostle, while a Jewish text becomes a Christian text.

Ephesians 5:21–33; Moritz, *A Profound Mystery*; and Gregory W. Dawes, *The Body in Question: Metaphor and Meaning in the Interpretation of Ephesians 5:21–33*, BibInt 30 (Leiden: Brill, 1998), all seem to presuppose a post-Pauline setting, none treat the authorship question directly, and so read it independent of Paul's other letters.

[105] For the data from 2009 to 2013, including from other 'Paul' sections, see White, *Remembering Paul*, 183–9.
[106] Sanders, *Paul and Palestinian Judaism*, 431–2.
[107] Richard A. Horsley, *Paul and Politics: Ekklesia, Israel, Imperium, Interpretation. Essays in Honor of Krister Stendahl* (Harrisburg: Trinity Press International, 2000), 12.
[108] Fredriksen, *Paul*, 169.

Not all scholarship maps so neatly, of course. Sanders, it turns out, really does think that for Paul the church is a third race, and that Ephesians modifies this by incorporating gentiles into Israel (à la Baur/Käsemann).[109] For John Barclay, a new social setting explains the shift: Paul's concern in Rom 11 has happened—gentile pride perhaps causing a Jewish 'self-distancing'—and Eph 2.11-22 puts its (Paul's) finger in the dike (à la Pfleiderer/Käsemann).[110] Only Lloyd Gaston thinks Eph 2.11-22 gets Paul exactly right—a manifesto of Paul's reception of gentiles *qua* gentiles, with no application for Jews.[111] So: is Eph 2.11-22 a Judaizing of a Christian Paul (Baur/Käsemann/Sanders)? A Christianizing of a Jewish Paul (Fredriksen/Horsley)? An *aggiornamento* of Paul for a new situation (Barclay)? Or just a right reading of Paul (Gaston)? One searches in vain for coherence to this scholarly quagmire, except this: each knows that Paul did not write it, that it is late, and that (save Gaston) it gets Paul wrong. This is the power of a split corpus and a settled reading order.[112] When one knows Ephesians is late, Eph 2.11-22 becomes a supple instrument that tends to take the inverse form of a given scholar's view of Jew, gentile, and ἐκκλησία in Paul—tossed to and fro in the cross-currents of varied Paulinisms. The consensus, that is, shapes exegesis as much as it results from it.

The Quest's Fragility and Failure

Prima facie, then, Ephesians and Paul seem ripe for a comparative rereading. Instead, the opposite situation obtains: the 175-year-old parting of Paul and Ephesians continues apace. This is a good place to pause, then, and reflect on the fragility and failure of the above quest—to make explicit what a modern way of (not) reading a collection does to Ephesians. Recall the three basic moves: discrete letters are (1) raw data to be (2) chronologically rearranged for the sake of (3) biographical and

---

[109] E. P. Sanders, *Paul, the Law and the Jewish People* (Philadelphia: Fortress, 1983), 172.
[110] Barclay, *Paul and the Gift*, 524 n. 9.
[111] Gaston, *Paul and the Torah*, 90.
[112] Rather than critique Pauline monographs which largely ignore Ephesians, which would be superfluous, I offer Gaston's *Paul and the Torah* and Matthew Thiessen's *Paul and the Gentile Problem* (New York: Oxford University Press, 2015) as models for how, to my mind, scholars committed to the consensus should engage Ephesians. Neither think Paul wrote Ephesians (Gaston, 90; Thiessen, 3 n. 8), nor make extensive use of it. But both draw it in when it illuminates their discussion of another Pauline text. Gaston, for instance, is absolutely right, to my mind, to use Eph 2.1-3 and 4.17-19 to clarify Rom 1.18-32 as a catalogue of *gentile* sin (66 n. H; cf. 69); right to see Eph 3.3-6 as an accurate summary of Paul's self-understanding and mystery vis-à-vis Gal 1.15-16 (79); and far better than Sanders and Fredriksen on Eph 2.11-22 relative to Jew/gentile in Paul (90). Gaston can even refer to the author as 'a later reader who best understood Paul' (90). Thiessen uses Ephesians with even greater frequency: Eph 2.11 confirms for him that Paul can use περιτομή/ἀκροβυστία to signify Jew/gentile (cf. Gal 2.7-8), thus solving the 'riddle' of 1 Cor 7.19 (9); Eph 4.17-19 clarifies Rom 1.18-32 (50); Eph 3.16-17 explicates the more terse Gal 4.6 (cf. 3.1-5, 14), that Christ enters the gentiles *pneumatically* (111); and Thiessen cites Eph 1.13-14 repeatedly, alongside Rom 8.23; 2 Cor 1.20, 22; and 5.5, to defend the claim that, for Paul, the *pneuma* makes gentiles Abraham's seed and heirs of God's promises, and guarantees their resurrection (135, 151, 160). If the present space between Paul and Ephesians is not to be wholly artificial—constructed by ignoring Ephesians or focusing myopically on difference—more Pauline monographs will need to follow Gaston and Thiessen, and learn to read Ephesians again.

historical narration. How does this work vis-à-vis Ephesians, the *corpus Paulinum*, and Paul? Is the rhetorical confidence of the consensus matched by strong evidence and a rigorous mode of argument?

With regard to (1), Ephesians offers virtually nothing of the sort—not even, in the earliest manuscripts, an address (𝔓46 ℵ* B* 6. 1739).[113] It claims Paul as its author (1.1; 3.1), prison as its setting (3.1; 4.1; 6.20), and Tychicus as its carrier (6.21–22). The author has likely not met his recipients (1.15; 3.2; 4.21), who are largely, if not exclusively, gentiles (2.11; cf. 2.1-3; 4.17-19). Anything more is mirror-reading, not from polemic (difficult) but from largely generalized content (intractably difficult)—a challenge only intensified if Ephesians is, indeed, a pseudepigraphon.[114] From what *Sitz im Leben*, then, does Ephesians emerge?—49/50 (Apamea),[115] the early 50s (Ephesus),[116] the late 50s (Caesarea),[117] the early 60s (Rome),[118] the 80s/90s,[119] between 100 and 110,[120] or post-125 (as a product of, or response to, Marcion)?[121] More fundamentally, what *is* Ephesians?—a theological treatise,[122] a wisdom discourse,[123] a liturgy (tied to baptism? the Eucharist? Pentecost?),[124] a sermon/homily,[125] a collage of prayers or hymnic fragments,[126] an honorific decree negotiating divine/human benefaction[127]—all of the above play-acting as a letter—or is it just a letter?[128] In sum: Ephesians is a piece of Christian literature from 50–150 CE. At this level, the project has to be deemed a transparent failure, at least if one wants any specificity. In 1931, in

---

[113] The problem is well known—the lack of ἐν Ἐφέσῳ in the earliest manuscripts—and the literature extensive. Beside the critical commentaries, see the summary and bibliography in Ernest Best, 'Recipients and Title of the Letter to the Ephesians: Why and When the Designation "Ephesians"?', *ANRW* 25.4 (1987): 3247–79. Lightfoot, 'Destination of Ephesians', is a concise and plain presentation of the data.

[114] So rightly, David Lincicum, 'Mirror-Reading a Pseudepigraphal Letter', *NovT* 59 (2017): 171–93; cf. John M. G. Barclay, 'Mirror-Reading a Polemical Letter: Galatians as a Test Case', *JSNT* 31 (1987): 73–93.

[115] Campbell, *Framing Paul*, 276 and 318–20.

[116] Deissmann, *Light from the Ancient East*, 237–9.

[117] Reicke, *Re-examining Paul's Letters: The History of the Pauline Correspondence*, ed. David P. Moessner and Ingalisa Reicke (Harrisburg: Trinity Press International, 2001), 78–85; John A. T. Robinson, *Redating the New Testament* (London: SCM, 1976), 62–7.

[118] This is the traditional position for those who think Paul wrote it. See, e.g., the commentaries of Abbott, Hort, and Robinson, and now O'Brien, Hoehner, Thielman, Arnold, and Cohick.

[119] And this for those who think he did not. See, e.g., the commentaries of Schnackenburg, Lincoln, Best and Sellin.

[120] Baur, 'Einleitung', 327–8.

[121] Most recently, R. Joseph Hoffmann, *Marcion, On the Restitution of Christianity: An Essay on the Development of Radical Paulinist Theology in the Second Century* (Chico: Scholars Press, 1984), 268–80. Much earlier, Bruno Bauer, *Kritik der paulinischen Briefe* and key figures in the Dutch Radical School each placed all of Paul's letters in the mid-second century. See Hermann Detering, 'The Dutch Radical Approach to the Pauline Epistles', *Journal of Higher Criticism* 3 (1996): 163–93.

[122] Käsemann, 'Das Interpretationsproblem', 517, 520; Andreas Lindemann, 'Bemerkungen zu den Adressaten und zum Anlaß des Epheserbriefes', *ZNW* 67 (1976): 240.

[123] Schlier, *Brief an die Epheser*, 21–2.

[124] Nils A. Dahl, 'Dopet i Efesierbrevet', *STK* 21 (1945): 85–103; Kirby, *Ephesians, Baptism and Pentecost*.

[125] Gnilka, *Epheserbrief*, 33; Lincoln, *Ephesians*, xxxix.

[126] Jack T. Sanders, 'Hymnic Elements in Ephesians 1–3', *ZNW* 56 (1965): 214–32.

[127] Holland Hendrix, 'On the Form and Ethos of Ephesians', *USQR* 42 (1988): 3–15.

[128] Hoehner, *Ephesians*, 77. For description of the above forms, with copious bibliography, see Hoehner, *Ephesians*, 74–6.

the final edition of his *Einleitung*, Adolf Jülicher predicted this inconclusive state of affairs—Ephesians will *always* be 'rätselhaft'—and in 1970, Werner Kümmel lamented it.[129] What does one do with a letter that does not give what a letter is meant to give?

The problem of this lack of data (1), though, grows exponentially in view of the modern concern for a letter's setting and chronological position (2). When letters contain dates, (1) offers (2) on its face, which paves the way for biographical/ historical narration (3). With Ephesians, however, the lack of (1) makes (2) impossible—Ephesians contains no hard links by which to position it chronologically within the corpus. What, then, does one do?—exactly what Baur, Hilgenfeld, Weizsäcker, Pfleiderer and Käsemann do: use one's Paulinism and a schema of Christian origins (3) to place Ephesians (2) in order to interpret the data (1). That is, the preferred order runs backwards: (3), (2), (1).[130] And here is where modern judgments about Ephesians get fragile, for the sheer scale of (3) makes it, inevitably, a construct—a piece of art. How and where one begins and ends a narrative—be it historical or biographical—is an evaluative choice that shapes the data.[131] And a text as pliable as Ephesians is uniquely susceptible to this shaping.

Take, first, the historical construct and its frame. At the heart of Baur's project lies a vanishingly simple question: how did mid-first-century primitive Christianity become third-century Catholic Christianity?[132] I have already shown what this way of framing the question does to Ephesians in Baur and his followers, but it is worth returning briefly to Pfleiderer's *Paulinismus*, which traces Paul and Paul's legacy from the 'original Pauline doctrine' to the 'common consciousness of the Roman Catholic Church'.[133] Paulinism, that is, from Paul to Rome—these are the poles within which he sets Ephesians. In a strict sense, of course, Ephesians belongs in this temporal frame, but what is striking is the subtle way the frame shapes Pfleiderer's analysis. Recall his conclusion about Ephesians, quoted above: 'Nicht mehr, wie zur Zeit des Paulus, um die Möglichkeit des Heidenchristenthums handelt es sich jetzt, sondern um die Herbeiführung der vollen Einheit desselben mit dem Judenchristenthum, also um die Verwirklichung der allgemeinen Kirche'.

To begin, both *Heidenchristenthum* and *Judenchristenthum* belong to the reconstruction, not Ephesians, which speaks serially of gentiles, once of Israel, and never of Jews. Lexical choices which evoke later Christianity are here applied to Ephesians, creating the impression of development. Ephesians is now about the unity of two groups of which it never speaks. More telling still, however, is Pfleiderer's apposition: this unity is 'die Verwirklichung der allgemeinen Kirche'. Again, Ephesians never

---

[129] Jülicher, *Einleitung*, 142; Werner Georg Kümmel, *Das Neue Testament im 20. Jahrhundert: Ein Forschungsbericht*, SBS 50 (Stuttgart: Verlag Katholisches Bibelwerk, 1970), 54: 'Die genauere Bestimmung des literarischen Charakters und der geschichtlichen Stellung des Epheserbriefes ist… noch nicht überzeugund gelungen'. Both cited in Merkel, 'Epheserbrief', *ANRW* 25.4:3157.

[130] Merkel, 'Epheserbrief', *ANRW* 25.4:3175–76 sees the conundrum.

[131] Annette Yoshiko Reed, 'Christian Origins and Religious Studies', *SR* 44 (2015): 307–19 (here 312). For the particular challenges here vis-à-vis Christian origins, see William Arnal, 'What Branches Grow Out of This Stony Rubbish? Christian Origins and the Study of Religion', *SR* 39 (2010): 549–72 (here 555–6).

[132] Hefner, 'Baur Versus Ritschl', 259–60.

[133] Pfleiderer, *Paulinism*, iv. For Pfleiderer as a devotee of Baur's project, see his *Primitive Christianity*, vii.

speaks of the 'allgemeine Kirche', nor even of the church (ἐκκλησία) in the passage from which Pfleiderer derives this conclusion (2.11–22). Finally, and most subtly, the two halves of the apposition do not obviously relate—apart, that is, from Baur's account of origins. The narrative frame, not Ephesians, explains how the 'volle Einheit' of Jew and gentile equates, without defense, to the 'allgemeine Kirche'. And *pace* Pfleiderer, Ephesians nowhere raises 'die Idee der Katholicität'. What all of this reveals is the power of the historical frame to shape what appears, at first glance, to be straightforward exegesis. The frame is leveraged to locate a setting, which then powerfully shapes exegetical conclusions, often providing the vocabulary itself. Look closely, however, and we are here a long way from Ephesians.

Or take, second, the priority of how one configures Paulinism. Baur straightforwardly admits that he prefers the *Hauptbriefe* and judges the others on their basis.[134] The process is only slightly more subtle in Käsemann, who nowhere situates Ephesians via direct historical links, but by reading it genetically against the Paulinism he discovers in the undisputeds. This happens most directly in the reappropriated ecclesiological metaphors discussed above. For Käsemann, a metaphor differently applied signals a 'shift in the centre of interest', by which he means *historical* interest. Harmonizing is disallowed: 'Historical criticism will insist that it is the texts themselves that are decisive, not an image of Paul which we find desirable.'[135] The irony here is rich, given the image of Paul that drives Käsemann's project, but he is not wrong: Ephesians does make Christ the head of the body in a way that Romans and 1 Corinthians do not. What Käsemann never argues, however, is why the shift must run in *this* direction and not the reverse, the hidden premise of which is an implied reading order (2). And *that* depends on Käsemann's Paulinism and the trajectory he sees in early Christianity (3). For Käsemann, Paul deigns no ecclesiology. He has a Christology (Christ's 'exclusive lordship') and an anthropology (the 'freedom of the Christian man'). So when Käsemann finds ecclesial interest, he sees early catholicism. Ephesians is thus displaced due to its 'total ecclesiastical consciousness'.[136] *Pace* Käsemann, the texts are not 'decisive' here, but rather an image of Paul and Christian origins that lets him use a shift in a metaphor as a historical wedge to (dis)place Ephesians. It is this sense in which, as Albert Schweitzer says of nineteenth-century work on Paul, an a priori Paulinism is 'deceptive' for historical research.[137]

All of that is to say, given the lack of (1), judgments about Ephesians' setting and purpose are fragile, and inevitably so. The rhetorical strength of the consensus belies judgments that are evidentially weak, both in data and mode of argument. These judgments, at bottom, presume a shared discourse about Paul and Christian origins—one that no longer holds sway. For all the hand-wringing in Pauline scholarship over the legacy of the 'Lutheran Paul', today's scholarly consensus on Ephesians depends

---

[134] Baur, *Paul*, 1:256 and 2:106 and 115.
[135] Käsemann, 'Paul and Early Catholicism', 244.
[136] Käsemann, 'Theological Problem', 120–1: 'The thematic treatment of the concept of the church cannot be called Pauline. Wherever ecclesiology moves into the foreground, however justifiable the reasons may be, Christology will lose its decisive importance.... That very thing has already happened in the letter to the Ephesians'.
[137] *Paul and His Interpreters*, 68.

almost entirely on it.[138] That Ephesians remains confidently non-Pauline when scholarly accounts of Paul and Christian origins are fragmenting testifies to the force of scholarly tradition. History, it turns out, is just as tenuous a map for Ephesians as the collection. And this may explain why very few attempts to locate Ephesians as a pseudepigraphon appeal firstly to any specific historical links, but rather to a genetic reading of Ephesians against Pauline source material—typically, x, y, or z theme in the *Hauptbriefe* or Colossians. Literarily dislodged, Ephesians gets offloaded into a historical and authorial vacuum: the Pauline *Schule* of the 80s/90s—a group and time about which, vis-à-vis Paul, we know almost nothing. Duly located, Ephesians is now late enough for alleged development, and early enough to be alluded to/cited in the Apostolic Fathers. As Edgar Goodspeed writes, though, 'It is no solution of Ephesians to say that it is the work of a Paulinist in the eighties'.[139] Indeed, it is no solution at all, just a circle.

An Alternative Not Followed

Where, then, does this leave us? And is there a better way forward? In 1969, Jewish scholar Samuel Sandmel turned his eye to the study of Christian origins and wrote as follows:

> I have a conviction that for every fact about the first Christian century that I can be sure about, there are nine pseudo-facts that I am unsure of; and great as is the collective knowledge in modern scholarship, the areas where we lack knowledge are immensely greater. If this contention is right, as I believe it is, it will also follow that much of the effort of scholars to provide correlations, and to make inferences from such alleged correlations, and to trace supposed developments, is at the minimum subject to substantial challenge, and at the maximum must necessarily be characterized as imaginative and ingenious and, at the same time, at least a little bit unsubstantial.[140]

In a beautiful irony, Sandmel pens these words two years before Robinson and Koester publish their *Trajectories through Early Christianity*—a work that illustrates well the perilous scaffolding that holds up Ephesians. To be clear, to say that early Christianity developed is to state the obvious; what is not clear is that Ephesians helps trace this, or sits as a data point on a 'trajectory'. Correlations, inferences and developments are in the eye of the beholder—'imaginative and ingenious' to be sure—but in the end, 'at least a little bit unsubstantial'. In closing, then, I sketch three modern readers of Ephesians who offer a better way forward. The power of these examples is that they disagree about authorship and setting, yet each, to my mind, gets Ephesians hermeneutically exactly right. My argument, again, is not about authorship, but how

---

[138] Over five pages of incisive writing, Barth, *Ephesians*, 1:44–9 sees the issues with particular clarity.
[139] Goodspeed, 'Place of Ephesians', 211.
[140] Sandmel, *First Christian Century*, 8. See also Chadwick, 'Absicht des Epheserbriefes', 145, who makes the same point vis-à-vis Ephesians.

to read Ephesians vis-à-vis the *corpus Paulinum*, whether Paul wrote it or not. To that end, I take Edgar Goodspeed, Nils Dahl, and Douglas Campbell as luminaries for a new quest.

On one level, Goodspeed's literary depiction of early Christianity is precisely the sort of inferential guesswork against which Sandmel cautions.[141] Moreover, Goodspeed stridently opposes nebulous accounts of Ephesians' setting,[142] which is why Jülicher's desideratum hangs as an epigraphic challenge to his 1933 *Meaning of Ephesians*: 'Eine klare Vorstellung über die Situation, in der ein Paulus redivivus den Eph. verfasst hat, ist bisher nicht beschafft worden'.[143] Goodspeed hardly backs away; his setting is as particular as one could want for such a general letter. Despite all of this, what Goodspeed sees more clearly than any other modern reader of Ephesians is its inseparability from the *corpus Paulinum*: 'The problem of Ephesians', he writes, 'is inextricably intertwined with that of the Pauline corpus; it cannot be dealt with apart from it'.[144] His reconstruction is elegantly simple, and almost certainly wrong: after Paul's death, he and his letters are forgotten, and the publication of Acts spawns new interest; having read Acts, an admirer familiar with Colossians searches for other letters, and, finding them, pens an epistolary introduction (Ephesians) and arranges and publishes the entire set—thus the revival of interest in Paul in Christian texts from the mid-90s on.[145]

Goodspeed's edifice, on the whole, is a house of cards, but how he reads Ephesians, as a frontispiece for the corpus, is suggestive. He writes:

> Ephesians is a mosaic of Pauline materials; it is almost a Pauline anthology; it is altogether built of Pauline elements, even though the writer goes well beyond Paul in the use he makes of them. Indeed, it may be doubted whether Paul himself was ever in such a position to survey and summarize his own thought and message as the author of Ephesians was. It has been well said that Ephesians reads like a commentary on the Pauline letters.[146]

Goodspeed's Ephesians is indeed a Pauline mosaic. He divides it into 618 textual fragments, 550 of which enjoy a Pauline parallel.[147] This is surely extravagant, but also a useful shock treatment for scholars not used to reading Ephesians alongside Romans and Galatians. And the result is a deeply ironic conclusion: Ephesians is too Pauline to be by Paul.

---

[141] As will soon be clear, Ephesians and the publication of Paul's letter collection are a watershed in Goodspeed's telling of this history. See particularly his 'A New Organization for New Testament Introduction', and *Meaning of Ephesians*, 1–17. A distillation is in *The Key to Ephesians* (Chicago: University of Chicago Press, 1956).

[142] See particularly Goodspeed, *Meaning of Ephesians*, 9, 13–15.

[143] From the fifth edition of Jülicher's *Einleitung* (1906), 127; cf. Goodspeed, *Meaning of Ephesians*, 15.

[144] Goodspeed, *Meaning of Ephesians*, 9.

[145] Goodspeed, *Meaning of Ephesians*, 3–17. See also his 'Editio Princeps of Paul', *JBL* 64 (1945): 193–204, and 'Ephesians and the First Edition of Paul', *JBL* 70 (1951): 285–91.

[146] Goodspeed, *Meaning of Ephesians*, 8; cf. 10. Sixty years later, Daniel Boyarin says much the same: 'Let me emphasize once more that Colossians and Ephesians may be the best *commentaries* on Pauline doctrine that we possess' (*A Radical Jew*, 310 n. 25).

[147] Goodspeed, *Meaning of Ephesians*, 9. See his synopsis at pp. 79–165.

In all of this, Goodspeed uncouples two questions that Paul's modern readers reflexively correlate: a text's origin and its co-texts. For modern critics, locating Ephesians in the 80s/90s means lifting it out of the collection and reading it alongside a new set of co-texts. Goodspeed's *Sitz im Leben*, on the other hand, is really a *Sitz im Buch*.[148] Despite its post-Pauline setting, Goodspeed's Ephesians still demands to be read vis-à-vis the corpus of church letters it introduces.[149] To take just one example, Eph 1.3–14 is 'a glorious prelude to the Pauline letters'—not just Ephesians, but the *corpus*—and so offers 'the heart of the Pauline message, the leading ideas of his letters stripped of the occasional and personal, and presented in their larger general aspect'.[150] Rather than casting Ephesians as a piece of polemic, so in vogue given recent accounts of pseudepigraphy, Goodspeed allows Ephesians to be what it so obviously is: the most generalized of Pauline letters. As such, it constitutes 'a summary of Pauline Christianity'.[151]

The same is true of Douglas Campbell's reading of Ephesians, albeit via a very different route. Compared to Goodspeed, Campbell's reconstruction is involved and complex, but something like it is also more possibly right.[152] It runs, skeletally, as follows: in early 50, heading west to Ephesus shortly after the Jerusalem council, Paul is imprisoned in the Lycus Valley nearby Colossae and Laodicea (Phlm 22; Col 4.13, 15–16; cf. 2 Cor 11.23); from here he engages in a 'proxy mission' to Colossae via Epaphras (Col 1.7; 4.12–13); just beyond, in Laodicea, lay a Christ-assembly of pagan converts unknown to Paul, and he to them (Eph 1.15; 3.2; 4.21; 6.21–22); this group, likely from a 'more observant Jewish context than not', required Paul's gospel but Paul was in prison.[153] Thus, the stage is set: Laodiceans (= Ephesians) is a Pauline 'account of pagan Christian identity'—that is, Paul's gospel *in absentia* by letter.[154]

The differences between Goodspeed and Campbell are obvious, but vis-à-vis Paul and the other letters, they read Ephesians in largely the same way. Compare, for instance, Goodspeed's 'summary of Pauline Christianity' with Campbell's conclusion: 'If this reconstruction holds good, then we would observe in Laodiceans as in no other epistolary situation…a relatively straightforward account of Paul's missionary

---

[148] I owe this language to the work of James D. Nogalski, and particularly his essay 'One Book and Twelve Books: The Nature of the Redactional Work and the Implications of Cultic Source Material in the Book of the Twelve', in *The Book of the Twelve and Beyond: Collected Essays of James D. Nogalski*, AIL 29 (Atlanta: SBL Press, 2017), 83–114 (here 100–108).

[149] One need not follow Goodspeed's conjecture that Ephesians introduced an early edition of the collection, for which there is no evidence, to recognize the hermeneutical fruit that results from it.

[150] Goodspeed, *Meaning of Ephesians*, 20 and 24.

[151] Goodspeed, *Meaning of Ephesians*, 20, referring specifically to Eph 1–2.

[152] See Campbell, *Framing Paul*, 309–38, although given that his provenance largely hangs on data from Colossians and Philemon, 254–338 in its entirety is vital.

[153] The major work here happens from pp. 254–83, 304–20, 336–8 (quotations at 261 and 336). The critical move is identifying Ephesians as Laodiceans (310–13), since it weaves Ephesians, Colossians, and Philemon into a '*single extended epistolary event*' (319, emphasis original), and furnishes Campbell with more data. Like every reconstruction of Ephesians aimed at specificity, Campbell's is tenuous, and depends on a host of what are, at best, possibilities. That said, Campbell marshals *far* more data than others do for more traditional settings. If Ephesians is authentic, I find something like his setting (early to Laodicea) far more plausible than a late missive to Ephesus from Rome. Moreover, his suggestion about the letter's purpose (Paul's *kerygma* via letter) is highly suggestive for further research.

[154] Campbell, *Framing Paul*, 314 and 319.

agenda in relation to pagan conversion—a presentation, he might say, of his gospel'.[155] Campbell never systematically reads Ephesians alongside Pauline co-texts, but the implication of this setting is clear.

> Of all the Pauline letters examined thus far, Laodiceans was elicited by particular circumstances that called most directly for an exposition of Paul's most coherent concerns.... It seems possible that the echoes of Laodiceans found in the undisputed letters are not evidence of the later influence on 'Ephesians' of the authentic Paulines so much as the filtering through of many of Paul's most significant concerns from Laodiceans to the letters he was forced to write in 51 and the spring of 52 in various rather more difficult and specific circumstances.... This would explain the heavy interdependence evident between the undisputed letters and Laodiceans.[156]

With this, Campbell turns virtually the entire history of Ephesians scholarship on its head. Although they argue the literary relationship in exactly opposite directions, Campbell and Goodspeed end up in the same place: reading the corpus through the lens of Ephesians. Campbell recognizes the consequence: 'Ultimately, this position will result in a more "Ephesiocentric" account of Paul's thought than might otherwise be the case'.[157] Eighty years later, Ephesians scholarship has its new Goodspeed.

Compared to the idiosyncratic Goodspeed and Campbell, Nils Dahl is in many respects quite typical, not least in his 'Einleitungsfragen zum Epheserbrief', the introduction to his never-finished commentary.[158] Dahl places Ephesians ca. 80, written likely to Laodicea and Hierapolis (and possibly other cities) by a young, Jewish-Christian Paulinist.[159] The letter is broadly 'utopisches' and reflective of 'einer späteren Generation' for reasons that are, by now, conventional: the fading of the Jew/gentile controversy (2.11–22; 3.5–7); the elevated *Paulusbild* (3.2–13); the focus on the church's unity, universally conceived; the retrospective valorization of 'apostles and prophets' (2.20; 3.3); and the stereotyped portrayal of heresy (4.14).[160] Moreover, Dahl has a lengthy section on similarities in Ephesians to the Apostolic Fathers and later New Testament texts,[161] and he sees an interpretive line from Paul through Ephesians to both early catholicism and Gnosticism.[162] The author, Dahl thinks, is 'ein Mann der Übergangszeit'—a line that echoes Hilgenfeld, and recalls Baur and Käsemann.[163]

All of this suggests that Dahl's judgments share in the fragility discussed earlier, and as a matter of 'Einleitungsfragen' they do. But in exegetical practice, Dahl draws

---

[155] Campbell, *Framing Paul*, 314.
[156] Campbell, *Framing Paul*, 325–6.
[157] Campbell, *Framing Paul*, 326.
[158] Previously unpublished, the work is now available in Dahl, *Studies in Ephesians*, 3–105.
[159] On authorship, see Dahl, 'Einleitungsfragen', 48–60; on addressees, 60–72; and on time and situation, 72–81. Dahl is meticulous and balanced; his own judgments appear at pp. 63 and 72.
[160] Dahl, 'Einleitungsfragen', 54. Dahl calls the letter utopian at 80–1; cf. Dahl, 'Fictional and Real Setting', in *Studies in Ephesians*, 453.
[161] Dahl, 'Einleitungsfragen', 28–37.
[162] Dahl, 'Einleitungsfragen', 54–5; cf. Dahl, 'Fictional and Real Setting', 452; and idem, 'Interpreting Ephesians: Then and Now', in *Studies in Ephesians*, 461–4.
[163] Dahl, 'Einleitungsfragen', 54.

back and rarely if ever leverages this setting for interpretation, precisely because he sees how fragile any setting is. Dahl himself is equivocal. That date?—it turns out two options are viable, a Pauline 'Mitarbeiter' writing in 60 (at Paul's behest) *or* 80 (after Paul's death), and that literary and theological criteria cannot adjudicate the question.[164] Dahl opts for the latter not for reasons of theological development, but because he detects daylight between the letter's real and fictional settings.[165] Those dual trajectories?—they are real, but also derive in part from the later use of a uniquely pliable text.[166] And those late co-texts?—Paul's letters remain the primary parallel material, since Ephesians belongs to the 'Pauline circle'.[167] Dahl's circumspect hermeneutic thus runs opposite to most recent work on Ephesians: he painstakingly works the letter's setting as far as it allows, offers his tentative solution, and then makes very little exegetically of it. This is Dahl's great virtue: he refrains from over-interpreting in the face of limited evidence.

So what *is* Ephesians for Dahl? It is a letter of congratulations—a reminder to gentiles of their newfound soteriological gift and a call to live accordingly.[168] To this end, Ephesians takes up Pauline themes, not least pre-Pauline baptismal motifs, and puts them to use in quite traditional ways for new gentile converts.[169] For the early Dahl (1945/1951), this is Paul himself, and for the later Dahl, it is a Paulinist.[170] Authorship aside, Dahl's description of the letter is apt: 'Ephesians combines "pre-Pauline", Pauline, ultra-Pauline and non-Pauline elements under a post-Pauline perspective'.[171] We are here a long way from today's stock judgments of developed Paulinism. If Dahl is right, the *modus operandi* for reading Ephesians vis-à-vis Paul will not do. Dahl is free to read Ephesians alongside Paul's letters for a simple reason: it is awash in Paulinism, just as it is for Goodspeed and Campbell. Three very different settings, in the end, give way to three near-identical ways of reading Ephesians vis-à-vis Paul. Theirs, I suggest, is a notable alternative to the regnant hermeneutic, and a promising way forward.

Conclusion

It is not, however, one that has been taken. If Ephesians scholarship of the past 175 years shares anything in common, it is the ubiquitous belief, across the ideological spectrum and whatever one's view of authorship, that Ephesians depicts development of/away from Paul. So, the German Catholic Joachim Gnilka: 'Der Vergleich dieser

---

[164] Dahl, 'Einleitungsfragen', 72; 'Fictional and Real Setting', 451.
[165] See here 'Einleitungsfragen', 76–81; 'Fictional and Real Setting', 451–9.
[166] See here specifically 'Einleitungsfragen', 55 and 80–1 (#5). Moreover, Dahl rejects any straight line of development over Ephesians to the Pastorals ('Fictional and Real Setting', 458), and suggests that, in many ways, Ephesians 'holds the middle position' between the undisputeds and Colossians (458).
[167] Dahl, 'Einleitungsfragen', 54; cf. 37–48, particularly the list on 38.
[168] Dahl, 'Einleitungsfragen', 81; 'Fictional and Real Setting', 453; 'Ephesians: Then and Now', 471–2.
[169] See Dahl, 'Fictional and Real Setting', 452. On this score—Ephesians using traditions less creatively/originally than Paul—Dahl is very similar to Käsemann, 'Ephesians and Acts', 288–9.
[170] Dahl's early articles are 'Dopet i Efesierbrevet' [1945] and 'Adresse und Proömium des Epheserbriefes', *TZ* 7 (1951): 241–64. His shift is evident in 'Ephesians', *IDBSup*, 268–9 [1976] and the essays in *Studies in Ephesians*. Dahl makes a few autobiographical comments on the question in 'The Concept of Baptism in Ephesians', trans. Bruce C. Johanson, in *Studies in Ephesians*, 414–15.
[171] Dahl, 'Fictional and Real Setting', 452; cf. idem, 'Einleitungsfragen', 54, 77–8.

Briefe mit Paulus läßt bemerkenswerte Entwicklungslinien in Erscheinung treten'.[172] Or again, the Northern Irish Presbyterian Ernest Best: '[The author of Ephesians] began with a situation he saw needed addressing and because he was a Paulinist he dealt with it in Pauline terms and so extended Paul's theology. Of course if Paul is the author he will naturally be adapting and developing himself'.[173] Or defending its authenticity, the Swiss Lutheran Markus Barth: 'Certainly those doctrinal differences between Ephesians and the homologoumena that have been mentioned so far can be explained as results of a late stage of theological development reached by the apostle himself'.[174] Or the American Baptist Harold Hoehner: 'In conclusion, the letter to the Ephesians may exhibit differences from other letters by Paul. However, they are differences in emphasis possibly due to differences in circumstances.... Paul was not a static but creative thinker and as new situations and/or problems arose, it is not unreasonable to suggest that there would have been development in his thinking'.[175] This is enough to prove the point. Vis-à-vis the *Hauptbriefe*, Ephesians is displaced even by those who think Paul wrote it.

This is not to say that it has been placed. The variety of proposed settings puts the lie to Hilgenfeld's judgment that Ephesians is only 'geschichtlich begreiflich...als die Schrift eines asiatischen Pauliners der gnostischen Zeit'.[176] On the contrary, scholars post-Baur have found it comprehensible anywhere from 50 to 150. What is true, however, save a precious few voices, is that Ephesians has been only 'intelligible' as a piece of developed Paulinism. For most modern scholars, Ephesians represents the first layer of a canonical misunderstanding of Paul. Here I have begun to argue the opposite: that the modern dismembering of the letter collection, while not in itself unjustified, is the gateway to misunderstanding Ephesians.[177] To echo Mary Beard's judgment (*mutatis mutandis*) about scholarly readings of Cicero, 'There is more than a hint in my argument that modern orthodoxies in interpreting [Paul]...are not unconnected with the order in which we have chosen to read [his letters]'.[178] The judgment that Ephesians is advanced, developed, catholicized Paulinism, in other words, is a construct of modern criticism. In our ecumenical age, the language since Baur and Käsemann grows more subtle, but the meaning is the same. Sometimes, however, scholars still say directly what they mean. So, Robert Morgan: 'Catholicism can convincingly appeal to Ephesians, but Protestantism draws its ecclesiology and much of its practice from the real Paul reflected in his authentic epistles'.[179] The myth of modern criticism here finds a worthy voice, but a myth it remains. Change the reading order and modify the Paul, and Ephesians looks quite different—or at least, that is the *Wirkungsgeschichtliche* argument of the next two chapters.

---

[172] Joachim Gnilka, 'Das Paulusbild im Kolosser- und Epheserbrief', in *Kontinuität und Einheit: Festschrift für Franz Mussner zum 65. Geburtstag*, ed. Paul-Gerhard Müller and Werner Stenger (Freiburg: Herder, 1981), 179. Gnilka writes here of both Ephesians and Colossians.
[173] Best, *Ephesians*, 71.
[174] Barth, *Ephesians*, 1:36.
[175] Hoehner, *Ephesians*, 58.
[176] Hilgenfeld, *Einleitung*, 677.
[177] For this argument in detail with respect to a particular text (Eph 3.1–13), see Chapter 5.
[178] Beard, 'Ciceronian Correspondences', 115.
[179] Morgan, 'Paul's Enduring Legacy', 252.

Part 2

READING PAUL AND EPHESIANS IN LATE ANTIQUITY

Chapter 3

ASSEMBLING PAUL

When Schleiermacher opens his ancient editions of Plato, he sees only 'disarrangement'.[1] When Baur opens those of Paul, he finds only a 'confused web of artificial combinations'.[2] Were an ancient editor like Porphyry, however, to open Schleiermacher or Baur's work, he would no doubt return the favor. As Porphyry writes of his editorial work for Plotinus, 'He himself left to us to produce the arrangement and correction of his books, and while he was living, I promised him and offered to his other pupils that I would do this. First, then, I did not think it right to leave the books in chronological confusion, as they were published.'[3] As Plotinus's self-appointed editor, for Porphyry to leave his works κατὰ χρόνους would be to leave them φύρδην, in utter confusion.[4] It would be, that is, an act of editorial neglect. The juxtaposition of ancient and modern is striking. Chronology is *not* king. Prime facie, then, and *pace* Schleiermacher, the 'natural order' of a collection is not natural; it is a socially constructed choice, a 'cultural preference'.[5]

Arrangement, of course, requires the prior act of collection—a point made programmatically by Ps.-Plutarch: 'In regard to education...it is useful, or rather it is necessary, not to be indifferent about acquiring the works of earlier writers, but to make a collection of these, like a set of tools in farming. For the corresponding tool of education is the use of books, and by their means it has come to pass that we are able to study knowledge at its source.'[6] This act of 'acquiring the works of earlier writers' brings us back to what Kenneth Dover calls the 'data of history': 'what we can see and touch and smell'.[7] Vis-à-vis Paul, it means a return to texts like 𝔓46, Vaticanus, and 1739 with which I began. Pace Dover, however, this too is construction. To 'make a collection' involves a series of choices—which texts? what order? and how much (para)textual intervention?—that guide interpretation.[8] Paul *may* have written, say,

---

[1] Schleiermacher, 'General Introduction', 26; cf. 14, 21 and 24.
[2] Baur, *Paul*, 2:111.
[3] *Plot.* 24.2–7. The translation is my own.
[4] LSJ, s.v. φύρδην 1. As becomes clear in his work that follows, Porphyry's editorial motive is not to set the chronological record straight, but to offer a new order that *escapes* the confusion of chronology. See my discussion below.
[5] Gibson, 'Ancient Letter Collections', 72.
[6] *Lib. ed.* 8B (Babbitt, LCL).
[7] Dover, *Lysias and the Corpus Lysiacum*, 1.
[8] See here the incisive comments of Beard, 'Ciceronian Correspondences', 120–1.

thirty-one letters; we do not know. He probably wrote at least one more than we have (1 Cor 5.9), and possibly two (Col 4.16). Regardless, the choice of ten, or thirteen, or fourteen (with Hebrews) is a choice. So too with the arrangement. The canon does not reflect the order in which he wrote the letters. The choice to arrange them by decreasing length, to pair the Corinthian and Thessalonian correspondence, and to separate church and individual letters, is, again, a choice. So too with the text itself. When Tertius transcribed Romans (16.22), he presumably wrote in *scriptio continua* without any paratextual markers to guide reading. And so, again, the choice to provide such—via textual division, ὑποθέσεις, κεφάλαια, etc.— is a choice.

In ways large and small, then, assembling a corpus, just like deconstructing it, is manifestly a case of 'editorial hermeneutics'.[9] The point is not simply to preserve, but to mediate: to facilitate interpreting *Homerum ex Homero*,[10] or, in our case, *Paulum ex Paulo*. For that, one needs the collection. To be sure, echoing Ps.-Plutarch, the collection offers 'knowledge *at its source*' (i.e. the letters), but *it* offers 'knowledge at its source'. This chapter exposes this late-antique way of reading Paul, not least its preference for the collection and non-chronological strategies for reading it. That is, it narrates how Paul's late-antique tradents assemble and read the only Pauls we have.

Reading Ancient Corpora

None of this, of course, is unique to Paul and his letters. The issue of collection itself is widespread in antiquity, and goes far beyond epistolary collections. To set the stage for Paul's late-antique readers, then, I show the above preferences in another series of late-antique corpora: the dialogues of Plato, the philosophical treatises of Plotinus, and the letter collections of Cicero, Pliny, and Sidonius Apollinaris.

Reading Plato in Antiquity

In his work on Plato, the third-century biographer Diogenes Laertius begins, as is his typical fashion, with a βίος (Diog. Laert. 3.1–47a). After Plato's biography, however, Diogenes turns to discuss the 'ordering [τάξις] of his dialogues', and in doing so attests to a robust ancient debate on how to arrange Plato's works (3.47).[11] Thrasyllus's tetralogies—the object of Schleiermacher's derision—enjoy the bulk of Diogenes's attention. Like Schleiermacher, Thrasyllus almost certainly pens an introduction to Plato (Τὰ πρὸ τῆς ἀναγνώσεως τῶν Πλάτωνος διαλόγων), which offers a biography (Diog. Laert. 3.1) and adjudicates questions of authenticity and arrangement (3.57–61).[12] Then as

---

[9] Eric W. Scherbenske, *Canonizing Paul: Ancient Editorial Practice and the Corpus Paulinum* (New York: Oxford University Press, 2013), 3–5.
[10] On this principle and its origin, see Christoph Schäublin, 'Homerum ex Homero', *MH* 34 (1977): 221–7. See also Rudolf Pfeiffer, *History of Classical Scholarship* (Oxford: Clarendon, 1968), 1:225–7; and succinctly, Jaap Mansfeld, *Prolegomena: Questions to Be Settled Before the Study of a Text*, Philosophia Antiqua 61 (Leiden: Brill, 1994), 204; cf. 178–9.
[11] On the order in which an author's works should be read as a standard topic of prolegomena in antiquity, see Mansfeld, *Prolegomena*, 10–11.
[12] We know Thrasyllus's work on Plato largely through Diogenes's *Lives of Eminent Philosophers* 3 Plato, easily accessible in LCL 184. For secondary discussion of Thrasyllus, his editorial work on the *corpus Platonicum*, and his impact on the subsequent interpretive tradition, see Harold

now, it appears, identifying and excluding spurious works begins the interpretive task.[13] For Thrasyllus, Plato's genuine dialogues are thirty-six in total (3.57). The critical move, though, is the next one, when Thrasyllus offers his order (τάξις) of reading. On analogy to the corpora of the tragic poets, Thrasyllus gathers Plato's works into tetralogies, or nine groups of four (3.56–61).[14] Intriguingly, for the symmetry to work, Thrasyllus must count Plato's *Epistles*, which he places last in his ninth tetralogy, as a single work.[15] Beside the 'common subject' of the first tetralogy (*Euthyphro, Apology, Crito, Phaedo*), which deals with the life of the philosopher, Diogenes does not report how (or whether) Thrasyllus's tetralogies represent any sort of progression. But the structure as a whole is undoubtedly Thrasyllus's attempt to outline a curriculum of reading for the would-be Platonist.[16]

Other options exist, of course.[17] Aristophanes of Byzantium arranges the dialogues in five trilogies (Diog. Laert. 3.62), within which the *Letters* again constitute a single unit. The second-century CE Middle Platonist Albinus offers one curriculum for the amateur (*Greater Alcibiades, Phaedo, Republic,* and *Timaeus*), and another for the aspiring Platonist (*Prol.* 5–6).[18] This latter order, consisting of twenty-eight dialogues, is explicitly a curriculum: the 'one who undertakes the study of Plato' begins with dialogues of a type that purify and prepare the reader before moving on to Platonic doctrine and logic proper (*Prol.* 6); the 'order of instruction' (διάταξις διδασκαλία) that Albinus seeks, then, is not chronological, but 'according to wisdom' (κατὰ σοφίαν; *Prol.* 4.16–17).[19] A simpler scheme is offered by the Neoplatonist Iamblichus, who settles on twelve dialogues for his program (*Anon. proleg.* 24–26). All together, eleven dialogues head an arrangement of Plato in antiquity: the nine listed by Diogenes, the *Epistles,* and *Parmenides* (Diog. Laert. 3.62; cf. Alb., *Prol.* 4; *Anon. proleg.* 24). Plato's ancient readers may enjoy a robust debate vis-à-vis his arrangement, then, but chronology hardly emerges as a fruitful possibility.[20] What matters is the collective: to gain a paideia in

---

Tarrant, *Thrasyllan Platonism* (Ithaca: Cornell University Press, 1993), 89–98, 179–99, and 201–6; and Mansfeld, *Prolegomena,* 59–74, and 89–97. The connection of biography and bibliography in editions of ancient figures is ubiquitous. On this convergence in ancient literary criticism generally, see D. A. Russell, *Criticism in Antiquity* (Berkeley: University of California Press, 1981), 159–64; and in specifically isagogical works, Mansfeld, *Prolegomena,* 179–91.

[13] Diogenes, for instance, lists ten Platonic dialogues widely acknowledged as spurious (3.62). See further Russell, *Criticism in Antiquity,* 159–61.

[14] The tetralogies' origin is discussed in Michael R. Dunn, 'The Organization of the Platonic Corpus Between the First Century B.C. and the Second Century A.D.' (PhD diss., Yale University, 1974), 51–9, and more indirectly by Tarrant, *Thrasyllan Platonism,* 11–17, 58–84, 89–107.

[15] Like the other letter collections outlined below, Plato's *Epistles* are arranged non-chronologically and have been subjected to modern re-ordering. See the discussion in A. D. Morrison, 'Narrativity and Epistolarity in the "Platonic" Epistles', in *Epistolary Narratives in Ancient Greek Literature,* ed. Owen Hodkinson, Patricia A. Rosenmeyer, and Evelien Bracke, Mnemosyne Supplements 359 (Leiden: Brill, 2013), 107–31 (here 108–9).

[16] Mansfeld, *Prolegomena,* 67–8, 93–5.

[17] The most extensive discussion is in Dunn, 'Organization of the Platonic Corpus'.

[18] Albinus's student—the physician-cum-philosopher Galen—does the same for his own corpus in his *De ordine librorum* and *De libris propriis,* on which see Mansfeld, *Prolegomena,* 117–31.

[19] The text of Albinus's *Prologos* is in Olaf Nüsser, *Albins Prolog und die Dialogtheorie des Platonismus,* Beiträge zur Altertumskunde 12 (Stuttgart: Teubner, 1991), 30–4.

[20] The sixth-century CE *Anonymous Prolegomena to Platonic Philosophy* attests the existence of two such orders, but rejects them as well as Thrasyllus's tetralogies in favor of the Iamblichian canon (24–6).

Platonism, a suitably arranged collection is paramount. On this way of reading, the discrete dialogue gives way to the macrostructure of the corpus—hermeneutically, no small thing.

Porphyry's (Fl. 234–305 CE) Vita Plotini

The same is true of Porphyry's work on the philosophical treatises of Plotinus, only now we have Porphyry's first-hand account of his work. More than the Latin, the Greek title—Περὶ τοῦ Πλωτίνου βίου καὶ τῆς ταξέως τῶν βιβλίων αὐτοῦ—reveals its scope.[21] Issued in the early years of the fourth century, Porphyry's edition of Plotinus comprises (1) a βίος (*Plot.* 1–23); (2) a bibliographical catalogue of the authentic corpus, with Porphyry's arrangement (τάξις) thereof (*Plot.* 24–26); and (3) the works (βιβλία) themselves, edited by Porphyry. As we saw above, Porphyry's editorial task was twofold: 'the arrangement (διάταξις) and correction (διόρθωσις) of his books' (24.2–5). On the latter, Porphyry's intervention is extensive, and necessarily so. Plotinus's compositional habits (forming letters, syllables, and spelling) were, to put it politely, idiosyncratic (8.4–6), and he refused to edit (8.1–4). Add to this the obscurity of Plotinus's thought, and Porphyry's editorial guidance runs the gamut: from punctuation (στίγμα) and correction (διορθόω) to make the text legible, to the provision of headings (κεφάλαια) and summaries (ἐπιχειρήματα) to make Plotinus intelligible (26.32–40). Reading Plotinus, not least in his own ill-formed *scriptio continua*, was difficult—a fact already acknowledged in antiquity—and so Porphyry's work, in large part, seeks to render him accessible.[22]

Not just accessible, though, but elegant. No intervention is more editorially disruptive than how one arranges a set of works (διάταξις). So what is Porphyry's choice here? Critically, he knows their chronological order, but does not follow it.[23] In his βίος, Porphyry delineates Plotinus's authorial activity in three stages—those treatises written prior to, during, and after Porphyry's period of study with Plotinus in Rome (263–68 CE)—and lists the relevant works chronologically within each stage (*Plot.* 4–6).[24] Plotinus wrote fifty-four works in total, and their 'power' (δύναμις) varies according to when they were written: the twenty-one of the early period are 'lighter in power' (ἐλαφροτέρας δυνάμεως), or easier to understand; the twenty-four of the middle period depict the 'prime of his power' (τὸ ἀκμαῖον τῆς δυνάμεως); and the final nine, written in illness at the end of his life, reveal Plotinus's 'abating of power' (ὑφειμένης τῆς δυνάμεως). Yet despite such insider knowledge, which to modern sensibilities is pregnant with possibilities for tracing philosophical development, Porphyry rejects

---

[21] The critical edition is Paul Henry and Hans-Rudolf Schwyzer, eds., *Plotini Opera I* (Oxford: Clarendon, 1964). Section and line references are to this edition. For English translation, see Plotinus, *Porphyry on Plotinus, Ennead I*, trans. A. H. Armstrong, LCL 440 (Cambridge, MA: Harvard University Press, 1989).

[22] Marie-Odile Goulet-Cazé makes this point with respect to Porphyry's inclusion of ὑπομνήματα, κεφάλαια, and ἐπιχειρήματα in 'L'arrière-plan scolaire de la Vie de Plotin', in *Travaux préliminaires et index grec complet*, ed. Luc Brisson et al., vol. 1 of *Porphyre: La Vie de Plotin*, Histoire des doctrines de l'Antiquité classique 6 (Paris: J. Vrin, 1982), 305–6.

[23] Porphyry may also know a chronological *edition* that precedes his own (26.32–35). See Goulet-Cazé, 'L'arrière-plan scolaire', 287–94.

[24] For discussion, see Goulet-Cazé, 'L'arrière-plan scolaire', 296–7.

chronology. To leave them κατὰ χρόνους, as we have seen, would consign them to 'utter confusion' (φύρδην; 24.5–7). So Porphyry organizes the works by subject matter, drawing together those treatises (πραγματεῖαι) of 'related topics' (οἰκείας ὑποθέσεις; 24.6–11). In doing so, he divides (διαιρέω) the *corpus Plotinicum* into six sets of nine (ἐννεάδαι; 24.12). Rather than begin with the ἐλαφροτέρας δυνάμεως of Plotinus's early years, Porphyry places the 'lighter *problems*' first (ἐλαφροτέροις προβλήμασιν), and progresses through a paideia in Neoplatonic philosophy.[25] Pedagogy is his focus, with obvious consequences for arrangement.[26] Porphyry also delights in the macrostructure as a whole. Beyond the perfection of the numbers six and nine (24.13–14), the *physical* design is elegant: the six ἐννεάδαι are split into three σωμάτια ('volumes')— three in volume one, two in volume two, and one in volume three (26.1–7). From διόρθωσις to διάταξις and everything in between, Porphyry guides the *what* and *how* of reading Plotinus. From the reader's perspective, Plotinus simply *is* now an elegantly designed collective—an editorially mediated book, or series of books.

Cicero, Pliny, Sidonius and Ancient Letter Collections

But what do we mean by book (βίβλος/βιβλίον; *liber/volumen*)? In classical Greek, βιβλίον/βίβλος typically refers to the papyrus roll that houses a work rather than the work itself, and the same is generally true of the Latin *volumen* and *liber*.[27] Inscribed on a single roll, a work *could* be called τό βιβλίον; equally, a longer work could span several βιβλία. But to call a work of literature (e.g. the *Aeneid*) a book was exceedingly rare in antiquity.[28] Where τό βιβλίον is reserved for the artefact (e.g. Plato [Diog. Laert. 3.65]) or the individual works that comprise a collection (e.g. Plotinus [*Plot.* 24.2–7]), then, my interest is not in the lexeme itself, but in the impulse toward collectivity and reading strategies that privilege it. In letter collections, however, the lexeme dovetails with the divisions of the collection itself. Far from a functional reference to the roll/codex, τό βιβλίον now marks off a hermeneutical boundary.[29] *This* set of letters constitutes a collected unit of meaning (τό βιβλίον), and so should be read together.

So, Cicero's 435 letters to friends (*ad Familiares*) are divided into sixteen βιβλία, as are his 426 letters to Atticus (*ad Atticum*).[30] Pliny himself arranges his 247 letters

---

[25] Porphyry identifies the subject of each ennead in his introductory comments to each (*Plot.* 24–26).
[26] This is most evident through a simple comparison of the lists in *Plot.* 4–6 (chronological) and 24–26 (enneadic). A useful table is in Plotinus, *The Enneads*, trans. Stephen MacKenna, 3rd ed. (London: Faber, 1962), 629; cf. the discussion in Mansfeld, *Prolegomena*, 111–13.
[27] LSJ, s.v. βιβλίον/βυβλίον II.1–2 and βύβλος/βίβλος I.1–4; Lewis and Short, s.v. *volumen* I and *liber* I, II.A-C. For helpful introduction to ancient book culture, see Bernard M. W. Knox and Patricia E. Easterling, 'Books and Readers in the Greek World', in *Greek Literature*, ed. Patricia E. Easterling and Bernard M. W. Knox, vol. 1 of *The Cambridge History of Classical Literature* (Cambridge: Cambridge University Press, 2008), 1–41; and E. J. Kenney, 'Books and Readers in the Roman World', in *Latin Literature*, ed. Wendell Clausen and E. J. Kenney, vol. 2 of *The Cambridge History of Classical Literature*, 3–32. On the early Christian side, the classic work is Gamble, *Books and Readers*. On the question of linguistic clarification, see Kenney, 'Books and Readers', 15 and 30.
[28] Kenney, 'Books and Readers', 15.
[29] If τό βιβλίον/*volumen* was purely functional, one would expect that a letter collection's books would house roughly the same number of letters, but this is demonstrably not the case. Within the collection of Ambrose, e.g., Book 10 makes up nearly a third of the collection. See further Gérard Nauroy, 'The Letter Collection of Ambrose of Milan', in *LALC*, 147.
[30] Two smaller collections (*ad Quint. Fratr.*; *ad Brut.*) contain 52 more letters spread across five books.

into nine books, with his 121-letter correspondence with Trajan appended (likely) posthumously as Book 10. Pliny almost certainly published these books in stages, thus sanctioning the letter *book's* priority, before completing the project with an 'omnibus' edition, now placing each book in a new nine-book hermeneutical collective.[31] Data like this can be multiplied: Seneca's 124 letters are published in 20 books; Fronto's 348 letters in 14 books; Symmachus's 902 letters in 10 books; and Sidonius Appolinaris's 147 letters in 9 books, to name a few.[32] This is drawn largely from the manuscript divisions, but other ancient sources also witness to the book as the primary unit of division. In his *Ep.* 32, Ambrose writes to his friend Sabinus, 'This letter that I have sent to you is a first attempt, which I plan to insert in the books [*libros*] of my letters, if you agree, and I will include it so that your name will recommend my collection'.[33] In the early fourth century, in Egypt, a certain Pachomius writes a series of letters to the fathers of his monasteries, who, believing a collection would be beneficial, ask him to make 'a book [βίβλιον] of those spiritual writings'.[34] Finally, some ways to the north, Rufinus reports that Cyprian's letters may be found in a bookseller's shop in Constantinople, sold 'in uno codice'—a reference to their physical collection in a particular kind of book.[35] Whether the work of an author, editor, or later collector-editor, and whether attested via manuscripts or secondary reference, letters from antiquity are arranged in a collective routinely called τό βιβλίον/*libri*.

So far, collectivity—but what of the editorial design of such letter books? Just here, as Mary Beard, Roy Gibson, and others have shown, ancient letter writers and their collectors are more or less disinterested in chronology.[36] The dominant organizing principle, rather, is by addressee or theme, and within this by what Gibson calls 'artful variety' or 'significant juxtaposition'.[37] Three of Cicero's entire collections, in fact, stem from correspondence with a single addressee: Atticus, Quintus, and Brutus. In Cicero's sixteen book *ad Familiares*, Books 1, 3, 14 and 16 gather letters to a single individual; Book 13 is thematic, collocating Cicero's letters of recommendation; and

---

[31] For a lengthy overview of publication, see John Bodel, 'The Publication of Pliny's Letters', in *Pliny the Book-Maker*, ed. Ilaria Marchesi (Oxford: Oxford University Press, 2015), 13–108, with summary at 105–8. The argument for a nine-book omnibus edition is that of Charles E. Murgia, 'Pliny's Letters and the *Dialogus*', *HSCP* 89 (1985): 171–206. Roy K. Gibson and Ruth Morello, *Reading the Letters of Pliny the Younger: An Introduction* (Cambridge: Cambridge University Press, 2012), 251–63, have recently argued that Pliny published Book 10 himself.

[32] Gibson, 'Ancient Letter Collections', treats all four, with bibliography there. See also the respective essays of Cristiana Sogno (on Symmachus) and Sigrid Mratschek (on Sidonius) in *LALC*.

[33] Cited and translated in Nauroy, 'Collection of Ambrose', 148.

[34] *Life of Pachomius*, in François Halkin, ed., *Sancti Pachomii: vitae Graecae*, Subsidia Hagiographica 19 (Brussels: Société des Bollandistes, 1932), 66–7; cited in Malcolm Choat, 'From Letter to Letter-Collection: Monastic Epistolography in Late-Antique Egypt', in *Collecting Early Christian Letters: From the Apostle Paul to Late Antiquity*, ed. Bronwen Neil and Pauline Allen (Cambridge: Cambridge University Press, 2015), 82.

[35] Rufinus, *De adult. libr. Orig.* 41–43; cited in Michele Renee Salzman, 'Latin Letter Collections Before Late Antiquity', in *LALC*, 28.

[36] Of the eleven collections studied in Gibson, 'Ancient Letter Collections', only Seneca's is truly chronological, and even this only in a 'somewhat qualified sense' (61). The multi-book collections of Cicero's *ad Atticum*, Pliny, and Sidonius progress roughly chronologically across books, but the books themselves are typically governed by an alternative arrangement (Gibson, 'Ancient Letter Collections', 61–2, 67–9). On the utility of Cicero's *ad Atticum* for historical narration, see the famous comment of Cornelius Nepos, *Att.* 16.3–4.

[37] Gibson, 'Ancient Letter Collections', 64–9.

Book 7 straddles the line, written to six or seven addressees, all Epicureans.³⁸ This is not banal—a facile shortcut to organize a large group of letters while giving them the imprimatur of design. Beard's reading of the subtle relational politics of Book 16—twenty-six letters from Cicero and family to his (ex-)slave Tiro—interwoven with Rome's own declining politics in the critical years 53, 50/49, and 45/44 BCE puts the lie to this suggestion.³⁹ More broadly, by selecting Cicero's letters to elite Romans, arranged by addressee, the collector highlights Cicero's political significance in the elite circles of Rome—a form of panegyria via letter collection.⁴⁰ Cicero's English readers, of course, miss this, since they meet him in an anthology or a chronologically revised edition, both of which efface the traditional book divisions.⁴¹

Cicero may have revised a portion of his letters, but the bulk of the work for publication was likely done by a later editor.⁴² But the avoidance of chronology can hardly be assigned to the foibles of such an editor. This is clear from the case of Pliny, who edits his own correspondence, and famously opens his collection as follows in a letter to Septicius Clarus: 'You have often urged me to collect and publish any letters of mine which were composed with some care. I have now made a collection, not keeping to the original order [*temporis ordine*] as I was not writing history, but taking them as they came to my hand' (*Ep.* 1.1.1 [Radice, LCL]).⁴³ Naturally, Pliny knows the chronology of his letters, but his project is not historiographical, so he chooses against it as an organizing principle. To be sure, the claim to ad hoc arrangement is a Plinian ruse: there is a rough chronological shape across Pliny's nine books, but internally, the letter books tend to be thematic, with an eye to artistic effect.⁴⁴ As Gibson and Ruth Morello show, Pliny juxtaposes Book 6, focused on issues of work (*negotium*), with Book 7, dominated by a concern for matters of leisure (*otium*).⁴⁵ Book 8 has its own internal juxtapositions—twenty-four letters that navigate, and repeatedly revisit, questions of authority and disparity in social relations.⁴⁶ Finally, with the inclusion of Book 9, Pliny creates a macrotextual inclusio—his collection tracing a 'path from light to dark'. Or at least, that is what the names of the addressees of the first and last letter suggest: to Septicius *Clarus* (*Ep.* 1.1) and *Fuscus* Salinator (*Ep.* 9.40). In so doing, Pliny places a 'hermeneutic burden' on the reader, whom he invites to read the collection again with this fresh (if delayed) revelation of canonical shape.⁴⁷

---

³⁸ Beard, 'Ciceronian Correspondences', 129–30; Gibson, 'Letters into Autobiography', 392–3.
³⁹ Beard, 'Ciceronian Correspondences', 130–43.
⁴⁰ See Gibson, 'Ancient Letter Collections', 73–7 (cf. 67), on the didactic, biographical, and encomiastic functions of ancient letter collections.
⁴¹ Beard, 'Ciceronian Correspondences', 106–15 (directly at 109) and 130; Gibson, 'Ancient Letter Collections', 62–3. No English translation exists, in fact, which retains Cicero's collections in the book form of their original publication (Beard, 'Ciceronian Correspondences', 114 and 143).
⁴² The relevant primary text is *Att.* 16.5.5. See Beard, 'Ciceronian Correspondences', 117–18, on the publication of the letters.
⁴³ Pliny's protestation of editorial innocence here echoes Ovid, *Pont.* 3.9.51–54.
⁴⁴ Theodor Mommsen, 'Zur Lebensgeschichte des jüngeren Plinius', *Hermes* 3 (1869): 31–136 first showed the broadly chronological shape of Pliny's collection, confirmed by A. N. Sherwin-White, *The Letters of Pliny: A Historical and Social Commentary* (Oxford: Clarendon, 1966).
⁴⁵ Compare Gibson and Morello, *Reading the* Letters, 36–73 (Chapter 2) and 169–99 (ch. 6); cf. 234.
⁴⁶ Ruth Morello, 'Pliny Book 8: Two Viewpoints and the Pedestrian Reader', in *Pliny the Book-Maker*, 146–86, here esp. 183 and 185.
⁴⁷ Gibson, 'Ancient Letter Collections', 68. The first to see this was Alessandro Barchiesi, 'The Search for the Perfect Book: APS to the New Posidippus', in *The New Posidippus: A Hellenistic Poetry Book*,

As with Plato and Plotinus, so also with Cicero and Pliny: the preference for the collectivity of a corpus pairs with non-chronological ways of reading it. On this score, the 147-letter collection of Sidonius Apollinaris is a good place to close. In a letter to Constantius, placed first in the collection, Sidonius sets the stage for the whole: 'You have this long while been pressing me...to collect all the letters making any little claim to taste that have flowed from my pen on different occasions as this or that affair, person, or situation called forth, and to revise [*retracto*] and correct [*enucleato*] the originals and combine [*includo*] all into a single book [*volumen*]' (*Ep.* 1.1 [Anderson, LCL]). The editorial work Sidonius envisions recalls the work of Porphyry on Plotinus,[48] and the process involves a somewhat complex series of events.[49] The result, however, is not complex: discrete *epistula*, revised, corrected, and collected in multiple *volumina*, which together form an *editio* (*Ep.* 8.16; cf. 1.1). Following his model Pliny, Sidonius opts for a nine-book collection, with a non-chronological aesthetic design throughout.[50] And in a particularly suggestive allusion, Sidonius addresses the final letter of his collection (*Ep.* 9.16) to a certain Firminus. The collection's arc is now not from 'light' to 'dark' (à la Pliny) but from 'constancy' to 'firmness'.[51] To get this, however, one needs to pay attention to the *editio*. It enjoys hermeneutical priority.

Books of letters proliferate in late antiquity.[52] Individual letters, while important, represent moments in a larger plot, whose design operates at the level of τό βίβλιον and, beyond that, the collection. This is neither haphazard nor artless. It evinces a 'strong cultural logic'—a set of 'aims, assumptions and priorities' that the modern project of disassembly ignores.[53] This twin impulse, which privileges collectivity and avoids chronology, is evidently at play in Plato, Porphyry, Cicero, Pliny and Sidonius (et al.). The question now is whether it is true of the still more famous ancient letter collection of Paul of Tarsus.

Reading Paul in Late-Antique Editions

In one sense, obviously so: Paul's letters come down only *as* a collection, none of which is chronologically arranged. The collection itself, as Nils Dahl suggests, is born likely

---

ed. Kathryn Gutzwiller (Oxford: Oxford University Press, 2005), 330–1, discussed further in Ilaria Marchesi, *The Art of Pliny's Letters: A Poetics of Allusion in the Private Correspondence* (Cambridge: Cambridge University Press, 2008), 249–51.

[48] See also the editorial work envisioned by Cicero for his own letters in *Att.* 16.5.5 (*perspicio/corrigo*), and what Fronto claims to do for Cicero's works in *ad Am.* 2.2 (*emendo/distinguo/noto*), as well as the discussion of Euthalius and Priscillian below, with bibliography there.

[49] Various letters in Sidonius's collection offer a window into the process (*Ep.* 1.1; 8.16; 9.1; and 9.16.3). See the outline in Sigrid Mratschek, 'The Letter Collection of Sidonius Appolinaris', in *LALC*, 310, 312–13.

[50] Mratschek, 'Collection of Sidonius', 310.

[51] On Pliny's collection as an exemplar for Sidonius, see Roy Gibson, 'Reading the Letters of Sidonius by the Book', in *New Approaches to Sidonius Appolinaris*, ed. Johannes A. van Waarden and Gavin Kelly (Leuven: Peeters, 2013), 195–219 (here 217–19).

[52] Possible reasons for this are discussed in Sogno, Storin, and Watts, 'Introduction', 6–9.

[53] Beard, 'Ciceronian Correspondences', 115.

in an effort to overcome the letters' particularity, precisely the thing moderns prize.[54] On arrangement, the lack of diversity is its own striking fact.[55] As we will see, Paul's late-ancient readers are not ignorant of his chronology; they just do not arrange his editions this way, opting instead for declining length. This may seem mundane, but my interest is not in the motivations of the earliest collector(s), to which our only access is the collection itself. My question, rather, is for Paul's later, specifically late-antique, readers: do *they* notice and make anything of Paul's letters as a collective, and of their arrangement? To this we do have access: first via two remarkable editions themselves, and second via a host of late-antique commentary that tries to make sense of the collection.[56]

The Euthalian Edition of the *Corpus Paulinum*

Sometime late in the fourth century, a Pauline tradent named Euthalius issued an edition of Paul's letters, followed shortly by editions of Acts and the Catholic epistles.[57] His prologue to Acts mentions his work on Paul, and so is a useful place to begin.

> First then, for my part, having read and written the apostolic book [τὴν ἀποστολικὴν βίβλον] in lines [στιχηδὸν], I sent it recently to one of our fathers in Christ… For I do not know of anyone anywhere, of all who act as ambassadors of the divine word, who has to this point composed, with great

---

[54] Nils A. Dahl, 'The Particularity of the Pauline Epistles as a Problem in the Early Church', in *Studies in Ephesians*, 165–78. Dahl cites a suggestive set of primary texts that show concern for the catholicity of the collection at 165–7.

[55] While overstated along these lines, see Trobisch, *Paul's Letter Collection*, 18–26.

[56] As far as I can see, this sort of explicit editorializing of an ancient letter collection, where we get overt *ancient* discussion of arrangement, is unique. This makes the *corpus Paulinum* a pregnant, untapped resource for the recent shifts in classical epistolography detailed above.

[57] The *editio princeps* of the paratexts associated with each is that of Lorenzo Zacagni, *Collectanea Monumentorum Veterum Ecclesiae Graecae Ac Latinae. Quae Hactenus in Vaticana Bibliotheca Delituerunt* (Rome: Typis Sacrae Congreg. de Propag. Fide, 1698), 403–708, from which J. P. Migne (Euthalius Diaconus, *Opera* [PG 85:628a–790a]) is essentially a reprint. Citations below are from Migne's Patrologia Graeca volume. Early work on the Euthaliana (1890–1910) focused on questions of the authorship, dating, and scope of the original edition, and remain fraught. I refer to the author as Euthalius, recognizing that the author's identity is essentially veiled. On dating, recent scholarship largely agrees in assigning it to the late fourth century (Willard, Dahl, Blomkvist, Scherbenske), following Günther Zuntz, *The Ancestry of the Harklean New Testament*, The British Academy Supplemental Papers 7 (London: Oxford University Press, 1945). As for scope, the material I treat below is uncontroversial, although some undoubtedly (κεφάλαια) or possibly (ἀναγνώσεις) precedes Euthalius, and is taken over by him. A history of research up to 1970, along with a thorough review of the edition's component parts (and subsequently attached traditions), is in Louis Charles Willard, *A Critical Study of the Euthalian Apparatus*, ANTF 41 (Berlin: de Gruyter, 2009 [1970]). Further histories of research, with discussion of the relevant critical issues, are in James Armitage Robinson, *Euthaliana: Studies of Euthalius, Codex H of the Pauline Epistles, and the Armenian Version* (Cambridge: Cambridge University Press, 1895), 1–10; Nils A. Dahl, 'The "Euthalian Apparatus" and the Affiliated "Argumenta"', in *Studies in Ephesians*, 231–4; Vemund Blomkvist, *Euthalian Traditions: Text, Translation and Commentary*, TUGAL 170 (Berlin: de Gruyter, 2012), 3–33; and now Scherbenske, *Canonizing Paul*, 117–52. The last two named, following Dahl's 2000 essay (above), turn helpfully to the relationship of text and paratext (adopting Gérard Genette's terminology), with Scherbenske the first to argue that Euthalius's purposes are catechetical in orientation (*Canonizing Paul*, 122–74, directly at 122–3 and 173–4).

effort, the shape [σχῆμα] of this writing. Nor was there a man so stubborn nor bold as to insult mercilessly, via the tolerable divisions of our unlearned reading [ταῖς...ἀναγνώσεως τομαῖς], the toils of others which have been composed quite competently.[58]

The ἀποστολικός βίβλος is his edition of Paul, and with appropriate deference to his editorial forebears, Euthalius hints at the novelty of his project: a new σχῆμα of Paul's writings. The ambiguity is clarified shortly after, with reference to his work on Acts:

> For that very reason, being very much a φιλόλογος, celebrating this task (indescribably!) as a friend, and above all, praising it always, you recently ordered me, brother Athanasius, my best friend, to read [ἀναγνῶναί] both the book of Acts and the Catholic letters with reference to prosodic features [κατὰ προσῳδίαν], in some way to draw up summaries [ἀνακεφαλαιώσασθαι], and to divide [διελεῖν], in great detail, the sense of each of these. And having done this, zealously and without hesitation, and having organised the text of these in rows [στιχηδόν] according to my own arrangement for the sake of intelligible reading [εὔσημον ἀνάγνωσιν], I sent each to you quickly.[59]

The work is technical, and mirrors what an ancient grammarian (γραμματικός) would do with a text. Euthalius inserts prosodic signs (κατὰ προσῳδίαν; accentuation, breathing marks, etc.), punctuates his text (διελεῖν), and arranges it in sense lines (στιχηδόν)—each a pedagogical response to an uninterpreted text. By undoing *scriptio continua*, Euthalius's σχῆμα—his textual division and layout—mitigates the need for prior knowledge of the text, and paves the way for 'intelligible reading' (εὔσημον ἀνάγνωσιν).[60]

---

[58] Euthalius, *Opera* (PG 85:629ab). All translations of Euthaliana are my own unless otherwise noted.
[59] Euthalius, *Opera* (PG 85:633bc).
[60] Zuntz, *Harklean New Testament*, 89, 99–104 saw Euthalius's indebtedness to the reading practices of ancient grammar clearly. Reading κατὰ προσῳδίαν, for instance, is the grammarian's first task according to the famous definition of Dionysius Thrax. For description, see Alan Kemp, 'The TEKHNĒ GRAMMATIKĒ of Dionysius Thrax: English Translation with Introduction and Notes', in *The History of Linguistics in the Classical Period*, ed. Daniel J. Taylor, Studies in the History of the Language Sciences 46 (Amsterdam: Benjamins, 1987), 169–89 (here 186). More generally, though, this work of annotating and dividing a text in order to facilitate ease of reading is precisely the job of the ancient γραμματικός, not least in response to what William Johnson (*Readers and Reading Culture*, 17–31; cf. 129–30) calls the intentionally difficult (elite) activity of reading *scriptio continua*. Galen (*De ind.* 14) thinks the proper punctuation of *scriptio continua* so vital that it substitutes for interpretation itself. Euthalius's punctuations (διαιρέω), divisions for reading (τομαί ἀναγνώσεως), and arrangement in sense lines (στιχηδόν) all point in this direction (see LSJ, s.v. διαιρέω VI; τομή IV.2; στιχηδόν) as does his use of σχῆμα (LSJ, s.v. 7d). On the need for *some* knowledge of a text prior to reading, given the challenges of *scriptio continua*, see Quintilian, *Inst.* 1.8.1–2; 2.5.1–9; and Aulus Gellius, *NA* 13.31.5. Without reference to Euthalius (or Priscillian, see below), the work of Raffaella Cribiore, *Gymnastics of the Mind: Greek Education in Hellenistic and Roman Egypt* (Princeton: Princeton University Press, 2001), 185–219 (esp. 189–92); and Catherine M. Chin, *Grammar and Christianity in the Late Roman World* (Philadelphia: University of Pennsylvania Press, 2008), helps set the editorial work of both in particularly stark relief. The seminal work on ancient education, still useful, is Henri Irénée Marrou, *A History of Education in Antiquity*,

Bare transmission, though, however skillfully composed, is not enough, and so Euthalius also tags the letters themselves with a robust work of editorial synthesis (ἀνακεφαλαιώσασθαι). This ambiguous reference in his prologue to Acts is clarified by a similar claim in Euthalius's prologue to Paul.

> In the following, we prefixed to each letter, concisely, the table of the chapters [τὴν τῶν κεφαλαίων ἔκθεσιν], which had been made by a certain one of the wisest of our fathers, a Christ-lover. Not only that, but also, by going over the reading of the [textual] web, working systematically, we drew up summaries [ἀνεκεφαλαιωσάμεθα] of the most accurate division of the readings [τὴν τῶν ἀναγνώσεων ἀκριβεστάτην τομὴν],[61] and the accepted list of the divine testimonies [τὴν τῶν θείων μαρτυριῶν εὐαπόδεκτον εὕρεσιν]. We will set this out, then, immediately after the prologue.[62]

Like Porphyry for Plotinus, Euthalius mediates Paul via a set of paratextual tables: κεφάλαια (chapter headings), ἀναγνώσεις (lection-style readings), and μαρτυρίαι (citations largely from the Old Testament). And it is in the latter two that Euthalius's cognisance of Paul as a collection begins to emerge.[63] Tables 2 and 3 give a sense for how these paratexts work for Euthalius, using Galatians as an example.

Table 2. Ἀνακεφαλαίωσις τῶν Ἀναγνώσεων [PG 85:716b–720b]

> In the letter to the Galatians, 2 readings, 12 chapters, 11 quotations, 293 lines.
> The first reading, six chapters, #1, #2, #3, #4, #5, #6; six quotations, #1, #2, #3, #4, #5, #6; 130 lines.
> The second reading, six chapters, #7, #8, #9, #10, #11, #12; five quotations, #7, #8, #9, #10, #11; 163 lines.

Table 3a. Ἀνακεφαλαίωσις Θείων Μαρτυριῶν
(SHORT LIST) [PG 85:720d–724c]

> In the letter to the Galatians, 11 [quotations]. Genesis, *4*: #1, #2, #7, #9; Leviticus, *1*: #10; Deuteronomy, *2*: #3, #6; Habakkuk the prophet, *1*: #4; Isaiah the prophet, *1*: #8; Ezekiel the prophet, and Deuteronomy, *1*: #5; the Apocryphon of Moses, *1*: #11.

---

trans. George Lamb (London: Sheed & Ward, 1956), with his description of the grammatical and rhetorical schools at 150–75.

[61] Following Zuntz, *Harklean New Testament*, 105 n. 7, where ἀνάγνωσις is plural in the Euthaliana, I take it to refer to the lection-style divisions of the manuscripts (see Table 2) rather than the layout of the text itself (signaled by the singular in the prologue to Acts); so also Willard, *Euthalian Apparatus*, 28.

[62] Euthalius, *Opera* (PG 85:708a).

[63] For discussion of all three, see Willard, *Euthalian Apparatus*, 22–56; Dahl, 'Euthalian Apparatus', 242–50; Scherbenske, *Canonizing Paul*, 136–46. Of the three, the interest of the κεφάλαια is most clearly text-internal, and so I do not discuss them here.

Table 3b. Ἀνακεφαλαίωσις Θείων Μαρτυριῶν (LONG LIST) [PG 85:725d–745d]

In the letter to the Galatians, 11 [quotations].
#1. Genesis, #9. 'And Abraham believed God, and it was reckoned to him as righteousness'.
#2. Genesis, #10. 'All nations will be blessed in you'.
#3. Deuteronomy, #9. 'Cursed is everyone who does not observe and obey all the things written in the book of the law'.
#4. [Etc.]

---

a. The text of Tables 3a/b is in Euthalius, *Opera* (PG 85:717b [3.1], 721b [3.2a], and 737a-c[3.2b]).
b. In the long and short lists (3.2a/b), the underlined numbers (rubricated in Euthalius) signify the order of the citations in a given letter. In the short list, the bold italicized numbers (black in Euthalius) depict the total citations of a given Old Testament book in that letter, while in the long list, they signify how many times Paul has cited that book to that point in his corpus.

Close textual division (διαιρέω, στιχηδόν) here gives way to broader editorial fragmentation.[64] On one level, Euthalius retains a focus on the discrete text: *Galatians* has 2 ἀναγνώσεις, 12 κεφάλαια, 11 μαρτυρίαι, and 293 στίχοι. By the end, though, Euthalius has these data for the whole corpus: 'In all of the fourteen letters, 31 readings, 147 chapters, 127 quotations, 4936 lines'.[65] The same is true of Euthalius's μαρτυρίαι: the short list offers a snapshot of Paul's citation practice in a given letter, which again gives way to the meta-data of the corpus: 13 citations from Genesis, 8 from Exodus, 1 from Leviticus, 1 from Numbers, 15 from Deuteronomy, and so on, 127 quotations in all.[66] Paul is a series of letters to be sure, but he is also a singular body of knowledge.

Nowhere is this more the case than in Euthalius's ἐπιτομή, a part of his prologue to Paul, which serves to abridge a larger work.[67] Here, Euthalius's ἐπιτομή works on two levels at once. First, in language deeply indebted to the ancient epistolary handbooks, Euthalius abridges each individual letter in a sentence or two.[68] As Euthalius describes

---

[64] Euthalius's work is a near perfect example of the sort of 'compilatory aesthetic'—or the obsessive 'reconfiguration of pre-existing texts'—that Jason König and Tim Whitmarsh call a 'major intellectual project' in the late Roman world ('Ordering Knowledge', in *Ordering Knowledge in the Roman Empire*, ed. Jason König and Tim Whitmarsh [Cambridge: Cambridge University Press, 2007], 3 and 29).

[65] Euthalius, *Opera* (PG 85:720b).

[66] Euthalius, *Opera* (PG 85:724b). Euthalius's indexing system, then, assumes the collection as a single entity—an observation already made in 1895 by Robinson (*Euthaliana*, 19).

[67] The ἐπιτομή can be found in its entirety at Euthalius, *Opera* (PG 85:701a–708a). Translation and discussion are in Blomkvist, *Euthalian Traditions*, 104–7, 206–11; and Scherbenske, *Canonizing Paul*, 127–36. See also Dahl, 'Euthalian Apparatus', 237–9.

[68] The handbooks are those of Ps.-Demetrius (Τύποι ἐπιστολικοί) and Ps.-Libanius (Ἐπιστολιμαῖοι χαρακτῆρες), with text and translation in Abraham J. Malherbe, *Ancient Epistolary Theorists*, Sources for Biblical Study 19 (Atlanta: Scholars Press, 1988). My muse here is Dahl, 'Euthalian Apparatus', 258–9, who briefly compares the language of the secondary Euthalian ὑποθέσεις to these handbooks and finds suggestive overlap. To my knowledge, the same has not been done for the ἐπιτομή.

it, Paul's action(s) in six of the letters match(es) a letter-type in one of the handbooks exactly (1 and 2 Corinthians; 1 and 2 Thessalonians; 2 Timothy; and Philemon).[69] Even in those letters without a specific type, Euthalius's descriptions echo the handbooks (Romans; Galatians; Philippians; Colossians).[70] Yet the language Euthalius uses to describe each letter is almost never actually present in the letter itself. Time and again, Euthalius's ἐπιτομή is more indebted to the meta-terminology of the handbooks than to the letters themselves. The effect is significant. On this epistolographical map, the malleability of Paul is on full display; Euthalius envisages Paul as the writer of all *kinds* of letters, which makes the collection itself a multi-faceted epistolary intervention. There is something here for all.

The second level, however, is still more fundamental, evident in how Euthalius bookends his ἐπιτομή: Paul's letter collection, in its entirety, is about πολιτεία, a way of life.[71] He begins: 'On the whole [ὅλως], throughout the web [ὑφῆς] of these fourteen

---

[69] Reference to the handbooks below are to page and line number in Malherbe, *Ancient Epistolary Theorists*, with the letter-*type* underlined. For easily accessible text and translation of Euthalius's ἐπιτομή, see Blomkvist, *Euthalian Traditions*, 104–6. For Euthalius, in 1 Corinthians, Paul 'finds fault' (ἐπιμέμφομαι → μεμπτικός) with the Christ-assembly there (μεμπτικός: 30.27; 32.27; 66.15; 68.13; 74.14), while in 2 Corinthians, he 'promises' (ἐπαγγέλω) and 'threatens' (ἀπειλέω → ἀπειλητικός) his presence (ἀπειλητικός: 30.28; 36.1; 66.16–17; 68.23; 74.37). 1 Thessalonians 'comprises praise' (περιέχω ἔπαινος → ἐπαινετικός) of their obedience in the face of persecution (ἐπαινετικός: 30.28; 36.14; 66.21; 70.14, 16, 18; 78.25), after which Paul 'comforts' (παρακαλέω → παρακλητικός) them (παρακλητικός: 66.15; 68.14; 74.16), and 2 Thessalonians 'comprises testimony' (περιέχω μαρτυρία → μαρτυρικός) of their progress and 'teaching' (περιέχω διδασκαλία → διδασκαλικός) about the end (διδασκαλικός: 66.21; 70.20; 78.28). 2 Timothy is rife with the language of the epistolary handbooks: in a letter that 'comprises praise' (περιέχω ἔπαινος → ἐπαινετικός) for Timothy's ancestral faith, Paul nevertheless 'accuses' (κατηγορέω → κατηγορικός) Timothy's fellows in Asia (κατηγορικός: 30.29–30; 38.28), 'impels' (προτρέπω, see n. 70 below) Timothy to avoid worldly desires, and 'reminds' him (ὑπομιμνήσκω → ὑπομνηστικός) and 'calls him to witness' (μαρτύρομαι → μαρτυρικός) to the κήρυγμα (ὑπομνηστικός: 66.24; 72.1; 80.26; μαρτυρικός = παραγγελματικός: 68.26). Finally, Philemon is an epistolary intervention in which Paul 'negotiates' (πρεσβεύω → πρεσβευτικός) on behalf of Onesimus (πρεσβευτικός: 66.21; 70.13; 78.20).

[70] Paul's catechesis in Romans takes the form of an ἀπόδειξις ('proof'), a form Paul also uses to confute the Galatians (ἀπόδειξις: Dem. 18.26, 30; 40.2, 3; ἀποδείκνυμι: Dem. 18.30; 40.26). When Paul 'impels' (προτρέπω) the Philippians, he does precisely what is expected in an 'advisory' (συμβουλευτικός) or 'paraenetic' (παραινετικός) letter (προτρέπω: 36.20; 68.1; προτροπή, in fact, constitutes one of the two parts of παραίνεσις for Ps.-Lib.). And in Colossians, Paul instructs Archippus to 'order' (παραγγέλλω) the Christ-assembly there to observe what he has written (παραγγέλλω: 68.25; παραγγελματικός: 66.17; 68.25; 76.5). Among the church letters, only Ephesians and Hebrews are described in language entirely devoid of resonance with the handbooks.

[71] This ethical emphasis is also evident in how Euthalius opens his account of Paul's epistolary activity in his ἐπιτομή: Paul 'offers many exhortations about life and virtue' (πολλὰς ... παραινέσις ὑπέρ τε βίου καὶ ἀρετῆς ... ἐποιήσατο) and 'guides people with respect to how to act' (περὶ τῶν πρακτέων τοῖς ἀνθρώποις εἰσηγήσατο). The description is largely generic. Antiquity attests all manner of figures engaging in such activity, often in language identical to Euthalius's. That is, neither the παραίνεσις nor the πολιτεία that Euthalius attributes to Paul is explicated, at this point, in Christian terms (Blomkvist, *Euthalian Traditions*, 207). Like Thucydides's Phormis (2.88.1; cf. 8.76.3), Polybius's Hannibal (3.62.2; cf. Scipio in 15.11.1), Josephus's Moses (*Ant.* 3.p.11; cf. Sentius Saturninus in 19.166.5) Plutarch's Nicias (*Vit. Nic.* 26.6), and Dio Cassius's Caesar and Pompey (41.57.3), Paul simply 'makes exhortations' (ποιέω + παραίνεσις). For the also-typical collocation of εἰσηγέομαι and πρᾶξις, see, e.g., Ps.-Clem. 4.15; Gregory Nazianzus, *Comp. vit.* 110 (= *Carm. mor.* 8); Sopater, *Diair. zēt.* (in Walz, *Rhet. Graec.* 8.154.7); and Libanius, *Decl.* 24.2.25. The point here is only that the locus in which Paul does these things, for Euthalius, is the collection.

epistles, [Paul] delineates for people the whole way of life [πολιτείαν].⁷² Crucially, here the corpus as such is the object of Euthalius's ἐπιτομή.⁷³ His interest here is not just collectivity, but also arrangement. The ἐπιτομή doubles as his discussion of reading order. This is implicit throughout, and explicit in closing: 'Thus, the whole book [ἡ πᾶσα βίβλος] comprises every aspect of how to live [πολιτειῶν], arranged according to progress [κατὰ προσαύξησιν]'.⁷⁴ Euthalius either misses, or lacks interest in, the principle of declining length. To his mind, the collection narrates the growth of progressively mature Pauline churches, and so he traces this across his ἐπιτομή: the story of the 'progress [αὔξησις] that is characteristic of each community'.⁷⁵ As in Plato, Plotinus, Cicero, Pliny and Sidonius, so also in Paul: Euthalius privileges Pauline collectivity (πᾶσα βίβλος) and a non-chronological hermeneutic (κατὰ προσαύξησιν). The path he traces, however, is not 'light to dark' (à la Pliny) or 'constancy to firmness' (à la Sidonius) but something like infancy to adulthood.

In all of this, Euthalius does what his modern counterparts do: he constructs a map and delineates the corpus accordingly. Like chronology, Euthalius's epistolo-graphical and ethical map is a critical imposition *ab extra*, and shapes what he sees in each letter. It both illuminates and occludes. But vitally, it *is* a map that can deal with difference. Euthalius handles Pauline variability—an unavoidable feature of the letters in their collected form, and which, in modern criticism, jettisons deutero-Paul from the corpus—via epistolary classification and ethical progression. By making Paul a writer of different kinds of letters, attentive to the situation and stage of his audience, Euthalius simultaneously renders null the problem of difference and celebrates what Paul's corpus offers in its totality. Its readers enjoy nothing short of a catechesis in Pauline πολιτεία—a life modeled, negatively and positively, by Paul's churches. For this project, the variability of the letters and the singularity of the corpus are both eminently useful. Discrete letters matter, but primarily as data points in the larger story told by the corpus.

What one needs, then, *materially*, is the letters together, which is what Euthalius provides. Collectivity, finally, is ensconced in the physical artefact itself. Euthalius relativizes particularity by rendering Paul as a single edition, and a robust one at that.⁷⁶ His readers open a substantial codex that contains (1) a lengthy prologue, including a *prooemium*, a βίος, an ἐπιτομή, a notice detailing the editor's work, and less certainly, a chronological account of Paul's preaching;⁷⁷ (2) tables of κεφάλαια, μαρτυρίαι, and ἀναγνώσεις for each letter; and (3) the text itself divided into sense lines. The point is not to sheer the real Paul off the rock of tradition, but to tradition the letters so as to mediate the real Paul. To this end, Euthalius builds what Baur disassembles. His hermeneutical locus is different: not the letter, but the book—ἡ βίβλος τοῦ Παύλου.

---

⁷² Euthalius, *Opera* (PG 85:701a). On πολιτεία in Euthalius, see Scherbenske, *Canonizing Paul*, 125, 134–6.
⁷³ Dahl, 'Euthalian Apparatus', 239; Blomkvist, *Euthalian Traditions*, 211.
⁷⁴ Euthalius, *Opera* (PG 85:708a).
⁷⁵ Euthalius, *Opera* (PG 85:705a).
⁷⁶ The paratexts alone run nearly 200 pages in Zacagni's edition and 100 columns in Migne's, although this includes a series of secondary ὑποθέσεις (see my final section below).
⁷⁷ See Dahl, 'Euthalian Apparatus', 235–7 and 240, and Blomkvist, *Euthalian Traditions*, 196–7, for arguments against the authenticity of this potted chronology of Paul's life.

Priscillian of Avila's *Canones Epistularum Pauli Apostoli*

Around the same time, in Latin Gaul, the layman-turned-bishop Priscillian of Avila (fl. ca. 340–ca. 385 CE) was also busy assembling Paul.[78] His purpose, however, was not catechetical but apologetic: a 'dearest brother' had requested the 'strongest bulwark' (*propugnaculum*) against the crafty heretics, and Priscillian responds, in effect, by sending an edition of Paul's letters.[79] Not just a bare edition, though: the heretics are hermeneutically crafty, twisting the Scriptures to and fro, and so Priscillian inscribes an editorially guided reading of Paul within the confines of a technologically savvy Pauline book.[80] He does this, as the title implies, via a series of ninety canons: short syntheses of Paul's thought, inserted *en bloc* before the letters, and paratextually keyed to them. Unlike Euthalius, Priscillian never discusses the letters' arrangement, nor calls the collection a *liber*. But he does treat them as a collective, erasing epistolary boundaries and aggregating his Pauline data for the sake of generalized synthesis. How, then, does this work?

Priscillian's procedure can be summarized from his own preface.[81] His work in the text of Paul involves three tasks: *distinguere*, *ordinare*, and *supernotare*. The first is the most invasive, and the sine qua non of his project. As in the Greek East, the Latin West adopted *scriptio continua*, and so Priscillian's first task is to punctuate (*distinguo*) his text.[82] The language recalls Euthalius's project (διελεῖν ... τὸν νοῦν),[83] but whereas Euthalius sought to enable reading, Priscillian facilitates interpretation, and

---

[78] Priscillian is perhaps best known as the first person to be executed as a heretic by imperial order in 385 CE. On Priscillian and the controversy, see Sulpicius Severus, *Chronicles* 2.46–51. Henry Chadwick, *Priscillian of Avila: The Occult and the Charismatic in the Early Church* (Oxford: Clarendon, 1976), offers a modern study (pp. 58–62 treat his *Canons* of Paul). In addition to his *Canons* on Paul (see the body of my text, below), Priscillian authored a series of eleven *Tractates*, a work on the Trinity, and a series of prologues to the gospels. Text and translation of each, with introduction, is in Marco Conti, ed. and trans., *Priscillian of Avila: The Complete Works*, Oxford Early Christian Texts (Oxford: Oxford University Press, 2010). The *Canons* themselves, extant in twenty-two Vulgate manuscripts (Conti, *Priscillian*, 27), have drawn virtually no attention from patristic or biblical scholars, apart from the printed editions of Angelo Mai, *Spicilegium Romanum*, vol. 9 (Rome, 1843), 744–63; Georg Schepss, *Priscilliani quae supersunt*, CSEL 18 (Vienna, 1889), 109–47; J. Wordsworth and H. J. White, *Novum Testamentum Domini Nostri Iesu Christi Latine secundum editionem Sancti Hieronymi*, vol 2.1 (Oxford: Clarendon, 1913), 17–32; and Donatien de Bruyne, *Préfaces de la Bible latine* (Namur: Godenne, 1920), 224–34. Schepss, *Priscilliana quae supersunt*, xxviii–xliiii, discusses the *Canons*' textual tradition and reception (cf. Conti, *Priscillian*, 17–19, 27–8), and the recent work of T. J. Lang and Matthew R. Crawford, 'The Origins of Pauline Theology: Paratexts and Priscillian of Avila's *Canons on the Letters of the Apostle Paul*', NTS 63 (2017): 125–45, to which I am indebted, is now the first in biblical studies to engage the *Canons* at length.

[79] Schepss, *Priscilliani*, 110; Conti, *Priscillian*, 165 and 167. Here and below, I note the citation in both the Latin text of Schepss and the Latin/English text of Conti.

[80] For Priscillian's description of heresy as fundamentally a textual phenomenon (i.e. heretics as perverse *readers*), see his preface in Schepss, *Priscilliani*, 110; Conti, *Priscillian*, 167.

[81] Schepss, *Priscilliani*, 110–12; Conti, *Priscillian*, 165–7. See also Lang and Crawford, 'Origins of Pauline Theology', 130–4.

[82] Lewis and Short, s.v. *distinguo* I.B.2.α. On the Latin adoption of *scriptio continua*, see Kenney, 'Books and Readers', 17.

[83] Unsurprisingly, *distinguo* and διαιρέω overlap perfectly in meaning. In addition to the relevant entries in Lewis and Short and LSJ, see the Latin–Greek lexicon of Benjamin Hederich, *Novum Lexicon Manuale Graeco-Latinum et Latinum-Graecum*, 3 vols. (Leipzig: Gleditsch, 1825): 1:828, s.v. διαιρέω 2.

so he divides his text into larger sense units—what he calls *testimonia*.[84] If this seems banal, it is anything but. As Thomas O'Loughlin writes of ancient textual division, 'Where one divides determines what one reads'.[85] It is, therefore, the fundamental hermeneutical act. Priscillian imposes order on his otherwise undifferentiated text, delimiting its basic units of meaning. The next two tasks follow quickly on: Priscillian numbers (*ordinare*) his testimonies consecutively within each letter, and annotates (*supernotare*) his text of Paul accordingly. So, Romans comprises 125 testimonies, 1 Corinthians 105, 2 Corinthians 61, etc., 566 in total.[86] Priscillian's technical work, along with the language he uses to describe it, matches precisely that of the ancient grammarian.[87] Moreover, systems of textual division and excerpting like this are ubiquitous in antiquity, not least in Latin manuscripts of Paul.[88] That said, Priscillian's work *is* distinctive: his 566 *testimonia* represent the most pervasive fragmentation of Paul's letters in antiquity.

This is far from trivial for the second half of Priscillian's project: his collocation and synthesis of these testimonies into ninety canons.[89] Again, Priscillian describes his working method: 'By gathering (*decerpens*) certain words from the testimonies themselves, I have fit together (*concinnaui*) canons which are in accord with the same flavours (*saporibus*) of the testimonies themselves'.[90] His text divided, Priscillian now fragments it again, plucking (*decerpo*) words from a series of corresponding testimonies, writing a fresh synthesis (*concinno*) of these texts, and then noting (*superadnotaui*) the supporting texts by letter and number beneath each canon. He then numbers the canons in red (1 to 90), and places this rubricated number alongside the relevant testimonies in his text of Paul if they were particularly indispensable.[91]

---

[84] A table of the *testimonia* with modern chapter/verse equivalent is in Schepss, *Priscilliani*, 169–74. Priscillian's *testimonia* typically fall between two and four modern verses, although Hebrews is partitioned into much larger sections (Lang and Crawford, 'Origins of Pauline Theology', 134).

[85] Thomas O'Loughlin, 'De Bruyne's *Sommaires* on its Centenary: Has its Value for Biblical Scholarship Increased?', introduction to Donatien de Bruyne, *Summaries, Divisions and Rubrics of the Latin Bible*, Studia Traditionis Theologiae 18 (Turnhout: Brepols, 2015), xxvi.

[86] See Tables 5 and 6 in Chapter 4 for other relevant data on the *Canons*.

[87] In addition to n. 60 above, see Suetonius, *Gramm.* 24, where Marcus Valerius Probus corrects (*emendare*), punctuates (*distinguere*), and annotates (*adnotare*) ancient books, which Suetonius says belongs to the domain of grammar (*grammatica*). Kenney, 'Books and Readers', 18, calls these acts of textual emendation an ancient commonplace.

[88] See the indispensable collection of de Bruyne, *Summaries, Divisions and Rubrics*, 527–49, which places Priscillian's *testimonia* alongside other systems of Latin textual division. Cyprian's *Testimoniorum libri tres ad Quirinum*, in which he excerpts 700 *testimonia* from across the biblical canon and juxtaposes them in lists under dogmatic headings, is similar to Priscillian's work; cf. Augustine, *Spec.*, although here primarily to condense each biblical book. See Paul J. Griffiths, *Religious Reading: The Place of Reading in the Practice of Religion* (Oxford: Oxford University Press, 1999), 164–72 for overview of both. Outside of early Christian circles, see Shane Butler's 'Cicero's *capita*', in *The Roman Paratext: Frames, Texts, Readers*, ed. Laura Jansen (Cambridge: Cambridge University Press, 2014), 73–111.

[89] That is, the secondary synthesis depends on Priscillian's novel system of textual division (so Lang and Crawford, 'Origins of Pauline Theology', 133, 144–5).

[90] The translation is my own, with Latin text in Schepss, *Priscilliani*, 111.

[91] For examples of Priscillian's system of annotation in manuscripts, see Codex Cavensis (C), Theodulfianus (Θ), and Toletanus (T). Descriptions with links to online images are in Hugh A. G. Houghton, *The Latin New Testament: A Guide to its Early History, Texts, and Manuscripts* (Oxford: Oxford University Press, 2016), 255, 277, and 280.

Text and paratext are thus deeply interwoven. As T. J. Lang and Matthew Crawford note, 'One can read Priscillian's work from the canonical synthesis back to the Pauline data or from the Pauline data back to the canonical synthesis'.[92] This is what I mean when I call it a technologically savvy book that editorially mediates Paul. Most critically, however, the Paul that is mediated is one in which the particularity of the letters (or the discrete testimony) is effaced—traded for the homogeneity of Priscillian's Pauline synthesis.

We can see this clearly if we turn to a specific canon. Here I treat Canon 15, which introduces a series of seven *testimonia* that depict the revelation of Paul's mystery.

Table 4. Priscillian's Canon 15

Can. XV. Quia sacramentum olim filiis hominum absconditum, nunc per apostolum sanctis manifestatum sit et quod Christus sapientia nuncupetur, quam nemo principum huius mundi cognouit.	Canon 15. Why the mystery was once hidden from the sons of men, and now is manifested to the saints through the apostle, and why Christ is called wisdom that none of the rulers of this world knew.
Cor. I. 9. 10.	1 Cor 2.1–7; 2.8–9
Eph. 2. 11. 13.	Eph 1.3–10; 3.1–5[*hom.*]; 3.9–13
Col. 10. 13.	Col 1.26–27; 2.2–3

As Table 4 shows, Canon 15 contains two main propositions (*quia sacramentum ... et quod Christus*).[93] On its surface, Canon 15 is manifestly Pauline; as he claims, Priscillian adheres closely to Paul's language. When one reads Canon 15 against Priscillian's Old Latin source texts, however, the shaping power of his synthesis becomes clear.[94]

I begin, then, with the two clauses of Priscillian's first proposition. The main subject, *sacramentum*, is one possible translation of the Greek μυστήριον, the others being *testimonium* and *mysterium*. Μυστήριον, in fact, occurs in the Greek text of each of the cited testimonies except 1 Cor 2.8–9 (10), and is translated each time as

---

[92] Lang and Crawford, 'Origins of Pauline Theology', 133.
[93] Text and trans. of Canon 15 is in Conti, *Priscillian*, 172–5. For the sake of clarity, in what follows I cite modern chapter and verse first, followed by the number of Priscillian's *testimonium* in parentheses.
[94] The process is relatively straightforward, with the caveat that we do not know the extent of the revisions of Peregrinus, who claims to scrub the *Canons* of heresy (see Peregrinus's preface in Schepss, *Priscilliani*, 109). For each clause, I compare Priscillian's language in Canon 15 with the Old Latin text in the relevant volumes of Paul's letters in H. J. Frede, ed., *Vetus Latina* (Freiburg: Herder, 1962-98), specifically text-type I, identified as Priscillian's text by Frede, *Epistula ad Ephesios*, VL 24/1 (1962): 33, and confirmed by my work in several canons as well as the citations in Priscillian's *Tractate 1*. Every reference to the Latin text below is to text-type I ad loc. in the relevant Frede volume. Where Old Latin editions have not yet been published (vis-à-vis Canon 15, only 1 Corinthians is lacking), I compare to the Old Latin text in H. J. Frede, *Ein neuer Paulustext und Kommentar*, 2 vols., AGLB 7–8 (Freiburg: Herder, 1973–74), and, for reference, Wordsworth and White's volume on 1 Corinthians.

mysterium in Priscillian's Old Latin text.[95] Priscillian, then, has collocated a set of texts that share a common lexeme (*mysterium*), which he then appears to replace with his preferred lexical choice, *sacramentum*.[96] If this is right, from where does Priscillian draw his language of a *mysterium absconditum*? The phrase is in 1 Cor 2.7 (9), Eph 3.9 (13), and Col 1.26 (10), but Priscillian is probably influenced by Ephesians, since only in Eph 3.5 (11) is the mystery hidden *filiis hominum*. Elsewhere, the *mysterium* is hidden *a saeculis* (Eph 3.9 [13]), *a saeculis saeculorum et a generationibus* (Col 1.26 [10]), or does not have an object (1 Cor 2.7 [9]). Priscillian's first clause, then, largely conflates Eph 3.5 (11) and 3.9 (13), drawing the *mysterium absconditum* from 3.9 and the *filiis hominum* from 3.5. The second clause, *nunc per apostolum sanctis manifestatum sit*, is more difficult. In Priscillian's cited testimonies, *manifestatum* only appears in variants to Eph 3.3 and 5 (11), but contra Canon 15, the *mysterium* there is revealed to Paul (*mihi*, 3.3) and *sanctis eius et prophetis* (3.5).[97] Other recipients also emerge: in Eph 1.9 (2), the *mysterium* is *notum nobis faceret*, while in 3.9 (13), in language that contradicts Canon 15, Paul 'illuminates *all*' with the *mysterium* (*inluminare omnes*). On the other hand, Col 1.26 (10) agrees with Canon 15 on the object of the revelation (*sancti*), but not the means: *God* (not Paul) reveals the *mysterium* in Col 1.26–27.[98] Strictly speaking, then, no text lies directly behind Priscillian's second clause; it is a mash-up of the textual fragments he has to hand, and elides the particularities of each.

Priscillian's second full proposition is somewhat clearer, and depends mainly on 1 Cor 2.7–8 (9 and 10) and Col 2.2–3 (13). He lifts his final clause, *quam nemo principum huius mundi cognouit*, directly from 1 Cor 2.8 (10).[99] The problem, though, is that Christ is not 'called wisdom' (*sapientia nuncupetur*) in 2.7 (9) as Priscillian suggests. Budapest Anonymous reads the *sapientia* of 2.7 as Christ,[100] and if Priscillian does the same, then 1 Cor 2.7–8 sits behind his second proposition in full. But again, *sapientia* in 2.7 itself is ambiguous. Only Col 2.2–3 (13) actually connects Christ and wisdom. There Christ is the *mysterium*, in whom *sunt omnes thensauri sapientiae ... absconditi*. In his final proposition, then, Priscillian again draws together two texts with a common lexical base—*sapientia*, *mysterium*, and *condo*—only to elide their idiosyncracies. These two texts *do*, however, offer some clue as to the structure of Canon 15 as a whole. Each speaks of the hiddenness (*condo*) of *sapientia* in close proximity to the *mysterium*, which for Col 2.2–3 is Christ—just as Priscillian's structural parallel suggests.

---

[95] The one exception is 1 Cor 2.1 (9), where μυστήριον is rendered *testimonium*.

[96] The other option is that Peregrinus emended Canon 15 in this direction. In the Vulgate of Priscillian's Canon 15 testimonies, *sacramentum* translates μυστήριον at Eph 1.9; 3.3 and 9; and Col 1.27.

[97] The variant with *manifestatum* in Eph 3.5 (text-type I) omits *apostolis* (cf. Greek: τοῖς ἁγίοις ἀποστόλοις αὐτοῦ καὶ προφήταις), which brings the text closer to Priscillian's in Canon 15, except the agent of revelation in 3.5 is not Paul (Priscillian's *per apostolum*) but the Spirit.

[98] Moreover, the participle in Col 1.26 is *declaratum*, not *manifestatum*. To be sure, Col 1.25 implies a role for Paul in this, and so Priscillian's synthesis is closest to the totality of the Colossians text. That said, Col 1.25 belongs to Test. 9, a text Priscillian does not even cite in its defense.

[99] In both the Old Latin text of Budapest Anonymous and the Vulgate, Priscillian's only modification would be to insert *mundi* for *saeculi*, but the former may have been in Priscillian's Old Latin text itself.

[100] Frede, *Ein neuer Paulustext*, 102. Commenting on *sapientam* at 2.7, Budapest writes, 'Id est Christum'.

What, then, can we say of Priscillian's work? After his pervasive work of textual division, Priscillian's mind is now a Pauline map, or better, a concordance.[101] In Canon 15, he collocates texts that share a common lexeme (*mysterium*) and a common way of speaking about it: that the *mysterium* was hidden and is now revealed. The texts are not, however, everywhere the same: they differ regarding from whom (or when) the *mysterium* is hidden; to whom and by whom it is revealed; and most notably, on the content of the *mysterium* itself. For the reader of Priscillian's edition, however, they do *not* differ. As the structural symmetry of Canon 15 suggests, Priscillian's *mysterium* is Christ. *Pace* Priscillian, this is only the case in Col 2.2 (13), and there not even a mystery revealed. Priscillian, though, does not want the particular but the homogeneous Paul. So he reads the *mysterium* of Col 2.2 over the *mysteria* of his other texts, effacing their own depictions of the *mysterium*. On Priscillian's scheme, Paul may say *x* in 1 Cor 9 and 10, *y* in Eph 2, 11 and 13, and *z* in Col 10 and 13, but what he really *means* is Canon 15. By fragmenting, juxtaposing, and then synthesizing diverse textual fragments, Priscillian homogenizes Paul.[102] His project thus eviscerates the letters as meaningful hermeneutical units, and replaces them with 566 discrete *testimonia*. Through *them*, he construct his canons—a new Pauline collective. In the face of the heretics, Priscillian makes Paul speak with a single voice.

When Paul Was a Book

Like editors of other ancient corpora, Euthalius and Priscillian configure Paul's letters as a collective, and editorially mediate them as such. This does not mean that Paul's late-antique readers have no interest in textual origins or chronology. They do, and this section shows that, primarily from the Greek and Latin commentary tradition. But what they do with this interest is very different from Paul's modern readers, since it consistently gives way, in the end, to the collection's priority, evidenced not least by their tendency to designate the collection a book (τὸ βίβλιον/*liber*). Rather than a counterfactual to the argument above, then, the work below is further evidence of it.

A Counterfactual? On Textual Origins and Chronology

To begin, however, with another ancient corpus: the fifty-eight speeches of Demosthenes. Some 700 years after Demosthenes, at the request of Lucius Caelius Montius,

---

[101] Of the seven *testimonia* on which I have worked (Canons 8, 9, 10, 15, 24, 25, and 78—all of which cite Eph 1.3–10[2]), Priscillian appears to gather his testimonies on the basis of shared lexemes in five (8, 10, 15, 24, 78). Moreover, Cyprian advocates reading by excerpt/textual division for precisely this reason, as an *aide-mémoire*. He writes, 'A tenacious memory holds on to what has been read in a cleverly ordered compendium' (*Test.* 1.Pref. 3; cf. *Test.* 2.Pref. 73; both cited in Griffiths, *Religious Reading*, 168). More broadly, see Johnson, *Readers and Reading Culture*, 118–20.

[102] In this, the *Canons* are a remarkable example of how Chin, *Grammar and Christianity*, 11–38, describes the work of the late-antique grammarian. She writes, 'The practice of reading via fragmentation and disarticulation is a creative process, enabling the reader to imagine juxtaposed fragments as part of larger homogeneous wholes' (66; cf. 14, 18, and 25). The result is that the 'original literary text is…subordinated to the production of the knowledge of which it is the object' (18). This is precisely Priscillian's objective. The words of the *testimonia* are many, and too supple to be safe, so Priscillian creates a *propugnaculum* (his *Canons*) to protect them.

the proconsul of Constantinople, the Antiochene rhetor Libanius composes a set of ὑποθέσεις to each speech.[103] The purpose, Libanius writes, is to provide the sort of cultural, historical, and linguistic data that would pave the way for a 'more exact knowledge of the speeches'.[104] And so Libanius sends an entire book (σύνταγμα) of *hypotheses*, prefaced by a biography (Pref. 2–13) and a potted history of Athens and Greece at the time of Demosthenes (Pref. 14–21). The whole thing is manifestly what we would call special introduction, meant to guide this native Latin through the challenges of the greatest of the classical Athenian orators (so Quintilian, *Inst.* 10.1.76). The same interest is evident in a series of *argumenta* (Gk. *hypotheses*) attached to Old Latin editions of Paul as early as the second century.[105] In relatively set form, the *argumenta* briefly introduce each letter's addressees, situate their relationship with Paul, and outline his reasons for writing, thus facilitating reading of the individual letter. A set of Greek *hypotheses* are more robust still. Associated from early on with Euthalius, these *hypotheses* detail each letter's (1) provenance, and Paul's relation to the addressees; (2) occasion (πρόφασις); and (3) a summary of moderate length.[106] Like Libanius, the author's focus is clearly text-internal. The purpose is to aid the reader of the individual letter as such.

So when, at the turn of the fifth century, the so-called Budapest Anonymous opens his prologue to the corpus by stating that the interpreter's first task is to determine 'to whom and for what' (*quibus vel pro qua re*) Paul writes, he is not idiosyncratic.[107] Origen, Chrysostom, Theodore, Ambrosiaster and Jerome each have their own version of this programmatic concern for a text's origin. For Chrysostom, Paul always responds to 'a certain cause and subject' (αἰτίας τινὸς καὶ ὑποθέσεως); for Theodore, meaning never derives 'simply and accidentally' (*absolute ... fortuitu*), by which he means apart from a historical occasion; for Ambrosiaster, 'In order to have an understanding of things, one needs to grasp their origins'; and Jerome, following Origen, interprets each letter in view of the 'distinctive character' of its addressees.[108] In the

---

[103] The text is in R. Foerster, ed., *Libanii Opera*, vol. 8 (Leipzig: Teubner, 1915), 575–681, with English translation in Craig Gibson, trans., 'Libanius' *Hypotheses* to the Orations of Demosthenes', in *Dēmos: Classical Athenian Democracy*, ed. C. Blackwell (A. Mahoney and R. Scaife, eds., *The Stoa: A Consortium for Electronic Publication in the Humanities* [www.stoa.org], 2003). For an overview, and an argument for Libanius's pedagogical purpose throughout, see Craig A. Gibson, 'The Agenda of Libanius' Hypotheses to Demosthenes', *GRBS* 40 (1999): 171–202.

[104] Gibson, 'Libanius' *Hypotheses* to the Orations', 4.

[105] The Latin text of these so-called Marcionite Prologues is conveniently set out in Alexander Souter, *The Text and Canon of the New Testament* (New York: Scribner's, 1913), 205–8. The bibliography on their origin is lengthy; see Scherbenske, *Canonizing Paul*, 88–92; and Dahl, 'Origin of the Earliest Prologues', 180–2, for overview. Dahl (203–4) argues for their origin in a seven-churches edition of Paul, while Scherbenske (91–3, 237–42) attributes them to Marcion.

[106] The text is in Euthalius, *Opera* (PG 85:748a–788a), as well as Blomkvist, *Euthalian Traditions*, 73–89, with translation. The secondary status of the *hypotheses* was already seen in 1698 by Zacagni; for discussion, see Willard, *Euthalian Apparatus*, 69–72.

[107] Frede, *Ein neuer Paulustext*, 15.

[108] John Chrysostom, *Hom. Rom.* Arg. 2; Theodore of Mopsuestia, *Comm. Eph.* Arg; here I follow the suggestion of Rowan A. Greer in Theodore of Mopsuestia, *The Commentaries on the Minor Epistles of Paul*, trans. with introduction by Rowan A. Greer, Writings from the Greco-Roman World (Atlanta: SBL, 2010), 179; Ambrosiaster, In Rom. Arg. 1; Eng. trans. of Theodore S. de Bruyne, *Ambrosiaster's Commentary on the Pauline Epistles: Romans*, with introduction by de Bruyne, Stephen A. Cooper, and David G. Hunter, Writings from the Greco-Roman World 41 (Atlanta:

latter case, this is because Paul, like a good physician, does not wish to 'heal the eyes of everyone with the same eye-salve'.[109] In what could be the epigraph to a critical *Einleitung*, Jerome writes, 'In conformity with the diversity of places, times, and people to whom they have been written, they must also have diverse themes, subjects, and origins'.[110] Meaning emerges from setting. As we will see below, there is more here than just history, but there is certainly not less.

This interest in a text's origins also enjoys a correlative late-antique interest in Pauline chronology. Here, Rufinus's prologue (*Primum quaeritur*) to his Vulgate revision of Paul is a good place to begin, since Budapest Anonymous and Pelagius cite it nearly verbatim in their own commentaries.[111] After addressing the physical position of the *corpus Paulinum* in the New Testament, Rufinus turns to the shape of the collection itself: 'Furthermore, it disturbs certain ones why the letter to the Romans has been placed at the beginning, when judgment shows clearly that it was not written first'.[112] Intriguingly, Rufinus's circle contains those who think Paul's letters should be arranged chronologically. Rufinus does not, and I return to his solution below; for now, it is worth highlighting that the problem also emerges elsewhere. The fifth-century bishop of Cyrus Theodoret, for instance, spends virtually the entire prologue to his commentary on the fourteen letters working out their chronological order. He writes, 'First, however, I will attempt to show the chronological arrangement [τὴν κατὰ τὸν χρόνον τάξιν] of the apostolic letters. On the one hand, the blessed Paul has written fourteen letters; on the other, I regard the arrangement which they have in the books [τὴν δὲ τάξιν ἣν ἐν τοῖς βιβλίοις ἔχουσιν] not to have been produced by him'.[113] Then follows a lengthy chronology of Paul's epistolary career, dovetailing Paul's scant references to his travel schedule and the Jerusalem collection with data from Acts.

If Theodoret is cognizent of the problem, and Rufinus's circle troubled by it, Chrysostom's readers appear to be duped by it. In the *hypothesis* to his homilies on Romans, Chrysostom proposes to settle the letter's date: 'For it is not, as most think (ὡς πολλοὶ νομίζουσι), before all the others, but before all that were written from Rome, yet subsequent to the rest, though not to all of them'. Chrysostom, it turns out, is not

---

SBL, 2017), 3; for Origen and Jerome's discussion, see Ronald E. Heine, *The Commentaries of Origen and Jerome on St. Paul's Epistle to the Ephesians*, Oxford Early Christian Studies (Oxford: Oxford University Press, 2002), 76.

[109] Heine, *Ephesians*, 76. On Chrysostom's use of the physician-*topos* applied to Paul, see Margaret M. Mitchell, '"A Variable and Many-sorted Man": John Chrysostom's Treatment of Pauline Inconsistency', *JECS* 6 (1998): 93–111 (here 102–3).

[110] Heine, *Ephesians*, 76.

[111] On the production of the *Primum quaeritur* for the Vulgate revision of Paul's letters, see H. J. Frede, ed., *Epistulae ad Philippenses et ad Colossenses*, VL 24/2 (Freiburg: Herder, 1966–71), 42–3; and on Rufinus as its author, Scherbenske, *Canonizing Paul*, 183–4, with bibliography. Text of the *Primum quaeritur* is in Wordsworth and White, *Novum Testamentum*, 1–5, with translation in Scherbenske, *Canonizing Paul*, 186–8. The prologue of Budapest Anonymous is in Frede, *Ein neuer Paulustext*, 15–18, and of Pelagius, in Alexander Souter, *Pelagius's Expositions of Thirteen Epistles of St. Paul*, 3 vols., Texts and Studies 9 (Cambridge: Cambridge University Press, 1922–31), 2:3–5.

[112] Trans. Scherbenske, *Canonizing Paul*, 187 (slightly revised); cf. Frede, *Ein neuer Paulustext*, 17; Souter, *Pelagius's Expositions*, 4.

[113] Theodoret, *Interpr. XIV Epist. S. Pauli Apostoli* (PG 82:37b). Eng. trans. Theodoret of Cyrus, *Commentary on the Letters of St. Paul*, trans. with introduction by Robert Charles Hill, 2 vols. (Brookline, MA: Holy Cross Orthodox, 2001).

concerned with a precise date, but with the letter's position relative to the others. His ὡς πολλοὶ νομίζουσι clearly implies that some are reading the collection as if arranged chronologically. Chrysostom knows it is not, and so he proceeds to offer a standard chronology of the letters. This is not, he insists, 'beside the point' (πάρεργον) or 'needlessly superfluous' (περιεργίας περιττῆς), but is vital for interpretation. For when Chrysostom finds difference between letters, as he does in Paul's *halakhic* judgments in Rom 14.1–2 and Col 2.20–23, his first recourse is to assign them to different periods of the apostle's career.[114] Here textual origins and chronology matter a great deal; to get Paul right depends on them.

Reversion to the Norm: The Corporeal Paul

And yet, such textual archaeology is never the end of the story. To return to Libanius's *hypotheses*, for all his obvious interests in textual origins, he neither chronologically arranges his *hypotheses* nor uses them to reorder the corpus.[115] Chronological narration does not follow from his textual archaeology. Via Libanius's work, Montius is well-positioned to read Demosthenes's speeches on their own terms, but he still reads them as arranged in his non-chronological edition. The same is true of the so-called Marcionite Prologues, which introduce Paul's letters but nowhere rearrange the corpus. Instead, these *argumenta* follow the order of the collections they introduce, and in their early form, likely preface the collection as a whole, thus functioning as both canonical *and* epistolary prolegomena.[116] What of the Euthalian *hypotheses*? Together with two other paratextual traditions (Τάδε ἔνεστιν and Διὰ τί), they likely belong to a separate edition of Paul, and these two other traditions offer a counterbalance to the *hypotheses*' focus on the discrete letter.[117] Τάδε ἔνεστιν is a bare bibliographical catalogue, introducing the collection via a table of contents: ἡ πρὸς Ῥωμαίους, ἡ πρὸς Κορινθίους, etc. But Διὰ τί goes further, querying the edition's title: 'Why are they called the fourteen letters of Paul (Παύλου Ἐπιστολαὶ Δεκατέσσαρες)'? The answer drops the Ἐπιστολαὶ Δεκατέσσαρες and appeals to the Παύλου, the thing that makes them a collective: 'Because the apostle himself writes them with his own hand'. The letters belong together because they are *Paul's* letters; this edition, to echo Ps.-Plutarch, offers 'knowledge at its source'.[118] When the origins of Paul's discrete letters have been pursued and described, that is, the question of the collection still remains.

Theophylact, for instance, that great medieval compiler of patristic exegesis, notes the (chronologically) odd position of Romans in the corpus, and then lists the letters that ought to precede it. Nevertheless, Theophylact muses, Romans remains first.

---

[114] John Chrysostom, *Hom. Rom.* Arg (PG 60:392–93; *NPNF*[1] 11:336–37). See further Mitchell, 'Variable and Many-sorted Man', 101–3.

[115] Gibson, 'Agenda of Libanius' Hypotheses', 176–8, shows at length that Libanius's *hypotheses* follow the order in his collection.

[116] On both points, see Dahl, 'Origin of the Earliest Prologues', 188–93 (esp. 192–3). All agree that their order presupposes an arrangement as we have in Marcion's *Apostolikon*, an argument which goes back to Donatien de Bruyne, 'Prologues bibliques d'origin Marcionite', *RBén* 24 (1907): 1–16.

[117] Text in Euthalius, *Opera* (PG 85:745c-d [Τάδε ἔνεστιν], 748a [Διὰ τί]). On the connection of the ὑποθέσεις with Τάδε ἔνεστιν and Διὰ τί in a separate edition, see Dahl, 'Euthalian Apparatus', 253–5, 259.

[118] On this point, see Blomkvist, *Euthalian Traditions*, 147–8.

Why is this so? 'Because in Scripture', he writes, 'there is no need to follow such a sequence'—a conclusion he grounds, following Chrysostom, in the order of the Book of the Twelve.[119] Theophylact may write in the eleventh century, but his hermeneutical two-step reflects a widespread late-antique tendency to acknowledge the letters' chronology and then revert to the corpus' arrangement for commentary, typically by appeal to scriptural precedent. For Chrysostom, dating and chronology are vital, but the collection itself need not share this concern. When his chronological outline is complete, Chrysostom pulls back: 'But if they have another arrangement (τάξιν) in the books (ταῖς βίβλοις), that is not at all astonishing, since the twelve prophets, who are not next to one another chronologically (οὐκ ἐφεξῆς ἀλλήλοις ὄντες κατὰ τοὺς χρόνους) but stand at great distance from one another, are placed consecutively in the arrangement of the books (ἐν τῇ τῶν βιβλίων τάξει ἐφεξῆς εἰσι κείμενοι)'.[120] Paul's letters have a canonical shape that is to be respected. Rather than bemoan this, Chrysostom finds scriptural precedent in another composite work, the Book of the Twelve. Theodoret, on the other hand, finds it in the editorializing of David's psalms in the Psalter: 'Just as the divine David composed the sacred Psalms...and others, at a later time, gathered them together as they pleased (συνήρμοσαν δὲ τούτους ἀλλήλοις), disrupting their chronological arrangement (τὴν ἀπὸ τοῦ χρόνου δὲ τάξιν οὐκ ἔχουσιν), one can also see this occurring with the apostolic letters'.[121] So Theodoret reconstructs Paul's chronology, but when he finishes he returns to his Pauline codex and comments on the letters in their canonical order.[122] The collection and *its* arrangement takes priority. Theodoret's job is to write on Paul as he finds him, not Paul as he reconstructs him.

The same is true in Rufinus's *Primum quaeritur*, and thus how Vulgate readers meet Paul ever after. Rufinus's solution to the strange position of Romans is not to reconstruct a new order but to make sense of the traditional one—to ask basic questions about its purpose, scope, and shape. The *Primum quaeritur* opens, in fact, with the first of these: 'First, it is to be asked why, after the gospels, which are the fulfillment of the law and in which examples and precepts for living are most plentifully arranged for us, the apostle wanted to send these letters to individual churches'.[123] The reference to individual churches should not obscure the fact that Rufinus positions Paul's letters firstly as a collective vis-à-vis the gospels. The *why* of Paul's letters is a why *of the collection*, and Rufinus answers, again, by appeal to scriptural precedent. The Pauline collection, like the prophetic books of the Old Testament, buttresses a fledgling people in the wake of divine speech (Moses/Jesus): ὁ ἀπόστολος supplements τό εὐαγγέλιον.

---

[119] Theophylact, *Comm. Rom.* Arg (PG 124:336ab). Trans. Blomkvist, *Euthalian Traditions*, 286. While Theophylact's subsequent appeal to the Book of the Twelve depends on Chrysostom, this line appears to be his own (compare PG 60:393).

[120] Chrysostom, *Hom. Rom.* Arg (PG 60:393). The translation is my own.

[121] Theodoret, *Interpr. XIV Epist. S. Pauli Apostoli* Pref. (PG 82:37b). The translation is my own.

[122] Theodoret, *Interpr. XIV Epist. S. Pauli Apostoli* Pref. (PG 82:44b). Theodoret suggests two possible reasons for the priority of Romans which have currency in his day: its comprehensive doctrinal value and the apologetic value of fronting Paul's letter to *Rome* (Theodoret, *Letters of St. Paul*, 1:39).

[123] Pelagius asks the same question (Souter, *Pelagius's Expositions*, 2:3), as does Budapest Anonymous (Frede, *Ein neuer Paulustext*, 15). Trans. here and below is that of Scherbenske, *Canonizing Paul*, 186–8; cf. 181–98 on the editorial hermeneutics at play across the *Primum quaeritur*.

Rufinus's next question follows, now about the collection's scope: 'Then it is to be asked why he wrote no more than ten letters to churches'. The answer is, by now, predictable: Paul's church letters comprise a new Decalogue, offering guidance to those newly freed from the devil and idolatry. Discrete letters will not do; only as a collective do they offer a catechesis in holiness. With this we come full circle, for herein lies Rufinus's answer to the collection's shape. Romans is first 'so that [the reader] may come by steps through each individual letter to the more perfect'.[124] Brief *argumenta* for each of the ten church letters follow, Romans through Hebrews, detailing precisely these steps. Like the reader of a Euthalian edition, the reader of the Vulgate learns to read Paul as a book—one that, across its pages, facilitates growth in Christian perfection.

What, then, of Jerome, whose statement cited above, that the letters' varied 'places, times, and people' elicit 'diverse themes, subjects, and origins', looks so distinctively modern? Here too, it turns out, Jerome reverts to the collection. Paul's letters are akin to John's mini-corpus in Rev 2–3: 'Just as the blessed John, writing to the seven churches in his Apocalypse, either reproved the vices or approved the virtues in each of them, so also the holy apostle Paul heals the wounds which have been inflicted on the individual churches'. Jerome follows with the aforementioned physician trope: '[Paul] does not wish, like an inexperienced physician, to heal the eyes of everyone with the same eye-salve'.[125] In the end, Jerome's concern with textual particularity serves his purposes of Pauline panegyric. The 'diversity of places, times, and people' suggests the variability of diseases that Paul treats, and the 'diverse themes, subjects, and origins' depict the malleability of Paul's cure. The collection is now a medical manual capable of treating myriad ecclesial diseases. The corpus in its totality does what no letter on its own can do.

In late antiquity, then, Paul's letters are viewed as a collective, and this may explain an intriguing feature of this period—namely, just how many commentators write on every letter: Theodore, Theodoret, and Budapest Anonymous on fourteen, and Ambrosiaster and Pelagius on thirteen.[126] Perhaps before these Pauline tradents consider themselves readers of a given letter, they reckon themselves interpreters of a collection. For all their very real interest in the letters' origins and chronology, the corpus is prior and hermeneutically meaningful. And this explains why Paul's late-antique readers can work out his chronology, but never comment on the letters in that order. As Richard Layton writes, their job is not 'to establish the corpus' order, but to explain it'.[127] Above, we have seen several such attempts. In the eleventh century,

---

[124] See, again, the same in Pelagius (Souter, *Pelagius's Expositions*, 2:4) and Budapest Anonymous (Frede, *Ein neuer Paulustext*, 17).

[125] Heine, *Ephesians*, 76.

[126] Marius Victorinus also writes on the first six letters (Galatians; Ephesians; and Philippians extant) in canonical order, and almost certainly set out to write on all (so Stephen A. Cooper, *Marius Victorinus' Commentary on Galatians: Introduction, Translation, and Notes*, Oxford Early Christian Studies [New York: Oxford University Press, 2005], 3–5 [directly at 5]). This impulse to treat the letters in a single commentary, which begins with Ambrosiaster, may be mostly confined to Latin Pauline exegesis (Cooper, *Galatians*, 5–9), but Theodoret wrote on all fourteen together, and in his prologue explicitly calls his a 'commentary on the apostle' (Theodoret, *Letters of St. Paul*, 1:35). Jerome, moreover, says that Theodore wrote on Matthew, John, '*et in apostolum*' (*Vir. ill.* 90).

[127] Richard A. Layton, 'Origen as a Reader of Paul: A Study of His *Commentary on Ephesians*' (PhD diss., University of Virginia, 1996), 333.

Theophylact offers another at the close of his *hypothesis* to Romans. After echoing Theodoret, that Paul writes here to the 'protectors of the whole world', Theophylact adds his own interpretive gloss, a sort of exegesis of the corpus: 'For he who supports the head, supports the whole body as well'.[128] The *corpus Paulinum* is now the *corporeal* Paul, a unified epistolary body. It is also, as we will now see, a book.

Paul, the Book

This is clear, in a general sense, from the weight Paul's late-antique readers give to the order of the collection itself. But is it also true in a more specific sense? Here, two questions emerge. First, in late antiquity, do Paul's readers encounter him *materially* as an independent collection, or simply within the New Testament? And second, do they ever call this collection, *linguistically*, a book, akin to Cicero and Pliny?

The first is, in a real sense, a false choice. The sixth-century pseudo-Athanasian *Synopsis Scripturae Sacrae*, for instance, refers to the 'fourteen epistles of the Apostle Paul, counted as one book' [βιβλίον], and later designates Paul's letters 'Book Seven' [Βιβλίον ξ'] of an eight-book New Testament.[129] The earlier *Synopsis Scripturae Sacrae* of pseudo-Chrysostom does the same: the 'fourteen letters of Paul' are one of the 'new books' (τῆς καινῆς βιβλία) of Scripture.[130] The same logic is at work in Vaticanus, in which the chapter numbers run consecutively across Paul's corpus rather than starting fresh with each letter. That is, the collection retains its integrity even in a whole-Bible pandect. With this proviso, the vast majority of Paul's ancient readers, at least up to the ninth century, read his letters in an independent collection. While the fourth and fifth centuries see the production of the four major uncial pandects—Sinaiticus (ℵ), Alexandrinus (A), Vaticanus (B), and Ephraemi (C)—these deluxe editions are far from the norm, and similar efforts are exceedingly rare until the eleventh and twelfth centuries.[131] Even the more limited compilations of Acts, the Catholic letters and Paul appear only in the ninth century and later.[132] Until that time, it seems, the norm was to produce independent editions of Paul—data that stretches, in Greek manuscripts, from 𝔓46 (ca. 200) to a tenth-century uncial (0243) through such notables as 𝔓99 (ca. 400), Freerianus (I 016; fifth century), Claromontanus (D 06; sixth century), Coislinianus (H 015; sixth century), Augiensis (F 010; ninth century), and Boernerianus (G 012; ninth century).[133] The same is true in Latin manuscripts, where we find editions of the *corpus Paulinum* that range from the fifth to the eleventh century.[134] In late antiquity, reading Paul physically within a New Testament would have been exceedingly rare.

---

[128] Theophylact, *Comm. Rom.* Arg (PG 124:336B). Trans. Blomkvist, *Euthalian Traditions*, 287.

[129] Ps.-Athanasius, *Synopsis Scripturae Sacrae* (PG 28:292, 412).

[130] Ps.-Chrysostom, *Synopsis Scripturae Sacrae* (PG 56:317).

[131] For description of the four Greek Bibles just named, see Metzger, *Text of the New Testament*, 42–9. Here and below, I follow the dating in NA²⁸. In Greek, the only other extant (near) comprehensive versions of the New Testament prior to the eleventh century are Ψ (044) and 33; in Syriac, see the Peshitta and Philoxenian and Harklean versions; and in Latin, the Vulgate editions of the whole Latin Bible (A, C) and New Testament (D, F).

[132] See, e.g., in Greek, L (020), 049, 81, 221, 326, 1175, 1739, 1841, 1891.

[133] See also the myriad Greek manuscripts listed in NA²⁸ that contain multiple Pauline letters, and therefore that almost certainly represent a whole collection (e.g. 𝔓92, 𝔓61, 0285 [081], 0278, and 0243).

[134] ar 61, b 89, d 75, f 78, g 77, m 86, r 64, and t 56.

The readers of a Euthalian or Priscillianist edition certainly did not. Nor, apparently, did a host of Paul's more well-known readers, who quite clearly read him within the confines of an independent book, and call it such. Here we begin to answer our second question above. Some evidence is suggestive, but in the end ambiguous. In the famous trial of twelve North African Christians in Carthage in 180 CE, when the proconsul Saturninus abruptly queries Speratus, the group's leader, as to the contents of his satchel, Speratus replies, 'Books and letters [*Libri et epistulae*] of a just man named Paul'.[135] The referent of *libri* is ambiguous, but it is possible that Paul is the subject of both, with the *et* functioning epexegetically: 'Books, that is, letters…'[136] Roughly two centuries later, in a letter to Sabinus (*Ep.* 37), Ambrose of Milan lauds his epistolographic forebears, of whom Paul is one such, as the authors of 'rich little books' (*codiculos*), who spread the faith via their letters.[137]

If the *Acts of the Scillitan Martyrs* and Ambrose are ambiguous, others are unequivocal. We have, in fact, already seen this: the *Synopses* of pseudo-Athanasius and pseudo-Chrysostom count the letters as one book (βιβλίον); both Chrysostom and Theodoret reference the letters' arrangement 'in the books' (τὴν τάξιν … ἐν τοῖς βιβλίοις); and in the Epistles of Paul and Seneca, Seneca refers to a Pauline collection as a *libellus*.[138] Seneca himself, in fact, plays the role of Paul's editor, dividing and arranging the corpus for a hearing with Nero. Under Seneca's watchful eye, what began as a series of *volumina* (Ep. Paul Sen. 3) becomes a *libellus*—a little book, indeed, when stood next to Cicero or Pliny, but a book nonetheless. It was some such book that Ponticianus finds on Augustine's gaming table in the famous garden scene in the *Confessions* (8.8.19–8.12.30, but here 8.6.14). Augustine's existential turmoil, of course, has him in his garden, where he hears a child say *tolle lege*, which he takes as a divine command to 'open the book' (*codicem*; 8.12.29): 'I hurried back to the place where Alypius was sitting. There I had put down the book of the apostle [*codicem Apostoli*] when I got up. I seized it, opened it and in silence read the first passage on which my eyes lit' (*Conf.* 8.12.29).[139] The text, of course, is Rom 13.13–14, but the book is a Pauline codex—one which, apparently, he kept on his table.

The same is true of Chrysostom, who calls Paul's heart '[Christ's] heart, a tablet of the Holy Spirit, and a book [βιβλίον] of grace'.[140] This might be ambiguous, were it not that elsewhere, in his *Propter fornicationes uxorem*, a Pauline book serves as a

---

[135] *Acts of the Scillitan Martyrs* 12. Eng. trans. in Herbert Musurillo, ed. and trans., *The Acts of the Christian Martyrs* (Oxford: Clarendon, 1972).

[136] Lewis and Short, s.v. *et* II.A. One could also read this to refer to the letters *themselves* as books, to gospel books, or to non-scriptural *libri* altogether. See briefly Houghton, *Latin New Testament*, 4–5. On the first, I have not found any other ancient source that refers to a discrete Pauline letter as a book. On the second, it arises from an assumption that assigning *libri* to Paul is a problem that requires an alternative explanation. Given the below, I suggest it is not a problem at all.

[137] Ambrose, *Epistle* 37, 6. Text in Karl Schenkl, *Sancti Ambrosii Opera*, CSEL 82 (Leipzig, 1897), 2.22, lines 38–46; cited in Nauroy, 'Collection of Ambrose', 150.

[138] Ep. Paul Sen. 1. I discuss this reference further in my Introduction.

[139] Text in Hammond, LCL 26; cf. 8.6.14; 8.12.30. Eng. trans. from Saint Augustine, *Confessions*, trans. with introduction and notes by Henry Chadwick, Oxford World's Classics (Oxford: Oxford University Press, 1998), 142. I am grateful to Joshua Bruce for bringing this passage to my attention. More broadly, see now Ian N. Mills, 'Pagan Readers of Christian Scripture: The Role of Books in Early Autobiographical Conversion Narratives', VC 73 (2019): 481–506.

[140] *Hom. Rom.* 32 (PG 60:680).

talisman for the man caught in the love-magic of prostitutes and mistresses: 'opening the book, and taking Paul as mediator ... the flame [will be] extinguished' (καὶ τὸ βιβλίον ἀναπτύξας τοῦτο, καὶ λαβὼν Παῦλον μεσίτην ... κατάσβεσον τὴν φλόγα).[141] In his fifth-century *Historia ecclesiastica*, Socrates Scholasticus relays a similar, albeit deeply ascetic, use of Paul's book. Convinced by his relatives to take a wife, the devout Egyptian monk Ammoun leads his bride to the nuptial couch, where they consummate their marriage in a rather unconventional way: 'Taking the apostolic book [βιβλίον λαβὼν ἀποστολικόν], he read Paul's letter to the Corinthians' and convinced her of the virtue of marital chastity' (4.23).[142] Finally, writing around the same time, Hesychius introduces his edition of the twelve books of the prophets, arranged 'by lines' (στιχηδὸν), as modeled on a similarly arranged edition of 'the apostolic book' (τὴν ἀποστολικὴν βίβλον)—likely a Euthalian edition of Paul.[143]

All of this, then, brings us back to the Euthaliana. In addition to the indirect evidence tallied earlier,[144] Euthalius refers five times to Paul's collection as the βίβλος, and never in the plural. We already saw two of these: in his prologue to Acts, Euthalius recalls reading and writing 'the apostolic book' (τὴν ἀποστολικὴν βίβλον) in lines, and in his *epitomē* of Paul, 'the whole book' (ἡ πᾶσα βίβλος) contains all πολιτεία.[145] He has read, that is, the 'book of Paul' (τὴν Παύλου βίβλον), as he puts it in his prologue to Acts.[146] In his Paul volume, Euthalius again reports arranging in lines 'the whole apostolic book' (πᾶσαν τὴν ἀποστολικὴν βίβλον),[147] and at the close of his prologue to Paul, Euthalius notes its length, calling the object of his labours not a series of letters but a book: 'The prologue prefixed to τῆς βίβλου Παύλου τοῦ ἀποστόλου, stichoi 300'.[148] It is little surprise, then, that a colophon to the Euthalian edition, likely secondary, picks up on just this way of referring to Paul's collection: 'This book [βίβλος] was collated against a copy in Caesarea from the library of the holy Pamphilus and copied by his hand'.[149] From the colophon itself, the reader would never know that what follows is a series of letters. All the reader knows is that the work in her hands is a book, the βίβλος τοῦ Παύλου.

As with Cicero, Pliny, and Sidonius, Paul's late-ancient readers repeatedly call his letters a book, and in so doing grant it hermeneutical pride of place. The origin of this linguistic designation is not clear, but it seems to be a product of the fourth century.[150] The colophon's linking of a Euthalian edition, where this language is

---

[141] *Propt. forn. uxor.* (PG 51:215).
[142] Socrates Scholasticus, *Hist. ecc.* 4.23.11 (contra the trans. in *NPNF*² 2:106).
[143] Hesychius, Στιχηρὸν τῶν ιβ' προφητῶν (PG 93: 1340f); cited in Robinson, *Euthaliana*, 36.
[144] I refer here to Euthalius's provision of various textual data for the corpus as a whole.
[145] Euthalius, *Opera* (PG 85: 629a; 708a).
[146] Euthalius, *Opera* (PG 85:629b). Interestingly, Euthalius never describes the Catholic epistles as ἡ βίβλος, but always with the plural ἐπιστολὰς. See PG 85:629b; 633bc; 668b.
[147] Euthalius, *Opera* (PG 85:720b).
[148] Euthalius, *Opera* (PG 85:713b).
[149] The colophon is found already in the earliest attested Euthalian manuscript, Codex Coislinianus. For translation and discussion, see Scherbenske, *Canonizing Paul*, 116 and 150–2.
[150] Outside of the ambiguous reference in the *Acts of the Scillitan Martyrs*, I have not found any reference to Paul's letters collectively as a βιβλίον/βίβλος/*liber* prior to the fourth century, even in a discussion where we might otherwise expect it (e.g. the Muratorian Canon or Tertullian's *Marc.* 5). That said, in his useful essay 'Greek Patristic Commentaries on the Pauline Letters', in *Dictionary of*

frequent, to Caesarea is suggestive. For it is here that Christian scholars such as Origen, Eusebius, and Pamphilus were involved in something of a revolution in book-making.[151] Wherever and whenever it started, though, one thing is sure: by the fourth century, Paul is a book.

Conclusion

None of this is to suggest that interest in the individual letters was lost, nor that Paul's late ancient and modern readers are wholly different. This is manifestly not the case. It is remarkable, in fact, how many genres of modern scholarship have late-antique antecedents.[152] Differences between the periods can be overdrawn, not least when evaluative epithets like critical and pre-critical become ciphers for entire eras. Such coded language is lazy, encourages the cessation of thought, and should be rejected. The actual reading practices of late-antique and modern criticism are more alike than we often imagine.[153] And where they do differ, it is facile to label the fault lines pre-critical and critical; they are simply '*differently critical*'.[154]

In this chapter, I explore where this difference actually lies. And the answer I propose is that lying beneath not dissimilar reading practices is a foundational disagreement about the object of Pauline study: Is it the βίβλος or the ἐπιστολή? or better, the ἐπιστολή within the βίβλος, or the ἐπιστολή within ἱστορία? The difference, that is, lies in how to read a letter collection. Is it hermeneutically meaningful in itself, or an obstacle to be discarded in pursuit of history? Two Pauline tradents separated by 1,300 years neatly encapsulate the difference. On the one side, Theodoret recognizes the value of Pauline chronology, but in the end falls back on the collection's priority. Letters *written* in a certain order need not be *read* in that order. J. D. Michaelis, on the other hand, sees a possible organizing principle in the collection (descending rank of cities), but opts instead for chronology. Letters *arranged* in a certain order need not be *read* in that order. Here are two astute readers, both aware of alternative ways to read a collection, who both nevertheless opt for the one native to their reading culture.

With this, we are already some way toward explaining the Jerome quote that stands at the head of this book. When Jerome writes that Ephesians 'stands in the

---

the Bible, ed. James Hastings, 5 vols. (New York: Scribner's, 1904), 5:484–531, C. H. Turner collects references from the second century and later to Paul's corpus as simply ὁ ἀπόστολος (484).

[151] See Anthony Grafton and Megan Williams, *Christianity and the Transformation of the Book* (Cambridge, MA: Harvard University Press, 2006), passim, but directly at 6 and 15–16. This singularly helpful work illuminates several strands of the discussion above.

[152] To put it baldly, the *Einleitung* (ὑπόθεσις/*argumentum*), *Life and Letters* (Euthalius's βίος and ἐπιτομή), *Theology* (Priscillian's *Canons*), *Chronology* (Chrysostom/Theodoret), and division of chapter and verse (Euthalius's κεφάλαια/Priscillian's *testimonia*) all have late-antique antecedents.

[153] For an excellent essay along these lines, see Francis Watson, 'Does Historical Criticism Exist? A Contribution to Debate on the Theological Interpretation of Scripture', in *Theological Theology: Essays in Honour of John B. Webster*, ed. R. David Nelson, Darren Sarisky, and Justin Stratis (London: Bloomsbury T&T Clark, 2015), 307–18 (esp. 308–10).

[154] John C. Cavadini, 'Exegetical Transformations: The Sacrifice of Isaac in Philo, Origen, and Ambrose', in *In Dominico Eloquio—In Lordly Eloquence: Essays on Patristic Exegesis in Honor of Robert Louis Wilken*, ed. Paul M. Blowers et al. (Grand Rapids: Eerdmans, 2002), 48–49. Emphasis mine. I am grateful to T. J. Lang for drawing my attention to this reference.

middle in concepts as well as in order', he reflects a reading culture attuned both to the physical dimensions and the hermeneutical possibilities of a letter collection. To be sure, Jerome calls Ephesians Paul's 'heart' because of its difficulty and profundity, but he gets there via allusive reference to its position in the book: it sits 'after the first epistles' and is 'longer than the final ones'.[155] That is, Jerome opens his edition of Paul and makes something, hermeneutically, of the book lying open on his desk. Which is to say, Jerome is a late-antique reader. The question now is what effect this has on how Ephesians is read vis-à-vis Paul.

---

[155] Heine, *Ephesians*, 77.

Chapter 4

PLACING EPHESIANS

In late antiquity, Paul's letter collection is not incidental to interpreting Paul. The book is neither just a composite nor an aggregate of missives; it has hermeneutical integrity in its own right. The collection, together with the paratextual traditions that mediate it, provides Paul's late-antique readers a map for reading Paul—a way of ordering Pauline knowledge.[1]

This chapter asks what this means for Ephesians—a letter that modern criticism finds frustratingly unsatisfying. Toward this end, a series of questions guides the work that follows: do late-antique interpreters give any evidence of reading Ephesians within the frame of the collection? And if so, what (if any) bearing does this have on interpretation? How do discussions of the corpus' order impinge on Ephesians? Alternatively, in what ways (if any) do proposals about the letter's provenance shape interpretation? Beyond these obvious questions, a few more subtle questions emerge: what co-texts is Ephesians most frequently read alongside? And what effect does this have on the relevant passages from Ephesians? Perhaps most interesting given contemporary judgments, how do Paul's late-antique readers handle variability within the corpus, specifically that of Ephesians with the other letters? If, as Margaret Mitchell rightly notes, Pauline variability is only *available* via the corpus—the very thing which late antiquity privileges—do they notice it?[2] And what are their strategies for dealing with it? All of these questions, then, are different ways of asking this chapter's central question: what does it mean to read Ephesians within Paul's corpus, against the backdrop of this map?

Textual Origins and Ephesians

First, however, what does it not mean? As the last chapter shows, it does not mean a lack of interest in textual origins, and this is the case not least with respect to Ephesians, where Paul's early readers grapple with the fragility of basic issues of prolegomena. Origen famously reads a text of Ephesians that lacks ἐν Ἐφέσῳ at 1.1, which leads to a clever bit of intertextual exegesis: the Ephesians are 'those who are' (τοῖς οὖσιν;

---

[1] König and Whitmarsh, 'Ordering Knowledge', 27–30 and 34–9.
[2] Mitchell, 'Variable and Many-sorted Man', 110: 'The inconsistency of Paul…is in some measure the predictable result of the hermeneutical shift occasioned by the collection of occasional writings into a corpus'.

1.1), derived from the one 'who is' (ὁ ὤν; Exod 3.14).³ The omission must have been widespread for a bibliophile like Origen not to encounter a text that read otherwise. In addition to the manuscript evidence (𝔓46 ℵ* B* 6. 1739), Basil of Caesarea confirms this in the fourth century: ἐν Ἐφέσῳ may be in his text, but he has searched, and it is absent 'in those copies which are ancient' (ἐν τοῖς παλαιοῖς τῶν ἀντιγράφων; adv. Eun. 2.19). In the West, as early as the second century, Marcion knows it as Laodiceans, and in defense of an Ephesian address Tertullian appeals to the tradition of the church and charges Marcion with falsifying the title (*titulum ... interpolare*)—not, in fact, the text itself (*Marc.* 5.11 and 17).⁴

The fragility is tied not only to the address, but also when and why Paul wrote. Staying in the West, the three-stage development of the Old Latin prologues attests a struggle along these lines. Did Paul write from Ephesus to Laodicea to combat false apostles (stage 1)? Or to Ephesus to combat false apostles (stage 2)? Or from Rome to Ephesus to praise the faith of the Ephesians (stage 3)?⁵ These forerunners of the *Einleitung* struggle to decide. That said, by the early fifth century, the matter is settled in the West: Ambrosiaster, Jerome, Budapest Anonymous, and Pelagius all follow the then-codified tradition of the prologues (stage 3).⁶ The debate rages on in the East, however, not least in Antioch, where it is tied to two questions: did Paul write before or after John's arrival in Ephesus, and before or after his own visit? For Severian of Gabala, the answer is after John and before his own; for Theodore, before John and before his own; and for Theodoret, before John and after his own.⁷ The Euthalian *hypothesis* and its (bizarre) setting rounds out the picture: from Rome to Ephesus, to a community Paul had yet to meet.⁸ Whatever else one may say, these tradents' belief in Paul's authorship of Ephesians stunts neither their pursuit of, nor varied proposals for, the letter's setting. On the contrary, they attest nearly every possible permutation within the boundaries of Paul's life.

Further, while none of these settings are overly specific, they *are* critically derived, in that each reckons with the available evidence. Theodoret, for instance, argues largely from Acts 15 and 19 to establish John's presence in Jerusalem during Paul's initial evangelization of Ephesus, and then connects Ephesians to 2 Timothy via their shared reference to Tychicus (Eph 6.21–22; 2 Tim 4.12), which places the whole set

---

³ The entire discussion is in Heine, *Ephesians*, 80, with Greek text in J. A. F. Gregg, 'The Commentary of Origen upon the Epistle to the Ephesians', *JTS* 3 (1902): 233–44 (235).
⁴ On the data above, see Lightfoot, 'Destination of Ephesians', 377–83.
⁵ The text of the original prologue is reconstructed by de Bruyne, 'Prologues bibliques', 14 (cf. 4–6 and 10). The prologue to Marius Victorinus's Ephesians commentary attests the second stage, which shifts the address but retains the content; so Karl Schäfer, 'Marius Victorinus und die marcionitischen Prologe zu den Paulusbriefen', *RBén* 80 (1970): 7–16. The third stage is the now-extant prologue; text in de Bruyne, 'Prologues bibliques', 15. See the discussion in Dahl, 'Origin of the Prologues', 191–3.
⁶ See the prefaces to the commentaries of each.
⁷ For Severian, see Karl Staab, *Pauluskommentare aus der Griechischen Kirche*, 2nd ed. (Münster: Aschendorff, 1984), 304; Theodore, *Comm. Eph.* Arg (Theodore, *Minor Epistles*, 175); Theodoret, *Comm. Eph.* Hyp. (Theodoret, *Letters of St. Paul*, 2:31–33). Chrysostom, *Hom. Eph.* Arg (PG 62:9; NPNF¹ 13:49) is somewhat ambiguous, although probably envisions it before John and after his own.
⁸ Euthalius, *Opera* (PG 85:761c).

near Paul's death (cf. 2 Tim 4.6–7).[9] Severian and Theodore, on the other hand, rightly highlight the author's seeming ignorance of his recipients (Eph 1.15; 3.1; 4.21), a strange conundrum on Theodoret's proposal, and which helps them situate the letter early.[10] But on their reading, what of the reference to Tychicus married to the data of 2 Timothy? On this score, the Euthalian *hypothesis* looks *most* logical, except it is diametrically opposed to Acts. The question is largely where one begins, and what data one privileges. All of this brings us back to the central point of Chapter 2—namely, the fragility of any setting for Ephesians. Late-antique judgments do not escape but rather share in these ambiguities.

But what is the interpretive effect of this? In one sense, quite little: Paul's early readers tend not to read Ephesians in light of an overly specified setting. Which is to say, they do escape *interpretation* that depends on an ambiguous setting. Instead, insofar as textual origins matter, their reading of Ephesians turns on two very general axes: Paul's relationship to, and the character of, his addressees. On the first, the vital question is whether or not Paul has met the Ephesians prior to writing. For Severian, Theodore, and the Euthalian ἐπιτομή and ὑποθέσεις, he has not, and this explains the letter's tone and content. When Paul's first contact with a community is via epistle, he writes a general letter. For the Euthalian *hypothesis*, this makes Ephesians a 'catechetical letter' (τὴν ἐπιστολὴν κατηχητικήν), written to strengthen the faith of new believers.[11] In his *epitomē*, Euthalius calls Ephesians 'first principles for catechumens and introductions for believers' (ἀρχαὶ κατηχουμένων καὶ πιστῶν εἰσαγωγαί), similar to Romans.[12] For Theodore, it makes Ephesians (and Romans and Colossians) nothing less than Paul's apostolic *kerygma*, focusing exclusively on the greatness of Christ and his work.[13] Rather than displace Ephesians, the letter's distinctiveness is explained via the most general of settings.

On the other hand, Origen, Jerome, Chrysostom, the *Primum quaeritur*, Budapest Anonymous, and Pelagius all appeal to the Ephesians themselves to explain the letter's content. In the latter three, virtuous recipients require no correction—the Ephesians receive 'no blame' and 'much praise'—which explains the letter's noticeable lack of polemic.[14] For Chrysostom, it is not the virtue but the nobility of the Ephesians that explains the letter they receive. Given the political, cultic, philosophical, and apostolic heritage of Ephesus, Paul shoulders a weight in writing there, so he offers them his 'profoundest conceptions' in a letter 'full of sublime thoughts and doctrines'. In fact, what he 'scarcely so much as utters anywhere else, he here plainly declares'.[15] Origen and Jerome, too, tie the letter's profundity to the character of its recipients, only now with reference to the past from which they have been delivered. Both lean heavily on Acts 19–20 to describe the Ephesians' former life—one of slavery to a host of deities

---

[9] Theodoret, *Letters of St. Paul*, 2:31–33 (cf. 1:38–39).
[10] Staab, *Pauluskommentare*, 304 (on Severian); Theodore, *Minor Epistles*, 171.
[11] Euthalius, *Opera* (PG 85:761c).
[12] Euthalius, *Opera* (PG 85:704a).
[13] Theodore, *Comm. Col.* Arg, here with reference to Ephesians and Colossians. See further my section on Theodore below. Severian's statement along these lines is in Staab, *Pauluskommentare*, 304.
[14] See Wordsworth and White, *Novum Testamentum*, 1–5 (*Primum quaeritur*); Frede, *Ein neuer Paulustext*, 18 (Budapest Anonymous); and Souter, *Pelagius's Expositions*, 5.
[15] Chrysostom, *Hom. Eph.* Arg. (PG 62:9–10; NPNF[1] 13:49).

due to their pagan catechesis in the Artemis cult—in order to make sense of the letter's obscurity.[16] Ephesians reveals Paul's deepest mysteries to those able to comprehend them—a healthy patient delivered from paganism into the pneumatic life.

Late antique and modern criticism may share an interest in textual origins, then, but that interest is not everywhere the same. What can we say of the effect on Ephesians of how Paul's late ancient readers construe its setting? With the partial exception of Origen and Jerome, these readers are remarkably content to admit the obvious generality of Ephesians. They posit varied settings, but always to explain the letter's generality rather than to create a polemical Ephesians out of whole cloth. It is little surprise, then, that so many of the judgments above call to mind the conclusions of Goodspeed, Dahl, and Campbell. For Paul's early readers, a general letter is not a problem to begin with, and so does not require a solution. Paul, it turns out, is not always a polemicist; if the situation calls for it, he can also play the catechist.

Ephesians in Late-Antique Editions of Paul

In fact, the catechetical and apologetic potential latent in Paul's letter collection is precisely what interests Euthalius and Priscillian, in large part as we will see, to the exclusion of Pauline polemics. How, then, does each deploy Ephesians? And what does Ephesians look like on these particular maps?

The Euthalian Edition

Euthalius maps Paul, as we have seen, both epistolographically and ethically. Paul writes all kinds of letters, which, when collected, narrate all πολιτεία, conveniently arranged on the principle of growth. What, then, of Ephesians on this dual schema? The data are minimal, and reducible largely to the few-sentence description of Ephesians in the *epitomē*.

> Πέμπτη ἡ πρὸς Ἐφεσίους κεῖται, πιστοὺς ἀνθρώπους καὶ παραμένοντας, ἧς ἐν τῇ προγραφῇ τὸ μυστήριον ἐκτίθεται, παραπλησίως τῇ πρὸς Ῥωμαίους · ἀμφοτέροις δὲ ἐξ ἀκοῆς γνωρίσμοις. Καὶ εἰσὶν αὗται πρὸς ἀντιδιαστολὴν ἀρχαὶ κατηχουμένων, καὶ πιστῶν εἰσαγωγαί.[17]

Vis-à-vis the other letters, the lack of illocutionary language in Euthalius's description of Ephesians stands out.[18] Paul does not *do* anything in Ephesians—a point buttressed by the fact that, with Hebrews, Euthalius's Ephesians is unique among Paul's church letters in lacking any linguistic overlap with the epistolary handbooks.[19] These missives, it seems, stretch the bounds of letter-writing. Ephesians is not so much epistolary intervention as it is Pauline prolegomena, which is exactly what Euthalius says. Ephesians and Romans are 'distinct' (ἀντιδιαστολή) within the corpus, for here

---

[16] Jerome, *Comm. Eph.* 1.Prol (Heine, *Ephesians*, 77–8).
[17] Euthalius, *Opera* (PG 85:704a).
[18] On the dominance of this language in the secondary *hypotheses*, see Dahl, 'Euthalian Apparatus', 258–9.
[19] 1 Timothy and Titus among the personal letters also lack this linguistic resonance.

Paul writes to those he has only heard of (ἐξ ἀκοῆς γνωρίμοις). These letters comprise first things (ἀρχαί ... καὶ εἰσαγωγαί) for catechumens and faithful alike (κατηχουμένων καὶ πιστῶν), and share a similar description of Paul's μυστήριον—presumably what other churches received via his initial preaching.[20] All of this may suggest that Ephesians belongs with Romans near the front of Paul's corpus, and Euthalius's own language implies this. Opening his *epitomē*, he writes that in the collection Paul 'guides people how to live' (περὶ τῶν πρακτέων τοῖς ἀνθρώποις εἰσηγήσατο), only to go on to use the nominal form to describe Ephesians as the initial form of that guidance (εἰσαγωγαί).[21] If Euthalius was arranging it, one suspects Romans and Ephesians would head the corpus, with the growth of Paul's churches narrated from there.

Euthalius, however, is not the letters' collector but the collection's interpreter, and as he finds it, Ephesians sits fifth (πέμπτη). Why? Because the collection's order is, for Euthalius, κατὰ προσαύξησιν. On this rubric, the Ephesians fall squarely in the middle, one of three churches marked by πίστις, whose letters mark the collection's center: the Ephesians are 'faithful and standing fast' (πιστοὺς καὶ παραμένοντας); the Philippians 'faithful and fruitful' (πιστοὺς καὶ καρποφόρους); and the Colossians 'faithful and steadfast' (πιστοὺς καὶ βεβαίους).[22] Παραμένοντες is not an obvious description of the Ephesians, and only loosely grounded in the text (Eph 6.10–17), but Euthalius highlights it in order to render Ephesians intelligible within a collection that, for him, delineates progress in virtue. That story begins with Roman initiates and Corinthian/Galatian backsliders, proceeds with three faithful (if untested) churches, and closes with the Thessalonians, who grow even in the face of suffering.[23] To say it slightly differently, then, the book (and its arrangement) shapes what Euthalius finds in Ephesians. If the collection narrates ethical growth, and if Ephesians sits fifth, the letter can be neither overtly polemical (à la Corinthians/Galatians) nor laudatory (à la 1 and 2 Thessalonians). And since the map is not chronological, Ephesians does not dangle at the edge of a Pauline timeline, nor does development come into play. Instead, Ephesians is basic to Pauline πολιτεία: via its physical position, roughly halfway along, and via its relation to its auditors, fundamental. Rather than a postlude, then, Ephesians is Pauline prelude (ἀρχαί ... καὶ εἰσαγωγαί), albeit entrenched in the heart of an ethically mapped corpus. Every map illuminates and occludes, and Euthalius's

---

[20] Euthalius says Paul describes it in Ephesians' προγραφή, which is ambiguous. The question of which texts in Romans and Ephesians resemble (παραπλησίος) one another, however, depends on identifying it. Blomkvist (*Euthalian Traditions*, 209 n. 316) opts for Eph 1.9–10 (cf. 3.4–5) and Rom 16.25–27 (both use μυστήριον), on the assumption that προγραφή equals *proemium* (i.e. Eph 1.3–14). Contra Blomkvist, however, Paul himself speaks explicitly of his μυστήριον with reference to a προγραφή at Eph 3.3 (κατὰ ἀποκάλυψιν ἐγνωρίσθη μοι τὸ μυστήριον, καθὼς προέγραψα ἐν ὀλίγῳ), which likely looks back to 2.11–22—a section that Paul tersely summarizes in 3.6 as his μυστήριον (3.3–4). If this is right, the more apt Romans parallel is 11.7–32, which also culminates in Paul's elucidation of the μυστήριον. And if this is correct, then in this allusive suggestion Euthalius collocates and reads similarly two texts (Eph 2.11–22; Rom 11.7–32) that modern scholarship tends to read via difference and development.

[21] Euthalius, *Opera* (PG 85:701a).

[22] Euthalius, *Opera* (PG 85:704a-b).

[23] It is not clear how Hebrews and the personal letters fit into Euthalius's scheme (if at all), nor precisely how Euthalius structures the progress of the corpus. For the main options, which read it either across individual letters (Dahl) or within and across subgroups of letters (Blomkvist), see Dahl, 'Euthalian Apparatus', 238, and Blomkvist, *Euthalian Traditions*, 207–10.

engagement with Ephesians is hardly robust. But for those late-ancient readers who meet Paul via Euthalius, the juxtaposition to Paul's modern readers is stark. Faced with where to begin reading, Ephesians and Romans are the letters of choice, far better than Corinthians and Galatians, which give only the Paul of controversy. What one wants in a letter turns not least, that is, on what one wants from the collection.

Priscillian's *Canones*

The situation in Priscillian is in principle the same, and in method quite different. Where modern criticism privileges the letter, and Euthalius the collection, Priscillian privileges the textual excerpt (*testimonium*). His Pauline map is neither history nor ethics, but dogmatics, constructed via the creative collocation of 566 discrete data points. Once divided into testimonies, the letters as such recede and are of limited value. That is, Priscillian does not interpret Ephesians (or Romans, etc.) but *Paul*, and for that purpose, the decontextualized fragments stand on their own. Epistolary boundaries are thus effaced, and Paul is a book, quite literally, of 566 textual excerpts. The question, then, is not how Priscillian reads Ephesians (he does not), but how the Ephesians testimonies function for him: how frequently he uses them, what co-texts he places them alongside, and what work they do on a Priscillianist map?

To begin, a simple look at the data is telling (Tables 5 and 6).[24] Priscillian divides Ephesians into 41 testimonies, which he cites 96 times in defense of 45 canons.

Table 5. Priscillian's Use of Pauline *Testimonia* in his Canons

Pauline Letter	Number of *Testimonia*	Number of References in Canons	Number of Canons Represented
Romans	125	243	66
1 Corinthians	105	184	57
2 Corinthians	61	105	44
Galatians	38	72	27
Ephesians	41	96	45
Philippians	25	43	26
1 Thessalonians	22	45	26
2 Thessalonians	10	21	14
Colossians	34	74	43
1 Timothy	31	62	32
2 Timothy	26	49	25
Titus	15	26	17
Philemon	5	6	5
Hebrews	28	112	52
Total	566	1138	

[24] Tables 5 and 6 represent my own original work, collating data available in the Schepss edition (*Priscilliani*, 112–47, 169–74), as well as in de Bruyne, *Summaries, Divisions, and Rubrics*, 527–49. Table 4.1 now also appears in Lang and Crawford, 'Origins of Pauline Theology', 136.

Half of his canons, therefore, make some appeal to an Ephesians testimony, less only than Romans (66), 1 Corinthians (57), and Hebrews (52). Given their length, the total references for Romans (243), 1 Corinthians (184), and 2 Corinthians (105) are unsurprising, but adjusted for length, Priscillian cites Ephesians more frequently per testimony than any letter in the corpus, save Hebrews.[25] To compare Priscillian's Paul to the seven-letter Paul of modern criticism, he cites Ephesians more than Philippians, 1 Thessalonians, and Philemon combined (i.e. the non-*Hauptbriefe* undisputeds; 96 → 94), more frequently (96 → 72) and in defense of more canons (45 → 27) than Galatians, and for more canons than 2 Corinthians (45 → 44). As Table 4.1 makes clear, Ephesians is a pregnant source for Priscillian. This is still more apparent in the frequency with which Priscillian uses individual testimonies, catalogued by letter (Table 4.2).

Table 6. Number of *Testimonia* that Reach Certain Citation Thresholds in the Canons

Letter | Use	3+	4+	5+	6+	7+	8+	9+	14+
Romans	28	9	2	1	0	0	0	0
1 Corinthians	20	3	1	0	0	0	0	0
2 Corinthians	9	5	1	0	0	0	0	0
Galatians	7	2	1	1	1	0	0	0
Ephesians	11	7	3	2	1	0	0	0
Philippians	5	1	0	0	0	0	0	0
Colossians	12	4	0	0	0	0	0	0
1 Thessalonians	9	0	0	0	0	0	0	0
2 Thessalonians	3	2	0	0	0	0	0	0
1 Timothy	8	3	0	0	0	0	0	0
2 Timothy	7	5	1	1	0	0	0	0
Titus	3	1	0	0	0	0	0	0
Philemon	0	0	0	0	0	0	0	0
Hebrews	19	11	8	5	4	4	2	1
Total	141	53	17	10	6	4	2	1

Leaving aside Hebrews for a moment, the data for Ephesians vis-à-vis the rest of the corpus are striking: Ephesians contains seven (Eph 1.3–10 [2]; 2.1–3 [6]; 2.4–10 [7]; 3.1–5a [11]; 3.5b–8 [12]; 3.9–13 [13]; and 4.17–19 [22]) of Priscillian's 42 testimonies cited 4+ times;[26] three (1.3–10 [2]; 2.1–3 [6]; and 2.4–10 [7]) of his nine cited

---

[25] While the function of Hebrews in Priscillian's scheme is outside of my scope, it is worth noting that he divides Hebrews into far longer *testimonia* than the other letters (see Schepss, *Priscilliani*, 169–74), which may lead to its relative linguistic absence in the canons themselves. In the seven canons I worked on, Priscillian rarely draws his language from Hebrews.

[26] Only Romans with nine has more. The others are Rom 1.24–27 (9); 4.23–5.2 (34); 5.16–19 (38); 5.20–6.2 (39); 6.3–5 (40); 6.23 (47); 8.5–9 (54); 8.15–17 (59); 8.34–39 (68); 1 Cor 6.13–14 (33); 7.7–8 (37); 7.28–35 (43); 2 Cor 4.2–3 (22); 4.18–5.9 (29); 5.15–6.1 (32); 10.2–7 (46); 13.1–4 (60); Gal 2.15–3.7 (10); 5.16–21 (30); Phil 3.17–4.2 (20); Col 1.15–16 (5); 1.26–2 (10); 2.9–10 (16); 2.11–12

5+ times;[27] two (1.3-10 [2]; 2.1-3 [6]) of his five cited 6+ times;[28] and Eph 1.3-10 (2), with Gal 5.16-21 (30), is Priscillian's most frequently cited text, cited in seven canons. Put differently, Priscillian uses much of Eph 1-3 repeatedly across his canons, with the only other extended Pauline section that approaches this level of use being Rom 5-8.[29] Marry this to the overwhelming data from Hebrews, and the point is a simple one. If one comes to the collection not for the polemics of history but for a synthetic account of Pauline dogma, the least particular letters (Romans, Ephesians, and Hebrews) serve one well. For a project aimed at fragmenting, decontextualizing, and homogenizing Paul, Priscillian finds Ephesians a far more amenable source than Galatians or 2 Corinthians.

To be more specific still, when Priscillian synthesizes Paul's soteriology (Eph 1.3-10; 2.4-10), hamartiology (2.1-3), and biography (3.1-9), he repeatedly reaches for his Ephesians testimonies.[30] If one starts with these Ephesians testimonies, and traces them through the canons they buttress, one gets a near-complete picture of Priscillian's Pauline synthesis of the dogmatic loci in question. Ephesians 3.5b-9a (12), for instance, leads the reader to a set of canons (71, 73, and 75) on Paul's apostolic vocation,[31] which in turn key the reader to a comprehensive set of co-texts. In Canon 71, Priscillian juxtaposes Paul's trope of being the least of the apostles with his heavenly ascent in 2 Cor 12.1-6, which Priscillian takes as the context for Paul's receipt of his gospel. Together, 1 Cor 15.9-11 (82); 2 Cor 12.1-6 (54); Gal 1.11-20 (5-6); and Eph 3.1-9 (11-12) all speak to this. Canon 73 then fills this out by detailing the method and scope of Paul's apostolic vocation—Paul proclaims the gospel in lands hitherto unreached—leaning on Rom 15.19-24 (117); 1 Cor 1.14-17 (3); 2 Cor 2.11-13 (12); 4.2-4 (22); 10.16-11.2 (48); Gal 1.13-20 (6); and Eph 3.5-9 (12). Finally, Canon 75 specifies Paul as the *gentile* apostle, which entailed negotiation with the other apostles—so Rom 1.11-15 (4); 11.11-14 (86-87); 15.14-16 (115); Gal 1.21-2.14 (7-9); and Eph 3.1-9 (11-12). On the obvious point, Priscillian is a remarkably good collector of texts relevant to Pauline biography. And while Canons 41, 72, and 74 (cf. 76 and 78) fill out the picture, none of the textual data these canons add match the frequency with which Priscillian uses Eph 3.1-9 for his Pauline portraiture. In fact, in the three canons (71, 73, and 75) that narrate Paul's apostolic identity most robustly, Eph 3.5b-9a is the only shared link, while Eph 3.1-5a is present in two (71 and 75). A text (Eph 3.1-9) that modern scholars take to betray a pseudo-Paulinist's attempt at verisimilitude is, for Priscillian, quintessentially Pauline.[32]

---

(17); 2 Thess 1.1-6 (1); 2.12-17 (5); 1 Tim 1.5-7 (3); 4.1-2 (15); 5.4-15 (19); 2 Tim 1.8 (6); 2 Tim 1.8[sed]-14 (7); 2.23-26 (17); 3.1-9 (18); Tit 3.3-7 (12).

[27] The others are Rom 34 (4.23-5.2); 8.5-9 (54); 1 Cor 7.28-35 (43); 2 Cor 10.2-7 (46); Gal 5.16-21 (30); and 2 Tim 1.8 (6).

[28] The others are Rom 8.5-9 (54); Gal 5.16-21 (30); and 2 Tim 1.8 (6).

[29] Eight of the 34 testimonies that comprise Rom 5-8, for instance, are cited 4+ times (Test. 34, 38-40, 47, 54, 59, and 68) and another ten cited 3+ times (Test. 37, 41-43, 48, 50, 53, 55, 62, 64).

[30] Given the ease of locating the relevant canons in the Schepss (Latin) and Conti (English) editions, I do not cite page numbers in each below. The Latin/English text with accompanying textual references is at Schepss, *Priscilliani*, 109-47, and Conti, *Priscillian*, 164-209.

[31] It is also cited in Canon 10, on the inscrutability of God's ways (see Eph 3.8).

[32] For this judgment among modern interpreters, see my Chapter 5.

The same sort of argument can be made for Eph 2.1–3 (6), which draws the reader to a series of six canons (5, 22, 28, 29, 89, and 90) that depict Paul's view of sin and evil, and into dialogue with a host of Pauline co-texts.[33] In Canons 22, 28, and 29, for instance, Priscillian gathers texts that contain a set of terms (sin, death, desire, flesh, law, nature) that Paul reckons 'inimical to God' (29), 'adverse to holy will' (28), and that 'reduce the soul to slavery' (22). In Canons 89 and 90, on the other hand, resurrection reverses both the corruptibility of bodies (90) and all that is 'ephemeral', 'harmful', 'malicious', and 'foolish' in the world (89). Behind all of this, for Priscillian's Paul, lie the specious gods listed in Canon 5, which draws heavily on Eph 2.1–3 (6). In terms of quantity, Romans testimonies dominate Priscillian's dogmatic account of sin and evil, not least a series of texts across Rom 5–7. Moreover, any sketch of Priscillian's account would have to include Canons 6, 26, and 79 (cf. 32, 38, and 66). But what intrigues, again, is what a large number of texts Eph 2.1–3 can be drawn alongside and stand in for. As Priscillian has it, virtually all of Rom 5–7 is encapsulated in this more succinct testimony. Save Gal 5.16–21 (30), no text is cited more frequently on these topics than Eph 2.1–3 (6). As with Pauline biography, so also with humanity's plight: Priscillian calls time and again on Eph 2.1–3 as a quintessentially Pauline text.

Finally, what does Priscillian do with Eph 1.3–10 (2), his most oft-cited text in a thirteen-letter corpus? The case is more difficult here, in no small part because the text itself ranges so broadly. Tracing Eph 1.3–10 through the canons leads to dogmatic syntheses that range from theology proper (Canons 8, 9, and 10) to soteriology (Canons 15, 24, 25, and 78), or more specifically, the (in)scrutability of God generally, and his electing/salvific purposes specifically. The textual abutment is expansive and diverse. These canons call on every letter except 1 Thessalonians, 1 Timothy, and Philemon. Priscillian, moreover, does a variety of things with this textual base to construct his univocal Paul. He straightforwardly synthesizes broadly similar texts via shared lexemes (Canons 8, 10, 15 and 78);[34] he pairs diverse textual excerpts in a single canon to complement one another (Canon 9);[35] he orders his excerpts to allow one to exegete the other (Canon 24),[36] or for all to illuminate each other (Canon 10);[37]

---

[33] Rom 5.12–15 (37); 5.20–6.2 (39); 6.6–7.25 (41–51); 8.2–10a (53–55); 8.11–13 (57); 8.19–27 (61–64); 9.16–29 (74); 12.1–12 (92); 16.5–16 (122); 16.19–20 (124); 1 Cor 3.19–23 (18); 7.28–35 (43); 11.31–32 (70); 15.24–30 (88–89); 15.36–45 (93); 15.50–16.7 (95–99); 2 Cor 2.10 (11); 4.2–3 (22); 4.18–5.9 (29); 7.8–12 (38); 10.16–11.1 (48); 12.7–8 (55); Gal 1.2–5 (2); 5.16–21 (30); 6.7–10 (34); Eph 1.19b–23 (5); 2.4–10 (7); 6.10–11 (38); Col 2.13 (18); 1 Thess 2.13–3.5 (6–8); 2 Thess 1.1–10 (1–2); 2.12–17 (5); 1 Tim 2.11–15 (12); 6.13–16 (29); 2 Tim 1.8–14 (7); 2.20–26 (16–17); Titus 2.11–12 (9); 3.3–7 (12); Heb 6.4–7.28 (10–12); 10.35–11.34 (19).

[34] In Canon 8, via *omnis/universa*; in Canon 10, via *investigabilis/inscrutabilis/incomprehensibilis*; in Canon 15, via *mysterium*; and in Canon 78, via *baptismus/baptizo, lavacrum/lavo*.

[35] In Canon 9, e.g., Priscillian juxtaposes the language of Eph 1.3–10 (2) with Rom 1.20 (7) to suggest that humanity's relation to and knowledge of God is mediated both via divine gift (of *sapientia, gratia*, and *benedictio*) and the created order (*per ea quae facta*).

[36] In Canon 24, Priscillian begins with 1 Cor 2.7 (9) to make the basic point—God's *sapientia* is shrouded in a *mysterium* from eternity past (*ante saecula*) for our glory (*in gloriam nostram*)—before exegeting Paul's *nostram* by appeal to Eph 1.4 (2), namely, those *quos ante constitutionem mundi elegit*.

[37] Canon 10's testimonies all address the hiddenness of God's work, signaled by his use of *similiter*. Whether his *iudicia* or *viae*, the *divitiae Christi* or *multiformis sapientia*, God's action is *investigabilis, inscrutabilis*, and *incomprehensibilis*.

he follows the language of one almost entirely, using the others as support, and can blatantly read the program of one letter (Hebrews) over that of another (Romans; Canon 25).[38] All of these are Priscillian's responses to the problem of a variable corpus, and to heretics who twist Paul out of shape. In response, Priscillian simply twists Paul together using a variety of hermeneutical tools at his disposal.

What, though, of Eph 1.3–10 (2) in this twisting? Beyond his various means of synthesizing, Priscillian is consistently indebted to the language of Romans and, slightly less so, Ephesians. He draws together fragments from both to construct Canons 8, 9, and 10 (cf. 25), while using 1 Cor 2.1–7 (9) and Eph 1.3–10 to create Canon 24. Besides Canon 24, however, and possibly Canon 9, what Priscillian is not indebted to is the actual language of Eph 1.3–10, which is surprising given that it is his most oft-cited testimony. The manuscripts, however, tell another story. Here, the rubricated numbers of Canons 24 (at 1.3–4), 25 (at 1.4), 78 (at 1.6–7b), and 15 (at 1.7c–9) sit in the margin of Eph 1.3–10, signaling the importance of this text for these canons.[39] The sixty-four testimonies listed under the seven canons that cite Eph 1.3–10, it seems, are a diverse bunch, which Priscillian negotiates into seven sparsely worded canons. Priscillian may not gather these words from Eph 1.3–10, but he evidently thinks it supports the syntheses he creates. Or again, when one's project is to generalize Paul, it is hardly a surprise that the most generalized passage in the most general letter shows up time and again. Like Goodspeed's Pauline map, Priscillian's not only creates space for Eph 1.3–10, it privileges it.

Ephesians in Late-Antique Commentaries on Paul

Neither Euthalius nor Priscillian systematically reads *Ephesians*, however. So what do we find in Paul's late-antique commentators who do? How do they read Ephesians, and alongside what? What do they do with the 'inconsistency' that is the 'predictable result' of the shift from reading an individual letter to reading a corpus?[40] In short, what do they make of Ephesians, and how do they make it?[41] To answer, I turn first

---

[38] Both of these occur in Canon 25, which is Priscillian's dogmatic synthesis of Rom 9–11. As such, he follows his Romans *testimonia* almost exclusively, except at a key point: the source of unbelievers' hardening (*induratio*) is *sin* (*peccatum*), as Heb 3.13 (7) has it, rather than the work of God himself, as Paul depicts in Rom 11.7 and 25 (84 and 89).

[39] This is the case in both Codex Cavensis (C) and Theodulfianus (Θ).

[40] Mitchell, 'Variable and Many-sorted Man', 110.

[41] It will be useful to distinguish my purpose and method below from two other types of studies of Pauline reception and/in patristic exegesis. On the one hand, this is not a study of how each of the authors below negotiates Paul's thought/theology, either broadly or in Ephesians itself. Most important along these lines is Maurice F. Wiles, *The Divine Apostle: The Interpretation of St. Paul's Epistles in the Early Church* (London: Cambridge University Press, 1967), although see also, with narrower chronological focus, Lindemann, *Paulus im ältesten Christentum*; William S. Babcock, ed., *Paul and the Legacies of Paul* (Dallas: Southern Methodist University Press, 1990); Pervo, *Making of Paul*; Michael F. Bird and Joseph R. Dodson, eds., *Paul and the Second Century*, LNTS 412 (London: T&T Clark International, 2011); and now the volumes on Tertullian (2013), the Apostolic Fathers (2016) and Irenaeus (2020) in the *Pauline and Patristic Scholars in Debate* series edited by Todd D. Still and David E. Wilhite (New York: Bloomsbury T&T Clark). It is also not, on the other hand, a study of patristic exegesis per se. Here see, e.g., Karlfried Froehlich, trans. and ed., *Biblical Interpretation in the Early Church* (Philadelphia: Fortress, 1984); Manlio Simonetti, *Biblical Interpretation in*

to the Greek commentaries, and to the golden-mouthed rhetor of Antioch, John Chrysostom.[42]

John Chrysostom (Fl. ca. 349–407 CE)

In the previous chapter, we saw Chrysostom refer to Paul's corpus as a book, and show awareness of its arrangement. As far as I can tell, the latter never impinges on his reading of Ephesians, nor on the other hand does his chronological interest lead him to read development in Ephesians.[43] The book itself, however, does impinge. For Chrysostom, as with Paul's other late-antique readers, the collection's priority poses the problem of Paul's variability particularly starkly, for difference must be interpreted within rather than excised from the corpus.[44] And Chrysostom recognizes this variability, that is, how hermeneutically supple the collection is: 'Those who are battling with one another', he writes, 'all use [Paul]'. Like Priscillian's opponents, Chrysostom's heretics 'cut up' (κατατέμνειν) Paul, excerpting his letters and reading the resultant fragments out of context.[45] Also like Priscillian, however, Chrysostom responds in kind, excerpting the letters (and Scripture as a whole) and using these newly constructed fragments to underpin his reading of a given passage. In just the first three verses of Eph 1, for instance, Chrysostom cites twenty scriptural co-texts.[46] His pace slows down, but his homilies feel in many places like a catena of Pauline (and scriptural) fragments.

What work does this do for Chrysostom? In places, his concatenation of texts resembles free association—a window into Chrysostom's creativity, to be sure, but little more. Elsewhere, though, Chrysostom collocates texts in Paul to allow one to interpret another.[47] When he arrives at the 'gift given to each one of us' (ἑνὶ δὲ ἑκάστῳ ἡμῶν ἐδόθη ἡ χάρις) in Eph 4.7, for instance, he calls up Paul's more expansive discussion of χαρίσματα in 1 Cor 12, thinking the Ephesians faced a similar challenge

---

the Early Church: An Historical Introduction to Patristic Exegesis (Edinburgh: T. & T. Clark, 1993); and Charles Kannengieser, *Handbook of Patristic Exegesis*, 2 vols., Bible in Ancient Christianity 1 (Leiden: Brill, 2004). In what follows, my interest lies closest to that of Frances Young, *Biblical Exegesis and the Formation of Christian Culture* (Cambridge: Cambridge University Press, 1997), who identifies the actual exegetical practices that patristic exegetes share in common, and which she roots in the grammatical and rhetorical schools. It is these raw mechanics of interpretation, including such paratextual features as ὑποθέσεις/*argumenta*, that I attend to below for how they help situate Ephesians vis-à-vis the other letters.

[42] For still useful overview, see Turner, 'Greek Patristic Commentaries', 484–531. The Greek authors treated below are at 490–6 (Origen), 501–7 (Chrysostom), 508–12 (Theodore), and 516–17 (Theodoret).

[43] Chrysostom thinks Paul wrote Ephesians from Rome. See his *Hom. Eph.* Arg (PG 62:9).

[44] Mitchell, 'Variable and Many-sorted Man', 110–11, makes the same point, and with respect to synthesizing Paul's letters with Acts as well.

[45] *Hom. 2 Cor* 21.4 (PG 61:545). Trans. and discussion in Mitchell, 'Variable and Many-sorted Man', 97. My numbering for the homilies here and below follows the critical edition of Frederick Field, *Interpretatio omnium epistolarum paulinarum*, 7 vols. (Oxford: Academiae Typus, 1845–62), with homily number followed by paragraph number.

[46] Chrysostom, *Hom. Eph.* 1.1 (PG 62:9–11).

[47] Countless examples could be listed here. Beside the two discussed in the body of the text, see, e.g., Chrysostom's exegesis at Eph 1.11 (vis-à-vis Rom 8.28–30) and 6.13 (vis-à-vis Gal 1.4) in *Hom. Eph.* 2.1 (PG 62:17) and 22.3 (PG 62:159).

as the fractious Corinthians.⁴⁸ Nothing in Ephesians suggests this, but it gives Chrysostom interpretive purchase on the otherwise terse and uninterpreted χάρις of Eph 4.7.⁴⁹ Faced a few verses later with the obscure christological exegesis of Ps 68.19 in Eph 4.9–10, Chrysostom appeals to Phil 2.5–8 to see here an example of humility: 'That very argument', he writes, '[Paul] is also insisting on here'—thus reducing the christological claim of Eph 4 to the ethical exhortation of Phil 2.⁵⁰ In both instances, Chrysostom reads an opaque text in Ephesians towards a more limpid Pauline co-text,⁵¹ not a little ironic since Chrysostom argues in his *hypothesis* to Ephesians for the letter's essential clarity vis-à-vis the others.⁵²

In places, however, difference forces itself upon Chrysostom and cannot be ignored, and in a few of the clearest examples, he seems to prefer the articulation of Ephesians to that of Romans.⁵³ In his exposition of Eph 2.11–3.13 across *Homilies* 5 and 6, for instance, Chrysostom clarifies relentlessly the newness of the Jew/gentile entity that results from God's creative act.⁵⁴ The product is a genuine *tertium quid*. The problem arises in that elsewhere Paul speaks more weakly of a 'grafting in'—a clear allusion to Rom 11, although Chrysostom never says so.⁵⁵ Chrysostom, of course, is not about to jettison Romans. Both belong to Paul, but he never resolves the issue. He names the disparity and moves along, perhaps one of the conveniences of his genre, although he hardly veils his preference. Later, however, in *Homily* 13, Chrysostom explicitly privileges Ephesians when faced with a variable Romans co-text. Ephesians 4.19 is clear enough: the gentiles 'gave themselves up' (οἵτινες … ἑαυτοὺς παρέδωκαν) to immorality of every stripe. The problem is that in Rom 1.26, Paul says that '*God* gave them up' (παρέδωκεν αὐτοὺς ὁ θεός). Which one is it? Really, the former: 'Whenever then you hear that "God gave them up to a debased mind"', Chrysostom writes, '*remember this expression*, that "they gave themselves up"'.⁵⁶ Read Romans in light of

---

⁴⁸ 'For', Chrysostom writes, 'this subject was continually carrying away both the Ephesians themselves, and the Corinthians' (*Hom. Eph.* 11.1 [PG 62:80–81; *NPNF*¹ 13:103]).

⁴⁹ '[Paul] enters indeed into the subject more fully in the Epistle to the Corinthians, because it was among them that this malady most especially reigned: here however he has only alluded to it' (*Hom. Eph.* 11.1 [PG 62:80–81; *NPNF*¹ 13:103]).

⁵⁰ *Hom. Eph.* 11.2 (PG 62:81 [*NPNF*¹ 13:103]).

⁵¹ See also *Hom. Eph.* 18.3 (PG 62:124–25), in which Chrysostom uses Rom 1.25 to explain the ambiguous πλεονέκτης, ὅ ἐστιν εἰδωλολάτρης of Eph 5.5.

⁵² 'Thoughts which he scarcely so much as utters anywhere else, he here plainly declares' (*Hom. Eph.* Arg. (PG 62:9–10; *NPNF*¹ 13:49]). Chrysostom then lists Eph 2.6; 3.5; and 3.10 as three such instances. In fact, though, when Chrysostom reaches 3.8–11 in *Homily* 7, he directs the reader to Romans, for Paul unfolds the nature of the οἰκονομία (3.9) more clearly there (*Hom. Eph.* 7.1 [PG 62:50]).

⁵³ Mitchell calls Chrysostom 'boldly honest in bringing apparent contradictions to the attention of his hearers' ('Variable and Many-sorted Man', 98). For the rhetorical background of Chrysostom's attempts to adjudicate perceived differences in the corpus, see Mitchell, 'Variable and Many-sorted Man', 98–104.

⁵⁴ See especially on 2.14–15 in *Hom. Eph.* 5.2–3 (PG 62:38–40). His comment on 2.15 (ἵνα τοὺς δύο κτίσῃ ἐν αὐτῷ ἕνα καινὸν ἄνθρωπον) is representative: 'Observe that it is not that the Gentile has become a Jew, but that both the one and the other enter into another condition. It was not with a view of merely making [the Gentile] other than he was, but rather, in order to create the two anew' (*Hom. Eph.* 5.3 [PG 62:40; *NPNF*¹ 13:72]).

⁵⁵ *Hom. Eph.* 6.1 (PG 62:44).

⁵⁶ *Hom. Eph.* 13.1 (PG 62:93; *NPNF*¹ 13:112). Emphasis mine.

Ephesians, Chrysostom encourages his auditors. In the end, however, Chrysostom cannot admit an outright contradiction, so via a questionable bit of lexical work—παρέδωκεν actually means συγκεχώρηκεν ('he permitted to be given')—Chrysostom avoids the troubling conclusion that his textual juxtaposition suggests.

Chrysostom may regard Ephesians as Paul's 'profoundest conceptions', but little in the *Homilies* bears this out. Instead, what stands out is the degree to which Paul is, for Chrysostom (à la Priscillian), a series of decontextualized excerpts. To this point, I have written as if Chrysostom cites Pauline co-texts by chapter and verse, but this is only for my reader's convenience. Chrysostom himself does not have this luxury,[57] so instead he strings together textual fragments, and only rarely introduces a citation by letter. In this way, he subsumes all of his fragments under the banner of a singular personage. The boundary between letters is thus virtually non-existent. The reader does not meet the Paul of Romans (or Corinthians, et al.), but simply Paul. Paul says certain things here, there, and elsewhere, but the frame is always Paul, the product of all his textual parts. This neither privileges nor relativizes Ephesians. It is just to say, to steal one of Paul's own images, that Paul is circumscribed within his corpus, of which Ephesians is a member.

Theodore of Mopsuestia (Fl. 350–428 CE)

In Theodore, we return to a form of interpretation that feels somewhat more familiar, and that retains a stronger focus on the individual letter as such.[58] After two pages adjudicating the John/Paul question vis-à-vis Ephesians, for instance, Theodore admits that the result is hermeneutically profitless, and promises instead a close philological and narrative reading of the letter.

> More attention must be paid to a detailed interpretation by which it is possible for us to discern the wisdom of the apostle's meaning.... This letter plainly also poses great difficulty in its language, so that it is not easy for someone who wishes to interpret it to make its meaning clear. For this reason I have thought it best not only to supply a general interpretation but also to explain the obscure words where the text requires me to do this. For in this way it will be clear to everyone who wants to analyze this scripture how the meaning of the apostle's understanding can be kept clear. I think this is to be honored before everything else.[59]

The letter here *is* the primary unit of meaning, and the focus of Theodore's interpretation. Meaning derives from a close reading of the language and structural form of

---

[57] This point is obscured (helpfully) in the *NPNF*[1] translation, which cites modern chapter and verse in parentheses behind each quotation.

[58] Only Theodore's work on the minor epistles (excluding Romans; 1–2 Corinthians; and Hebrews) remains, and only in Latin translation, with Greek fragments extant. The critical edition is Henry B. Swete, ed., *Theodori episcopi Mopsuesteni In epistolas b. Pauli commentarii*, 2 vols. (Cambridge: Cambridge University Press, 1880–82), with introduction at 1:ix–lxxxvii. English translation, with facing Latin (and Greek) text and briefer introduction is in Theodore, *Minor Epistles*.

[59] Theodore, *Minor Epistles*, 179.

the text itself, in concert with a subordinate concern for the historical occasion.[60] And this leads to Theodore's succinct statement of the letter's *argumentum*, which is more epistolary summary than critical prolegomena: 'the teaching of those good things [*bonorum*] plainly bestowed on us by Christ's coming and expounded in the form of a thanksgiving is the proof of the doctrines [*dogmatis*], while it also unfolds the exhortation of what pertains to virtue (*virtutem*)'.[61] Written to a community unknown to him, Ephesians is Paul's account of the christological goods that belong to believers, first laying the groundwork of doctrine (Eph 1–3), on which the ethics of Eph 4–6 rest. In all of this, Ephesians is like Romans (and Colossians), a point Theodore argues across his preface. They share a setting (unknown auditors), subject matter (Christ's gifts), and structure (doctrine/ethics).[62] Even Romans, however, involves some polemic, with Paul engaged in a careful argument against both gentile and Jewish interlocutors. Ephesians, on the other hand, takes the form of a thanksgiving, loose and overflowing.[63] Sixteen hundred years before Dahl, Theodore thus anticipates his conclusion: Ephesians is a general thanksgiving for Christ's gifts written to a group of Christ-followers of whom Paul just became aware.

For Dahl, of course, this lacks a certain particularity he expects of Paul. The letter is too 'utopisches'.[64] What, though, of a different era, where the problem is not generality but particularity? As one might expect, Theodore's judgment is quite different. The problem for Theodore, in fact, is not a letter like Ephesians, but one like Philemon. Theodore's preface to Philemon is his longest, taken up with the question of why this brief, personal, and seemingly private letter ought to be read to begin with.[65] Theodore's first reply, a non sequitur from a modern point of view, emphasizes its necessity for Paul's collection to be complete: 'All the letters of Paul are fourteen in number'. In response to the problem of particularity, Theodore posits the catholicity of the corpus. He goes on, however, to distinguish between Paul's personal and church letters, and it is the latter in particular that address all. Theodore clearly privileges the church letters for the ongoing life of the church: 'Indeed, we are both provided with doctrines [*dogmata*] set forth in them with exactness and are taught by them the practice of a right way of life [*rectae institutum*]. For anyone will find both of these things written in all the letters more or less fully expounded.'[66] All the letters may

---

[60] On Theodore's exegesis, see Swete, *Theodori episcopi Mopsuesteni*, 1:lxv–lxxi; Greer, 'Introduction', in *Minor Epistles*, xiii–xx; and Simonetti, *Biblical Interpretation*, 69–74. Both Swete (1:lxvii–lxix) and Greer (xiv–xx) highlight Theodore's concern for the logical sequence/narrative form (*historiam*) of the text, with a secondary interest in history, particular in his ὑποθέσεις. On the use of ὑποθέσεις in Antiochene exegesis, see Frances Young, 'The Rhetorical Schools and Their Influence on Patristic Exegesis', in *The Making of Orthodoxy: Essays in Honour of Henry Chadwick*, ed. Rowan Williams (Cambridge: Cambridge University Press, 1989), 190–1; and idem, *Biblical Exegesis*, 173–5.
[61] Theodore, *Minor Epistles*, 175.
[62] See Theodore, *Minor Epistles*, 171–3. His programmatic statement of how Paul writes to a community he does not know is in his *argumentum* to Colossians (*Minor Epistles*, 363).
[63] Theodore, *Minor Epistles*, 171–3.
[64] Dahl, 'Einleitungsfragen', 80–1.
[65] The question is posed this way by a certain Cyrinus for whom Theodore writes the commentary (*Minor Epistles*, 773). The full prologue runs from 773–85.
[66] The portion of Theodore's response that I summarize and cite above is at *Minor Epistles*, 775.

contain such help, but not equally. Theodore's language here hews more closely to his description of Ephesians' central purpose quoted above than of any other letter. For Theodore, all the letters offer doctrine and ethics, but Ephesians does this principally, untrammeled by particularity. The very thing which gave Dahl pause makes Ephesians uniquely attractive to Theodore.[67]

This does not mean Theodore uses it as a gateway into the collection. Given his concern for the integrity of each letter, he does not cite Pauline co-texts frequently. That said, his Paul is a more univocal figure than Chrysostom's. Theodore never draws attention to difference in his Ephesians commentary, and this has a harmonizing effect not least on the letter's eschatology. Despite the clear tense (aorist) of the main verbs in Eph 1.3–6, Theodore reads the εὐλογία πνευματική of 1.3 as future, partly by appeal to 1 Cor 15.42–44 and Paul's distinction there between the present and future bodies of believers.[68] Rather than admit difference, or the incongruity of his comparison, Theodore reads the logic of 1 Corinthians over that of Ephesians, assimilating the latter thereto. Elsewhere, however, Theodore's futurist impulse, and the co-texts he cites toward this end, reveal a point strangely missed by much modern scholarship—that Ephesians contains its *own* future eschatology.[69] For Theodore, Paul's reference to believers' being sealed (σφραγίζω) by τό πνεῦμα τῆς ἐπαγγελίας ὁ ἅγιος has both a present and a future logic, which he elicits by appeal to Rom 8.23, where the Spirit is the firstfruit (ἀπαρχή) of the eschatological 'redemption of our bodies' (ἡ ἀπολύτρωσις τοῦ σώματος ἡμῶν). This leads Theodore back to Eph 1.14a, where the Spirit's sealing is the 'pledge of our inheritance' (ἀρραβὼν τῆς κληρονομίας ἡμῶν), which Theodore reads as a reference to the same event as Rom 8.23. Weaving exegesis of Rom 8.23 and Eph 1.13–14 together, Theodore draws out the interplay of present and future in both.[70]

Vis-à-vis Ephesians' eschatology, then, in places Theodore's co-texts obscure and in others they illuminate. The book as such does not feature explicitly in Theodore's exegesis, but as his preface to Philemon makes clear, it does signal the hermeneutical boundaries of what counts for Paul. The letters are fourteen. More important, however, is what Theodore expects from this book. By focusing on what all the letters contain, Theodore privileges generality over particularity. Again, it is telling that Philemon provokes Theodore's lengthiest prologue. A general letter of thanksgiving, on the other hand, needs no apology. It works quite well given Theodore's own hermeneutical priorities.

---

[67] The same is true in reverse vis-à-vis Philemon. Different presuppositions about what makes for an acceptable Pauline letter dictate which letters requires special querying.

[68] Here at 1.3, Theodore writes, 'It is just as [Paul] plainly said in the letter he wrote to the Corinthians in his argument about the resurrection' (*Minor Epistles*, 185). For another instance, see his comments on Eph 1.22b–23, where he cites 1 Cor 12.13 (pp. 209–11).

[69] This is most stark in Lindemann, *Die Aufhebung der Zeit*, but see also, e.g., Gnilka, *Epheserbrief*, 122–28; and Muddiman, *Ephesians*, 108–9. Lincoln, *Ephesians*, 105–9, is better, although his continued use of the language of 'realised eschatology' obscures what is actually an *ecclesiological* claim in Eph 2.6.

[70] Theodore, *Minor Epistles*, 201–3.

Theodoret of Cyrus (Fl. 393–457 CE)

Theodoret's interpretive focus, on the other hand, is more limited, evident not least in the modest size of his Ephesians commentary—a mere twenty-six (Greek) columns in Migne, as opposed to the eighty-four of Chrysostom's homilies and the eighty-five pages for Theodore in Swete's edition.[71] This is both intentional—Theodoret values brevity for his readers—and a function of his labors: he is the first Greek to write a single volume on the entire series of letters.[72] Theodoret's comments on individual lemma, then, are largely paraphrase, and not terribly involved. But his scope and arrangement—all fourteen letters in canonical order—do have one vital effect: Theodoret comes at Ephesians immediately in the wake of writing on Romans, Corinthians, and Galatians, which in many respects makes itself felt more acutely than does his posited setting for the letter itself.[73] That is, Theodoret's own compositional setting, writing on the letters in quick succession, closes down the historical space he otherwise opens up between Paul's myriad compositional settings.[74] Despite placing Ephesians at the very end of Paul's life, Theodoret never appeals to development in Ephesians. The fourteen letters are rather equal and alternative points of access to Paul.

This does not mean that Theodoret cites other textual data frequently. When he does, however, he typically draws these co-texts from Paul's letters. Such collocations can draw relatively straightforward connections: the 'fullness of the times' in Eph 1.10 echoes the same in Gal 4.4; the promise for the gentiles (Eph 3.7) is that which belongs to Israel (Rom 9.4); and Paul's exhortation to grow in love (Eph 4.15) appears also in Rom 12.9 and 2 Cor 6.6.[75] But Theodoret can also interpret the ambiguous in Ephesians by appeal to clearer texts elsewhere in Paul. Like Theodore, Theodoret appeals to texts in Corinthians (now 1 Cor 13.12 and 2 Cor 5.7), with their sense of delayed expectation, to draw out the same future hope in Eph 2.7, and cements this with an appeal to 2 Tim 2.11–12.[76] Elsewhere, Theodoret uses two terse excerpts from Romans to describe the problem (8.22) and anticipation (8.19) to which the ἀνακεφαλαίωσις of Eph 1.10 is the answer, drawing Heb 2.19 alongside as a parallel.[77] Theodoret offers here a sort of Pauline soteriology by textual excerpt, and one deeply indebted to Ephesians for its culmination. Lastly, Theodoret's project, with its interpretive gaze on the collection, can ride roughshod over real variability in the letters. As does Chrysostom, Theodoret reads the παρέδωκεν of Rom 1.26 as divine consent (συγχώρησις), since Paul teaches clearly in Eph 4.19 that the gentiles hand *themselves*

---

[71] Compare Theodoret, *Interpr. XIV Epist. S. Pauli Apostoli* (PG 82:505–58) with Chrysostom, *Hom. Eph.* (PG 62:9–176) and Theodore, *Comm. Eph* (Swete, *Theodori episcopi Mopsuesteni*, 1:112–96).

[72] On Theodoret's brevity, see his *Letters of St. Paul*, 1:36, and Hill's discussion at 1:5–7, 13–15.

[73] Which is late in Paul's life, from a Roman imprisonment (*Letters of St. Paul*, 2:33).

[74] For the dating of Theodoret's commentary, see Hill, 'Introduction', in *Letters of St. Paul*, 1:1–2, who places the whole set within a few years in the mid-440s, although a decade earlier is possible.

[75] See Theodoret, *Letters of St. Paul*, 2:34, 42–3, 47 (PG 82:512b, 528b, 536d–537a). In each, Theodoret links Ephesians to its co-text by some variation of a simple introductory formula ('As Paul says in his letter to...'), which gives the impression of sameness: what Paul says here, he also says there.

[76] Theodoret, *Letters of St. Paul*, 2:39 (PG 82:520d–521a).

[77] Theodoret, *Letters of St. Paul*, 2:34 (PG 82:512b-c). In other words, 'All creation needed the remedy of the Incarnation', Theodoret writes, and Eph 1.10 describes that remedy.

over to impurity.⁷⁸ Romans here succumbs to the force of Ephesians. Elsewhere, Theodoret assimilates Ephesians to 1 Corinthians, quoting three clipped fragments of 15.26–28 to explain Paul's words at Eph 1.22–23. Theodoret writes, 'His teaching was similar, remember, in the letter to the Corinthians, where he says, "The last enemy destroyed is death", and "He put all things under his feet", and at the end he said, "So that God may be all in all"'.⁷⁹ If this was all Paul says in 1 Cor 15, Theodoret's collocation would hold. The problem, of course, as Origen and Jerome already noticed, is that the final subjection of all things in 1 Cor 15 is undeniably future, while Eph 1.22–23 on its own leaves no hint that this subjection is anything but a full and final reality now.⁸⁰ The parallel depends on Theodoret's careful excerpting of these (and only these) texts from 1 Cor 15. Like Priscillian, Theodoret's textual fragmentation and juxtaposition homogenizes Paul.

In large part, the scope of Theodoret's project explains this harmonizing impulse. It is much easier to admit difference if one has been disciplinarily trained to read each letter on its own terms—still more, as a discrete and in principle separable element entirely. If, on the other hand, Theodoret's knowledge of Paul comes via the collection, then its rough edges of difference represent an ever-present problem in need of smoothing. The project's scope also explains, in part, Theodoret's provenance for Ephesians, the critical data for which is the shared reference to Tychicus in Eph 6.21–22 and 2 Tim 4.12. Again, in modern terms, Theodoret's data is suspect, but if the collection is prior, then his setting is probably the most cogent one available. Where one begins—with the discrete letter or the book—is a hermeneutical choice of real consequence. Baur displaces Ephesians by driving a wedge between Paul and the disputeds/Acts; Theodoret places Ephesians by synthesizing those very same data. As Theodoret shows, one can do textual archaeology and chronology and not displace Ephesians. The modern wedge between Paul and Ephesians depends not on historical study per se, then, but on the particular historical stories modern scholarship tells, and how it uses Paul's corpus to tell them. Theodoret's commitment to the collection closes down that space.

Marius Victorinus (Fl. 290–364 CE)

In Gaius Marius Victorinus, we come to the head and probably most sophisticated representative of Latin exegesis of Paul.⁸¹ By 354 Rome's own teacher of rhetoric, and a senator with a statue in Trajan's forum, Victorinus shortly thereafter converted to

---

⁷⁸ See Theodoret, *Interpr. XIV Epist. S. Pauli Apostoli* (PG 82:540a), where he writes at Eph 4.19 vis-à-vis Rom 1.26, Ἐνταῦθα γὰρ σαφῶς ἐδίδαξεν ὡς ἑαυτοὺς παρέδωκαν τῇ ἀσελγείᾳ. Hill seems to have missed this line in his translation (*Letters of St. Paul*, 2:48), which makes it appear as if Theodoret allows the difference to go uncommented on. In fact, Theodoret reads Romans towards Ephesians here.
⁷⁹ Theodoret, *Letters of St. Paul*, 2:38 (PG 82:517b-d).
⁸⁰ I discuss Origen and Jerome's solution to this below (Heine, *Ephesians*, 115).
⁸¹ Alexander Souter, *The Earliest Latin Commentaries on the Epistles of St. Paul* (Oxford: Clarendon, 1927), introduces the major figures, with Victorinus at pp. 8–38. On Victorinus as the head of this resurgence, see Bernard Lohse, 'Beobachtungen zum Paulus-Kommentar des Marius Victorinus und zur Wiederentdeckung des Paulus in der lateinischen Theologie des vierten Jahrhunderts', in *Kerygma und Logos*, ed. A. M. Ritter (Göttingen: Vandenhoeck & Ruprecht, 1979), 351–66, although the notion of a 'rediscovery' has been rightly questioned.

Christianity, penned a series of Trinitarian treatises in the late-350s, and turned his attention to Paul shortly afterward (mid-360s).[82] In doing so, he applied to his study of Paul a principle he learned from his work on Cicero (*Inv.* 2.117), to interpret *Paulum ex Paulo*.[83] For Victorinus, this entails not just restricting his co-texts nearly exclusively to Paul's letters, which drew Jerome's derision, but also setting out to write on all the letters in their canonical order.[84] As Stephen Cooper writes, Victorinus's project bespeaks 'an intensive focus on the Pauline corpus as an integral whole'.[85]

As we have seen repeatedly, however, such a project does not fail to attend to the individual letter, and Victorinus's interpretive attention focuses largely here.[86] To look ahead, then, what intrigues in Victorinus is not that he exhaustively reads Ephesians alongside Paul's letters, but rather what he expects and rewards in a letter, and which Ephesians clearly contains. Victorinus begins the prologue to his Ephesians commentary, for instance, this way: 'The letter to the Ephesians contains the chief point [*summam*] which must always characterize the whole teaching [*totius disciplinae*]'.[87] He then immediately explicates this chief point (*summa*) as a double knowledge, both theological (*theologiae*) and ethical (*ad praecepta vivendi*), which corresponds to the letter's two halves, and then specifies each of these further in the most general terms. The theological knowledge that Ephesians offers is 'knowledge of God and Christ, of his mystery and advent', while its ethics are both general (pertaining to all Christians), and particular (pertaining to master/slave, father/son, and husband/wife).[88] In his first two sentences, then, Victorinus casts the Paul of Ephesians as the purveyor of complete knowledge—a total philosophy that pervades the letter from front to back.[89] More interesting still, Victorinus associates this with Paul's *summa* in writing, in contrast to Galatians, where Victorinus ties the letter's *summa* more closely to its historical occasion.[90] For Victorinus, Paul's purpose in writing the Ephesians

---

[82] Biographically, our meager access is through Jerome, *Vir. ill.* 101, and Augustine, *Conf.* 8.2.3–4. Cooper, *Galatians*, has biography (16–40), with lengthy introduction to the Pauline commentaries at pp. 88–248. See also Stephen Andrew Cooper, *Metaphysics and Morals in Marius Victorinus's Commentary on the Letter to the Ephesians: A Contribution to the History of Neoplatonism and Christianity*, AUS 5/155 (New York: Peter Lang, 1995), 1–42.

[83] Victorinus wrote a commentary on Cicero's *De inventione rhetorica*. See his comments on the relevant section in Cicero (*Inv.* 2.117) in Cooper, *Galatians*, 107–8. I discuss the hermeneutical principle, with bibliography, in Chapter 3 (n. 10).

[84] Cooper calls this focus on the corpus a 'notable departure from the tradition of Christian commentary' that precedes him (*Galatians*, 109; cf. 105–10). Cooper cites only Origen in defense, but be that as it may, as we saw in Chapter 3, it is not unique from the tradition that *post-dates* him, which is the period of my study. On Jerome's derision of Victorinus's lack of scriptural knowledge, see his *Comm. Gal.* 1.Prol.

[85] Cooper, *Galatians*, 107.

[86] Cooper, *Galatians*, 88–100 (cf. 114–16) argues that Victorinus's theory of *interpretatio* focuses on the text itself (88), while his actual method is akin to paraphrase (101), indebted to the grammatical and rhetorical schools. Cf. Souter, *Latin Commentaries*, 21–7.

[87] The critical edition is *Marii Victorini opera pars II opera exegetica*, ed. Franco Gori, CSEL 83/2 (Vienna: Hoelder-Pichler-Tempsky, 1986), with Latin text cited from here. Throughout, I follow the English translation of Cooper, *Metaphysics and Morals*, 43–114, with valuable analysis at 115–232.

[88] Cooper, *Metaphysics and Morals*, 43.

[89] See Cooper, *Metaphysics and Morals*, 115–17, with particular reference to Cicero's similar concern for the union of theoretical and practical knowledge (115).

[90] Compare here the first paragraph of each preface in Gori, *Marii Victorini*, 1 (Ephesians) and 95 (Galatians); Eng. trans. in Cooper, *Metaphysics and Morals*, 43, and idem, *Galatians*, 249.

is the pure explication of knowledge. This is vital, for identifying a letter's *summa* provides the reader a hermeneutical governor, regulating all subsequent exegesis.[91] To be sure, Victorinus parrots his Old Latin prologue to suggest an anti-Judaizing strand in Ephesians, but by 1.23 he abandons it and never returns.[92] Instead, his subsequent exegesis tends to conform to his account of Paul's most general purpose in writing.

For Victorinus, Paul relays this theological knowledge most transparently in Eph 1.4–23. At 1.4, Victorinus offers his Neoplatonically informed paraphrase of the following section, linking it explicitly to Paul's *summa*: all things were made by Christ; preexistent souls entered the world and were freed from it; Christ is now reconciling all things back to God in himself so that all might be one.[93] Ephesians 1.4–23, in other words, offers a window into the heart of Paul's theological knowledge—a condensed form of what we meet elsewhere in the other letters. Just before this, in fact, Victorinus offers another summary of the passage, now under the heading of Paul's *mysterium*. He writes,

> This is a discourse about divinity and a short explanation of the whole mystery, in which the following is established: that Christ existed before the world; that the world has been made; that there were souls before the world; that the world exists by God's dispensation; that souls both came into the world and are being freed from the world by God's dispensation; and all that is done is the will of God; and that for those living in accordance with Christ there is a reward so that sins may be forgiven and we may participate in the glory of God. *This we have also dealt with in Paul's other letters.*[94]

Victorinus then explicates the *summa* in nearly identical terms (see above), calling it the source of this mystery. The point is this: Victorinus's account of Eph 1 evokes for him a set of themes that pervade the other letters, but here in Ephesians, these themes are the letter's *summa*—its chief point. Like Priscillian and Goodspeed, Victorinus sees in Eph 1 an apt summary of Paul's theological knowledge—which he variably calls Paul's *summa*, *mysterium*, and a *magnificum argumentum* ('weighty argument').

This brings us close to Theodore's conception in the East—Ephesians as the most general of letters—albeit a generation earlier. Victorinus's claim, however, goes one step further. Ephesians offers not just christological goods but total knowledge, canvassing both theology and ethics. Again, in a scholarly age whose interpretive slogan is that Paul is *not* a systematic theologian, this may seem hopelessly naive,

---

[91] So Cooper, *Galatians*, 94–5, referencing the work of Pierre Hadot, *Marius Victorinus: Recherches sur sa vie et ses œuvres* (Paris: Études augustiniennes, 1971).

[92] In addition to the preface, see Victorinus's commentary at 1.1–2 and 23, and the oblique reference at 2.5 (Cooper, *Metaphysics and Morals*, 45, 63, and 66).

[93] Cooper, *Metaphysics and Morals*, 47, with Victorinus's Neoplatonism discussed at 15–22; cf. Stephen Cooper, 'Philosophical Exegesis in Marius Victorinus's Commentaries on Paul', in *Interpreting the Bible and Aristotle in Late Antiquity: The Alexandrian Commentary Tradition between Rome and Baghdad*, ed. Josef Lössl and John W. Watt (Farnham, Surrey, UK: Ashgate, 2011), 67–89.

[94] Gori, *Marii Victorini*, 6. Eng. trans. Cooper, *Metaphysics and Morals*, 46–7. Emphasis mine.

or confirm its own bias against the letter. But Victorinus is not a modern critic, nor beholden to its interpretive priorities, and so Ephesians' generality is not a problem to be solved in the first place.

Ambrosiaster

If Victorinus's philosophically inclined exegesis feels foreign to modern readings of Paul, the Pauline exegesis of the anonymous Latin commentator Ambrosiaster feels more familiar. In the opening line of his Romans commentary, he programmatically connects meaning and textual origins, and this bears itself out in his perceptive reading of the social dimension of Paul's arguments vis-à-vis Jews and gentiles across his commentaries.[95] That said, in the scope of his work, Ambrosiaster is distinctively late antique. By the mid-380s, within two decades of Victorinus's work, Ambrosiaster provides the first extant commentary in Latin or Greek on the corpus in its entirety.[96] This scope, however, is not immediately felt: Ambrosiaster does not write a prologue to the corpus, and never comments on its arrangement. His interpretive focus is largely the individual letter, with short prologues (*argumenta*) to each followed by concise running commentary.[97] Moreover, Ambrosiaster's *non*-Pauline scriptural citations in his work on Ephesians, concentrated in the Psalms, Matthew, John, and Acts, outnumber his citation of *Pauline* co-texts,[98] and where he does cite Paul's letters, he is not reticent to acknowledge difference (on both, see below).[99] The collection is neither impermeable nor univocal. In both of these cases, Ambrosiaster's practice recalls that of Paul's modern critics, and so poses the authorship question particularly starkly: what allows Ambrosiaster to retain Ephesians where moderns displace it?

---

[95] Ambrosiaster writes, 'In order to have an understanding of things, one needs to grasp their origins' (In Rom. Arg. 1). On the sociological makeup of the Roman church, see his In Rom. Arg. 2–3 (*Ambrosiaster's Commentary: Romans*, 3–4).

[96] The critical edition is *Ambrosiastri qui dicitur Commentarius in Epistulas Paulinas*, ed. H. J. Vogels, 3 vols., CSEL 81 (Vienna: Hoelder-Pichler-Tempsky, 1966–69). Eng. trans. Ambrosiaster, *Commentaries on Romans and 1–2 Corinthians*; and idem, *Commentaries on Galatians–Philemon*, trans. and ed. Gerald Bray, Ancient Christian Texts (Downers Grove: InterVarsity, 2009). All translations below are taken from these volumes. A new English translation is in process, the first volume of which is the already cited *Ambrosiaster's Commentary: Romans*. A second volume on the remaining letters is forthcoming. For matters of critical introduction, particularly date and authorship, see Souter, *Latin Commentaries*, 39–49; Bray, 'Translator's Introduction', in *Romans and 1–2 Corinthians*, xvi; and now Hunter, 'The Author, Date, and Provenance', in *Ambrosiaster's Commentary: Romans*, xxiii–xxix.

[97] On Ambrosiaster's exegetical method and the form of his commentary, see Souter, *Latin Commentaries*, 63–78; and Cooper, 'Ambrosiaster's Exegesis of the Pauline Epistles', in *Ambrosiaster's Commentary: Romans*, lxi–lxxv.

[98] This is conveniently visible in Bray's footnotes. Cooper, 'Ambrosiaster's Exegesis', in *Ambrosiaster's Commentary: Romans*, lxxiii–lxxiv lists Ambrosiaster's most oft-cited non-Pauline scriptural books.

[99] He can also harmonize. At Eph 1.4, he reads God's eternal choice (ἐκλέγομαι) as God's foreknowledge (προγινώσκω), citing Rom 8.29 and 9.24 in defense, which allows him not only to revise Ephesians toward his preferred soteriology, but also to clarify the *object* of God's foreknowledge—the ambiguous ἡμᾶς of Eph 1.4 is the Jew/gentile assembly of Rom 9.24 (Ambrosiaster, *Galatians–Philemon*, 36).

Here, the social location and larger project of Paul's readers is vital, since both differently shape otherwise similar approaches to the data. Ambrosiaster's co-texts for Eph 1.19–21, which details Christ's resurrection, ascension, and heavenly rule, offer a good example of this. A natural Pauline text to cite here would be 1 Cor 15, but Ambrosiaster opts instead for Jn 17.24; Ps 85.11; Jn 16.24; and Mt 26.25 to link Paul's Christology to that of the Psalms and Jesus himself.[100] In James Moffatt's *Introduction*, christological overlap between Ephesians and the Johannines relocates Ephesians to the late first century within his account of origins;[101] in Ambrosiaster, this overlap confirms Ephesians' (and Paul's) christological orthodoxy, not trivial within the christological debates of the late fourth century.[102] What in one instance displaces Ephesians in another keeps it within the fold.

It is also telling, along these lines, how Ambrosiaster deals with difference, be it literary (between letters) or historical (between text and reader). At Eph 2.20, Ambrosiaster reads the 'apostles and prophets' as metonyms for the Old and New Testaments. He recognizes, however, that 1 Cor 12.28, in which Paul says that God appoints '*first* apostles, *second* prophets…', calls this into question, since it suggests both groups are Paul's contemporaries. Ambrosiaster picks the lock by arguing that 1 Corinthians clarifies the church's order while Ephesians depicts its foundation.[103] The latter is not, however, a later catholicizing of the church's charismatic beginnings; Paul simply has different purposes in each. That said, Ambrosiaster does not ignore historical distance between his world and Paul's. At Eph 4.11–12, he recognizes distinctions between his own preferred late-antique Roman ecclesial polity and that of Paul's text. But critically, all of Paul's letters, Eph 4.11–12 included, depict the *primitive* end of that spectrum. As Ambrosiaster writes, 'Not everything written by the apostle coincides with the order of things which now exists in the church, because the apostolic writings describe what happened at the beginning.'[104] The same text that for Käsemann throws light on the letter's early catholicism reveals for Ambrosiaster the church's charismatic beginnings.[105] The text, of course, stays the same, but the readers change, and the judgments of each say less about the text than about their own ecclesial anxieties. The social location from which, and the larger hermeneutical frame *within* which, one reads Ephesians matters a great deal.

Neither of these lead Ambrosiaster to displace Ephesians to a later stage of developing Christianity. And while he also does not read it explicitly via its place in the collection, there are signs that the order in which he reads the collection has an impact

---

[100] Ambrosiaster, *Galatians–Philemon*, 38.
[101] See Moffatt, *Introduction*, 383–5.
[102] Cooper, 'Ambrosiaster's Theology', in *Ambrosiaster's Commentary: Romans*, lxxvii. More broadly, see J. N. D. Kelly, *Early Christian Doctrines*, rev. ed. (San Francisco: Harper & Row, 1978), 280–309.
[103] Ambrosiaster, *Galatians–Philemon*, 42. Elsewhere, Ambrosiaster appeals to Trinitarian theology to deal with Eph 5:2, which speaks of Jesus doing something that Rom 8:32 attributes to God (*Galatians–Philemon*, 54–5).
[104] Ambrosiaster, *Galatians–Philemon*, 49.
[105] So, Ambrosiaster: 'It was to allow the people to grow and multiply that at the beginning everyone was allowed to evangelize, to baptize and to expound the Scriptures in the church. But when the church became established in every place, congregations were formed and rectors and other officials were appointed, with the result that after that no clerk who was not ordained would dare perform a function which was not appointed or assigned to him' (*Galatians–Philemon*, 49).

on his reading of Ephesians. And this, I suggest not with a little irony, is why his reading of Ephesians is so suggestive to present scholarship on Paul. More than any other late-antique Paulinist, Ambrosiaster reads the Jew/gentile question pervasively across Ephesians—partly, I suggest, because he reads Ephesians on the heels of Romans and Galatians.[106] He is alone in late antiquity, for instance, in distinguishing an ethnically Jewish 'we' in 1.11–12 and a gentile 'you' in 1.13.[107] Paul's prayer beginning in 1.15, then, is one of gratitude for *gentile* πίστις, and his abrupt shift to 'you' in 2.5 reckons God's χάρις particularly incongruous for *gentiles*.[108] Ambrosiaster is not alone in reading Eph 2.11–22 vis-à-vis Jew and gentile—the text demands it—but in some ways his reading depends on an exegetical imagination shaped by Romans and Galatians. The 'enmity' (ἔχθρα) in view in 2.14 is born from a conflict over circumcision; the 'law of commandments in ordinances' (τὸν νόμον τῶν ἐντολῶν ἐν δόγμασιν) set aside in 2.15 is not a religious system *in toto* but the specifically Jewish practices of 'circumcision, new moons, food laws, sacrifices and the sabbath'; and at 3.5–7, Ambrosiaster insists that the Old Testament prophets did not see Paul's *particular* gospel coming, since they foresaw gentile inclusion, but via circumcision, and certainly not apart from 'works of the law'.[109] Tellingly, Ambrosiaster imports a phrase (ἔργα νόμου) famously absent from Ephesians, but central to the question of Paul's gospel in Romans and Galatians (Rom 3.20, 27–28; Gal 2.16; 3.2, 5, and 10). All of this suggests, as Ambrosiaster himself says at Eph 3.1, that the first two chapters of Ephesians comprise Paul's *gentile* gospel.[110]

To be sure, Ambrosiaster's perceptive focus on Ephesians' gentile audience could simply be his reading Eph 2.11 back over the earlier data, and he never explicitly appeals to Romans and Galatians to ground the gentile focus of Eph 1–2. Part of what I am suggesting, however, is that he does not have to. By publishing a commentary on the *corpus Paulinum*, Ambrosiaster and his readers arrive at Ephesians via Romans, 1 and 2 Corinthians, and Galatians. He may not pay hermeneutical homage to these letters, but he need not; his striking exegesis of Ephesians does it for him.

Origen (Fl. ca. 184/5–253/4 CE)

At some point between 386–388 CE, within a few years of Ambrosiaster, Jerome writes a series of commentaries on Galatians, Ephesians, Titus and Philemon.[111] At his own

---

[106] On Ambrosiaster's exegetical sensitivity to Jew/gentile questions, see Souter, *Latin Commentaries*, 65, 72–5; de Bruyne, Cooper, and Hunter, 'Polemical Aspects of the Commentary', in *Ambrosiaster's Commentary: Romans*, cii–cvii.
[107] Ambrosiaster, *Galatians–Philemon*, 37.
[108] Ambrosiaster, *Galatians–Philemon*, 37 (1.15) and 40 (2.5).
[109] Ambrosiaster, *Galatians–Philemon*, 41 (2.14–15) and 43 (3.5–7).
[110] He writes, 'Now that he has shown the dispensation of the divine mercy which had existed before the foundation of the world for the salvation of the Gentiles, Paul declares…' (*Galatians–Philemon*, 42).
[111] He did this at the request of his friends and patrons Paula and Eustochium, shortly after his arrival in Bethlehem in 386. See his *Comm. Gal.* 1.Prol and *Comm. Eph.* 1.Prol and 3.Prol (Souter, *Latin Commentaries*, 98–100; Heine, *Ephesians*, 7–9). The critical edition of his Ephesians commentary is Francesco Piere, 'L'esegesi di Girolamo nel Commentario a Efesini. Aspetti storico-esegetici e storico-dottrinali' (PhD diss., Università degli Studi di Bologna, 1996/1997), although Jerome, *Opera Omnia* (PL 26:439–554) is more accessible. English translations of Jerome's Pauline commentaries are in *St. Jerome: Commentary on Galatians*, trans. Andrew Cain, FC 121 (Washington, DC:

admission, Jerome's work on Paul derives largely from Origen.¹¹² For several reasons, then, this single work on Ephesians, in which we hear both Origen and Jerome's voice, brings this chapter to a fitting close. Chronologically and geographically, it spans a large portion of our period of interest and crosses the boundary of East and West. More importantly, Jerome and Origen's method is indisputably grammatical: they both use the grammarian's tools to facilitate reading (à la Euthalius),¹¹³ and fragment the text to elicit creative juxtapositions with other Pauline and scriptural excerpts (à la Priscillian). To be sure, the breadth of these co-texts explodes the collection and makes Scripture itself the locus for comparison. And yet, Paul's corpus retains hermeneutical integrity. Among late-antique commentators, only Origen and Jerome place Ephesians via its position in the collection.¹¹⁴ Their collection-attentive, grammatically shaped reading of Ephesians, then, makes my argument in these two chapters most thoroughly and explicitly. A different way of reading a letter collection privileges a different sort of letter and positions Ephesians very differently vis-à-vis Paul.

From a modern vantage point, the frequency with which Origen and Jerome use Paul's other letters to read a text from Ephesians is striking. If the pervasive reading of Ephesians alongside non-Pauline co-texts in modern criticism bends Ephesians away from Paul, the opposite is true in Origen and Jerome. Many of their Pauline citations offer simple comparison: what Paul says here recalls what he says elsewhere.¹¹⁵ Others, however, clarify ambiguity in Ephesians via appeal to allegedly clearer data in another letter. The ambiguous co-heirs (συγκληρονόμα) of the gentiles in Eph 3.6 is solved by appeal to Rom 8.17—the gentiles are 'co-heirs with Christ' (συγκληρονόμοι δὲ Χριστοῦ).¹¹⁶ At Eph 3.9, the αἰῶνες from whom the mystery is hidden is 'this present

---

Catholic University of America Press, 2010); *St. Jerome's Commentaries on Galatians, Titus, and Philemon*, trans. Thomas P. Scheck (Notre Dame: University of Notre Dame Press, 2010); and the already cited Heine, *Ephesians*.

¹¹² Jerome, *Comm. Eph.* 1.Prol lists his debt to Apollinarius, Didymus, and especially Origen (Heine, *Ephesians*, 78). See Heine, *Ephesians*, 5–7 and 18–22, with translation of relevant primary sources at pp. 273–81. The Greek fragments of Origen on Ephesians are conveniently collected in Gregg, 'Commentary of Origen', 233–44, 398–420, and 554–76, with Eng. trans. in Heine alongside that of Jerome. Heine's *Ephesians* is thus the indispensable source for what follows. All translations are from there unless otherwise noted, and vis-à-vis the task of identifying what in Jerome belongs (also) to Origen, I follow him throughout. Where we do not have the Greek text of Origen, but Jerome is clearly indebted to him, Heine italicizes his text of Jerome. Below, then, I refer to Origen when the text is his alone, to Origen and Jerome when the latter is dependent, and to Jerome when Heine's text of Jerome is not italicized.

¹¹³ Both Origen and Jerome consistently recognize and defend Paul's poor grammar on the grounds that he is 'untrained in speech' (2 Cor 11.6). See their comments at Eph 2.1–5; 3.1–3; 3.13. Usually, Origen and Jerome's work is to clarify Paul's indecorous style (see at 1.15–18a; 2.1–5, 14b–18; 3.1–3, and 16–19), but they can also address matters of syntax (at 1.3; 1.4b–5a; 1.8b–9a; 1.13; 3.6), etymology (2.1), and other grammatical ambiguities (3.13; 5.12). For Origen's grammatical exegesis, see Bernard Neuschäfer, *Origenes als Philologe*, 2 vols., Schweizerische Beiträge zur Altertumswissenschaft 18 (Basel: Reinhardt Verlag, 1987); and Peter W. Martens, *Origen and Scripture: The Contours of the Exegetical Life* (Oxford: Oxford University Press, 2012), 25–68.

¹¹⁴ Layton, 'Origen as a Reader of Paul', 314–19 and 331–5, and Heine, *Ephesians*, 22–35, both situate Origen/Jerome's comment about Ephesians being 'in the middle' within ancient discussions of a corpus' arrangement (τάξις/*ordo*). For the effect of the corpus' priority on Origen's and Jerome's reading of Ephesians, see Layton, 'Origen as a Reader of Paul', 311, 335–46.

¹¹⁵ See, e.g., at Eph 4.2 (with Gal 6.2); 5.11 (Gal 5.22); 5.16 (Gal 1.4; Heb 6.5); and 6.11 (Rom 13.14).

¹¹⁶ Heine, *Ephesians*, 146–7. Origen and Jerome both recognize that a clearer answer (Israel, 2.12) lies closer to hand, but opt nevertheless for the solution above.

wicked age' (τοῦ αἰῶνος τοῦ ἐνεστῶτος πονηροῦ; Gal 1.4), and all the 'spiritual and rational creatures' who live in it.[117] And Paul's cryptic ethnic slander in Eph 4.19, that the gentiles capitulate to 'every impurity in covetousness' (ἐν πλεονεξίᾳ), is a coded reference to sexual deviance, since in 1 Thess 4.3–8 Paul charges the Thessalonians not to defraud (πλεονεκτεῖν) their brothers—that is, to take their wives sexually (4.6).[118] Like Priscillian, lexical connections (συγκληρονόμοι, αἰών, πλεονεξία/πλεονεκτέω) make for suggestive Pauline co-texts for Origen and Jerome.

If the collection is the boundary, however, what do Origen and Jerome do with the inevitable variability within it? At the narrowly textual level, their options are several. They clarify syntax (Eph 1.8–9) or call forth other supporting texts (Eph 1.3) in order to dismiss the problem;[119] they draw philosophical distinctions so as to make the discrepancy only apparent (Eph 1.22);[120] and when these options fail, as they do for Origen at Eph 2.6 (vis-à-vis Rom 6.5), he simply collates contradictory texts into a new synthesis. Origen's Paul now envisages a two-stage resurrection—one present and spiritual (Eph 2.6), the other future and bodily (Rom 6.5).[121] When the corpus is primary, all the data count, even if it means expanding one's Paul.

This is not, however, a blanket invitation to harmonize. For to harmonize would be to run roughshod over the specific genius inscribed in the collection—Paul's ability to respond to specific ecclesial illnesses in kind.[122] Far from making Paul univocal, Origen and Jerome celebrate that the collection makes Paul polyvalent. They attribute difference to the churches addressed, which both absolves Paul from contradiction and garners him praise as a good physician. Paul is not a one-trick pony. Origen and Jerome know this because they see what is distinctive in each church and read its letter accordingly, which is to say, they read each letter within the integrity of the collection. And so, to turn to this book's epigraph and to say it directly, Ephesians is the heart of Paul's corpus because the Ephesians themselves are a church capable of receiving Paul's profundity. To be sure, Origen and Jerome partly derive this from a historical

---

[117] Heine, *Ephesians*, 149.
[118] Heine, *Ephesians*, 184–5. Cf. their exegesis at Eph 5.3 (209–10) and 5.5 (214–15), where they again appeal to 1 Thess 4.6 on the basis of a shared lexical base.
[119] At Eph 1.8–9, Origen and Jerome read ἐν πάσῃ σοφίᾳ καὶ πφονήσει with περισσεύω rather than γνωρίζω to avoid Paul suggesting an epistemological confidence that he elsewhere eschews (1 Cor 13.9 and 12; Heine, *Ephesians*, 93–5). At Eph 1.3, Origen and Jerome dismiss the problem of an overly realized soteriology by appealing to a set of Pauline (and scriptural) co-texts that locate the Christian's life in heaven, or in the Spirit (Phil 3.20; Jn 15.19; 1 Cor 15.49; Rom 8.9; Mt 6.20–21; Heine, *Ephesians*, 81–3).
[120] At Eph 1.3, Origen leverages his Neoplatonism to locate the blessings 'outside of sense perception' in the 'intellect', so making the past tense of the verb acceptable (Heine, *Ephesians*, 83–4). At 1.22, Origen and Jerome admit the difference between Heb 2.8/1 Cor 15.25 and Eph 1.22, but explain it via a contrast between ontology and volition: Ephesians depicts the subjection of all things in their *nature*, while Hebrews/1 Corinthians admit that not all do so, at present, by their own *choice* (Heine, *Ephesians*, 115).
[121] The discussion here is in Origen, *Comm. Rom.* 5.9 at his comments on Rom 6.5 (Origen, *Commentary on the Epistle to the Romans, Books 1–5*, trans. Thomas P. Scheck, FC 103 [Washington, DC: Catholic University of America Press, 2001], 368). Origen does not actually cite Eph 2.6, but his description of (and suggestion for how to read) present resurrection in Paul clearly alludes to it, and his exegesis of Eph 2.6 in his Ephesians commentary runs identically (Gregg, 'Commentary of Origen', 405 [fr. 10.141, lines 1–12]; Heine, *Ephesians*, 126–7).
[122] See Heine, *Ephesians*, 76.

setting (i.e. Acts 19–20), but more frequently, they discover this through a pervasive contrast with Paul's other churches, not least the Corinthians.[123] That is, Origen and Jerome read Ephesians against the backdrop of the collection, against which it stands out in high relief.

This elevation begins almost immediately. Origen's reading of Eph 1.1, which designates the Ephesians 'those who are' (τοῖς οὖσιν), raises a problem. Did Paul not say in 1 Cor 1.28 that God chose the 'things which are not' (τὰ μὴ ὄντα) to abolish the 'things which are' (τὰ ὄντα)? The key, for Origen, is in v. 29, 'that no flesh may boast before God'. If 'those who are' fail to attribute their being to its cause (the 'one who is'), they lose being and become those 'who are not' (τὰ μὴ ὄντα).[124] The Ephesians 'who are' (τοῖς οὖσιν), however, have avoided this trap. From 1.1, then, Paul declares them the most worthy sort of recipients, and confirms this in 1.13, again via a crucial Corinthian co-text. At 1.13, Paul writes that the Ephesians 'heard the word of truth, the good news of your salvation' (τὸν λόγον τῆς ἀληθείας, τὸ εὐαγγέλιον τῆς σωτηρίας ὑμῶν). On its face, the text is innocuous, but appealing to 1 Cor 2.4, Origen distinguishes between Paul's 'word' (λόγος) and his 'proclamation' (κήρυγμά), and celebrates the Ephesians for receiving not just the latter but the former as well, the totality of Paul's teaching.[125] Moreover, Paul's λόγος is nothing less than the revelation of Paul's mystic knowledge. It makes the Ephesians 'sharers in unutterable words [ἀπορρήτων λόγων], led by Paul'.[126] Origen's Greek clearly alludes to 2 Cor 12.4, and the ἄρρητα ῥήματα that Paul hears in his heavenly ascent.[127] Paul, of course, was forbidden to repeat those words, but Origen evocatively suggests that he did—*to the Ephesians*. The Ephesians alone are fit for Paul's heavenly mysteries, which is also what Jerome says in the prologue to Book 3 of his commentary.[128] In Origen and Jerome's scheme, Ephesians is the written testimony of what Paul heard in the third heaven, and so the substance of his apocalyptic gospel. Not the whole of Ephesians, however: as Paul himself suggests (3.3–4), Origen and Jerome find these mysteries especially in Eph 1–2.[129] Precisely those chapters that create insuperable difficulties for modern scholars are, for Origen and Jerome, a treasure house of Pauline mysteries.

---

[123] See Layton, 'Origen as a Reader of Paul', 335–46, who discusses many of the same examples I do below.

[124] Heine, *Ephesians*, 80. Jerome suggests this as a possibility, but then falls back on the straightforward reading, since he knows the text with ἐν Ἐφέσῳ in it.

[125] The discussion is in Heine, *Ephesians*, 101–3. The implication of citing the distinction of 1 Cor 2.4, particularly in light of the Ephesian/Corinthian contrast throughout, seems to be that the Corinthians only receive the κήρυγμά, although this is difficult to justify in the immediate context of 1 Cor 2 itself.

[126] See Origen's Greek at Gregg, 'Commentary of Origen', 242 (fr. 8.119, lines 11–12). I depart here from Heine's translation ('secret teachings' [101]), then, to draw out the connection to 2 Cor 12.4.

[127] See the full discussion of this section of Origen/Jerome in Layton, 'Origen as a Reader of Paul', 342–5.

[128] In *Comm. Eph.* 3.Prol (Heine, *Ephesians*, 201), Jerome says that Paul 'wrote to no other churches in such a mystical manner revealing the "mysteries hidden from the ages" (Eph 3.9)'.

[129] As Jerome writes at Eph 3.3–4, 'Truly if one will contemplate the preceding words of this epistle one will see mysteries revealed… This is what we meant in the preface when we remarked that no other epistle of Paul contains so many mysteries and is so wrapped in hidden meanings' (Heine, *Ephesians*, 143–4).

If in Eph 1-2 we have Paul's theology at its most sublime, for Origen and Jerome Eph 4-6 offers the apex of Paul's ethics. Unsurprisingly, this is because the Ephesians are fit recipients, seen now in contrast with the Corinthians.[130] This emerges first at Eph 5.1, where Paul exhorts the Ephesians, 'Be imitators of God'. Rather than read 5.1 relative to 4.32, as the οὖν suggests, Origen and Jerome turn to the parallel phrase in 1 Cor 11.1 ('Be imitators of me as I also am of Christ'), and draw a distinction between the Ephesians and Corinthians. The latter could only imitate the imitator, but the Ephesians imitate not Paul, nor even Christ, but God himself.[131] Origen and Jerome can only draw this conclusion, of course, because the interpretive locus for Eph 5.1 is not Ephesians itself but the collection.[132] The same is true at Eph 5.24, where Paul commands wives to submit to their husbands, 'just as the church submits to Christ'. For Origen and Jerome, the force of the connective (ὡς... οὕτως) requires that the husband/wife relationship be chaste, just as the Christ/church relationship is holy (i.e. passionless; Eph 5.27). This raises the problem of 1 Cor 7.5, however, where Paul allows husband and wife to 'come together again' (i.e. have intercourse) after time set apart for prayer. Why the difference? The answer lies in the capacity of Paul's addressees. 1 Corinthians 7.5 is a concession (συγγώμη) to moral neophytes, racked by 'dissensions and schisms' (1 Cor 1.11; 3.3) and tolerant of sexual impropriety of the worst kind (1 Cor 5.1-2). Paul's true marital-sexual ethic, on the other hand, is in Eph 5.24, where he addresses those of considerable moral progress.[133]

A final and lengthy example is in Eph 6.12,[134] where Paul identifies the Ephesians' opponents not as 'blood and flesh' (αἷμα καὶ σάρκα) but as a host of malevolent cosmological forces (ἀρχαι, ἐξουσίαι, κοσμοκράτορες, πνευματικὰ τῆς πονηρίας). This leads Origen and Jerome immediately to 1 Cor 10.13.

> I do not think Paul could have said, Your 'wrestling is not against blood and flesh', when writing to the Corinthians to whom he said, 'Let no temptation seize you except a human one...'. (1 Cor 10.13). I think, in fact, that the struggles which there are called human temptations are 'against flesh and blood'.

The critical link, for Origen and Jerome, is the 'blood and flesh' struggle of Eph 6.12 and the 'human temptations' of 1 Cor 10.13, which they both further explicate via the vice list of Gal 5.19-21. This 'blood and flesh' struggle belongs to the Corinthians, while the Ephesian struggle is spiritual (πνευματικὰ τῆς πονηρίας, κτλ.), and so more exalted. They do battle with Satan himself. In fact, the location of the struggle—Paul moves it out of the realm of αἷμα καὶ σαρξ—is paramount: 'Freed from bodies', they

---

[130] Layton, 'Origen as a Reader of Paul', 346.
[131] Heine, *Ephesians*, 208.
[132] Layton, 'Origen as a Reader of Paul', 346.
[133] The whole discussion is in Heine, *Ephesians*, 234-5.
[134] The discussion runs from Heine, *Ephesians*, 254-60. To modern eyes, the length may be surprising, but Eph 6.12 is in fact one of Paul's most oft-cited texts in late antiquity. See Jennifer R. Strawbridge, *The Pauline Effect: The Use of the Pauline Epistles by Early Christian Writers*, Studies of the Bible and Its Reception 5 (Berlin: de Gruyter, 2015), 11 n. 38, 62-9, and 210-17.

rise 'near to God', but also to that place 'full of contrary powers'.[135] That is, the location of the struggle and the nature of their opponents prove the Ephesians' righteous character. Jerome's keen canonical eye then finds both the Corinthian (Rom 8.35-37) and Ephesian (8:38-39) struggle in Paul's catalogue of what cannot 'separate us from the love of Christ' (8.35-39).[136] Once again, the Ephesians are elevated by reading Ephesians within the frame of the collection, which redounds positively to how Origen and Jerome perceive the letter itself, for whom it is Paul's theological and ethical magnum opus—the corpus' 'heart'.

This is not to say Ephesians is plain. Origen and Jerome repeatedly recognize the letter's obscurity and apologize for their convoluted comments, which they blame on the letter's complexity.[137] To use an apt Pauline metaphor, the Ephesians receive solid food while the Corinthians receive milk (1 Cor 3.2). To the degree that this makes the letters variable, Origen and Jerome absolve Paul from contradiction by spotlighting his pastoral duty to attend to his patients as he finds them. In the Ephesians, Paul finds a healthy patient, capable of receiving his heavenly *mysteria* (2 Cor 12.4). Far from displaced, Ephesians is elevated via this canonical map. Where Paul's modern readers see difference and read (historical) development, Origen and Jerome see uniqueness and read (spatial and epistemological) ascent. Ephesians is not late, it is heavenly, and so it belongs 'in the middle'—Paul's corporeal heart.

Conclusion

What does it do to Ephesians, then, to read it within Paul's book? The irony, of course, is that without the book there is no dilemma of Ephesians at all. An individual missive, received on its own, is self-evidently Pauline until one has other letters with which to compare it. As Mitchell rightly notes, the problem only emerges with the collection. Here, then, is another irony. The very thing that late antique tradents are busy producing (the collection), and which guarantees for them Ephesians' authenticity, creates in due course the possibility of critical scepticism. The question, from late antiquity to the present, is what to do with the 'inconsistency of Paul' (or more gently, variability) ensconced in the collection. Paul's modern readers homogenize Paul by rendering what is divergent *pseudo*-Paul—that is, by dividing the collection. Ephesians stands outside that homogeneity and becomes development. In late antiquity, this is evidently not an option. The collection itself guarantees that Ephesians belongs to Paul,[138] and so difference is explained on other grounds. Most typically, it is either that Paul had not met the recipients and so writes generally (Severian, Theodore,

---

[135] Heine, *Ephesians*, 255. Conversely, appealing to something like a moral-ontological gravity, Jerome says that the immoral (i.e. Corinthians) are 'dragged down' and remain nearer the earth—thus, their struggle is with αἷμα καὶ σάρξ (see Heine, *Ephesians*, 258-60).

[136] Heine, *Ephesians*, 260.

[137] See, e.g., their comments at Eph 4.19 and 6.12 (Heine, *Ephesians*, 185 and 260).

[138] The fact that late-antique readers regard Hebrews as Paul's despite its anonymity is largely attributable to its presence within Paul's corpus. On this point generally, see Scherbenske, *Canonizing Paul*, 6 and 42-6, and of Hebrews specifically, 189-90. The same can be said for the Epistle to the Laodiceans, which is attested in Latin Bibles beginning in the sixth century, as well as for 3 Corinthians, albeit less so (Houghton, *Latin New Testament*, 20 and 170).

Euthalius), or else that the Ephesians themselves are a model church and so Paul writes seminally (Origen, Jerome, Chrysostom, *Primum quaeritur*, Budapest Anonymous, Pelagius). The Paul of late antiquity tends to be more polyvalent than the Paul of modern criticism—the necessary result of a broader set of source material. Be that as it may, the same hermeneutic that compels the collection (i.e. catholicity) also privileges letters that offer Paul free of particularity. On this late antique rubric, Romans and Ephesians are frequently linked, and fare well—Galatians, less so. Different maps privilege different letters.

Safely nestled within the collection, Ephesians is read alongside a robust set of Pauline co-texts. Paul's late-ancient tradents close down space between Ephesians and the other letters by reading it within Paul's book, aided by reading practices that assimilate textual fragments into a new whole—*Paul*. In the case of Priscillian, this makes Ephesians quintessentially Pauline. Part of the utility of reading the Greek and Latin fathers reading Ephesians is watching Pauline exegesis happen with all the pieces on the table. This is not to say that their judgment about, nor way of reading Ephesians is correct. This chapter can hardly prove that. But it can reveal again the constructed nature of modern judgments. Illuminating a different interpretive horizon has a way of shedding light on our own as well. My purpose, however, has not been just a catalogue of reception, nor endless deconstruction, but a return to the text. Duly chastened, how does Eph 3.1–13—a text (de)formed by modern criticism—read when read alongside Pauline co-texts without prior assumptions of development? That is the task of Part 3.

Part 3

READING EPHESIANS AMONG THE PAULINES

Chapter 5

IMAGING PAUL IN EPHESIANS

Sometime in the early 50s CE, Paul found himself in an epistolary back-and-forth with the Christ-assembly in Corinth. The correspondence included intervening visits, and some in Corinth appear to have been nonplussed by the juxtaposition of the epistolary Paul and the man himself: 'His letters are weighty and strong', they muse, 'but his bodily presence is weak, and his speech contemptible' (2 Cor 10.10). For these first readers, the Paul inscribed in the letters did not match the physical reality. The disjunction is starker still for those who meet Paul only via the collection. The Paul of Galatians, a firebrand, insists on his gospel's priority and his mission's independence. The Paul of 1 Corinthians, an ecumenist, aligns that gospel and mission with a broader set of apostolic colleagues and forebears. The Paul of 2 Corinthians, to put it mildly, takes on a variety of personae. The Paul of Romans is expansive, universal—a priest of the gospel for gentiles the world over, with designs on provoking a homecoming of the Jews as well. The Paul of Philippians is a warm-hearted pastor of a particular local assembly, until he is not (Phil 3.2–11). And so on.

Who, though, is the Paul of Ephesians? The standard answer, read off the face of Eph 3.1–13, is not Paul at all, but an idealized Paul, with 3.1–13 a piece of Pauline hagiography. In the last fifty years, this judgment arises primarily in studies that focus on the images of Paul (*Paulusbilder*) inscribed in various acts of Paul's reception.[1] For all their sophistication, however, two problems plague these works: the implicit assumption that (1) such images belong only to reception of Paul, and (2) that the Paul of the so-called authentic letters is a univocal fixed point from which to trace divergent images. As the above already hints, both are false. Every act of Pauline writing, authentic or not, fashions a *persona Pauli*—an act of rhetorical (self-)construction. In the collection, those personae are several, but none offers Paul unvarnished, the 'real Paul'.[2] In the face of this challenge, Benjamin White urges a historiographical shift to the study of the letters as (and among) Pauline traditions, in search of their 'gist'—or the 'broad impressions' they share.[3] I think this is right, and this chapter offers one

---

[1] See my discussion of these works in Chapters 1 and 2.
[2] White, *Remembering Paul*, passim (but see directly at 180). This insight also emerges centrally in Margaret M. Mitchell, *Paul, the Corinthians, and the Birth of Christian Hermeneutics* (Cambridge: Cambridge University Press, 2010); and idem, *Heavenly Trumpet*, 428–33 (directly at 432). The implications of this insight, however, for the study of the Pauline pseudepigrapha have not yet been felt.
[3] White, *Remembering Paul*, 176–7 and 181.

such search, reading Eph 3.1–13 as a way in to Paul's sundry images inscribed in the collection.

It is not, however, just any search, nor is Eph 3.1–13 an arbitrary choice—one possible example among many—with which to close this study. Rather, it has borne the brunt of modern ways of reading Paul's collection in a particularly direct way. Extricated from the late first century, however, and placed back in the corpus, Eph 3.1–13 links to a set of Pauline co-texts at the heart of current debates about Paul's apostolic self-conception. This chapter asks where Eph 3.1–13 fits vis-à-vis these images of Paul. To anticipate the conclusion, not only does it sit particularly well among Paul's various personae in the *Hauptbriefe*, it holds together their diversity as well. Vis-à-vis Paul's apostolic identity, in fact, as we have it in these letters, Eph 3.1–13 looks a lot like its 'gist'.

Paul, the Apostle of the Church?

As we saw in Chapter 2, this is not the judgment of a host of works on Paul's reception. Take, for example, the conclusion of J. Christiaan Beker about the image of Paul in Eph 3:

> Paul's portrait in Ephesians conforms to its vision of the church as the *una sancta catholica et apostolica ecclesia*. Paul is portrayed here as remembered by his pupils after his death; a figure whose authority and stature have increased enormously over time. He is now nostalgically transmitted to the churches of Asia Minor as the apostle of sacred memory whose struggles with Judaism and Judaizers have been forgotten and whose apocalyptic yearnings have been displaced by an ecclesiology of triumphant eschatological fulfillment.[4]

And then also that of Gregory Sterling: 'Paul [in Ephesians] is no longer the Apostle to the Gentiles, he is the Apostle to the Church'.[5] These judgments are not unique, but only particularly colorful (Beker) and pithy (Sterling) examples of a pervasive scholarly consensus: in Eph 3.1–13, a later Paulinist both magnifies Paul and universalizes his apostolate.[6] The Paul of Ephesians, in other words, becomes *the* apostle of *the* church.

In Chapter 2, I critique the method of arriving at this judgment, but here it is worth showing, briefly, its extent. As the premier apostle, Paul is now the architect of the church's unity,[7] the theological guarantor of orthodoxy,[8] and a suffering redeemer

---

[4] Beker, *Heirs of Paul*, 72.
[5] Sterling, 'From Apostle to the Gentiles', 97.
[6] This judgment goes back to Baur, *Paul*, 2:32–3, and is nicely expressed in Käsemann, 'Ephesians and Acts', 293: 'For Ephesians Paul is the apostle per se, for whom the others are merely the foil'. For a good (and recent) example, see Shkul, *Reading Ephesians*, 142–72 (directly at 165–6).
[7] Barrett, 'Pauline Controversies', 239; Brown, *Churches the Apostles Left Behind*, 20–1; Beker, *Heirs of Paul*, 71–2; Furnish, 'Paul in His Place', 5 and 7; and Sterling, 'From Apostle to the Gentiles', 95–7.
[8] Marguerat, 'Paul après Paul', 322.

himself.⁹ For Robert Wild, Ephesians sketches a 'veritable "Paulology"'—a 'mythologized image of Paul'.¹⁰ No one, however, goes further than Richard Pervo, for whom the Paul of Eph 3.1–13 is the 'ideal Paul', the 'great apostle', the 'guarantor of apostolic tradition', the 'guardian of a mystery', and a 'martyr': 'The apostle', in fact, 'has become an archetype'.¹¹ In these works, a late setting leads directly to an inflated Paul, with the text of 3.1–13 left behind for more distorting sobriquets. The judgments are largely the same in Ephesians scholarship proper. In Eph 3.1–13, Paul is the 'ecclesiastical apostle par excellence' (Merklein) with 'outsanding apostolic authority' in the 'universal, ecumenical church' (Gnilka).¹² Here is an 'idealised picture of Paul' as an authoritative 'church theologian' (Schnackenburg)—a 'mystagogue' (Fischer).¹³ Paul in Ephesians is 'ins Überdimensionale gesteigert' (Ernst)—a 'revered figure, a dignitary', a 'pillar of the church' and the 'agent of an already-achieved unity' (Lincoln).¹⁴ In fact, the whole of 3.1–13 is a 'Paul-anamnesis', and so 'pseudonymity is at its most transparent here'.¹⁵ The idealized image of Paul in 3.1–13 gives the game away.

The Paul of Ephesians is thus an image, a portrait, a legend, and a figure of idealized hagiography. The one thing he is not is Paul. For all their genuinely learned insights elsewhere, vis-à-vis Eph 3.1–13 and its image of Paul, these scholars lapse consistently into caricature. If one knows Ephesians is late, one certainly can read Eph 3.1–13 as they do. But if one did not know, would this be the most natural way to read it? Does exegesis invite, much less demand, the ubiquitous verdict that Paul here is *the* apostle of *the* church? At the level of words, the striking thing is that Eph 3.1–13 uses neither ἀπόστολος nor ἐκκλησία—at least not with reference to Paul and the object of his labors.¹⁶ It may be time, then, to return to the text, and rather than plot it on a path to the second century, simply attend to the way the words actually run.

---

⁹ These three images are all spoken of in de Boer, 'Images of Paul', and MacDonald, *Pauline Churches*, 123–6. Penny ('Pseudo-Pauline Letters', 259–67) offers largely the same, albeit somewhat more balanced.
¹⁰ Robert A. Wild, S.J., 'The Warrior and the Prisoner: Some Reflections on Ephesians 6:10–20', *CBQ* 46 (1984): 289 and 294.
¹¹ Pervo, *Making of Paul*, 75–7.
¹² Helmut Merklein, *Das kirchliche Amt nach dem Epheserbrief*, StANT 33 (Munich: Kösel, 1973), 332–5, 337 and 343; Gnilka, 'Paulusbild im Kolosser- und Epheserbrief', 184 and 193; cf. Sellin, *Brief an die Epheser*, 57–8.
¹³ Schnackenburg, *Ephesians*, 131 and 136; Fischer, *Tendenz und Absicht*, 110.
¹⁴ Josef Ernst, *Die Briefe an die Philipper, an Philemon, an die Kolosser, an die Epheser*, RNT (Regensburg: Friedrich Pustet, 1974), 331; cited in Lindemann, *Paulus im Ältesten Christentum*, 41; Lincoln, *Ephesians*, lxiii and 172.
¹⁵ The label of 3.1–13 as 'Paul-anamnesis' is that of Schnackenburg, *Ephesians*, 143, and the transparency of pseudepigraphy in 3.1–13 that of Lincoln, *Ephesians*, 168 and 176. For works that regard the letter as post-Pauline, but tend to stress continuity here, see Best, *Ephesians*, 42–4, 292–4 (directly at 44), and Michael Gese, *Das Vermächtnis des Apostels: Die Rezeption der paulinischen Theologie im Epheserbrief*, WUNT 2/99 (Tübingen: Mohr Siebeck, 1997), 246–7.
¹⁶ So rightly, Muddiman, *Ephesians*, 146.

The Image of Paul in Ephesians: Reading Ephesians 3.1–13 among the Paulines

So how do those words run? Who *is* the Paul of Eph 3.1–13? Cutting through the thicket, a fairly straightforward answer is possible: Paul is a διάκονος τοῦ εὐαγγελίου (3.6–7) with a particular οἰκονομία (τῆς χάριτος τοῦ θεοῦ, 3.2), which he later simply calls his χάρις (3.8). This οἰκονομία-χάρις is twofold: to herald Christ-πλοῦτος to the ἔθνη (3.8) and to shed light on the management of a μυστήριον (3.9)—a mystery defined in 3.6, and revealed to Paul κατὰ ἀποκάλυψιν (3.3). All of this is placed in the frame of Paul's imprisonment (3.1 and 13)—suffering he envisages as part and parcel of his task of dispensing the Christ-gift to gentiles. Again, no ἀπόστολος, nor ἐκκλησία. Whatever Paul is, he is for the gentiles (3.1 and 8). To the degree that Eph 3.1–13 evinces an image of Paul, it does so through the key terms I have left untranslated. To those, then, we turn, and given the text's muddled syntax, it will be good to take all of this in stages: the detailed picture of 3.2–7, the summary of 3.8–9, and the frame of 3.1 and 13.

Paul: Courier and Fiduciary—The Image in Detail (Eph 3.2–3a and 6–7)

As of Eph 3.1, Paul has just spent twelve verses constructing a new kinship relationship for his gentile auditors (2.11–22).[17] Those who were outsiders to Israel's way of life (ἀπηλλοτριωμένοι τῆς πολιτείας τοῦ Ἰσραὴλ) and strangers to their promissory covenants (ξένοι τῶν διαθηκῶν τῆς ἐπαγγελίας, 2.12) had seen their position vis-à-vis Israel's God dramatically reverse (2.13). By the end, Paul declares these 'strangers and aliens' (ξένοι καὶ πάροικοι) to be 'co-citizens with the holy ones' (συμπολῖται τῶν ἁγίων, 2.19), and 'those without God' (ἄθεοι, 2.12) to be God's kin, drawn into the family lineage (οἰκεῖοι τοῦ θεοῦ, 2.19; cf. 3.15). As it does in 1.15, the reality of this new gentile situation leads Paul to appeal to God on their behalf (Τούτου χάριν, 3.1 and 14), but mention of his imprisonment for the gentiles leads him to break off to outline his role in actualizing the gentile solution just described. The first period, itself beset by digressions, runs as follows:

> —if indeed you have heard of the management of the gift [τὴν οἰκονομίαν τῆς χάριτος] of God which was given to me for you [ἔθνη], that the mystery [μυστήριον] was made known to me according to revelation [κατὰ ἀποκάλυψιν], as I have just written in brief. (When you read it, you will be able to understand my insight in the mystery of Christ, which was not made known to the sons of men in other generations as it has now been revealed to his holy apostles and prophets by the spirit.) The gentiles are co-inheritors, co-members of the body, and co-partakers of the promise in Christ Jesus through the gospel, of which I became a courier [διάκονος] according to the gracious gift of God which was given to me according to the working of his power. (Eph 3.2–7)

---

[17] On my use of the nomenclature of 'Paul' as the author of Ephesians, see the Introduction.

To begin, then, with a simple observation: amidst the various turns of this period, Paul's only nominative singular self-appellation is διάκονος (3.7). A long history of reading this word in the allegedly ubiquitous and mundane realm of humble service—so 'minister' (KJV, NASB) and 'servant' (NIV, NRSV)—has resulted in its being largely ignored in secondary discussion of Paul's image in 3.1–13.[18] There is nothing remarkable, so the thinking goes, about designating Paul subservient to his message.

As John N. Collins and Anni Hentschel have shown, however, the διακον- word group is neither ubiquitous nor mundane in antiquity, but a relatively rare way to describe specifically mediatorial work.[19] The διάκονος is a 'go-between' charged with executing a task on behalf of another, most typically the delivery of a message, and frequently between gods and humans—thus 'courier' above.[20] In his *Politicus*, Plato reckons διακονία a science (τέχνη) in which both prophets and priests participate. Prophets mediate in one direction, interpreting the gods' oracles to humans (μαντική), while priests work in both: via sacrifices, they offer human gifts to the gods, and via prayers, they request divine gifts for humans (*Pol.* 290c-e; cf. 299d-3). Prophets and priests, that is, occupy the liminal space separating gods and humans, doing the work of διακονία.[21] The most famous emissary along these lines from classical antiquity is Hermes, the διάκονος of Zeus, whose work has him traversing the vast space between heaven and earth, heralding messages to and fro (Aeschylus, *Pr.* 941–43; Lucian, *Char.* 1; *Dial. d.* 7.3; 24.1–2), and the same could be said for Michael, the chief angel of the Jewish God (*T. Abr.* 9.24).[22] Such figures need not be divine (or semi-divine). Paul's contemporaries Philo and Josephus label such notable figures of the Jewish past as Joseph, Moses, Aaron, and Jeremiah with this terminology to designate their role as mediators.[23] And Josephus even applies it to himself, casting his desertion to

---

[18] The key work here is Hermann W. Beyer's 1935 entry in the *Theologische Wörterbuch* ('διακονέω, διακονία, διάκανος', *TDNT* 2:81–93), whose judgment comes to structural expression in Johannes P. Louw and Eugene A. Nida, *Greek–English Lexicon of the New Testament Based on Semantic Domains* (New York: United Bible Societies, 1988), §35.19–30. For the history of this linguistic decision, see Anni Hentschel, *Diakonia im Neuen Testament: Studien zur Semantik unter besonderer Berücksichtigung der Rolle von Frauen*, WUNT 2/226 (Tübingen: Mohr Siebeck, 2007), 11–24; and concisely, John N. Collins, 'A Monocultural Usage: διακον- Words in Classical, Hellenistic, and Patristic Sources', *VC* 66 (2012): 290–5. The commentaries almost universally opt for 'service' (e.g. Lincoln, *Ephesians*, 181–2; Schnackenburg, *Ephesians*, 135; Muddiman, *Ephesians*, 156) or 'minister' (e.g. O'Brien, *Ephesians*, 238–9) and are everywhere brief, and the works on Paul's image (noted above) make nothing of it. Best, *Ephesians*, 43 and 314–15, is better, cognisant as he is of Collins's work.

[19] The seminal work is John N. Collins, *Diakonia: Re-Interpreting the Ancient Sources* (New York: Oxford University Press, 1990), now confirmed by Hentschel, *Diakonia im Neuen Testament*, 34–85, in her work on Classical, Hellenistic, and Jewish sources. The table in Collins, 'Monocultural Usage', 295–6, gives concise summary.

[20] Collins, *Diakonia*, 77–95. I follow his recommended translations for verb, common and abstract noun throughout this chapter (335). My focus (given Eph 3.7) is on the divine/human boundary, but this is not to suggest that the word is restricted to this arena. For its more mundane sense, see, e.g., Plato, *Rep.* 2.370e, 371a-e; Philo, *Jos.* 167; Jos., *Ant.* 18.262, 265, 269, 278, 283, and the discussion (on Plato's use) at Collins, *Diakonia*, 78–85.

[21] See Collins, *Diakonia*, 85.

[22] See Collins, 90–2. In *T. Abr.* 9.24a, dying Abraham asks Michael to 'deliver a message for me (διακονῆσαί μοι λόγον)' to God.

[23] Philo, *Jos.* 241–42; *Vit. Mos.* 1.82–84; Jos., *Ant.* 10.177; *War* 3.352–54; 4.622–29 [626]. Interestingly, such language is largely absent from the LXX (διάκονος: Esth 1.10; 2.2; 6.3, 5; *4 Macc.* 9.17; Prov 10.4; διακονία: 1 Macc 11.58).

the Romans in self-aggrandizing terms. Far from a traitor, he is the διάκονος of God, announcing to the Romans the 'things to come' (τὰ μέλλοντα εἰπεῖν)—a task for which he deems himself uniquely fit.[24] After a few of Josephus's prescient predictions, Vespasian apparently agreed, calling him the διάκονος τῆς τοῦ θεοῦ φωνῆς and releasing him from prison (*War* 4.622–29 [626]). We are here a long ways from mere service. To broker the relationship of gods and humans, and to traverse the middle space—this is what the διάκονος does.

This is also what the Paul of Eph 3.1–13 does. Collins, in his analysis of the verbal form, highlights five elements that recur repeatedly with it: (1) a form of διακον-; (2) the object delivered; (3) the one who mandates the delivery; (4) the recipients; and (5) in the case of a passive verb, the agent.[25] Given the nominal form in 3.7, the syntax is different, but all five are present in the near context: (5) Paul is (1) the courier of (2) good news, clearly heavenly in origin and (3) given by God as a gift, to be dispensed (4) to the gentiles. This good news of divine beneficence toward gentiles (so 1.3–14; 2.4–8 and 11–22), moreover, results in the reversal of the gentiles' status (2.11–13 and 19–22), which Paul tersely summarizes as his μυστήριον at 3.6 (thus διὰ τοῦ εὐαγγελίου). This mystery is not ecclesiological per se—as if Paul announces the unity of the church—but is relentlessly focused on the gentiles, both across 2.11–22 and in its summary in 3.6.[26] Paul is not the courier of a message about the church's unity, much less a servant of the (universal) church. Nor does he even, firstly, bear a message about the unity of Jew and gentile. Instead, that unity is the ground (γάρ, 2.14–18) of Paul's *gentile* gospel (2.11–13 and 19–22)—a point confirmed by the lack of named co-heirs in 3.6. Paul is not concerned in Ephesians with the other (Jewish) side of the equation.[27] Central to the image of Paul in Eph 3.1–13, substantively and structurally, is that Paul is the courier of the gentile gospel. Much as Josephus reckoned himself the διάκονος τῆς τοῦ θεοῦ φωνῆς to the Romans, the Paul of Ephesians fancies himself the διάκονος τοῦ εὐαγγελιου θεοῦ for gentiles.

Turning back to 3.2, Paul also reckons himself the fiduciary of a gift for these gentiles. The clauses of 3.2–3a, centered on Paul's οἰκονομία, and 3.6–7, on Paul as διάκονος, run parallel: both are defined relative to/as a gift given by God; each is picked

---

[24] Fit, that is, due to his priestly descent, and his skill in interpreting dreams, divining God's speech, and elucidating Israel's scriptures (Jos., *War* 3.352–53).

[25] Collins, 'Monocultural Usage', 300.

[26] For this way of reading 'Paul' vis-à-vis Ephesians, which goes back to Baur, see my Chapter 2. This impressionistic verdict continues to characterize works on Paul's reception (in addition to n. 7 above, see John W. Marshall, 'Misunderstanding the New Paul: Marcion's Transformation of the *Sonderzeit* Paul', *JECS* 20 [2012]: 25, 27–8), and while most Ephesians scholars rightly recognize the gentile focus of Ephesians, the language of the church as central to Paul's focus still persists (Lincoln, *Ephesians*, lxiii, 193–4; Hoehner, *Ephesians*, 111–12). Broader problems with translating ἐκκλησία 'church' in Paul are particularly pressing in Ephesians given the scholarly penchant to read in it a developed ecclesiology. For this reason, I refer to Paul's auditors as Christ-groups/assemblies throughout, following Anders Runesson, 'The Question of Terminology: The Architecture of Contemporary Discussions of Paul', in *Paul within Judaism*, 53–78; and Jennifer Eyl, 'Semantic Voids, New Testament Translation, and Anachronism: The Case of Paul's Use of *Ekklēsia*', *MTSR* 26 (2014): 315–39.

[27] As Dahl rightly suggests, 'If there were Christians of Jewish origins among the addressees, the author takes no account of them' ('Gentiles, Christians, and Israelites in the Epistle to the Ephesians', in *Studies in Ephesians*, 446).

up in 3.8-9 as half of that gift; and significantly, the terms are conceptually similar as well. Both position Paul in a mediatorial role situated between the gift-giving God on the one side and the newly gift-receiving gentiles on the other. Διάκονος designates Paul a courier of a divine message for these gentiles, while Paul's οἰκονομία has him managing a gift for the gentile portion of God's family lineage.

If the former is at home in the religious world of priests and prophets, the latter belongs to the economic world of estate management.[28] It denotes, most simply, the management of the ancient household, a matter of no small debate in the lengthy discussions of Xenophon and Aristotle on the topic (Xen., *Oec.* 1.1–4; Arist., *Pol.* 1253b). As John Goodrich shows, this base meaning can extend to include managerial work in other sectors, most notably in regal, civic, and private administrative contexts.[29] Real differences aside, in each the οἰκονόμος sits in the middle of a hierarchy, with charge over underlings on behalf of a superior, administering tasks which were frequently financial in scope.[30] Even where the object managed is metaphorical, the base meaning of οἰκονομ-language does not lose its basic managerial sense. To draw again on notable figures from the Jewish tradition: David may be gifted in the οἰκονομία of earthly affairs (Jos., *Ant.* 7.391), but God manages (οἰκονομέω) all things to their deliverance (Philo, *Dec.* 53); and Joseph may manage Egypt's grain on behalf of Pharaoh (Jos., *Ant.* 2.87–90, 93–94),[31] but Baruch is the 'manager of the faith' (οἰκονόμος τῆς πίστεως, *4 Bar.* 7.2), to whom Jeremiah disburses mysteries (μυστήρια)—an act which completes Jeremiah's own οἰκονομία (*4 Bar.* 9.29 and 31). The word is thoroughly at home in the world of ancient administration.

Paul's language in Eph 3.2 sits comfortably in this world as well, but this is precisely where it has not usually been read. Three mistakes persist here, each tied to overly theological readings of the key terms οἰκονομία and χάρις. In the first, οἰκονομία is read as essentially God's 'plan' of salvation history (*Heilsgeschichte*). Here οἰκονομία denotes the result of good management—i.e. orderly arrangement—which gets theologically translated to God's arrangement of salvation history.[32] In this reading, Paul's χάρις

---

[28] The seminal study is now John Goodrich, *Paul as an Administrator of God in 1 Corinthians*, SNTSMS 152 (Cambridge: Cambridge University Press, 2012). On estate (as opposed to regal and civic) management, the conceptual field within which he places Paul, see 71–102. More concisely, see Giorgio Agamben, *The Kingdom and the Glory: For a Theological Genealogy of Economy and Government*, trans. Lorenzo Chiesa with Matteo Mandarini (Stanford, CA: Stanford University Press, 2011), 17–20.

[29] Goodrich, *Paul as an Administrator*, 25–102, with useful summaries of each at 46–7, 69–70, and 102.

[30] Goodrich, *Paul as an Administrator*, 23.

[31] Unsurprisingly, Joseph is an obvious candidate to be linked to an οἰκονομία; see also *T. Jos.* 12.3; Jos., *Ant.* 2.57.

[32] So, BDAG, s.v. οἰκονομία 2b. The shift here is cogently described by Agamben, *Kingdom and the Glory*, 17–23 (directly at 20). From the second century on, Agamben finds this salvation-historical turn in οἰκονομία pervasive in early Christianity, but he criticizes reading it back into Paul, including all three uses in Ephesians (21–23). The latter is precisely what Oscar Cullmann does in his influential 1946 *Christus und die Zeit*, in which he makes *Heilsgeschichte* (οἰκονομία) central to his account of time in primitive Christianity, and appeals to Eph 1.10; 3.2 and 9; and Col 1.25 for its presence already in Paul (Eng. trans. *Christ and Time*, trans. Floyd V. Filson [London: SCM, 1962], 33 n. 17). Cullmann has been critiqued, but 'plan' remains the ubiquitous reading at Eph 1.10 and 3.9, if slightly less so at 3.2. Mitton, *Epistle to the Ephesians*, 93, takes οἰκονομία as 'plan' at 1.10; 3.2 and 9, and distinguishes Ephesians from Colossians on this score.

is rightly not read as (theological) grace, but Paul's gift *is* to witness to, or unveil, God's salvation-historical plan (οἰκονομία).³³ The second mistake has a similar result, but gets there from a different direction. These readers rightly give οἰκονομία its managerial sense, and make Paul its subject, but overly reify χάρις: Paul is now the steward of Christian grace, as opposed (so goes the implication) to a dispensation of works.³⁴ A third variation sits between the above, with the emphasis here on *God's* plan (οἰκονομία) to use Paul to preach (Christian) grace.³⁵ Each of the above, in its own way, sweeps Paul into the currents of *Heilsgeschichte* as the great apostle and executor of God's *Heilsplan*—in some respects an exalted image, but an increasingly unpopular one in post-War/Holocaust scholarship on Paul.

In the face of these misreadings, and in view of the repetition of οἰκ-terminology in 2.19–22 and the clear sense of χάρις as Paul's 'gift' at 3.8, I suggest that in 3.2 οἰκονομία does not mean *Heilsgeschichte* and χάρις does not mean grace.³⁶ As Giorgio Agamben rightly urges, we should not import a theological sense for οἰκονομία unless exegesis demands it.³⁷ In the case of Ephesians, exegesis does not demand (much less invite) it, and the same is true for χάρις. In Eph 2.19–22, Paul narrates how, in the body of the messiah, God has reversed gentile status, turning foreigners (πάροικοι) to kinsfolk (οἰκεῖοι), building them on an apostolic foundation (ἐποικοδομηθέντες) and into a dwelling place (συνοικοδομεῖσθε εἰς κατοικητήριον) for God—a construction (οἰκοδομή) that turns out to be that centerpiece of Israel's *cultus*, a holy temple (ναός ἅγιος). In Eph 3.2, Paul assumes (εἴ γε) that his gentile auditors have heard of his managerial role with respect to this household/building/temple.³⁸ Critically, however, and as with his role as διάκονος, Paul does not have managerial responsibility for the whole household, which would bring us back, in meaning if not in lexical choice, to Paul as *the* apostle of *the* church. Instead, he manages a gift given him to disburse *to the gentiles* (εἰς ὑμᾶς), one portion of God's family lineage. At the bookends of the opening sentence of Paul's digression (3.2–7), then, the image of Paul inscribed therein is clear: Paul is the courier of good news from Israel's God for gentiles, and the fiduciary of a gift which he manages for gentiles—precisely what 3.8–9 goes on to describe, and hangs on the singular peg of Paul's χάρις.³⁹ To be sure, even if circumscribed to the gentiles, this is no small (self-)image, but is it more outsized than elsewhere in Paul?

---

³³ Cullmann, *Christ and Time*, 223; Schnackenburg, *Ephesians*, 131. Even John Reumann, 'Oikonomia-Terms in Paul in Comparison with Lucan *Heilsgeschichte*', NTS 13 (1967): 147–67, who takes on Cullmann directly, and rightly emphasizes the administrative character of οἰκονομία, ends up falling back part way into this way of reading Eph 3.2 (163, although cf. his caution at 157), which he unsurprisingly regards as development away from Paul. For discussion of Reumann, with further bibliography, see Goodrich, *Paul as an Administrator*, 14–15.

³⁴ Lincoln, *Ephesians*, 174; Hoehner, *Ephesians*, 422–4. Contra Hoehner, Paul does not here speak of his 'administration regarding God's unmerited favor' (423).

³⁵ So, e.g., Robinson, *Ephesians*, 167; Best, *Ephesians*, 298–9.

³⁶ Better on all of this is Muddiman, *Ephesians*, 150; Thielman, *Ephesians*, 193–4.

³⁷ Agamben, *Kingdom and the Glory*, 22.

³⁸ On the function of εἴ γε, see BDF §454 (2). Interestingly, Paul can elsewhere appeal to what his auditors have heard (ἀκούω) as the basis for narrating their identity (Gal 1.13 and 23).

³⁹ For a similar argument relative to Paul's use of οἰκονομία in Col 1.25, see T. J. Lang, 'Disbursing the Account of God: Fiscal Terminology and the Economy of God in Colossians 1,24–25', ZNW 107 (2016): 116–36.

It is certainly not different from the role Paul envisages for himself vis-à-vis the Christ-assembly in Corinth. A striking passage in this regard is 1 Cor 3.5–4.5, in which Paul negotiates his identity in the context of Corinthian factionalism (1.10– 4.21). Paul almost certainly founded this assembly (3.6, 10; 4.15), and in a fleeting but suggestive statement connects his initial work in Corinth with the 'gift of God which was given to me' (τὴν χάριν τοῦ θεοῦ τὴν δοθεῖσάν μοι, 3.10). Paul moves quickly along, not defining his χάρις here, but the two self-appellations that bookend this section, and which Paul uses to clarify his role in their founding, are striking:

> What, then, is Apollos? What is Paul? Διάκονοι through whom you believed. (1 Cor 3.5)

> Let a person reckon us this way: as servants of Christ and οἰκονόμοι of the mysteries of God. (1 Cor 4.1)

That is, Paul explicates his role in their founding by appealing to his dual role as their διάκονος and οἰκονόμος, tied loosely to his χάρις.

The similarities run further, however. After 1 Cor 3.5, Paul shifts to an agricultural metaphor (3.6–9b) and then to an architectural one (3.9c–14), which leads him to self-identify as a 'wise architect' who laid the Corinthian foundation (3.10). In 3.9–14, in fact, Paul's repeated use of οἰκ-terms (5×) rivals the repetition in Eph 2.19–22, and ends in the same place: the Corinthian Christ-assembly is not just any construction, but that glorious οἰκοδομή of Israel's cult, the 'temple of God' (ναὸς θεοῦ) where the 'spirit of God dwells' (τὸ πνεῦμα τοῦ θεοῦ οἰκεῖ, 3.16). This is simply the programmatic vision of Eph 2.19–22 applied to a particular assembly. In a context of partisan identification, Paul's concern is with the unity of the assembly (3.17), not apostolic distinctions (3.21–22). *Pace* Barrett, if Paul is anywhere the 'great architect of the unity of the church', it is here in 1 Corinthians, not Ephesians. In any respect, what stands out is that in a setting where Paul clearly negotiates his own image, not least vis-à-vis his role in founding this Christ-assembly, he roots this founding in his God-given gift, defined via the two poles of that gift in Eph 3.2 and 7 (cf. vv. 8–9), his work as God's διάκονος and οἰκονόμος.[40] If 1 Corinthians and Ephesians are different on this score, it lies not in development, but in the difference between a programmatic description of Paul's gift (Ephesians) and his recollection of that gift in action (1 Corinthians).

The similarities run deeper still, in fact, to how Paul uses these two words across his Corinthian correspondence. As we would expect from Eph 3.6–7, Paul uses διακον-language in 1 and 2 Corinthians consistently to describe both his initial work in, and the message he brings to, Corinth. We saw this already at 1 Cor 3.5, a self-designation that results from the fact that Paul delivered (διακονέω) the Corinthians (2 Cor 3.3). This claim is so bold that he backs off to remind himself at whose commission he works (3.5), only to double down on his role as the διάκονος of a new covenant

---

[40] Nor are these idiosyncratic uses in 1 and 2 Corinthians. In addition to 1 Cor 3.5, Paul designates himself a διάκονος at 2 Cor 3.6; 6.4; and 11.23, and an οἰκονόμος again at 1 Cor 9.17 (after initially at 4.1).

(3.6)—one characterized by spirit, righteousness, and glory (3.7–21). Here in 3.7–21, Paul's role as courier links to his message, which he aptly summarizes as his διακονία (4.1), and later calls his διακονία of reconciliation (5.18), in which God's appeal to the Corinthians (and the world!) comes through Paul (5.20), just what we would expect of a διάκονος. In 1 and 2 Corinthians Paul nowhere ties his commission exclusively to gentiles,[41] but if the Christ-assembly in Corinth is predominantly gentile,[42] then all of the above depicts, again, the programmatic claim of Eph 3.6–7 in action. In Rom 11.13–14, however, Paul backs out again and conceives his apostleship in more general terms, mirroring Eph 3.7: Paul has a διακονία to the gentiles.

Equally striking, if less frequent, is Paul's use of οἰκονομ- language in 1 Corinthians, and what he links it to. Paul, as we already saw, is a manager of mysteries (1 Cor 4.1), which is exactly how the Paul of Ephesians goes on to clarify his οἰκονομία in Eph 3.3 and 9, albeit in the singular. The other use in 1 Cor 9.17 is notoriously vexed, but for my purposes, the point is clear enough: Paul ties his fiduciary task (οἰκονομία) explicitly to the compulsion (ἄκων) he is under to proclaim the good news (εὐαγγελίζωμαι), with εὐαγγελίζω/εὐαγγέλιον appearing repeatedly in these four verses (9.15–18). What is more, the entire point of this section, that Paul so vehemently argues, is that he has proclaimed his gospel to them 'free of charge' (ἀδάπανος). He has executed his fiduciary duty, one might say, as a gift. Again, and strikingly, Paul ties his οἰκονομία in 1 Corinthians to exactly those two tasks to which he connects them in Eph 3—his disclosure of mysteries (3.2–3) and his proclamation of the gospel (3.8). If the Paul of Ephesians is not Paul, he has imitated the Paul of 1 and 2 Corinthians remarkably well. The image of Paul in each is virtually identical.

Paul's Mystery: Do Others Know It?—The Image's 'Problem' (Eph 3.3b–5)

Paul's role as a διάκονος of the gospel with the οἰκονομία of a gift for gentiles is unproblematic, at least with respect to 1 and 2 Corinthians. In Eph 3.3–5, however, Paul immediately explicates his managerial task as having to do with a mystery he received according to revelation (κατὰ ἀποκάλυψιν, 3.3),[43] into which he enjoys particular insight (3.4), but which has also been revealed to a set of his co-religionists, God's 'holy apostles and prophets' (3.5). These few verses have proven fertile ground for speculations about the developed *Paulusbild* of Ephesians, although the fact that the alleged development runs in opposite directions—is Paul here valorized as *the* bearer of the mystery, to which the others are subordinate,[44] or is his gentile-mystery here assimilated to a broader set of apostolic colleagues (à la Acts), his primacy devalued?[45]—might suggest that the problem lay more with scholars' presuppositions about Paul than anything in Ephesians itself. That said, elements of Eph 3.3–5 look

---

[41] So, rightly, Watson, *Paul, Judaism, and the Gentiles*, 72.
[42] Gordon D. Fee, *The First Epistle to the Corinthians*, NICNT (Grand Rapids: Eerdmans, 1987), 4.
[43] The ὅτι of v. 3 picks up the ἠκούσατε of v. 2, and what follows stands in logical apposition to Paul's οἰκονομία (so, e.g., Best, *Ephesians*, 299).
[44] So Sterling, 'From Apostle to the Gentiles', 85–8 (directly at 88); Penny, 'Pseudo-Pauline Letter', 264.
[45] So Lincoln, *Ephesians*, 179. For a helpful discussion of Eph 3.1–13 in the context of other New Testament traditions about the origins of the gentile mission, see Ernest Best, 'The Revelation to Evangelize the Gentiles', in *Essays on Ephesians* (Edinburgh: T. & T. Clark, 1997), 103–38.

in some respects unique within Paul's collection. The challenge of 3.3–5 is not understanding what it says, but deciding whether Paul would say it. That is a question for comparative exegesis, reading these verses alongside the other letters. Toward this end, I begin by clarifying the challenge of 3.3–5—that is, where the questions actually lie.

The challenge is not, firstly, that the Paul of Ephesians mediates a μυστήριον per se. That claim is relatively commonplace in antiquity, in both Jewish and pagan circles alike. While the term is largely absent from the LXX, God gives Daniel insight into the μυστήριον of Nebuchadnezzar's dreams (LXX Dan 2.18, 27; cf. 2.1, 19, 28, 47), which turn out to be μυστήρια about the end of days (2.28–30).[46] In the apocrypha and pseudepigrapha, Enoch (*1 En.* 103.2; cf. *Jub.* 4.18), Levi (*T. Levi* 2.10), Jeremiah (*4 Bar.* 9.23, 29), and Ezra (*4 Ezra* 12.36–38) all receive revelation of divine mysteries, typically eschatological in orientation. For the sectarians of Qumran, the Teacher of Righteousness mediates mysteries (1QpHab 7; 1QH^a 9.21; 10.13–14; and 12.27–28),[47] and Philo is 'initiated into the great mysteries' by the great oracular figures of Israel's history, Moses and Jeremiah (*Cher.* 48–49).

More broadly, as James Constantine Hanges shows, claims to divine revelation are ubiquitous in pagan sources, specifically by those involved in relocating a god's cult.[48] The same is true of a group that Heidi Wendt loosely categorizes 'freelance religious experts'—independent purveyors in the competitive marketplace of ancient religion.[49] And as Sarah Rollens argues with respect to Greco-Roman associations in particular, such claims to revelation redound not just to the prestige of the recipient, but to the association founded on their basis as well, linking group members to each other (i.e. a shared identity) and to the past (i.e. to a divine revelation).[50] To be sure, virtually all of the Jewish and pagan data along these lines are retrospective, assigning such claims to figures of the (distant) past, and valorizing them for their heavenly insight.[51] And this may encourage the now-traditional way of reading Eph 3.2–13, as a testamentary tribute to a mythologized Paul, girded with a mystery to buttress the identity of later gentile assemblies.[52] But this fails to recognize, as Hanges, Wendt, and Rollens rightly acknowledge, that Paul makes such claims for *himself* in the other letters.[53] The simple

---

[46] On the Hebrew (סוד) and Aramaic (רז) terms behind μυστήριον here, see Markus N. A. Bockmuehl, *Revelation and Mystery in Ancient Judaism and Pauline Christianity* (Eugene, OR: Wipf & Stock, 2009), 15–16. On the avoidance of μυστήριον in the LXX, see 100–104.

[47] In a striking passage in the Rule of the Community, the *maskil* is enlightened פלאו מרזי, 'from his wondrous mysteries' (1QS 11.5)—mysteries which illuminate otherwise hidden salvation and knowledge (11.6), and the inheritance of the holy ones, who are a chosen and heavenly assembly (11.7–8; cf. Eph 1.11, 14, 18; 2.6; 3.5, 9–10).

[48] James Constantine Hanges, *Paul, Founder of Churches: A Study in Light of the Evidence for the Role of 'Founder-Figures' in the Hellenistic-Roman Period*, WUNT 292 (Tübingen: Mohr Siebeck, 2012), vii; cf. 69–77.

[49] Heidi Wendt, *At the Temple Gates: The Religion of Freelance Experts in the Roman Empire* (New York: Oxford University Press, 2016), 154.

[50] Sarah E. Rollens, 'The God Came to Me in a Dream: Epiphanies in Voluntary Associations as a Context for Paul's Vision of Christ', *HTR* 111 (2018): 41–65 (directly at 42).

[51] This is particularly true of the data studied in Hanges, *Paul, Founder of Churches*, and Rollens, 'The God Came to Me'.

[52] We have already seen this impulse above in Pervo, *Making of Paul*, 75–7, but this is also how Hanges, *Paul, Founder of Churches*, 440–1, reads Eph 3.1–13.

[53] Each of them does this by virtue of inscribing Paul into the picture they draw on the basis of other pagan sources. But Wendt sees this particularly clearly in her 'James C. Hanges, *Paul, Founder of*

fact, then, that in Eph 3.2-13 we meet Paul as the dispenser of a heavenly μυστήριον, in the midst of a larger digression about his gentile mission, cannot prima facie be a strike against it—as if these sorts of things only happen in retrospect. Ephesians 3.3-5 *could* be a testament to Paul, and a window into his post-mortem veneration/proto-catholic subsumption. It could also just be Paul, engaged in the fragile and complex art of negotiating a hearing with a gentile community that does not know him, but who seems to know something of him (3.2; cf. 6.21-22)—a particularly difficult task to undertake by letter.[54] Both are possibilities, and both are historically defensible. The proof is in the comparative exegesis. Even if not so directly, do we meet the core suggestions of Eph 3.3-5 elsewhere in Paul's letters?

I suggest that we do, but this requires clarifying the right questions to ask. In broad sweep, Eph 3.2-6 looks quite conventional in three respects. Elsewhere, Paul clearly thinks he has received divine mysteries, to which he enjoys privileged access (Rom 11.25; 1 Cor 2.1, 7; 4.1; 13.2; 15.51; cf. Col 1.25-26; 4.3). Equally, Paul fancies himself the recipient of an apocalyptic vision—one in which he saw Jesus and which he (at least retroactively) associates with the reception of his gentile mission (Gal 1.11-12, 16).[55] Lastly, Paul links his fiduciary task (οἰκονομία) with his access to mysteries (1 Cor 4.1). So when the Paul of Ephesians is the fiduciary of a gentile-gift, which is closely connected to a mystery he has by revelation (3.2-3), we are on familiar ground. That said, while the words all resonate in a Pauline register, the devil is in the details. In Eph 3.3-5, it is the *gentile*-μυστήριον (3.6) that Paul has by revelation, and which a set of his co-religionists share. The questions, then, are two: in Paul's other letters, does he receive his (gentile-)mystery via an apocalypse (3.3)? And does he think that other 'apostles and prophets' share knowledge of this mystery?

In a strictly lexical and syntactic sense, the answer to the former is (mostly) no, with only Eph 3.3 and Rom 16.25 linking Paul's μυστήριον directly with an ἀποκάλυψις (cf. more obliquely 2 Cor 2.1, 7 and 10). And given the regnant scholarly position on Rom 16.25-27, such a co-text for Eph 3.3 hardly inspires confidence.[56] While useful, however, a narrow focus on the lexical/syntactic question misses a larger point. If the μυστήριον in Ephesians, known to Paul κατὰ ἀποκάλυψιν, is gentile incorporation, then the real questions are whether Paul elsewhere (1) describes his mystery similarly, and (2) depicts his insight into *that* (i.e. gentile inclusion) as the result of revelation, whether he uses the language of a μυστήριον or not. And here we meet a conundrum. In Rom 11.25-26, Paul's μυστήριον resembles closely the picture of Eph 3.6,

---

Churches: A Study in Light of the Evidence for the Role of 'Founder-Figures' in the Hellenistic-Roman Period. A Review Essay', R&T 20 (2013): 292-302 (297).

[54] This is the line Campbell takes in his *Framing Paul*, 315-16. See more broadly Wendt, 'Review Essay', 296, and extending the courtesy to Ephesians.

[55] I am skeptical that we should distinguish between δι' ἀποκαλύψεως (Gal 1.12) and κατὰ ἀποκάλυψιν (Eph 3.3; cf. Gal 2.2), as Lincoln, *Ephesians*, 175, suggests (for criticism, see Thielman, *Ephesians*, 194-5). But even if we were to, the difference is negligible—the point in both cases is that Paul receives what he receives via an epistemological *novum*.

[56] On the secondary status of 16.25-27, see Robert Jewett, *Romans: A Commentary*, Hermeneia (Minneapolis: Fortress, 2007), 998-1002. T. J. Lang, *Mystery and the Making of a Christian Historical Consciousness: From Paul to the Second Century*, BZNW 219 (Berlin: de Gruyter, 2015), reads these texts as part of a developing 'mystery schema of revelation' (5; cf. 69-107, 110-17). See also Bockmuehl, *Revelation and Mystery*, 199-210.

but he does not connect this explicitly to revelation. In Gal 1.11–12 and 15–16, on the other hand, Paul's gospel comes to him δι' ἀποκαλύψεως, which propels him 'to gospel [Christ] among the gentiles', but nowhere is this Paul's μυστήριον. Finally, in 1 Cor 2.6–10, Paul speaks ἐν μυστηρίῳ the hidden wisdom of God (2.7), which God 'revealed to us by his spirit' (ἡμῖν δὲ ἀπεκάλυψεν ὁ θεὸς διὰ τοῦ πνεύματος), but which is not obviously related to the Jew/gentile question.[57] Notice, then, what we have. In Romans: Jew/gentile + μυστήριον; in Galatians: gentile + ἀποκάλυψις; in 1 Corinthians: μυστήριον + ἀποκάλυψις; and in Ephesians: μυστήριον + ἀποκάλυψις + Jew/gentile.

In these clearly overlapping texts, which deal variably with Paul's mystery, revelation, and the gentile question, Ephesians represents the center set. It gets none of the other texts exactly right, and all of them partly right. To state it this way, however, obscures the fact that none of the 'undisputed' texts match perfectly either. Remarkably, these texts converge in Ephesians where they diverge from each other. Conceptually, the language of Ephesians at this point maps quite cleanly onto the others in their totality. To identify the differences in Ephesians and label them development is, strictly speaking, arbitrary. Instead of a primitive/developed binary, it would be more accurate to say that the image of Paul in Ephesians here is general, where the others are ad hoc. Paul and his mystery in 3.3–4 and 6 has the air of the programmatic—a program met in action in the other letters.

What, then, of v. 5, and the claim that Paul shares his gentile-mystery, in some sense, with other apostles and prophets? That Paul thinks some such figures have access to *a* mystery (or mysteries) is straightforwardly unproblematic, and we know this most notably from 1 Corinthians. In 2.1, Paul prioritizes his position vis-à-vis the mystery—he came proclaiming the μυστήριον τοῦ θεοῦ to the Christ-assembly there—but by 2.6–16, and at his own admission, that mystery is far from his alone, as his shift to the plural implies: '*We* speak ἐν μυστηρίῳ the hidden wisdom of God' (2.7), which God 'revealed to *us* by his spirit' (2.10). This is, in fact, the same two-step as Eph 3.3–5—vis-à-vis the mystery, first Paul, then the group.[58] As of 1 Cor 2.10, Paul's 'we' is ambiguous, but as 4.1 clarifies, it includes at least Paul, Apollos, and Cephas, who are all 'managers of the mysteries of God' (cf. 3.22). And it is precisely the latter two that Paul elsewhere reckons fellow ἀπόστολοι (1 Cor 4.1 in view of 4.6 and 9; 9.5; 15.5–8 [cf. Gal 1.18–19; 2.8]). The connection is still more explicit for prophets, when in 1 Cor 13.2 Paul links the gift of προφητεία with knowledge of 'all μυστήρια'.

At the very least, then, Paul thinks God's mystery has been revealed to *some* figures he labels apostles, as well as to those with the gift of prophecy. It is probably no accident, then, that apostles and prophets head Paul's list of those God appoints in the Christ-assembly (1 Cor 12.29). Such figures are responsible to mediate a divine message, and so are well-positioned to receive and transmit mysteries. Obviously there is nothing as programmatic in 1 Corinthians as there is in Eph 3.5, but there is also nothing that diverges from it. And this is telling, for with respect to the recipients of the mystery, Eph 3.3–5 does diverge rather sharply from the Apostolic Fathers—precisely

---

[57] On the complex syntax of this section, 2.7 in particular, see Lang, *Mystery and the Making*, 54–60.
[58] *Pace* Sterling, 'From Apostle to the Gentiles', 85–8, then, Eph 3.3–5 does not require a redaction-critical reading vis-à-vis Col 1.26–27 to be explicable (i.e. 1 Cor 2.1–10).

that group of texts toward which Ephesians is ostensibly on a trajectory (see the following excursus). What displaces the 'apostles and prophets' in Eph 3.5, then, is not mistranslation (as in διάκονος), nor theological reification (as in οἰκονομία), but an imagined historical trajectory that reads the same words in Ephesians with a different referent than they have in Paul. Put simply, ἀπόστολοι καὶ προφῆται in Ephesians become a valorized magisterium, rather than people like Apollos and Peter (et al.), or the prophets of 1 Cor 13.2.

Excursus:
Mystery, Apostles, and Prophets in the Apostolic Fathers.

If Eph 3.3-5 shares conceptual overlap with 1 Corinthians on the question of who receives divine μυστήρια, how about with the Apostolic Fathers? Who receives or manages mysteries in these writings? Μυστήριον appears eleven times in this corpus (Ignatius, *Eph.* 19.1; *Mag.* 9.2; *Trall.* 2.3; *Didache* 11.11; *Diogn.* 4.6; 7.1-2; 8.10; 10.7; 11.2, 5), and is linked one time to prophets (*Did.* 11.11), never to apostles, and so never to the two together (as in Eph 3.5). In Ignatius (*Trall.* 2.3), διάκονοι mediate the μυστήρια of Jesus, and in every other text in which recipients are designated (or implied), it is always all Christians who receive or mediate the μυστήρια of God. In other words, relative to the mystery and its recipients, if Eph 3.5 represents a stage on the way ('trajectory') to the restriction of the μυστήριον to the magisterial few, it is a stage without a final destination. The evidence, in fact, points in the exact opposite direction: Paul keeps the circle relatively narrow (although they *mediate* the mystery to all), while the Apostolic Fathers—the *Epistle to Diognetus* in particular—throw the doors wide open. In this, the Apostolic Fathers follow the logic of texts like Col 1.26 (cf. Eph 1.9) much more closely than that of Paul in, say, 1 Corinthians. But the 'trajectory' runs the reverse of what most scholars assume, and Eph 3.5 lies much closer to Paul's words in 1 Corinthians than to the Apostolic Fathers, with whom its account of the μυστήριον, strictly speaking, shares nothing in common.

• • •

But does Paul think that these apostles and prophets share knowledge of the *gentile* mystery as he depicts it in Eph 3.6? Part of what displaces Eph 3.3-6 here is not just an imagined historical trajectory, but modern portraits of Paul that underwrite that trajectory. Pauline scholarship going back to Baur, allied to Paul's rhetoric in Gal 1, has a long history of reading Paul and his gentile gospel as if they are wholly unique within the early Jesus movement. Any suggestion, then, of a shared apostolic revelation about gentiles is designated a retroactive attempt to democratize the gentile mission, à la what Luke did for Philip (Acts 8) and Peter (Acts 10). The problem of Acts thus becomes the problem of Eph 3.3-5. On this way of reading the evidence, Eph 3.3-5 imposes a false unity, and papers over what was really conflict all the way down—a prime example of later orthodoxy strong-arming history.[59] And Gal 1-2 can

---

[59] This is most apparent in Lincoln, *Ephesians*, 179, but it is also present in Best, 'Revelation to Evangelize', 130-2, who thinks the author of Ephesians knows two traditions about the origins of the gentile mission (Paul and the Twelve) and combines them.

be read in such a way so as to support such a view of Pauline uniqueness: Paul with the εὐαγγέλιον τῆς ἀκροβυστίας, and Peter for the περιτομή (2.7); Paul and Barnabas εἰς τὰ ἔθνη, James, Peter and John εἰς τὴν περιτομήν (2.9; cf. 1.11–12, 16–17). There is a big difference, however, between dividing responsibilities and operating within hermetically sealed areas of revelation. The former follows from Gal 2.7–9; the latter does not. Moreover, one can acknowledge that the specifics of Paul's gentile-gospel may be idiosyncratic within the early Jesus movement, and at the same time say that something like Eph 3.5–6 is operative during Paul's career. In fact, I suggest that something like the μυστήριον of Eph 3.6—the ἔθνη as συγκληρονόμα καὶ σύσσωμα καὶ συμμέτοχα τῆς ἐπαγγελίας ἐν Χριστῷ Ἰησοῦ—*was* known more widely than Paul, and by precisely the sorts of figures Eph 3.5 envisages. What is more, we know this from Paul's other letters, where both key passages and passing references virtually demand this conclusion, and make little sense apart from it.[60] Ephesians 3.5, then, is not only not a problem, it clarifies Paul—making explicit a tacit assumption that we get only hints of elsewhere. Ephesians, in other words, may not blunt *Paul's* radicality, but it does blunt radical *Paulinists* who envisage Paul alone with the gentile-mystery.

This is arguable, in fact, from Gal 1–2 itself—that apogee of Pauline independence. After fiercely defending the autonomy of his reception of his (gentile-)gospel (1.11–23), not least its lack of reliance on other apostles (1.17), Paul goes to Jerusalem some (significant) time later with Barnabus and Titus (2.1) to do what he foreswore to do earlier: set before a larger group of apostles (οἱ δοκοῦντες, 2.2, 6 and 7) his gospel for the gentiles (τὸ εὐαγγέλιον ὃ κηρύσσω ἐν τοῖς ἔθνεσιν), in order to make sure that his work was not for nothing (εἰς κενόν, 2.2). How Paul recounts their response is telling: Titus, a Ἕλλην, was not 'compelled to be circumcised' (ἠναγκάσθη περτμηθῆναι, 2.3), which preserves the 'truth of the gospel' (2.5).[61] The anecdote about Titus is vital, for it suggests that Paul did not go to Jerusalem to argue *that* the gospel was for the gentiles, but to adjudicate a controversial facet of his iteration of this gospel—the non-circumcision of the ἔθνη, of which Titus was a living, breathing (foreskinned) example. On this score, it seems, he was able to garner Jerusalem's backing. They 'added nothing' to him (2.6), recognized his 'gospel for the foreskin' (2.7), and sent him back on his way (2.9).

What this suggests, however, is frequently lost, both in Paul's rhetoric and scholarship allied to it. On the broad question of gentile inclusion, Paul is far from idiosyncratic. In fact, the logic of Gal 2.1–10 demands this conclusion, since it is difficult to explain why Paul would risk going to Jerusalem in the first place unless he was confident of the outcome—that is, unless he knew that the apostles there already agreed with him on the basic premise of gentile inclusion, and so were in a position to adjudicate the matter. And as Paul leaves Jerusalem, it is difficult to envision any

---

[60] Thus, rightly to my mind, the discussion in Fredriksen, *Paul*, 95–7, of the Antioch incident, and the relative unity of the major players on the meta-level question of gentile inclusion (specifically 97; cf. 103; and strikingly on 146–7).

[61] Even if Gal 2.4–5 represents a digression in the text, depicting an earlier Antioch dispute (Watson, *Paul, Judaism, and the Gentiles*, 102–5), which may well be the case, in the narrative logic of Gal 2 itself, the preservation of the 'truth of the gospel' (2.5) is clearly tied, for Paul, to Titus retaining his foreskin (2.3).

conclusion other than something like Eph 3.5-6 in his head: the ἔθνη are in, and those ἀπόστολοι (at least James, Cephas, and John) know it. Paul, of course, knows that *he* did not disclose this to them (Gal 1.16-17), so Israel's God must have. Far from a late first-century imposition of unity, in terms of co-texts, Eph 3.3-5 fits much better in the mid-first, making explicit what is tacit in a text like Gal 2.

Elsewhere in Paul, moreover, it is not just tacit. At the very least Barnabas, whom Paul draws into the apostolic ambit (1 Cor 9.5-6), shares responsibility for the gentile-εὐαγγέλιον (Gal 2.9; cf. Acts 14.4 and 14), and the picture widens out from here. Paul's host of fellow-workers in the gentile mission would all presumably agree with a summary of the mystery such as we find in Eph 3.6. Admittedly, Paul labels very few of them ἀπόστολοι, but some are: Andronicus and Junia in Rome (Rom 16.7); Epaphroditus in Philippi (Phil 2.25-30; 4.18); and Silvanus in Thessalonica (1 Thess 2.7; cf. 1.1, 5, 7; 2.1, 4, 9, 13).[62] It is probably these figures, then, that we should call to mind in Eph 3.5, rather than an idealized magisterium viewed retrospectively from the late first century. This is not to say that Paul's gentile-gospel was shared in every particular by each of the figures mentioned so far. But Eph 3.5-6 does not say that either. What it does say is that key early figures (ἀπόστολοι καὶ προφῆται) in the Jesus movement now see the ἔθνη on new terms vis-à-vis God and Israel, and that Paul has particular insight into this. Both Gal 2 and Paul's role as the leader of a gentile mission, in which he has colleagues, are fully explicable in precisely these terms.

Widening the circle still further, even Paul's fiercest polemics in Galatians and 2 Corinthians confirm that Eph 3.5-6 sits comfortably in the mid-first century. That is, the very presence of Paul's opponents in these places, who offer alternative gentile εὐαγγέλια (Gal 1.6-9; 6.12-13; 2 Cor 11.4-5, 12-13), suggests their tacit agreement with Eph 3.6. Why, in other words, would figures like those Paul attacks in 2 Cor 11-12 and Gal 5-6 travel to Galatia and Corinth to compete for gentile converts if the claim of Eph 3.6 was non-operative among other apostolic figures during Paul's lifetime? And as Paul's epithets suggest (ὑπερλίαν ἀπόστολοι [2 Cor 11.5; 12.11]; ψευδοαπόστολοι [11.13]) these figures clearly carry out their gentile missions under the auspices of an ἀποστολή. Paul, of course, is adamantly opposed to these figures, and would never grant that the gentile-mystery was revealed to *them*. And this may account for the inclusion of the ἅγιος in Eph 3.5. God reveals the gentile-mystery to his '*holy* apostles and prophets', but not to the ψευδοαπόστολοι (2 Cor 11.13), the ὑπερλίαν ἀπόστολοι (2 Cor 11.5; 12.11), or the ψευδαδέλφοι (Gal 2.4-5).[63] Regardless, Paul's polemics make clear that the democratization of the gentile mission did not wait for the late first century, and so Eph 3.5-6 need not be pushed there either. On the contrary, in Eph 3.3-6, Paul may just be engaged in the same posturing that we find in Galatians and Corinthians, careful to privilege his insight while simultaneously allying himself to other figures of authority.

---

[62] See the useful table in E. Earle Ellis, 'Coworkers, Paul and His', in *DPL* (p. 184).
[63] This would be the same sort of triangulating in which Paul engages in a text like Gal 2, where his gospel is affirmed by the big three of James, Peter, and John (cf. Eph 3.5), but the 'false brothers' lie outside the pale, and Paul is the key figure in advancing this gentile-gospel (Gal 2.4-10; cf. Eph 3.3).

Stepping back from the gentile-mystery itself, we see exactly this two-step in 1 Cor 15.1–11, a suggestive co-text for Eph 3.3–6. In 1 Cor 15.1–11, the question relates to Paul and the apostles vis-à-vis the εὐαγγέλιον; in Eph 3.3–6, it relates to Paul and the apostles and prophets vis-à-vis the μυστήριον, but the two terms are closely parallel in both letters.[64] Notice specifically how Paul negotiates his image relative to the other apostles, the alleged problem of Eph 3.3–5. In the span of eleven verses, the Paul of 1 Corinthians insists on the primacy of his gospel (15.1–2), only to turn and immediately situate himself and his gospel as links in an apostolic chain (15.3a). He can thoroughly align his gospel with that of the apostles (15.3b–8), subordinate himself to them (15.9), re-assert his priority (15.10) and then relativize it again (15.11). What began with the absolute necessity of adhering to Paul's gospel (15.1–2) ends on the first-person plural, and the common gospel Paul and the apostles share: '*This* [i.e. 15.3–8] we preached and this you believed' (15.11).[65] Here is Paul, negotiating his image and authority within a broader effort to show the unity of the apostolic message.

A myopic focus on Gal 1.11–12 and 15–19, that admits wholesale Paul's rhetoric of autonomy, may seem a problem for Eph 3.3–5. But then, it also is for 1 Cor 15.1–11— and for Gal 2.1–10. If any Pauline text actually decenters Paul, and subordinates him and his gospel to a set of co-religionists, it is 1 Cor 15.1–11, not Eph 3.5, and this at his own admission, on his own pen, in an indubitably Pauline letter. And 1 Cor 15.1–3 is far more difficult to reconcile with Gal 1.11–12 than either is with Eph 3.3–5, which sits rhetorically in the middle. The short answer to the so-called problem of Eph 3.3–5, then, is that it is not a problem at all, so long as one's interpretive horizon expands beyond Gal 1. Paul is not a radical Paulinist. Instead, I suggest the following. The *Paulusbild* of Paul vis-à-vis the other apostles is complex, varied, and negotiated— in 1 Cor 15.1–11 (cf. 1.10–17; 3.5–4.5), in Gal 1.11–12, 15–19; 2.1–14, *and in* Eph 3.3–5. Paul's rhetorical purposes in each letter largely explain how he narrates this relationship. In Galatians, facing a group deserting his gospel, Paul insists on its divine origin (Gal 1.11–12, 15–17), and then carefully forecloses any thought that it may be idiosyncratic (Gal 2.1–10). Paul's gospel is distinctive, but not unique. In 1 Corinthians, facing a fractured assembly divided along partisan apostolic lines, Paul homogenizes the apostolate and its gospel to ground Corinthian unity (1 Cor 1.10–17; 3.4–4.5; 15.1–11). Paul's gospel is anything but unique (15.3–8, 11), although his work for them is distinctive (15.1–2, 10). In Ephesians, seeking to shape the identity of a gentile assembly he does not know, Paul declares the mystery of their inclusion (3.3–4 and 6).[66] But given that someone else founded this assembly (4.20–21), Paul knows that this mystery is shared more broadly (3.5). Paul's mystery is not unique, but his

---

[64] In 1 Corinthians, both are used to describe the content of Paul's initial proclamation (1 Cor 2.1; 15.1). For the close connection in Ephesians, see 3.2–3, 6–7, and most closely, 6.19 (τὸ μυστήριον τοῦ εὐαγγελίου).

[65] Οὕτως κηρύσσομεν καὶ οὕτως ἐπιστεύσατε. On the use of οὕτως adjectivally here, see BDF §434; and Anthony C. Thiselton, *The First Epistle to the Corinthians*, NIGTC (Grand Rapids: Eerdmans, 2000), 1213.

[66] So, Lincoln, *Ephesians*, lxxiv–lxxvii, who does not think Paul wrote it, and Campbell, *Framing Paul*, 315–16, who thinks he did, both suggest the letter is functioning this way.

insight is distinctive. In all three, Paul has a complex apostolic world to negotiate. And I, at least, cannot see how he negotiates it substantially differently in Eph 3.3–5 than he does in Gal 1–2 and 1 Cor 3–4 and 15.

Paul's Gift: The Image in Nuce (Eph 3.8–9)

Thus far, I have detailed the image of Paul in Eph 3.2–7. In 3.8–9, Paul takes the twin poles of 3.2–7—his role as a courier of the gospel and dispenser of the gentile-mystery—and hangs them on a single peg, his χάρις. In Eph 3.8–9, in other words, Paul states directly and unequivocally the gentile-gift he manages (3.2). Here, then, is the *Paulusbild* of Ephesians *in nuce*.

> To me—less than the least of all the holy ones[67]—this gift [χάρις] was given: to announce good news to the gentiles [τοῖς ἔθνεσιν εὐαγγελίσασθαι] of the incomprehensible wealth of Christ, and to bring to light [for everyone] what is the management of the mystery [φωτίσαι (πάντας) τίς ἡ οἰκονομία τοῦ μυστηρίου] hidden from the ages in God who created all things. (Eph 3.8–9)

Paul details his gift via two infinitives: εὐαγγελίσασθαι and φωτίσαι. The first recalls his role as a διάκονος of the gospel (v. 7); the second further clarifies his role vis-à-vis the mystery for which he has a fiduciary responsibility (vv. 2–3).

The first is relatively straightforward, but given the ubiquity of judgments about the developed *Paulusbild* of 3.1–13, the object and audience of Paul's εὐαγγέλιον in 3.8b are noteworthy—namely, Christ-capital (τὸ πλοῦτος τοῦ Χριστοῦ) for the ἔθνη. Readers of secondary scholarship could be forgiven if they expected to find Paul's gift narrated as follows: τῇ ἐκκλησίᾳ εὐαγγελίσασθαι τὰς παραδόσεις τῶν ἀποστόλων, 'to announce to the assembly the good news of the traditions of the apostles' (so, e.g., Pervo). Ironically, this would be a legitimate reading of the image of Paul in 2 Thessalonians (2.15; 3.6) and 1 Corinthians (11.2; cf. 15.1–11), where Paul actually says he mediates παραδόσεις. But the Paul of Ephesians emphatically does not articulate his χάρις this way. Instead, the first half of Paul's gift in Eph 3 is to herald good news about Christ to gentiles (v. 8b). How does this fit alongside Paul's other letters?

To begin, εὐαγγελίζω is a fitting verb to make central to Paul's gift, since Paul consistently uses it to depict his initial work in a city. In fact, as with other terms across Eph 3.2–13, Paul's concern 'to gospel' the gentiles in 3.8b is simply a programmatic statement of what he *does* in practice elsewhere. He reached Corinth first τῷ εὐαγγελίῳ τοῦ Χριστοῦ (2 Cor 10.14), 'gospeled the gospel' to them (τὸ εὐαγγέλιον ὃ εὐηγγελισάμην ὑμῖν, 1 Cor 15.1–2), and had designs to go further, 'to gospel [εὐαγγελίσασθαι] in places beyond you' (2 Cor 10.16). Enter Rome, one such 'place beyond'. Writing to the Christ-assembly there, Paul longs 'to gospel [εὐαγγελίσασθαι] to you who are in Rome' (Rom 1.15)—a strange thing to say to an established Christ-group, unless Paul reckons himself a particularly important broker of this εὐαγγέλιον.

---

[67] Much is typically made of Paul's self-designation as ἐλαχιστοτέρῳ—the impossible comparative of a superlative ('less than the least')—but in light of what follows, it is best read as a way of magnifying the gift (χάρις) by setting it in the starkest possible contrast to the worth of its recipient.

More telling still, though, is when the other letters make 'gospeling' (εὐαγγελίζω) similarly central to Paul's apostolic program. As the Paul of 1 Corinthians insists, Christ sent him οὐ…βαπτίζειν ἀλλ' εὐαγγελίζεσθαι (1.17). The Paul of Romans is 'set apart' for the gospel (Rom 1.1; cf. Gal 1.15–16) and a cultic mediator of it (λατρεύω, λειτουργός, Rom 1.9; 15.16), so woe to him if he does not announce it (1 Cor 9.16). And for the Paul of Galatians, the whole purpose of his revelation was just this, ἵνα εὐαγγελίζωμαι αὐτὸν ἐν τοῖς ἔθνεσιν (1.16; cf. 1.8, 11; 4.13). The phrase is strikingly similar to Eph 3.8b. Before anything else, Paul is a gospeler—a herald of good news.

And as Eph 3.8 and Gal 1.16 suggest, he heralds good news specifically to gentiles. The witness of the collection on this score, even beyond Romans and Galatians, is clear: as the Paul of 1 Timothy aptly puts it, I was appointed a 'herald and apostle…a teacher of the gentiles' (2.7; cf. 1 Thess 2.16; 2 Tim 4.17). Such a gentile *Paulusbild* is truly expansive, however, in Romans. Here Paul is a λειτουργός Χριστοῦ Ἰησοῦ εἰς τὰ ἔθνη (15.16), which drives him from Jerusalem, in a loop, all the way to Illyricum disbursing the εὐαγγέλιον τοῦ Χριστοῦ (15.19).[68] And as in 2 Cor 10, the Paul of Romans has ambition to go further: εὐαγγελίζεσθαι οὐχ ὅπου ὠνομάσθη Χριστός (15.20). One need only look at a map: if Paul is a 'catholic liturgist' in any of the letters (so Beker)—if he is anywhere a universal priest—he is so in Romans. The Paul of Romans is the εὐαγγελιστής of the gentiles in most of the habitable Roman world, with designs on reaching the rest. By comparison, the Paul of Ephesians looks quite ordinary.

But generically on point: Paul is a gospeler of gentiles, but what of the object of that gospeling, τὸ ἀνεξιχνίαστον πλοῦτος τοῦ Χριστοῦ (Eph 3.8b)? Is this also a laconic distillation of what we find elsewhere in Paul? The short answer is yes, although identifying it as Christ-*wealth* (πλοῦτος) is unique to Ephesians. While the verb (εὐαγγελίζω) typically lacks an object in Paul,[69] Christ is its object directly in Gal 1.16, and implicitly at Rom 15.19.[70] The noun can also be unmodified, but most frequently it is the εὐαγγέλιον τοῦ Χριστοῦ.[71] The implication of both the nominal and verbal forms, then, is that Paul's gospel disburses Christ, as is the case in 1 Cor 15.1–11, a description of Paul's gospel that trades also as a christological résumé. While the πλοῦτος τοῦ Χριστοῦ is unique as the object of Paul's gospel,[72] it is at least suggestive that Paul uses it twice in Rom 9–11 in connection with the gentiles: God endures the

---

[68] See also here Rom 1.13: καθὼς καὶ ἐν τοῖς λοιποῖς ἔθνεσιν.

[69] Of the 21 occurrences, twelve lack an object: Rom 1.15; 15.20; 1 Cor 1.17; 9.16 (2×); 9.18; 15.2; 2 Cor 10.16; Gal 1.8–9 (3×); and 4.13. For εὐαγγελίζω with εὐαγγέλιον as the object, 1 Cor 15.1; 2 Cor 11.7; Gal 1.11. See the discussion in Best, *Ephesians*, 318.

[70] Cf. 2 Cor 4.5, with a different verb: 'We proclaim (*kērussomen*) Jesus Christ as Lord'.

[71] For the 'good news of Jesus/Christ/his son', see Rom 1.9; 15.19; 1 Cor 9.12; 2 Cor 2.12; 4.4; 9.13; 10.14; Gal 1.7; Phil 1.27; 1 Thess 3.2; 2 Thess 1.8; cf. 2 Tim 2.8 for another terse summary. For the 'good news of God', see Rom 1.1; 15.16; 2 Cor 11.7; 1 Thess 2.2, 8–9; cf. 1 Tim 1.11.

[72] In Ephesians, the word is an economical way of signaling a broader complex of soteriological 'benefits' (εὐλογίαι, 1.3) that accrue to gentiles via the benefaction of Israel's God in Christ (Eph 1.3–14, 18–19; 2.4–7, 13–18). In 1.3–14, πλοῦτος occurs in connection with ἀπολύτρωσις and ἄφησις: the latter two are given in accordance with the 'wealth [πλοῦτος] of God's gift' (1.7). At 1.18, it is the πλοῦτος of the gentiles' (new) κληρονομία that is in view. And in 2.4–7, it is because God is πλούσιος ἐν ἐλέει (2.4) that he 'made us alive…and raised us and seated us together in Christ Jesus'—all so that in the coming ages he might show the πλοῦτος of his gift.

infidelity of 'vessels of wrath', in part, to make known 'the wealth [πλοῦτος] of his glory' for gentiles (9.23-24);[73] and Israel's 'loss' (ἥττημα) means πλοῦτος ἐθνῶν, 'wealth for gentiles' (11.12). Just this, then, is what Eph 3.8b says Paul travels the Mediterranean heralding: a new era of Christ-wealth for gentiles. The reader of Paul does not need Ephesians to know this. But nowhere save Gal 1.16 is it stated so directly. The Paul of Ephesians is no apostle of the church, but he is a gospeler of Christ-capital for gentiles.

What, then, of 3.9, and the second part of Paul's gift: φωτίσαι [πάντας] τίς ἡ οἰκονομία τοῦ μυστηρίου? If the first half of Paul's gift is straightforward, the second half is somewhat more complex. Vis-à-vis the image of Paul inscribed here, two decisions are critical, and a third thing vital to keep in mind: (1) the object of φωτίζω (i.e. the textual problem of πάντας); (2) the subject of the οἰκονομία (i.e. God or Paul) and its translation; and (3) the definition of the μυστήριον at 3.6. These decisions are vital because interpreters' language tends to get slippery here, with the text's (alleged) image of Paul swelling accordingly. To say it directly, and in reverse order: if (3) the μυστήριον is the unity of the (universal) church, and (2) οἰκονομία the salvation-historical plan through which God inaugurates it, and (1) πάντας is read, then it is difficult to avoid the images of Paul with which this chapter began—Paul as the great apostle and revealer of the Christian church. This is not, however, what Paul says, either in 3.2-7, or here in 3.9.

To begin, then, from the end. The μυστήριον of Eph 3.6 is not the ἐκκλησία,[74] but the new status of the ἔθνη: they are συγκληρονόμα καὶ σύσσωμα καὶ συμμέτοχα τῆς ἐπαγγελίας (3.6). Across 2.11-22, and then in the summary of 3.6, Paul never takes his rhetorical gaze off the gentiles. The effect of this is subtle but important for 3.9. What Paul sheds light on the οἰκονομία of is not the creation of the church as such,[75] but the οἰκονομία of gentile inclusion. This is no surprise. It has been the pervading thrust of Eph 3 to this point (vv. 1, 2, 3, 6, 8 and now 9), and exactly what he agreed to in Gal 2.9, where his gentile mission is similarly labeled his χάρις.

What, then, of οἰκονομία—its meaning and its subject? Commentators frequently take οἰκονομία as 'plan' here, with the result that the Paul of Ephesians here highlights God's salvation-historical plan that culminates in the church.[76] But there is no reason to take οἰκονομία here in any way other than its normal, active sense. The gentile-mystery, formerly hidden but now revealed (3.5 and 10), is being managed.[77] This, of

---

[73] Strictly speaking, the πλοῦτος is made known for 'us'—a Roman body composed of Jews and gentiles (9.24). But as the citations of Hos 2.23 and 1.10 go on to show (at 9.25-26), the focus here is on gentiles.

[74] *Pace* Schnackenburg, *Ephesians*, 134-5; and also the otherwise cogent essay of Nils Dahl, 'Das Geheimnis der Kirche nach Epheser 3,8-10', in *Studies in Ephesians*, 349-63. Although as v. 10 makes clear, the μυστήριον *does* reveal the unexpected ethnic makeup of that ἐκκλησία.

[75] Up to Eph 3.10, ἐκκλησία has featured only once in Ephesians (1.22), and never in the so-called ecclesiological section of 2.11-22, nor so far in Paul's depiction of his own role (3.1-9).

[76] Thielman, *Ephesians*, 214; Schnackenburg, *Ephesians*, 137. Worse still is Muddiman, *Ephesians*, 158, who has Paul here illuminating the 'secret plan of salvation'. Muddiman takes μυστήριον as an attributive genitive modifying οἰκονομία, and loses entirely the connection to 3.6. Better is Lincoln, *Ephesians*, 184.

[77] What Agamben, *Kingdom and the Glory*, 22 says of Col 1.24-25 applies equally to Eph 3.9: 'Nothing in the text authorizes us to relate *oikonomia* to a meaning that could perhaps belong only to *mystērion*'. Put otherwise, to read οἰκονομία as 'plan' makes it and μυστήριον essentially redundant.

course, raises the question of who manages it, and here 3.9 is different than 3.2. For in 3.2, it is the *gift* that is managed, and this is Paul's work (cf. 3.8–9), but in 3.9, it is the *mystery* that is managed, and in a wider view, this is clearly God's work.[78] For Paul, God hid the mystery (3.5 and 9b), revealed it (3.3 and 5), and now manages it (3.9a). Just as God has the οἰκονομία τοῦ πληρώματος τῶν καιρῶν (1.9), he also has the management of this particular age (αἰών) of gentile-incorporation. And he manages this age in a particular way, for the mystery is not just that the gentiles are in, but how they are in: ἐν Χριστῷ Ἰησοῦ and διὰ τοῦ εὐαγγελίου (3.6). To this management, Paul stands syntactically one step removed: God manages, and Paul sheds light on that management. The upshot of this way of reading 3.9, looking elsewhere in the collection, is that it makes Eph 3.9 and Rom 11 evocative co-texts. In a tight phrase, Eph 3.9 explains what Paul does in Rom 11. The latter is Paul's φωτισμός of the Christ-assembly in Rome about how Israel's God executes the gentiles' inclusion: his οἰκονομία τοῦ μυστηρίου (Eph 3.9). It is no surprise, then, that Paul encapsulates his argument in Rom 11 under the heading of a μυστήριον (11.25); nor that all of this indicates the πλοῦτος, σοφία, and γνῶσις of God (11.33; cf. Eph 3.8–10); nor that it represents the 'incomprehensibility' of God's generosity (ἀνεξιχνίαστος, Rom 11.33; cf. Eph 3.8)—the only other use of this rare word in Paul's letters. Romans 11.7–32, in other words, is Paul's χάρις dispensed.

But in Eph 3.9 who is this for? That depends entirely on how one answers the textual problem of 3.9a: whether or not to read the πάντας.[79] It is tempting to read the omission—it fits the context, the external data are relatively strong, it is the *lectio difficilior*, with scribes perhaps reading toward Col 1.28—thus circumscribing Paul's role at all points in Eph 3.1–13 to the gentiles. On balance, however, it is probably best to read πάντας: Paul sheds light for all on God's management of the mystery.[80] Is this, then, an unacceptable universalizing of Paul? It is not, it should be said, universal soteriological illumination, as if the sentence ended at πάντας.[81] Functionally, if not grammatically, the object of φωτίζω is the interrogative clause (τίς ἡ οἰκονομία τοῦ μυστηρίου) that follows—the key insight of those who read the text without πάντας.[82] Given what I argue above, then, Paul circumscribes even his more expansive project (for πάντας) to the gentile question—to enlighten all as to God's action for gentiles. But does Paul elsewhere broaden his gaze this way? He does, and in precisely that text we might expect, Rom 11. After articulating God's management of the gentile-mystery in a highly condensed form—Israel's trespass means πλοῦτος κόσμου, and Israel's loss, πλοῦτος ἐθνῶν (11.12)—Paul turns to those gentiles.

---

[78] So rightly, e.g., Lincoln, *Ephesians*, 184.
[79] The omission is in ℵ* A 6. 1739 and 1881. NA[28] places πάντας in brackets. The vast majority of contemporary commentators (Lincoln; Muddiman; Thielman; O'Brien) read πάντας, as does Bruce M. Metzger, *A Textual Commentary on the New Testament*, 2nd ed. (Stuttgart: Deutsche Bibelgesellschaft, 1994), 534. A few significant nineteenth-century commentaries omit it (Robinson; Abbott).
[80] See the discussion in Lincoln, *Ephesians*, 167.
[81] This is a somewhat odd suggestion by Best, *Ephesians*, 319, although he corrects himself when he gets to the clause οἰκονομία τοῦ μυστηρίου (320).
[82] Abbott, *Ephesians*, 87. Robinson, *Ephesians*, 170, references a suggestive parallel (grammatically) in LXX Judg. 13.8: φωτισάτω ἡμᾶς τί ποιήσωμεν τῷ παιδαρίῳ. The same is true in the parallel clause of Col 1.27, although there with γνωρίζω.

Now I say to you gentiles, in as much as I am, on the one hand, an apostle of the gentiles, I magnify my commission [διακονία], if somehow I might provoke my flesh (i.e. Jews) to jealousy and save some from them. (Rom 11.13–14)

Here, I suggest, is the same two-step. Paul, the apostle of the gentiles, with one eye firmly trained there (Eph 3.8), magnifying his διακονία (Eph 3.7) so as to catch the (soteriological) attention of his fellow Jews—that is, hoping that God's οἰκονομία τοῦ μυστηρίου will somehow redound to the benefit of 'all' (Rom 11.14; cf. Eph 3.9).

With this, Paul's gift has been defined, both in detail (3.2–7) and *in nuce* (3.8–9). I have treated all the key terms for this argument above, except χάρις itself.[83] So finally, then, is χάρις also central elsewhere to Paul's divinely sanctioned role? Many of the most critical co-texts treated above re-emerge here, so we can be brief. Four times outside of Ephesians Paul collocates χάρις with a passive form of δίδωμι to describe his vocation (Rom 12.3; 15.15; 1 Cor 3.10; Gal 2.9; cf. Eph 3.2, 7 and 8), and the similarly styled χάρις + λαμβάνω (Rom 1.5) functions the same way. A useful way into these texts, however, is 1 Cor 15.10, in which the centrality of χάρις to Paul's apostolic identity is signaled by its repetition: 'But by the gift [χάρις] of God I am what I am, and his gift [χάρις] to me was not empty. Instead, I worked harder than all of them, but not I, but the gift [χάρις] of God that is with me'. The text is somewhat ambiguous, and Paul's first and third uses of χάρις may well reflect a more properly theological notion of 'grace'. The second, though, is intriguing: it is *Paul's* gift (εἰς ἐμέ; cf. Eph 3.8, Ἐμοί), which may or may not produce a yield (οὐ κενὴ ἐγενήθη), and which Paul works hard at (περισσότερον...ἐκοπίασα). It is hard not to read something more specific here, not least in light of 1 Cor 3.10, where Paul narrates the origins of this assembly as the working out of the χάριν τοῦ θεοῦ τὴν δοθεῖσάν μοι. There is nothing programmatic in 1 Corinthians, but χάρις does constitute Paul's apostolic identity (15.10) and generate the yield of the Corinthian assembly itself (3.10).

We get something closer to the programmatic in Galatians. Why, in fact, do James, Cephas, and John affirm Paul and send him εἰς τὰ ἔθνη? Because they saw, and here is Paul's shorthand for it, the χάριν τὴν δοθεῖσάν μοι (2.9)—a gift manifestly associated with Paul's gentile mission (cf. 1.15–16). Vis-à-vis Paul, his gift, and the gentile mission, however, nowhere outside of Ephesians is Paul more expansive than in Romans. Negotiating his own image with a Christ-assembly he has not met, Paul leads with self-definition: he has received χάριν καὶ ἀποστολήν—a gift meant to bring about the 'obedience of faith' among gentiles (1.5).[84] This is why Paul wants to disburse a

---

[83] I have hinted at this along the way, but Paul's χάρις, here—not least with its connection to Christ-πλοῦτος—sits comfortably within the ancient world, now well-mapped, of gift-giving and divine benefaction. See G. W. Peterman, *Paul's Gift from Philippi: Conventions of Gift-Exchange and Christian Giving*, SNTSMS 92 (Cambridge: Cambridge University Press, 1997); Stephan Joubert, *Paul as Benefactor: Reciprocity, Strategy and Theological Reflection in Paul's Collection*, WUNT 2/124 (Tübingen: Mohr Siebeck, 2000); James R. Harrison, *Paul's Language of Grace in its Graeco-Roman Context*, WUNT 2/172 (Tübingen: Mohr Siebeck, 2003); Barclay, *Paul and the Gift*; and now, vis-à-vis Eph 3.1–13, Lang, *Mystery and the Making*, 98–9.

[84] See Don B. Garlington, *The Obedience of Faith: A Pauline Phrase in Historical Context*, WUNT 2/38 (Tübingen: Mohr Siebeck, 1991).

'pneumatic gift' (χάρισμα πνευματικόν) to these gentiles (1.11), 'to gospel' them (1.15), and ultimately to reap a gentile harvest (1.13) in Rome as he has elsewhere—his χάρις and ἀποστολή demand it.

Moreover, outside of Eph 3.8-9, Rom 15.15-16 is the closest we get to a definition of Paul's gift in the *corpus Paulinum*.

> Now I have written you more boldly…because of the gift [χάρις] which was given to me by God, to be a priestly aide of Christ Jesus to the gentiles [λειτουργός Χριστοῦ Ἰησοῦ εἰς τὰ ἔθνη], performing the gospel of God as a priest [ἱερουργοῦντα τὸ εὐαγγέλιον τοῦ θεοῦ], that the gentile offering might be acceptable, made holy by the holy spirit.

Paul has a gift: he is a λειτουργός Χριστοῦ Ἰησοῦ εἰς τὰ ἔθνη. The metaphor is now cultic and not economic, and so the imagery shifts accordingly.[85] What does not shift is who Paul's gift is for (the ἔθνη), what he connects it to (the εὐαγγέλιον), and how he uses it (to negotiate unity). As Rom 11.13-14 (and Eph 3.9) would have us expect, while Paul is a λειτουργός for gentiles, he exercises his gift with one eye on the larger question of Jew and gentile which bookends this section (15.7-13 and 25-29). Paul's disbursal of his gift—his 'priestly performance of the gospel' to make the 'gentile offering acceptable'—belongs to his attempt to forge a trans-local unity between his gentiles and the Christ-assembly in Jerusalem (15.25-27). Concern for such unity is the typical criticism of Ephesians, within which Paul's image is drawn maximally. In truth, such a concern is arguably more explicit in Romans. Regardless, in both, Paul occupies a central role on the soteriological map, and Paul's gift for gentiles is central to his image in each.

When it comes to Paul's gift, then, the five central texts (Rom 1.5; 15.15-16; 1 Cor 3.10; Gal 2.9; and Eph 3.8-9) show neither scrupulous uniformity nor wild diversity.[86] Where they do diverge, it is not contradiction or development that explains the shifting terminology, but the various metaphors Paul uses to designate his work—agricultural (1 Cor 3), architectural (Rom 15; 1 Cor 3; Eph 3 [cf. 2.19-22]), economic (Eph 3), and cultic (Rom 15). Ephesians 3.8-9 is not, in other words, an outlier. It *is* programmatic in a way that only Rom 15.15-16 approaches. In these texts, Paul is not a mediator of (soteriological) grace nor motivated by it.[87] He has a particular gentile-gift.[88] Apart from Eph 3.8-9, though, one could easily mistake 'gift' for 'grace'

---

[85] Vis-à-vis the εὐαγγέλιον, rather than heralding Christ-πλοῦτος, he is its priest (ἱερουργέω), bearing the acceptable gentile-offering (προσφορὰ τῶν ἐθνῶν, 15.16).

[86] In all five, it is a God-given gift, linked closely with mediating Christ. Four of the five connect Paul's gift directly to his gentile mission (Rom 1.5; 15.15-16; Gal 2.9; and Eph 3.8-9 [cf. 3.2]), while 1 Cor 3.10 does so implicitly. And four of the five situate Paul's χάρις within a broad concern for unity (save Rom 1.5), typically that of Jew/gentile (Rom 15.15-16; 1 Cor 3.10; Gal 2.9; Eph 3.8-9).

[87] Lincoln, *Ephesians*, 193, is representative. Speaking of what Eph 3.2-13 emphasizes, he writes, 'The first is Paul's indebtedness to the grace of God for his apostolic ministry (vv. 2, 7, 8). Ephesians has already stressed that salvation is all of grace (2:8-10). Now it makes clear that the apostleship which was instrumental in bringing that salvation to the Gentiles was also all of grace.' In a maximal sense, this is not objectionable, but it does conflate various types of 'gift' language in Ephesians, and misses the specificity of what Paul is saying in Eph 3.

[88] So rightly Barth, *Ephesians*, 358-9.

in these texts, and miss the specificity of Paul's claim. In this sense, Eph 3.8–9 works nicely not only as the image of Paul *in nuce* of Eph 3, but as the 'gist' of Paul's gift in the *Hauptbriefe* as well.

With 3.9, the image of Paul in the digression (3.2–13) is largely complete. That image, I argue, is not only unproblematic, but hermeneutically fruitful. In 3.10, however, we meet something genuinely new in Paul's letters—the ἐκκλησία as a sign to cosmic powers (ἀρχαὶ καὶ ἐξουσίαι) of the 'manifold wisdom of God'. On its face, 3.10 does not contribute to the text's image of Paul at all, but most commentator's read the ἵνα that opens v. 10 as picking up the entirety of vv. 8–9, specifically the infinitives that comprise Paul's gift.[89] The upshot of this is that the Paul of Ephesians becomes a cosmic prophet—the architect of a church that reverberates in the heavenlies.[90] Following T. K. Abbott, I suggest reading the ἵνα clause more narrowly, as the purpose not of Paul's gift, but of God's eternal concealing of the mystery, so picking up only v. 9b and following.[91] All of the necessary parallels to v. 10—the relevant features of the *Revelationsschema*—are found in v. 9b.[92] And the upshot of this is that Paul falls abruptly from view halfway through v. 9, with God taking center stage in vv. 9b–12. This, for Paul, is God's work: the hidden mystery, the revealed wisdom, the confounding of powers, and all of this (now and only now) 'through the assembly'. Here as elsewhere, Paul's breathless style runs him into a new point, with most readers missing the switch. In 3.8–12, Paul dispenses his gift, and God wraps it in a transtemporal and supramundane package. It is the *Gottesbild*, then, not the *Paulusbild*, that is (to recall Ernst) 'ins Überdimensionale gesteigert'.

Paul the Suffering Prisoner: The Image's Frame (Eph 3.1 and 13)

Finally, all of the above is set in a particular frame (3.1 and 13). In a stark juxtaposition, Paul narrates his exalted χάρις (3.2–9) within the confines of a much bleaker reality.

> For this reason, I, Paul, the prisoner [ὁ δέσμιος] of Christ Jesus on behalf of you gentiles [ὑπὲρ ὑμῶν τῶν ἐθνῶν]. (Eph 3.1)

> Therefore, I am asking not to grow weary in my afflictions for you [ἐν ταῖς θλίψεσίν μου ὑπὲρ ὑμῶν], which are your glory [ἥτις ἐστὶν δόξα ὑμῶν]. (Eph 3.13)

If anything, the compositional setting envisaged in 3.1 (cf. 4.1; 6.19) threatens to call into question Paul's legitimacy and the efficacy of his gift, and so needs to be redeployed. In Eph 3.1 and 13, then, Paul reconceptualizes his situation: he is the prisoner 'of *Christ*' (not Rome) and 'for you *gentiles*' (not any wrongdoing). In fact, these sufferings are necessary to bring about gentile-δόξα (3.13). Most readers of Ephesians, however, opt for an alternative reading, seeing in 3.1 and 13 a post-mortem

---

[89] So, e.g., Thielman, *Ephesians*, 215; Lincoln, *Ephesians*, 185; O'Brien, *Ephesians*, 244–5.
[90] This is particularly apparent in Gombis, 'Triumph of God', 95–9.
[91] Abbott, *Ephesians*, 88; cf. Lang, *Mystery and the Making*, 101 n. 124.
[92] All of this is outlined at Abbott, *Ephesians*, 88.

testament to '*the* prisoner', whose sufferings now take on a vicarious (salvific) quality.[93] Which is it?—Paul negotiating his own (incarcerated) image, or a clever Paulinist inflating the image of Paul after his death?

Two things need to be said here and the problem clarified before we attend to it. First, although the judgment is widespread, there is no good reason to label Paul's afflictions (θλίψεις) a retrospective allusion to his death—apart, that is, from the presumed setting.[94] Suffering is basic to Paul's own apostolic identity, not least as a way of identifying with the object of his proclamation—Christ himself (so, e.g., 2 Cor 1.3–11; 4.8–12; 6.4–5; 11.23–29). Moreover, as James Kelhoffer argues, properly deployed, suffering generates social capital that Paul can (and does) use elsewhere to confirm his credibility and leverage his authority.[95] For reasons both deep-seated and pragmatic, then, Paul utilizes his afflictions in his own acts of self-presentation.[96] That his θλίψεις appear in Eph 3.1–13, a central text of Pauline (self-)portraiture, is hardly surprising, nor a problem on its face. Second, and in keeping with the entirety of 3.1–13, Paul's afflictions are *for the* ἔθνη. Paul suffers, strictly speaking, not for the church, nor do his afflictions take on universal mediatorial significance. They belong to his gentile mission. That said, Paul's language *is* vicarious (ὑπέρ in both 3.1 and 13), as virtually all readers suggest. Paul's hardships, in some way, mediate gentile-δόξα. What does this mean, and does the Paul of the other letters believe this?

To this end, Eph 3.1 offers little by way of clarification. Paul is the prisoner, tersely and simply, 'on behalf of [ὑπέρ] you gentiles'. Ὑπέρ in Paul, when used with expressions of suffering, is typically reserved for Christ's action,[97] but can be used for Paul's own mediation (2 Cor 1.8; 12.15). We get more from 3.13, but this is also where the difficulty lies. The Greek of 3.13 is famously ambiguous: διὸ αἰτοῦμαι μὴ ἐγκακεῖν ἐν ταῖς θλίψεσίν μου ὑπὲρ ὑμῶν, ἥτις ἐστὶν δόξα ὑμῶν. The first verb lacks an object, the second a subject, and the meaning of δόξα is disputed. On the last point, Paul almost certainly means eschatological glory. Elsewhere when Paul links suffering and glory, he has such glorification in view (Rom 8.17–18; 2 Cor 4.17).[98] Whatever Paul requests in v. 13a, then, the result of his afflictions is δόξα for the gentiles (cf. Rom 9.23).

---

[93] On Paul as 'the prisoner', see Philip Esler, '"Remember my Fetters": Memorialisation of Paul's Imprisonment', in *Explaining Christian Origins and Early Judaism: Contributions from Cognitive and Social Science*, ed. Petri Luomanen, Ilkka Pyysiäinen and Risto Uro (Leiden: Brill, 2007), 231–58. For the language of Paul's vicarious suffering, see Sellin, *Brief an die Epheser*, 271; Fischer, *Tendenz und Absicht*, 104–7; Gnilka, 'Das Paulusbild', 190–2. Even Dassmann, *Der Stachel im Fleisch*, 53, who otherwise emphasizes continuity, sees divergence at precisely this point.

[94] Fischer, *Tendenz und Absicht*, 108: 'Die Deutung seines Leidens (= seines Todes) als stellvertretendes Opfer für die Gemeinde'. cf. Sellin, *Brief an die Epheser*, 58: 'Die Äußerungen zur Rolle un zum Selbstbild des Apostels setzen den Tod des Paulus indirekt voraus (3.1; 6.19)'.

[95] James A. Kelhoffer, *Persecution, Persuasion, and Power: Readiness to Withstand Hardship as a Corroboration of Legitimacy in the New Testament*, WUNT 270 (Tübingen: Mohr Siebeck, 2010). On suffering and Paul's apostolic identity, see also Scott J. Hafemann, *Suffering and the Spirit: An Exegetical Study of 2 Cor. 2:14–3:3 within the Context of the Corinthian Correspondence*, WUNT 2/19 (Tübingen: Mohr Siebeck, 1986); John T. Fitzgerald, *Cracks in an Earthen Vessel: An Examination of the Catalogues of Hardships in the Corinthian Correspondence*, SBLDS 99 (Atlanta: Scholars, 1988).

[96] Kelhoffer, *Persecution, Persuasion, and Power*, 61–7.

[97] BDAG, s.v. ὑπέρ A1e

[98] Lincoln, *Ephesians*, 191–2; Schnackenburg, *Ephesians*, 142; Thielman, *Ephesians*, 222.

What, then of v. 13a? Who is Paul asking (the object of αἰτέω) and who needs to not 'grow weary' (the subject of ἐγκακέω)? Nearly all commentators opt for Paul's gentiles on both counts—Paul asks his readers not to 'lose heart' in his sufferings.[99] This is grammatically viable, but the verb is a strange choice to apply to Paul's audience about his own sufferings. Given the setting envisaged by the letter itself (3.1; 4.1; 6.19), the verb makes better sense as self-referential, with Paul the subject of ἐγκακέω and God the (implicit) object of αἰτέω, as elsewhere in Paul.[100] Paul asks not to grow weary, and he does so because (1) his gentile-gift needs to be disbursed (thus, the διό of v. 13a), and (2) his endurance of hardship brings these gentiles glory (thus, the ἥτις of v. 13b). The logic of 3.13, then, coming out of 3.2–12, runs as follows: Paul begs (God) not to let him (Paul) grow weary, because he knows that his θλίψεις—those hardships he encounters as he dispenses his gentile-χάρις—are the cost for him of mediating eschatological deliverance to the ἔθνη. Given the ambiguity of v. 13, this reading of the grammar has to be provisional. But what if we read the *collection*? Do we find anything like this elsewhere?

I suggest we do. In fact, Eph 3.13 (in view of 3.1–12) sits remarkably closely to a series of texts across 2 Corinthians. Writing from Macedonia, Paul repeatedly catalogues the hardships he just endured in Asia (2 Cor 1.3–11; 4.8–12; 6.4–5; 11.23–29)—θλίψεις so pressing that he (and Timothy) had despaired even of life itself (1.8). Nearly overcome though he was, these afflictions clearly have vicarious (and salvific) benefit for the Corinthians: 'if we are afflicted [θλιβόμεθα], it is for your consolation and deliverance [ὑπὲρ τῆς ὑμῶν παρακλήσεως καὶ σωτηρίας]' (1.6)—a point he reiterates in 12.15, when he promises to 'spend and be spent *for your souls* [ὑπὲρ τῶν ψυχῶν ὑμῶν]'. Trade the noun for the verb, and δόξα for παράκλησις and σωτηρία (and ψυχή), and the Paul of Ephesians and 2 Corinthians say the same thing. Not only is Paul's suffering vicarious in 2 Corinthians, it also buttresses, time and again, a defense of his role as a διάκονος (cf. Eph 3.7, in view of 3.1 and 13). Notably, in 2 Cor 11–12, Paul's claim to be a better 'courier of Christ' (διάκονος τοῦ Χριστοῦ) than his opponents (ψευδαπόστολοι, 11.13; cf. 12.11) hinges on his sufferings (11.23–29; 12.7–10) and revelations (12.1–7), and when earlier he defends his διακονία (6.3), and commends himself as their διάκονος (6.4), he does so via a catalogue of his hardships (θλίψεις, κτλ., 6.5).

Paul's afflictions, then, are vicarious; they bring soteriological benefit to his auditors; and he deploys them to buttress his authority as their διάκονος. The most suggestive co-text for Eph 3.13, however, is 2 Cor 4.1, in view of what precedes it. After 1.3–11, Paul's suffering comes starkly back into view in 2.14–17, which leads in 3.4–18 to an extended description of his διακονία. This commission gives Paul 'confidence' (πεποίθησις, 3.4) and 'boldness' (παρρησία, 3.12) in his access to God—precisely what characterizes Paul and his gentile auditors in Eph 3.12—which then leads to his declaration of dogged intent: 'Therefore, having this commission [διακονία], inasmuch as we were shown mercy, *we do not grow weary* [οὐκ ἐγκακοῦμεν]' (2 Cor 4.1). A few verses later, Paul will say the same again, now on the back of the claim that, through

---

[99] See, e.g., Thielman, *Ephesians*, 220–21; Schnackenburg, *Ephesians*, 142; Lincoln, *Ephesians*, 191.
[100] On Paul as the subject of the rare verb ἐγκακέω, see 2 Cor 4.1 and 16 and my discussion below. For God as the implied object of αἰτέω, see Eph 3.20; Col 1.9. This way of reading 3.13 has the benefit of allowing αἰτέω and ἐγκακέω to share a subject—the most natural reading.

his *kerygma*, the gift (χάρις) multiplies to the many (4.13–15). Paul's response?—'Therefore, we do not grow weary [οὐκ ἐγκακοῦμεν]...for our slight momentary afflictions [θλίψεις] are producing for us an eternal weight of glory [δόξα] beyond measure' (4.16–17). The logic here is identical to Eph 3. Paul will not neglect his duty (2 Cor 4.13), nor grow weary in it (4.16), for his commission and the afflictions that come with it are bringing about eschatological glory—both of the Corinthians (3.18) and his own (4.17)—and the gift spreads across the Mediterranean (4.15).[101]

Ἐγκακέω, then, designates not a fate that threatens Paul's readers, but rather expresses Paul's own dogged determination to fulfill his apostolic task. Grammar may not decide the problem of Eph 3.13, but 2 Corinthians does. What Paul asks not to do in Eph 3.13 ('grow weary'), he insists he will not do in 2 Cor 4.1 and 16. If this is right, Eph 3.13 may belong alongside 2 Corinthians not only intertextually, but historically as well. And this is a fitting way to begin to draw to a close, for the above suggests the historical possibilities of reading Ephesians within the collection. Rather than presuming a location, driving a wedge between these texts, and creating a developed *Paulusbild* out of Eph 3.13, the above begins with the collection, finds evocative links therein, and ends with a suggestion about history. Whether Ephesians belongs compositionally next to 2 Corinthians or not, however, *the hermeneutical point remains the same*: the image of Paul in Eph 3.13 (and more broadly, vv. 1–13) is not developed, but rather pithy and programmatic. It says here, in fact, in one short verse, what the Paul of 2 Corinthians takes most of a letter to say.

Conclusion

To return, then, to where we began: is the Paul of Eph 3.1–13 '*the* apostle of the church' (Sterling)? No. Is Eph 3.1–13 a 'veritable "Paulology"' (Wild)? In a sense, yes, but that does not decide who wrote it, nor how to read it vis-à-vis the other letters. Paul's modern tradents read it as a *post*-Pauline Paulology, a judgment that depends largely on a displaced historical setting and a genealogical relationship of Eph 3.1–13 to Col 1.23–28—and thus, a redaction-critical reading of these texts.[102] That is, it depends on how to read a letter collection. With these decisions in hand, interpretation follows:

---

[101] Another obvious co-text, frequently discussed, is Col 1.24–29, which, while it lacks the ἐγκακέω, runs in the same direction as Eph 3.1–13 and the 2 Corinthians passages discussed above. Briefly, Paul, the διάκονος, bears fiduciary responsibility (οἰκονομία) for the μυστήριον of Christ-πλοῦτος (Χριστὸς ἐν ὑμῖν, ἡ ἐλπὶς τῆς δόξης) for gentiles (vv. 25–27), which he disburses via the sufferings of his apostolic labors (vv. 24 and 29), and in which he rejoices. On this way of reading Col 1.24–29, which both illuminates and is illuminated by Eph 3.1–13, see Lang, 'Disbursing the Account of God'. By leaving this Colossians co-text to a footnote, I am not denying its prominence nor its utility for understanding Paul's image in Eph 3. I am simply drawing attention to the fact that Paul's image in Eph 3 (and Col 1) sits squarely within the contours of a map drawn on the basis of the *Hauptbriefe*. Moreover, Eph 3 depicts this image more succinctly and directly, and so more obviously. To restrict its co-texts to allegedly deutero- or trito-Pauline texts and so displace Eph 3 is arbitrary. Finally, if Paul's role vis-à-vis the 'church' (ἐκκλησία) *is* to be taken as a marker of an inflated *Paulusbild*, it bears saying that this concern is more germane to Col 1.24–29 (see vv. 24–25) than to Eph 3.1–13, which nowhere depicts Paul's role vis-à-vis the church.

[102] As Sterling, 'From Apostle to the Gentiles', 76, acknowledges. His *Paulusbild* in Ephesians is entirely dependent on its authors' alleged redactions of Colossians.

οἰκονομία becomes salvation-history; χάρις becomes grace; ἀπόστολοι καὶ προφῆται become either a magisterium to whom Paul is assimilated, or else a Pauline foil; θλίψεις become Paul's death; the ἔθνη become the church; and Paul becomes ὁ ἀπόστολος. As I have tried to show in this chapter, Eph 3.1–13, read within the collection, neither requires nor invites any of these decisions. In fact, there is a deep irony here, for many of the Pauline images attributed to Ephesians apply far more directly to other (mostly) undisputed letters. Contemporary scholarship has misidentified its Pauline images. The Paul of Romans may be a 'catholic liturgist' (15.16, so Beker),[103] and the Paul of 1 Corinthians the 'great architect of the unity of the church' (3.10, so Barrett), and the Paul of 2 Thessalonians (and 1 Corinthians) the 'guarantor of tradition' (2 Thess 2.15; 3.6; 1 Cor 11.2; cf. 15.3, so Pervo), but the Paul of Ephesians is none of these things.

This suggests that Paul is a more complex figure than modern scholars allow. It also suggests that the seven letters are not so univocal a fixed point from which to judge Paul's reception—if they are a fixed point at all. We are left, then, with the collection, and a host of Pauline images inscribed in its pages. Whether Eph 3.1–13 is *Paulusbild* or *Selbstbild*, I suggest, is beside the point. That decision tells us nothing about how it sits vis-à-vis the other letters. And 2 Cor 10.10 always sits in the collection as a caution against overconfidence. Paul can so construct *himself*, it seems, so as to surprise his original hearers in person. Without access to Paul in the flesh, we have only the Paul of the collection. These are the data alongside which I have read Eph 3.1–13. After two generations of reading Eph 3.1–13 alongside Colossians, the Pastorals, and Acts, with somewhat contrived—and by now cliché—results, a raft of evidence from the *Hauptbriefe* suggests a more redolent set of co-texts. On this score, a late-antique Pauline tradent, Priscillian of Avila, may actually lead the way. After laboring through all of the letters—his textual division and summary leaving his brain a Pauline topography—it is perhaps not a surprise that Eph 3.5–9 (Test. 12) is the single textual link shared by his central canons on Paul's apostolic identity. For Priscillian, at least, Eph 3 is not the first stage in misunderstanding Paul, but gets him exactly, quintessentially, right.

---

[103] Beker, *Heirs of Paul*, 71–2.

CONCLUSION

In early 2015, a seemingly innocuous photograph of a dress became an overnight viral sensation, generating 10 million tweets in the week after its initial post to Tumblr and 37 million visits to the original article on *Buzzfeed*. The cause of the viral intrigue was simple: when looking at the photograph, some people saw a white dress with gold lace, while others saw a blue dress with black lace.[1] Within a few days, the retailer of the dress, *Roman Originals*, weighed in decisively: the dress was blue and black. White and gold was not even a product option at that time. The retailers' verdict, however, did nothing to stop the obvious next question for vision scientists: why did people *see* the dress in such starkly different colors?

The answer, it seems, lies at least partly in how the human eye and brain adjust ('correct') for how the objects we see are illuminated—what light we see them in. To put it simply, for those who saw the dress and assumed it was illuminated by natural light (blue), their brains corrected for blue, leading them to see a white and gold dress. For those, on the other hand, who saw the dress imagining it to be awash in artificial light (yellow), their brains corrected for yellow and they saw a blue and black dress. The vital point is this: the colors that one sees in the photographed dress are a function of assumptions one makes about how the dress is illuminated. What makes the photograph so unique, and what drives the divergence of people's visual perception of the dress, is that it essentially decontextualizes (ambiguates) the lighting in which the dress should be perceived. The photograph itself offers no clues (in fact, conflicting clues) as to whether the dress is illuminated by natural or artificial light, so the viewer must supply the conditions (i.e. assumptions) for perception.[2] Shorn of any context for the lighting in the room, people quite literally see differently: some blue and black, others white and gold.

Looking back over the argument of this book, I find this oddity of visual perception a near-perfect analogy for Ephesians and the now-2,000-year history of reading

---

[1] For summary, as well as the picture, see 'The dress', *Wikipedia*, https://en.wikipedia.org/wiki/The_dress; and Ian Sample, '#TheDress: have researchers solved the mystery of its colour?' *TheGuardian.com*, May 14, 2015, https://www.theguardian.com/science/2015/may/14/thedress-have-researchers-solved-the-mystery-of-its-colour. A later study of 1400 people revealed that 57% of participants saw the dress as blue/black, while 30% saw white/gold, 10% blue/brown, and approximately 10% could switch back and forth between color combinations.

[2] For brief overview of the science at work here, see again Sample, '#TheDress', and more extensively in Rosa Lafer-Sousa, Katherine L. Hermann, and Bevil R. Conway, 'Striking Individual Differences in Color Perception Uncovered by "The Dress" Photograph', *Current Biology* 25.13 (May 2015), https://doi.org/10.1016/j.cub.2015.04.053. I am grateful to Ben Shank, Lecturer in Physics at Hope College, for walking me through this material.

Ephesians. Ephesians *is* the dress—a letter that takes the form of the illuminating contexts within which we read ('see') it. On its face, Ephesians narrates the gospel of Christ-wealth for gentiles, an act of divine mercy that wraps this non-people into the lineage of God's people as a gift (Eph 1–3), and then delineates the social and ethical vision that characterizes the community whose life has been born from and re-configured on the basis of this gospel (Eph 4–6). Two thousand years later, of course, we do not have access to the dress in the conditions of the store, only in the context of the photograph. This challenge applies to any ancient text. The great hermeneutical challenge of *Ephesians*, however, is that it offers on its face no context for illumination—no obvious clues as to the light in which we should read it, or how we should adjust our eyes to read it well. Like the dress in the photograph, Ephesians is shorn of those very things on which the modern study of Paul so manifestly depends, and by which we typically learn to 'see' a letter.

Left with contextual ambiguity, we revert to socially patterned ways of reading the letter. For roughly 175 years, a certain configuration of Paulinism and a particular way of narrating Christian origins has combined with a 'natural' (i.e. chronological) way of reading the Pauline book to provide the illuminating context for reading Ephesians. The result has been to render the letter a text of early, nascent, developing catholicism. This is the story I told in Chapters 1 and 2. On the one hand, the sheer longevity of this way of reading Ephesians attests its plausibility. It is a perfectly intelligible way to read Ephesians, given the conditions modern criticism supplies to illuminate the letter. The historiographical frame of Christian origins, from Paul to Catholicism, is a powerful map within which to plot Ephesians—not least when wedded to a Paul reducible to the 'radical (i.e. Protestant) Paulinism' of Romans and Galatians. Set in a certain historical light, viewed from a certain Pauline angle, the dress (Ephesians) really does look white and gold (developed).

I have no interest in denying this, nor in questioning the sincerity of scholars who look at Ephesians and see Pauline development. What I have tried to show is that the data for this judgment, both in Ephesians and the first century, are remarkably thin—apart, that is, from the reading strategies outlined in Chapter 1. And it is just these reading strategies that struggle mightily with a text like Ephesians. Whatever one's view of the letter's author and setting, then, when it comes to Ephesians, Pauline scholars would do well to internalize Benjamin Jowett's caution regarding historical and chronological confidence, lest the space between Paul and Ephesians be deemed completely artificial. He writes, 'Real uncertainties are better than imaginary certainties, and general facts more trustworthy than minute ones, in those fields of history of which we know little'.[3] More still, as Henry Chadwick already saw so clearly a half-century ago, all attempts to derive a setting for Ephesians *historically* are 'hopelessly subjective'—rooted in assumptions about Paul and the first century that exceed our actual knowledge.[4] When scholars today confidently label Ephesians

---

[3] Jowett, 'Chronology', 151.
[4] Chadwick, 'Absicht des Epheserbriefes', 145: 'Der Brief an die Epheser ist bekanntlich eine der am schwersten zu erklärenden Urkunden des NTs. In einem augenfälligen Sinn ist diese Schwierigkeit verknüpft mit dem unlösbaren Problem seiner Verfasserschaft. Wenn ich "unlösbar" sage, so meine ich, daß es anscheinend keine Methode zur Entscheidung der Frage gibt, die nicht hoffnungslos

Pauline development, then, I simply suggest that such a judgment says more about the reader—and the 'sociology of reading' Paul in modern criticism (à la William Johnson)—than it does about the text of Ephesians. In Ephesians, we may just meet the limits of historical criticism.

That is not to say we meet the limits of interpretation, nor even the limits of a search for authorship and setting. Read the letter in a different light (map, etc.), with alternative illumination—say, within the confines of the collection—and Ephesians looks different. Or so goes the argument of my Chapters 3 and 4. Where modern scholars see white and gold, late-antique Paulinists see blue and black. With these early Pauline tradents, I have advocated a return to the collection as our primary co-texts for reading Ephesians, and then tested the utility of this approach on the *imago Pauli* in Eph 3.1–13, a text whose interpretation has been shaped deeply by modern ways of reading. Critically, my approach does not run roughshod over historical aims, nor is it a lapse into 'canonical' or 'pre-critical' exegesis.[5] It arose, rather, as I asked how best to treat this letter given what sort of letter it is, and when and how to attempt some tentative historical judgments. This is where I find Edgar Goodspeed so instructive, for across his decades of work on Ephesians—the main thesis of which is distilled in this book's epigraph—Goodspeed leaps the gap between canonical and historical exegesis, and shows how a text's origin need not determine its co-texts. For Goodspeed, 'The *problem* of Ephesians is inextricably intertwined with that of the Pauline corpus' for the simple reason that *Ephesians* is inextricably intertwined with the Pauline corpus.[6] I very much agree, and in Chapter 5 I showed how this was the case with respect to Paul's image in Eph 3.1–13, finding there the 'gist' of the collection's Pauline portraiture, not least of the *Hauptbriefe*, holding their tensions together.

Having done this, then, and somewhat to my surprise, I think it is now possible, in closing, to offer a few tentative suggestions about the possible setting I alluded to in the Introduction—an early missive of Paul to the Christ-assembly in Laodicea (cf. Col 4.16), written before but near in proximity to the *Hauptbriefe*.[7] With respect to Ephesians, in other words, I have found that while its (alleged) origin need not determine its co-texts, its most redolent Pauline co-texts may offer suggestive hints about its origin. And this, as Kenneth Dover suggests, is to 'take things in the right order' historiographically—to begin with the manuscript and end by assessing a few aspects of history.[8] To be clear, the exegetical sketches below do not depend on this setting;[9] rather, they have informed my view of this possible setting. If the reader

---

subjektiv wäre—die nicht annimmt, wir wüßten viel mehr als wir in der Tat wissen können über den Geist des ersten Jahrhunderts im allgemeinen und über den Geist des Paulus im besonderen'; cf. Sandmel, *First Christian Century*, 8.

[5] I use these scare quotes advisedly, since as I show in Chapters 3 and 4, late-antique interpretive method and practice can hardly be labeled 'pre-critical', just 'differently critical'; cf. Cavadini, 'Exegetical Transformations', 48–9.

[6] Goodspeed, *Meaning of Ephesians*, 9. Emphasis mine.

[7] The sketches below, then, begin to fill out Douglas Campbell's proposed setting, which goes back in general idea to Theodore of Mopsuestia. On this setting, see my section 'An Alternative Not Followed' in Chapter 2.

[8] Dover, *Lysias and the Corpus Lysiacum*, 1.

[9] For example, all of my exegesis in Chapter 5 (and #1 below) holds, to my mind, even if the letter could be confidently dated to the 80s/90s.

wonders why references to Philippians, Thessalonians, and the Pastorals are not more abundant below, the simple answer is that when one follows the language of Ephesians, it does not invite to be read (firstly) alongside these letters. On the contrary, parallels to the *Hauptbriefe* recur repeatedly. Time and again, then, the brief exegetical sketches below suggest to me the period between the Jerusalem council (Gal 2.1–10; Acts 15) and the writing of the *Hauptbriefe* as a setting pregnant with exegetical possibility—as a context which may illuminate. I offer the three sketches below, then, ranging more widely across the letter now, in the hope that it may spur further work in Ephesians by scholars whose Pauline portraits may incline them to explore the matters below in a letter they have hitherto ignored.[10]

1. **Paul's gentile-vocation (Eph 3.1–13):** This first sketch is largely review. As I showed in Chapter 5, the links between Eph 3.1–13 and the *Hauptbriefe* on the negotiation of Paul's apostolic identity are not just literarily but in the end historically suggestive. The key texts (Rom 1.5, 13–15; 11.13–14, 25–26; 15.14–21; 1 Cor 2.6–10; 3.5–4.5; 9.15–18; 15.1–11; 2 Cor 1.3–11; 4.8–12; 6.4–5; 10.13–18; 11.23–29; Gal 1.11–2.10; Eph 3.1–13) all share a common linguistic base applied to a diversity of metaphors for Paul's apostolic vocation vis-à-vis his churches. In Ephesians and 1 Corinthians, Paul describes his gentile-mission principally in terms of a διακονία and οἰκονομία, through which he establishes Christ-assemblies of (largely, although not exclusively) gentiles as God's temple, the place where God's spirit dwells (1 Cor 3.5–4.5; Eph 2.19–3.8; cf. Rom 11.13–14). More broadly, the proclamation of this gentile-εὐαγγέλιον is Paul's God-given χάρις (Rom 15.15; 1 Cor 3.10; Gal 2.9 [cf. 1.16]; Eph 3.2, 7–8), which forces him to negotiate a complex apostolic world vis-à-vis his reception of a gentile-μυστήριον (Rom 11.25; 1 Cor 2.1, 7; 4.1; Eph 3.3–4; cf. Col 1.25–26; 4.3; or ἀποκάλυψις, Gal 1.12). This is a task in which he labors yet which causes him no small opposition. Just here things turn historically suggestive: Paul's prayer (Eph 3.13) and resolve (2 Cor 4.1, 16–17) not to 'grow weary' (ἐγκακέω) in the midst of the suffering elicited by his gentile mission—suffering that results in gentile δόξα, παράκλησις and σωτηρία (Eph 3.13; 2 Cor 1.6)—evocatively links Ephesians and the Corinthian correspondence. And perhaps this is why, as admittedly different as the florid style of Ephesians' opening (1.1–14) is from Paul's style elsewhere in the corpus, it is in fact quite similar to the opening of 2 Corinthians (1.1–11).

---

[10] I am thinking here of the contemporary Pauline portraits described so well by Margaret Mitchell (*Heavenly Trumpet*, 423–8), and more specifically still of that more recent portrait that sketches Paul within Judaism in works like, e.g., Pamela Eisenbaum, *Paul Was Not a Christian: The Real Message of a Misunderstood Apostle* (New York: HarperOne, 2009); Fredriksen, *Paul*; Gager, *Reinventing Paul*; Caroline Johnson Hodge, *If Sons, then Heirs: A Study of Kinship and Ethnicity in the Letters of Paul* (New York: Oxford University Press, 2007); and Nanos and Zetterholm, eds., *Paul within Judaism*. In each, Ephesians is discussed only on the rarest of occasions (if ever), and typically dismissed for the usual reasons. Much better in this regard, from a reader sympathetic to the above works, is Matthew Thiessen, 'The Construction of Gentiles in the Letter to the Ephesians', in *The Early Reception of Paul the Second Temple Jew: Text, Narrative and Reception History*, ed. Isaac W. Oliver, Gabrielle Boccaccini, and Joshua Scott, LSTS 92 (London: T&T Clark, 2018), 13–25.

Might these two letters, then, have been written during (Ephesians) and shortly after (2 Corinthians) a spasm of particularly difficult opposition that landed Paul in prison (2 Cor 1.8–11; 4.8–12; 11.23–29; Eph 3.1; 6.19–20)—a sense of opposition only intensified as Paul learns of the new 'Colossian philosophy' threatening the infant Christ-assembly there (Col 2.8–23), so that his concern is not only for his own bodily welfare but for the spiritual health of his churches as well (2 Cor 11.28; cf. Col 1.24–2.5)? Put all of the above together, and might Eph 3.1–13 not just be Paul's distilled depiction of his gentile mission for a community he has not yet met (Eph 1.15; 3.2; 4.21)—a vocation tied to a χάρις, a μυστήριον, and a εὐαγγέλιον that, at the time of writing, he had already disbursed in Corinth and Galatia, and which he longed to disburse in Rome (Rom 1.15)? Is this a context which illuminates?

2. **Paul's gentile-gospel (Eph 1–2):** Working backward, if Eph 3.1–13 is a distilled form of the main contours of the collection's image of Paul, might Eph 2.11–22 (and more broadly, Eph 1–2) be a distilled form of Paul's gospel for gentiles—the *kerygma* he would typically share in person, and of which we have echoes in the other letters? This is certainly how the letter itself depicts its first two chapters. As Paul transitions to his own role in 3.1–13, he tells his readers that he has just described for them (προγράφω; Eph 3.3) his gentile-mystery—a gospel that links up, again, with a host of texts across the *Hauptbriefe*. Paul's gentile auditors were dead in characteristically gentile sin (Eph 2.1–3; 4.17–19; cf. Rom 1.18–32; Gal 2.15; 5.19–21), but Israel's God had mercifully brought them to life (Eph 2.4–9; cf. Rom 3.24–26; 4.16–18; 6.3–11; 8.9–11; Gal 2.17–21; 3.7–9, 13–14, 25–29); they were estranged from the πολιτεία of Israel (Eph 2.12), a child of the slave Hagar (Gal 4.23–24), a wild olive shoot (Rom 11.17), and a non-people (Rom 9.24–26) who were now, through the beneficence of Israel's God, fellow-citizens with the holy ones (Eph 2.17), children of the free woman Sarah and so of the Jerusalem above (Gal 4.26–31), grafted into the olive tree (Rom 11.17), and made a people (Rom 9.24–26). All of this happened for them in the body of the messiah (Eph 2.14–16; Gal 3.27–29) and through the presence of God's holy πνεῦμα, who wraps gentiles into Israel's lineage and guarantees (ἀρραβών) their resurrection (Eph 1.13–14; 2.18; Rom 8.23; 2 Cor 1.20, 22; 5.1–5; Gal 3.1–5, 14).

To be sure, when it comes to what Paul's new Christ-assemblies are, how they relate to the long story of Israel, and what all of this means for the ongoing ethnic status of those Jews and gentiles who comprise them, there is a certain ambiguity in Ephesians: are gentiles simply wrapped into the lineage of Israel, as reading straight from Eph 2.11–13 to v. 19 might seem to imply, or are Jew and gentile together made into something new (εἷς καινὸς ἄνθρωπος, 2.15), a third thing, as Eph 2.14–18 seems to suggest? This is no small question, since Ephesians has consistently been displaced just here. I do not deny the ambiguity; I only point out that Romans and Galatians share in precisely this same ambiguity. For the Paul of Galatians, are the gentiles simply now children of Sarah, Abraham's offspring, and so sharers of what Israel always enjoyed (Gal 3.29; 4.31), or is there 'no longer Jew or Greek…for all of you are one in Christ Jesus' (Gal 3.28)? For the Paul of Romans, have the gentiles simply been grafted (παρὰ φύσιν) into an olive tree to which Israel has not just temporal (Rom 11.17) but 'natural' priority (κατὰ φύσιν, 11.24), or is there 'no distinction between Jew and Greek' for 'the same Lord is Lord of all' (Rom 10.12; cf. 3.29–30)?

Or to press the point still further, if Ephesians 'trumpet[s] a new universal humanity, undoing the distinction between Israel and the nations' so vital to the 'historical Paul',[11] is this not exactly what Paul himself does in texts like Rom 9.22–24 ('…including *us* whom he has called, not from the Jews only but also from the gentiles') and 1 Cor 10.32 ('Give no offense to Jews or Greeks or to the ἐκκλησία of God'), *himself* 'undoing the distinction' by lexically distinguishing the 'called'/ἐκκλησία from the Jews on one side and gentiles on the other? And does this not make the 'in-Christ' identity of these Jews and gentiles more fundamental than their ethnic identity (even while still retaining it), and so rendering these ἐκκλησίαι (in some sense at least) not a *verus Israel* but at least a *tertium quid*?

Not denying for a moment the ambiguity of Ephesians on these questions, I only ask, do not Romans, Galatians, and Corinthians share in this ambiguity? And might this suggest not only the complexity of Paul's thought on this score,[12] but perhaps also that he is writing these letters around the same time, working in real time to articulate not only his gentile gospel but also to strengthen the status of his Jew/gentile Christ-assemblies vis-à-vis non-believing Israel on the one side (so, Rom 9, culminating in vv. 24–26) and pagan gentiles on the other (so, e.g., Rom 11.17–24; Gal 4.8–9, 28–31; Eph 2.11–13, 19–22)? Might Eph 1–2, then, not be developed, but rather the 'gist' of Paul's gentile gospel—a gospel that had, almost as a feature rather than a bug, certain tensions within it about the new status of gentiles-in-Christ vis-à-vis Israel? Is this a context that changes the color of the dress?

3. **Paul's gentile-ethics (Eph 4.17–5.14):** One final feature points further in the direction of Ephesians' connection to the period right before Paul composed the *Hauptbriefe*, and the hint comes not surprisingly from Nils Dahl. In a little-noticed essay from 1963, Dahl highlights the striking linguistic overlap between the paraenesis in Eph 5.5–11 and a series of short passages across 1 Cor 5–6 in which Paul recalls, then clarifies, his initial ethical instruction to the Christ-assembly in Corinth (1 Cor 5.9–10, 11; 6.9–10).[13] The key shared terminology across all four texts involves reference to a set of people (πόρνος, ἀκάθαρτος, πλεονέκτης, εἰδωλολάτρης) that Paul's in-Christ gentiles are not to associate with (μὴ συναναμίγνυσθαι/μὴ γίνεσθε συμμέτοχοι; 1 Cor 5.9, 11; Eph 5.7), as well as a warning that such people 'will not inherit the kingdom of (Christ and of) God'

---

[11] Fredriksen, *Paul*, 169.
[12] This is a good example, to my mind, of a place where Ephesians can draw attention to texts in the *Hauptbriefe* that certain strands of Pauline scholarship today would prefer to ignore. That is, it is a place alive to that potential that Markus Barth saw in Ephesians, 'to force extreme Paulinists of all times to revise their prejudices' (*Ephesians*, 1:48).
[13] Nils A. Dahl, 'Der Epheserbrief und der verlorene, erste Brief des Paulus an die Korinther', in *Studies in Ephesians*, 335–48. See especially the table on p. 337.

(1 Cor 6.9-10; Eph 5.5). What makes this overlap so suggestive, however, is that 1 Cor 5.9-10 is Paul's recollection of his paraenesis to the Christ-assembly in Corinth in his *first* (now lost) letter to the Corinthians. In the compositional situation I envisage for Ephesians, then, this would make it and the lost letter to Corinth more or less contemporaneous. And this is only reinforced by the overlapping content of their moral exhortation suggested by comparing 1 Cor 5.9-10 with Eph 5.5-11 (and more broadly, 4.17-5.14).

We can put this slightly differently, and be more specific still, by asking a simple question: using the hints of 1 Cor 5.9-10, what sort of ethical stance and tone must this first, lost letter to Corinth have contained so as to require the particular clarification Paul offers in v. 11, even as he reinforces unequivocally its basic moral vision in 1 Cor 6.9-10? More succinctly, what sort of letter would have generated the need for Paul to backtrack as he does in 1 Cor 5.11? I suggest that something like the paraenesis of Eph 4.17-5.14 (and more specifically, 5.5-11) almost perfectly fits the bill. Here, a typical Jewish conception of pagan immorality (4.17-19), combined with a strong sense of the pneumatic renewal undergone by his gentile converts (4.23-24; cf. 1.13-14), leads Paul to construct a rhetorical wall between the 'new self' of his gentiles and their 'old self' and 'former manner of life' (4.22). These gentiles must put away ψεῦδος, κλέπτης, λόγος σαπρός, πικρία, θυμός, ὀργή, κραυγή, and βλασφημία (4.25-31) and, coming nearer the lexical parallels in 1 Cor 5.9-10, completely reject πορνεία, πᾶσα ἀκαθαρσία, αἰσχρότης, μωρολογία, and εὐτραπελία (Eph 5.3-4). In Eph 5.5, the divide between the 'new self' of Paul's gentiles and the form of life of their pagan co-ethnics is unequivocal, and the lexical overlap with 1 Cor 5.9-10 complete: 'everyone who is πόρνος or ἀκάθαρτος or πλεονέκτης, which is εἰδωλολάτρης, has no inheritance in the kingdom of Christ and of God' (5.5; cf. 1 Cor 5.10, 11; 6.9-10). This divide, for Paul, is as clear as darkness and light (Eph 5.8-10), and so Paul's gentiles must not 'be associated with them' (5.7; cf. 1 Cor 5.9, 11) nor 'take part in the unfruitful works of darkness, but instead expose them' (5.11).

If the first, lost letter to Corinth mirrored this strongly ascetic and sectarian moral vision, Paul's backpedal in his follow-up communiqué (canonical 1 Corinthians) is hardly a surprise: Eph 4.17-5.14 contains precisely the sort of vigorous ascesis that we might expect would generate (gentile) Corinthian questions, and require some gentle revision in scope (1 Cor 5.11), even as he leaves the basic moral vision intact (6.9-10). If this is the case, might the close *linguistic* connections of these four texts (Eph 5.5-11; 1 Cor 5.9-10, 11; 6.9-10) be evidence that Ephesians belongs *historically* alongside the first, lost letter to Corinth, and so further evidence that Ephesians itself belongs to the period before the canonical Corinthian correspondence? Is this a context which illuminates?

With these sketches in place, we are now in a position briefly to summarize, and we can do so again in the form of a question. Looking back over the hints above (##1-3), gleaned from reading Ephesians alongside its most redolent Pauline co-texts, and then seeking to locate these hints historically, I pose the following question: was there a time in Paul's life when he would have been more apt to have been thinking deeply through (1) the precise configurations of his gentile gospel and the status of his gentile Christ-assemblies vis-à-vis Israel (#2 above, Eph 1-2); (2) the moral-ethical requirements for pagans who have received (and must now walk in) the πνεῦμα of Israel's God (#3 above, Eph 4.17-5.14); and (3) his own apostolic vocation vis-à-vis these gentiles, and how it relates to other key figures in the early Jesus movement (#1 above, Eph 3.1-13) than in the run-up to and aftermath of the Jerusalem council (Gal 2.1-10; Acts 15)? Is not Ephesians full of precisely the sort of things we would expect to be on Paul's mind after such an event?[14]

And if we are to take the lack of an address in our earliest manuscripts seriously, together with the link to Col 4.16 and the evidence of the earliest non-canonical tradition about the letter's destination,[15] and combine it with the slender evidence the letter itself provides as to its character, audience, and relationship to its recipients, does not the simplest reading of that evidence suggest that 'Ephesians' is Paul's gospel for an unknown gentile community in Laodicea, penned a short time after the Jerusalem council, together with Colossians and Philemon and before the *Hauptbriefe*? In his book *Framing Paul*, Douglas Campbell suggests that the *Hauptbriefe* are the filtering through, in response to more specific and urgent epistolary situations, of ideas first developed in Ephesians (Laodiceans).[16] My own Chapter 5, as well as the sketches above, suggest similarly. Might this shed fresh light, and should we look at the dress again?

...

I have tried to begin with the artefact and close with a few thoughts about history. As I have stressed throughout, any potential setting for Ephesians is fragile and tenuous at best, and I regard the possibility of an early missive to Laodicea no differently. The letter simply does not allow for confident placement, nor offer many clues on its face. And some of the clues it does offer seem to conflict.[17] The quest for the historical Ephesians is fraught with uncertainty, even when that quest is pursued via the pathways of the collection. Yet if the sketches above have proven fruitful or suggestive, then reading Ephesians alongside the collection, not least with recent Pauline portraits in view, introduces new data that should be considered—considerably more data, I suggest, than we have for a Roman imprisonment or a Pauline school in the 80s/90s, about which we know nothing. As Goodspeed saw, there may be historical fruit to pick by reading Ephesians within the collection.

---

[14] An event in which, collating the data of Galatians and Acts, Paul set forth his gentile gospel before the Jerusalem apostles (Gal 2.2), received the right hand of fellowship from them (2.9), and left accompanying a letter about the ethical implications of all of this for gentiles (Acts 15.22-29).

[15] I am thinking here of the earliest stage of the Old Latin prologues, in which the prologue for 'Ephesians' attests a Laodicean address (reconstructed by de Bruyne in 'Prologues bibliques', 14 [cf. 4-6 and 10]). In the mid-second century, Marcion knows the letter as Laodiceans as well (Tertullian, *Marc.* 5.11 and 17).

[16] Campbell, *Framing Paul*, 325-6.

[17] The presence of a *Haustafel*, for instance, which it shares in common with Colossians, Titus, and 1 Peter gives me pause, as does the exalted view of marriage in 5.22-33 (in contrast to 1 Cor 7).

To close, then: in his review of Adolf Harnack's famed *History of Early Christian Literature*, writing specifically of Ephesians, Caspar René Gregory laments, 'When will our science learn that it is the most unscientific thing in the world to give up a tradition, without severe compulsion, before we have anything to put in its place?'[18] Quite so, and the 125 years of scholarship on Paul and Ephesians since Gregory penned those words has done little to fill the gap. What felt like an assured result was, rather, a result of the sociology of modern reading. While plausible, I argue that this way of reading Ephesians, and the amount of space it opens up between Paul and Ephesians, is methodologically fragile, exegetically distorting, and ultimately circular and self-reinforcing. It is constructed space. This space needs closing, whether one thinks Paul wrote Ephesians or not. To this end, I have suggested a return to the Pauline book as an alternative context for illumination. The dilemma of Ephesians is inextricably intertwined with how to read that book. There is no guarantee, of course, what Paul's contemporary readers will find in Ephesians if they begin to read it alongside that book, now in light of our own portraits of Paul. But that is the pleasure of discovery, as each age reads Paul afresh in light of its own aims and purposes. If today's students of Paul start reading Ephesians with Paul again, I have a hunch that more than just Eph 3.1–13 may come to be seen as Paul's 'gist'. And if that were to happen, they would join a wide array of Paulinists from very different eras of reception (Origen, Jerome, Chrysostom, Victorinus, Ambrosiaster, Priscillian, Euthalius, Robinson, Dodd, Goodspeed, Caird, Dahl, Bruce, Gaston, Boyarin, Campbell and Wright) who have seen in Ephesians (or at least parts of Ephesians) something like the quintessence of Paul's gospel. No doubt that will mean something different today than it did for Origen or Priscillian or even Dodd. But whatever it will mean, I suspect it will take the fresh light of a very old way of reading to get there: to take up and read Paul's book.

---

[18] Review of *History of Early Christian Literature*, by Adolf Harnack, *AmJT* 2 (1898): 574–97.

BIBLIOGRAPHY

Primary Sources/Reference Works

Aland, K., B. Aland, J. Karavidopoulos, C. M. Martini, and B. M. Metzger, eds. *Novum Testamentum Graece*. 28th ed. Stuttgart: Deutsche Bibelgesellschaft, 2012.

Ambrosiaster. *Commentaries on Galatians-Philemon*. Translated and edited by G. L. Bray. Ancient Christian Texts. Downers Grove, IL: InterVarsity, 2009.

Ambrosiaster. *Commentary on the Pauline Epistles: Romans*. Translated with an introduction by T. de Bruyne, S. A. Cooper, and D. G. Hunter. Writings from the Greco-Roman World 41. Atlanta: SBL Press, 2017.

Ambrosiaster. *Commentary on Romans and 1–2 Corinthians*. Translated and edited by G. L. Bray. Ancient Christian Texts. Downers Grove, IL: InterVarsity, 2009.

Ambrosiastri qui dicitur Commentarius in Epistulas Paulinas. Edited by H. J. Vogels. 3 vols. Corpus Scriptorum Ecclesiasticorum Latinorum 81. Vienna: Hoelder-Pichler-Tempsky, 1966–69.

Ps.-Athanasius. *Synopsis Scripturae Sacrae*. Patrologia Graeca 28. Paris, 1887.

Augustine. *Confessions*. Translated by C. J.-B. Hammond. 2 vols. Loeb Classical Library 26–27. Cambridge: Harvard University Press, 2014–16.

Augustine. *Confessions*. Translated with introduction and notes by H. Chadwick. Oxford World's Classics. Oxford: Oxford University Press, 1998.

Barlow, C. W. *Epistolae Senecae ad Paulum et Pauli ad Senecam <Quae Vocantur>*. Rome: American Academy in Rome, 1938.

Bidez, J. and F. Cumont, eds. *Iuliani imperatoris epistulae, leges, poematia, fragmenta varia*. Paris: Société d'Édition 'Les Belles Lettres', 1922.

Blass, F., A. Debrunner, and R. W. Funk. *A Greek Grammar of the New Testament and Other Early Christian Literature*. Chicago: University of Chicago Press, 1961.

Cooper, S. A. *Marius Victorinus' Commentary on Galatians: Introduction, Translation, and Notes*. Oxford Early Christian Studies. New York: Oxford University Press, 2005.

Cooper, S. A. *Metaphysics and Morals in Marius Victorinus's Commentary on the Letter to the Ephesians: A Contribution to the History of Neoplatonism and Christianity*. American University Studies 5/155. New York: Peter Lang, 1995.

Danker, F. W., W. Bauer, W. F. Arndt, and F. W. Gingrich. *Greek-English Lexicon of the New Testament and Other Early Christian Literature*. 3rd ed. Chicago: University of Chicago Press, 2000.

de Bruyne, D. *Préfaces de la Bible latine*. Namur, 1920.

Diogenes Laertius. *Lives of Eminent Philosophers, Volume 1: Books 1–5*. Translated by R. D. Hicks. 2 vols. Loeb Classical Library 184. Cambridge: Harvard University Press, 1925.

Elliger, K. and W. Rudolph, eds. *Biblia Hebraica Stuttgartensia*. Stuttgart: Deutsche Bibelgesellschaft, 1983.
Euthalius Diaconus. *Opera*. Patrologia Graeca 85. Paris, 1864.
Field, F. *Interpretatio omnium epistolarum paulinarum*. 7 vols. Oxford: Academiae Typus, 1845-62.
Foerster, R., ed. *Libanii Opera*. Vol. 8. Leipzig: Teubner, 1915.
Frede, H. J. *Ein neuer Paulustext und Kommentar*. 2 vols. *Aus der Geschichte lateinischen Bibel* 7-8. Freiburg: Herder, 1973-74.
Frede, H. J., ed. *Vetus Latina: Die Reste der Altlateinischen Bibel*. 27 vols. Freiburg: Herder, 1962-98.
Fronto, M. C. *Correspondence*. Translated by C. R. Haines. 2 vols. LCL 112. Cambridge, MA: Harvard University Press, 1919-20.
Gibson, C., trans. 'Libanius' *Hypotheses* to the Orations of Demosthenes'. In *Dēmos: Classical Athenian Democracy*. Edited by C. Blackwell. In *The Stoa: A Consortium for Electronic Publication in the Humanities*. Edited by A. Mahoney and R. Scaife. www.stoa.org. 2003.
Gregg, J. A. F. 'The Commentary of Origen upon the Epistle to the Ephesians'. *Journal of Theological Studies* 3 (1902): 233-44, 398-420, and 554-76.
Halkin, F., ed. *Life of Pachomius*. In *Sancti Pachomii: vitae Graecae*. Subsidia Hagiographica 19. Brussels: Société des Bollandistes, 1932.
Hawthorne, G. F., and R. P. Martin, eds. *Dictionary of Paul and His Letters*. Downers Grove, IL: InterVarsity, 1993.
Hederich, B. *Novum Lexicon Manuale Graeco-Latinum et Latinum-Graecum*. 3 vols. Leipzig: Gleditsch, 1825.
Heine, R. E., ed. *The Commentaries of Origen and Jerome on St. Paul's Epistle to the Ephesians*. Oxford Early Christian Studies. Oxford: Oxford University Press, 2002.
Henry, P. and H.-R. Schwyzer, eds. *Plotini Opera I*. Oxford: Clarendon, 1964.
Hesychius. Στιχηρὸν τῶν ιβ΄προφητῶν. Patrologia Graeca 93. Paris, 1865.
Jerome. *Opera Omnia*. Patrologia Latina 26. Paris, 1845.
St. Jerome: Commentary on Galatians. Translated by A. Cain. Fathers of the Church 121. Washington, DC: Catholic University of America Press, 2010.
St. Jerome's Commentaries on Galatians, Titus, and Philemon. Translated by T. P. Scheck. Notre Dame: University of Notre Dame Press, 2010.
John Chrysostom. *Homilies*. Patrologia Graeca 60-62. Paris, 1862.
John Chrysostom. *Homilies on Galatians, Ephesians, Philippians, Colossians, Thessalonians, Timothy, Titus, and Philemon*. In vol. 13 of *Nicene and Post-Nicene Fathers*, Series 1. Edited by G. Alexander and P. Schaaf. Edinburgh: T. & T. Clark, 1994.
John Chrysostom. *Propter fornicationes uxorem*. Patrologia Graeca 51. Paris, 1862.
Kittel, G., and G. Friedrich, eds. *Theological Dictionary of the New Testament*. Translated by G. W. Bromiley. 10 vols. Grand Rapids, 1964-76.
Lampe, G. W. H., ed. *Patristic Greek Lexicon*. Oxford: Clarendon, 1961.
Lewis, C. T., and C. Short. *A Latin Dictionary: Founded on Andrews' Edition of Freund's Latin Dictionary. Revised, Enlarged and in Great Part Rewritten*. Oxford: Clarendon, 1900.
Liddell, H. G., R. Scott, and H. S. Jones. *A Greek-English Lexicon*. 9th ed. with revised supplement. Oxford: Clarendon, 1996.
Louw, J. P., and E. A. Nida. *Greek-English Lexicon of the New Testament Based on Semantic Domains*. New York: United Bible Societies, 1988.
Mai, A. *Spicilegium Romanum*. Rome, 1843.

Malherbe, A. J. *Ancient Epistolary Theorists*. Sources for Biblical Study 19. Atlanta: Scholars Press, 1988.
Marii Victorini opera pars II opera exegetica. Edited by F. Gori. Corpus Scriptorum Ecclesiasticorum Latinorum 83/2. Vienna: Hoelder-Pichler-Tempsky, 1986.
Meeks, W. A., ed. *The Writings of St. Paul: Annotated Text, Reception and Criticism*. 2nd ed. Norton Critical Editions. London: Norton, 2007.
Metzger, B. M. *A Textual Commentary on the New Testament*. 2nd ed. Stuttgart: Deutsche Bibelgesellschaft, 1994.
Musurillo, H., ed. and trans. *The Acts of the Christian Martyrs*. Oxford: Clarendon, 1972.
Nüsser, O. *Albins Prolog und die Dialogtheorie des Platonismus*. Beiträge zur Altertumskunde 12. Stuttgart: Teubner, 1991.
Origen. *Commentary on the Epistle to the Romans, Books 1–5*. Translated by T. P. Scheck. Fathers of the Church 103. Washington, DC: Catholic University of America Press, 2001.
Patrologia Graeca. Edited by J.-P. Migne. 162 vols. Paris, 1857–86.
Patrologia Latina. Edited by J.-P. Migne. 217 vols. Paris, 1844–64.
Piere, F. 'L'esegesi di Girolamo nel Commentario a Efesini. Aspetti storico-esegetici e storico-dottrinali'. PhD diss., Università degli Studi di Bologna, 1996/1997.
Plotinus. *The Enneads*. Translated by S. MacKenna. 3rd ed. London: Faber, 1962.
Plotinus. *Porphyry on the Life of Plotinus. Ennead 1*. Vol. 1 of *Enneads*. Translated by A. H. Armstrong. 6 vols. Loeb Classical Library 440. Cambridge: Harvard University Press, 1969.
Plutarch. *The Education of Children*. Vol 1. of *Moralia*. Translated by F. C. Babbitt. 15 vols. Loeb Classical Library 197. Cambridge: Harvard University Press, 1927.
Ps.-Chrysostom. *Synopsis Scripturae Sacrae*. Patrologia Graeca 56. Paris, 1859.
Schenkl, K. *Sancti Ambrosii Opera*. Corpus Scriptorum Ecclesiasticorum Latinorum 82. Leipzig, 1897.
Schepss, G., ed. *Priscilliani Quae Supersunt: Maximam Partem Nuper Detexit Adjectisque Commentariis Criticis Et Indicibus*. Corpus Scriptorum Ecclesiasticorum Latinorum 18. Vindobonae: F. Tempsky, 1889.
Schneemelcher, W., ed. *New Testament Apocrypha*. Translated by R. McL. Wilson. 2 vols. Cambridge: James Clarke, 1991–92.
Septuaginta: Vetus Testamentum Graecum. 3rd ed. 16 vols. Göttingen: Vandenhoeck & Ruprecht, 1990–.
Socrates Scholasticus. *Ecclesiastical History*. In vol. 2 of *The Nicene and Post-Nicene Fathers*, Series 2. Edited by P. Schaff. Edinburgh: T. & T. Clark.
Souter, A. *Pelagius's Expositions of Thirteen Epistles of St. Paul*. 3 vols. Texts and Studies 9. Cambridge: Cambridge University Press, 1922–31.
Staab, K. *Pauluskommentare aus der Griechischen Kirche*. 2nd ed. Münster: Aschendorff, 1984.
Swete, H. B., ed. *Theodori episcopi Mopsuesteni In epistolas b. Pauli commentarii*. 2 vols. Cambridge: Cambridge University Press, 1880–82.
Theodore of Mopsuestia. *The Commentaries on the Minor Epistles of Paul*. Translated with an introduction by R. A. Greer. Writings from the Greco-Roman World 26. Atlanta: Society of Biblical Literature, 2010.
Theodoret of Cyrus. *Commentary on the Letters of St. Paul*. Translated with an introduction by R. C. Hill. 2 vols. Brookline, MA: Holy Cross Orthodox, 2001.
Theodoret of Cyrus. *Interpretatio XIV Epistolarum Sancti Pauli Apostoli*. Patrologia Graeca 82. Paris, 1864.

Theophylact. *Commentarius in Omnes Divi Pauli Epistolas*. Patrologia Graeca 124. Belgium.
Tov, E., ed. *Discoveries in the Judean Desert*. 40 vols. Oxford: Clarendon, 1977.
Weichert, V. *Demetrii et Libanii qui feruntur* Τύποι ἐπιστολικοί *et* Ἐπιστολιμαῖοι χαρακτῆρες. Leipzig: Teubner, 1910.
Wordsworth, J., and H. J. White, eds. *Novum Testamentum Latine, Editio Maior: Pars Secunda— Epistulae Paulinae*. Oxford, 1913–41.
Zacagni, L. *Collectanea Monumentorum Veterum Ecclesiae Graecae Ac Latinae. Quae Hactenus in Vaticana Bibliotheca Delituerunt*. Rome: Typis Sacrae Congreg. de Propag. Fide, 1698.

Secondary Sources

Aageson, J. W. *Paul, the Pastoral Epistles and the Early Church*. Peabody, MA: Hendrickson, 2008.
Abbott, T. K. *A Critical and Exegetical Commentary on the Epistles to the Ephesians and to the Colossians*. International Critical Commentary. Edinburgh: T. & T. Clark, 1897.
Agamben, G. *The Kingdom and the Glory: For a Theological Genealogy of Economy and Government*. Translated by L. Chiesa with M. Mandarini. Stanford, CA: Stanford University Press, 2011.
Aletti, J.-N. *Saint Paul: Épitre aux Éphésiens: Introduction, Traduction et Commentaire*. Etudes Bibliques 42. Paris: Gabalda, 2001.
Alkier, S. *Urchristentum: zur Geschichte und Theologie einer exegetischen Disziplin*. Beiträge zur historischen Theologie 83. Tübingen: Mohr Siebeck, 1993.
Altman, J. G. 'The Letter Book as a Literary Institution 1539–1789: Toward a Cultural History of Published Correspondences in France'. *Yale French Studies* 71 (1986): 17–62.
Arnal, W. 'What Branches Grow Out of This Stony Rubbish? Christian Origins and the Study of Religion'. *Studies in Religion* 39 (2010): 549–72.
Arnold, C. E. *Ephesians*. Zondervan Exegetical Commentary of the New Testament. Grand Rapids: Zondervan, 2010.
Arnold, C. E. *Ephesians: Power and Magic. The Concept of Power in Ephesians in Light of its Historical Setting*. Society for New Testament Studies Monograph Series 63. Cambridge: Cambridge University Press, 1989.
Aune, D. E. 'Reconceptualizing the Phenomenon of Ancient Pseudepigraphy'. Pages 789–824 in *Pseudepigraphie und Verfasserfiktion in frühchristlichen Briefen*. Edited by J. Frey, J. Herzer, M. Janssen, and C. K. Rothschild. Wissenschaftliche Untersuchungen zum Neuen Testament 246. Mohr Siebeck: Tübingen, 2009.
Babcock, W. S., ed. *Paul and the Legacies of Paul*. Dallas: Southern Methodist University Press, 1990.
Bacon, B. W. *An Introduction to the New Testament*. New York: Macmillan, 1900.
Baird, W. *History of New Testament Research*. 3 vols. Minneapolis: Augsburg Fortress, 1992–2013.
Barchiesi, A. 'The Search for the Perfect Book: A PS to the New Posidippus'. Pages 320–42 in *The New Posidippus: A Hellenistic Poetry Book*. Edited by K. Gutzwiller. Oxford: Oxford University Press, 2005.
Barclay, J. M. G. 'Mirror-Reading a Polemical Letter: Galatians as a Test Case'. *Journal for the Study of the New Testament* 31 (1987): 73–93.
Barclay, J. M. G. *Paul and the Gift*. Grand Rapids: Eerdmans, 2015.

Barrett, C. K. *Paul: An Introduction to His Thought*. Louisville: Westminster John Knox, 1994.
Barrett, C. K. 'Pauline Controversies in the Post-Pauline Period'. *New Testament Studies* 20 (1974): 229-45.
Barth, M. *Ephesians: Introduction, Translation, and Commentary*. 2 vols. Anchor Bible 34A-B. Garden City, NY: Doubleday, 1974.
Barth, M. 'Traditions in Ephesians'. *New Testament Studies* 30 (1984): 3-25.
Bassler, J. M. 'Paul's Theology: Whence and Whither?' Pages 3-17 in *1 and 2 Corinthians*. Edited by D. M. Hay. Vol. 2 of *Pauline Theology*. Edited by J. M. Bassler, D. M. Hay, and E. E. Johnson. Minneapolis: Fortress, 1993.
Bassler, J. M. 'Preface'. Pages ix-xi in *Thessalonians, Philippians, Galatians, Philemon*. Edited by J. M. Bassler. Vol. 1 of *Pauline Theology*. Edited by J. M. Bassler, D. M. Hay, and E. E. Johnson. Minneapolis: Fortress, 1997.
Bassler, J. M., D. M. Hay, and E. E. Johnson, eds. *Pauline Theology*. 4 vols. Minneapolis: Fortress, 1991-97.
Bauer, B. *Kritik der paulinischen Briefe*. 3 vols. Berlin: Hempel, 1850.
Baum, A. D. 'Authorship and Pseudepigraphy in Early Christian Literature: A Translation of the Most Important Source Texts and an Annotated Bibliography'. Pages 11-63 in *Paul and Pseudepigraphy*. Edited by S. E. Porter and G. P. Fewster. Pauline Studies 8. Leiden: Brill, 2013.
Baum, A. D. *Pseudepigraphie und literarische Fälschung im frühen Christentum*. Wissenschaftliche Untersuchungen zum Neuen Testament 2/138. Tübingen: Mohr Siebeck, 2001.
Baur, F. C. 'Die Christpartei in der korinthischen Gemeinde, der Gegensatz des petrinischen und paulinischen Christenthums in der ältesten Kirche, der Apostel Petrus in Rom'. *Tübinger Zeitschrift für Theologie* 4 (1831): 61-206.
Baur, F. C. *The Church History of the First Three Centuries*. 3rd ed. Translated by A. Menzies. 2 vols. Theological Translation Fund Library. London: Williams and Norgate, 1878 [1853-1860].
Baur, F. C. 'Die Einleitung in das Neue Testament als theologische Wissenschaft. Ihr Begriff und ihre Aufgabe, ihr Entwicklungsgang und ihr innerer Organismus'. *Theologische Jahrbücher* 9 (1850): 463-566.
Baur, F. C. *History of Christian Dogma*. Translated by P. C. Hodgson and R. F. Brown. Oxford: Oxford University Press, 2014.
Baur, F. C. *Paul the Apostle of Jesus Christ: His Life and Work, His Epistles and His Doctrine. A Contribution to the Critical History of Primitive Christianity*. 2nd ed. Translated by E. Zeller. 2 vols. Theological Translation Fund Library 1. London; Edinburgh: Williams and Norgate, 1873 [1845].
Bauspiess, M., C. Landmesser, and D. Lincicum, eds. *Ferdinand Christian Baur und die Geschichte des frühen Christentums*. Wissenschaftliche Untersuchungen zum Neuen Testament 333. Tübingen: Mohr Siebeck, 2014.
Beard, M. 'Ciceronian Correspondences: Making a Book Out of Letters'. Pages 103-44 in *Classics in Progress: Essays on Ancient Greece and Rome*. Edited by T. P. Wiseman. Oxford: Oxford University Press, 2002.
Beare, F. W. Review of *Epistle to the Ephesians*, by C. L. Mitton. *Journal of Biblical Literature* 72 (1953): 70-72.
Beker, J. C. *Heirs of Paul: Paul's Legacy in the New Testament and in the Church Today*. Minneapolis: Augsburg Fortress, 1991. Repr., Grand Rapids: Eerdmans, 1996.

Beker, J. C. *Paul the Apostle: The Triumph of God in Life and Thought*. Edinburgh: T. & T. Clark, 1980.
Bessiéres, M. 'La tradition manuscrite de la correspondance de Saint Basile, Chapitre I'. *Journal of Theological Studies* 21 (1919): 9–50.
Best, E. *A Critical and Exegetical Commentary on Ephesians*. International Critical Commentary. Edinburgh: T. & T. Clark, 1998.
Best, E. *Essays on Ephesians*. Edinburgh: T. & T. Clark, 1997.
Best, E. 'Recipients and Title of the Letter to the Ephesians: Why and When the Designation "Ephesians"?.' *ANRW* 25.4:3247–79. Part 2, *Principat*, 25.4. Edited by H. Temporini and W. Haase. New York: de Gruyter, 1987
Best, E. 'Who Used Whom? The Relationship of Ephesians and Colossians'. *New Testament Studies* 43 (1997): 72–96.
Bird, M. F. and J. R. Dodson, eds. *Paul and the Second Century*. Library of New Testament Studies 412. London: T&T Clark, 2011.
Birks, T. R. *Horae Paulinae; ... by William Paley, D.D. with notes and a Supplementary Treatise entitled Horae Apostolicae by the Rev. T. R. Birks*. London: Religious Tract Society, 1849.
Blasi, A. J. *Making Charisma: The Social Construction of Paul's Public Image*. New Brunswick, NJ: Transaction, 1991.
Blomkvist, V. *Euthalian Traditions: Text, Translation and Commentary*. Texte und Untersuchungen zur Geschichte der altchristlichen Literatur 170. Berlin: de Gruyter, 2012.
Bockmuehl, M. N. A. *Revelation and Mystery in Ancient Judaism and Pauline Christianity*. Eugene, OR: Wipf & Stock, 2009.
Bodel, J. 'The Publication of Pliny's Letters'. Pages 13–108 in *Pliny the Book-Maker*. Edited by I. Marchesi. Oxford: Oxford University Press, 2015.
Bornkamm, G. *Bibel, das Neue Testament: Eine Einführung in seine Schriften im Rahmen der Geschichte des Urchristentums*. Stuttgart: Kreuz-Verlag, 1971.
Bornkamm, G. *Paul*. Translated by D. M. G. Stalker. London: Hodder & Stoughton, 1971.
Boyarin, D. *A Radical Jew: Paul and the Politics of Identity*. Berkley: University of California Press, 1994.
Brown, R. E. *An Introduction to the New Testament*. New York: Doubleday, 1997.
Brown, R. E.0 *The Churches the Apostles Left Behind*. New York: Paulist, 1984.
Brox, N. *Falsche Verfasserangaben: Zur Erklärung der frühchristlichen Pseudepigraphie*. Stuttgart: KBW Verlag, 1975.
Bruce, F. F. *Paul: Apostle of the Heart Set Free*. Grand Rapids: Eerdmans, 1977.
Buck, C. H., and G. Taylor. *Saint Paul: A Study of the Development of His Thought*. New York: Scribner, 1969.
Bultmann, R. *Theology of the New Testament*. Translated by K. Grobel. 2 vols. London: SCM, 1952.
Bultmann, R. 'Urchristliche Religion (1915–1925)'. *Archiv für Religionswissenschaft* 24 (1926): 83–164.
Butler, S. 'Cicero's *capita*'. Pages 73–111 in *The Roman Paratext: Frames, Texts, Readers*. Edited by L. Jansen. Cambridge: Cambridge University Press, 2014.
Cadbury, H. J. 'The Dilemma of Ephesians'. *New Testament Studies* 5 (1959): 91–102.
Cadbury, H. J. Review of *Epistle to the Ephesians*, by C. L. Mitton. *Journal of Bible and Religion* 20 (1952): 210, 212.
Caird, G. B. *The Apostolic Age*. Studies in Theology 53. London: Duckworth, 1966.
Campbell, D. A. *The Deliverance of God: An Apocalyptic Rereading of Justification in Paul*. Grand Rapids: Eerdmans, 2013.

Campbell, D. A. *Framing Paul: An Epistolary Biography*. Grand Rapids: Eerdmans, 2014.

Cavadini, J. C. 'Exegetical Transformations: The Sacrifice of Isaac in Philo, Origen, and Ambrose'. Pages 35–49 in Indominico Eloquio, *In Lordly Eloquence: Essays on Patristic Exegesis in Honor of Robert Louis Wilken*. Edited by P. M. Blowers, A. R. Christman, D. G. Hunter, and R. D. Young. Grand Rapids: Eerdmans, 2002.

Chadwick, H. 'Die Absicht des Epheserbriefes'. *Zeitschrift für die neutestamentliche Wissenschaft und die Kunde der älteren Kirche* 51 (1960): 145–53.

Chadwick, H. *Priscillian of Avila: The Occult and the Charismatic in the Early Church*. Oxford: Clarendon Press, 1976.

Childs, B. S. *The Church's Guide for Reading Paul: The Canonical Shaping of the Pauline Corpus*. Grand Rapids: Eerdmans, 2008.

Chin, C. M. *Grammar and Christianity in the Late Roman World*. Philadelphia: University of Pennsylvania Press, 2008.

Choat, M. 'From Letter to Letter-Collection: Monastic Epistolography in Late-Antique Egypt'. Pages 80–94 in *Collecting Early Christian Letters: From the Apostle Paul to Late Antiquity*. Edited by B. Neil and P. Allen. Cambridge: Cambridge University Press, 2015.

Cohick, L. H. *The Letter to the Ephesians*. New International Commentary on the New Testament. Grand Rapids: Eerdmans, 2020.

Collins, J. N. *Diakonia: Re-Interpreting the Ancient Sources*. New York: Oxford University Press, 1990.

Collins, J. N. 'A Monocultural Usage: διακον- Words in Classical, Hellenistic, and Patristic Sources'. *Vigiliae Christianae* 66 (2012): 287–309.

Colpe, C. 'Zur Leib-Christi-Vorstellung im Epheserbrief'. Pages 172–87 in *Judentum, Urchristentum, Kirche: Festschrift für Joachim Jeremias*. Edited by Walther Eltester. Beihefte zur Zeitschrift für die neutestamentliche Wissenschaft 26. Berlin: Töpelmann, 1960.

Conybeare, W. J., and J. S. Howson. *Life and Epistles of St. Paul*. London: Longman, Brown, Green, and Longmans, 1852.

Conti, M., ed and trans. *Priscillian of Avila: The Complete Works*. Oxford Early Christian Texts. Oxford: Oxford University Press, 2010.

Conzelmann, H. 'Paulus und die Weisheit'. *New Testament Studies* 12 (1965): 321–44.

Conzelmann, H. 'Die Schule Des Paulus'. Pages 85–96 in *Theologia Crucis—signum Crucis: Festschrift für E. Dinkler*. Edited by C. Andresen and G. Klein. Tübingen: Mohr Siebeck, 1979.

Cooper, S. 'Philosophical Exegesis in Marius Victorinus's Commentaries on Paul'. Pages 67–89 in *Interpreting the Bible and Aristotle in Late Antiquity: The Alexandrian Commentary Tradition between Rome and Baghdad*. Edited by J. Lössl and J. W. Watt. Farnham, Surrey, UK: Ashgate, 2011.

Cousar, C. B. *The Letters of Paul*. Interpreting Biblical Texts. Nashville: Abingdon, 1996.

Coutts, J. 'The Relationship of Ephesians and Colossians'. *New Testament Studies* 4 (1958): 201–7.

Credner, K. A. *Einleitung in das neue Testament*. Halle: Waisenhaus, 1836.

Cribiore, R. *Gymnastics of the Mind: Greek Education in Hellenistic and Roman Egypt*. Princeton: Princeton University Press, 2001.

Cullmann, O. *Christ and Time*. Translated by F. V. Filson. London: SCM Press, 1962.

Dahl, N. A. 'Adresse und Proömium des Epheserbriefes'. *Theologische Zeitschrift* 7 (1951): 241–64.

Dahl, N. A. 'The Concept of Baptism in Ephesians'. Translated by Bruce C. Johanson. Pages 413–39 in *Studies in Ephesians*.

Dahl, N. A. 'Dopet i Efesierbrevet'. *Svensk teologisk kvartalskrift* 21 (1945): 85–103.
Dahl, N. A. 'Einleitungsfragen zum Epheserbrief'. Pages 3–105 in *Studies in Ephesians*.
Dahl, N. A. 'Ephesians'. Pages 268–69 in *Interpreter's Dictionary of the Bible: Supplementary Volume*. Edited by K. Crim. Nashville: Abingdon, 1976.
Dahl, N. A. 'Ephesians and Qumran'. Pages 107–44 in *Studies in Ephesians*.
Dahl, N. A. 'The "Euthalian Apparatus" and the Affiliated "Argumenta"'. Pages 231–75 in *Studies in Ephesians*.
Dahl, N. A. 'Das Geheimnis der Kirche nach Epheser 3,8–10'. Pages 349–63 in *Studies in Ephesians*.
Dahl, N. A. 'Gentiles, Christians, and Israelites in the Epistle to the Ephesians'. Pages 441–49 in *Studies in Ephesians*.
Dahl, N. A. 'Interpreting Ephesians: Then and Now'. Pages 461–73 in *Studies in Ephesians*.
Dahl, N. A. 'The Letter to the Ephesians: Its Fictional and Real Settings'. Pages 451–59 in *Studies in Ephesians*.
Dahl, N. A. 'The Origin of the Earliest Prologues to the Pauline Letters'. Pages 179–209 in *Studies in Ephesians*.
Dahl, N. A. 'The Particularity of the Pauline Epistles as a Problem for the Ancient Church'. Pages 165–78 in *Studies in Ephesians*.
Dahl, N. A. *Studies in Ephesians: Introductory Questions, Text- & Edition-Critical Issues, Interpretation of Texts and Themes*. Edited by D. Hellholm, V. Blomkvist, and T. Fornberg. Wissenschaftliche Untersuchungen zum Neuen Testament 131. Tübingen: Mohr Siebeck, 2000.
Darko, D. K. *No Longer Living as the Gentiles: Differentiation and Shared Ethical Values in Ephesians 4:17–6:9*. The Library of New Testament Studies 375. London: T&T Clark, 2008.
Dassmann, E. *Der Stachel im Fleisch: Paulus in der frühchristlichen Literatur bis Irenäus*. Munster: Aschendorff, 1979.
Davidson, S. *An Introduction to the Study of the New Testament: Critical, Exegetical, and Theological*. 2nd rev. ed. 2 vols. London: Longmans, Green, 1882 [1868].
Dawes, G. W. *The Body in Question: Metaphor and Meaning in the Interpretation of Ephesians 5:21–33*. Biblical Interpretation Series 30. Leiden: Brill, 1998.
de Boer, M. C. *The Defeat of Death: Apocalyptic Eschatology in 1 Corinthians 15 and Romans 5*. Journal for the Study of the New Testament Supplement Series 22. Sheffield: Sheffield Academic, 1988.
de Boer, M. C. 'Images of Paul in the Post-Apostolic Period'. *Catholic Biblical Quarterly* 42 (1980): 359–80.
de Bruyne, D. 'Prologues bibliques d'origin Marcionite'. *Revue bénédictine* 24 (1907): 1–16.
de Bruyne, D. *Summaries, Divisions and Rubrics of the Latin Bible*. Studia Traditionis Theologiae 18. Turnhout: Brepols, 2015.
de Wette, W. M. L. *An Historico-Critical Introduction to the Canonical Books of the New Testament*. Translated by F. Frothingham. Boston: Crosby, Nichols, and Company, 1858. Translation of *Lehrbuch der historisch-kritischen Einleitung in die kanonischen Bücher des neuen Testaments*. 5th ed. Berlin: Reimer, 1846 [1826].
de Wette, W. M. L. *Kurze Erklärung der Briefe an die Colosser, an Philemon, an die Epheser und Philipper*. Handbuch zum Neuen Testament 2/4. Leipzig: Weidmann, 1843.
Deissmann, A. *Light from the Ancient East: The New Testament Illustrated by Recently Discovered Texts of the Graeco-Roman World*. Translated by Lionel R. M. Strachan. New York: Harper & Brothers, 1922.

Detering, H. 'The Dutch Radical Approach to the Pauline Epistles'. *Journal of Higher Criticism* 3 (1996): 163-93.
Dibelius, M. *A Fresh Approach to the New Testament and Early Christian Literature*. London: Nicholson and Watson, 1936.
Dibelius, M. *An die Kolosser, Epheser, an Philemon*. 3rd ed. Handbuch zum Neuen Testament 12. Tübingen: Mohr, 1953.
Dibelius, M. *Paul*. Translated by F. Clark. London: Longmans, 1953.
Dodd, C. H. 'Ephesians'. Pages 1222-37 in *The Abingdon Bible Commentary*. Edited by F. C. Eiselen, E. Lewis, and D. G. Downey. New York: Abingdon-Cokesbury, 1929.
Dover, K. J. *Lysias and the Corpus Lysiacum*. Sather Classical Lectures 39. Berkeley: University of California Press, 1968.
Dunn, J. D. G. *Christianity in the Making*. 3 vols. Grand Rapids: Eerdmans, 2003-15.
Dunn, J. D. G. *Jesus, Paul, and the Law: Studies in Mark and Galatians*. Louisville: Westminster John Knox, 1990.
Dunn, J. D. G. *Jesus Remembered*. Christianity in the Making 1. Grand Rapids: Eerdmans, 2003.
Dunn, J. D. G. *The New Perspective on Paul*. Rev. ed. Grand Rapids: Eerdmans, 2008.
Dunn, J. D. G. *The Theology of Paul the Apostle*. Grand Rapids: Eerdmans, 1998.
Dunn, J. D. G. *Unity and Diversity in the New Testament*. 3rd ed. London: SCM, 2006 (1977).
Dunn, J. D. G., ed. *The Cambridge Companion to St. Paul*. Cambridge: Cambridge University Press, 2003.
Dunn, M. R. 'The Organization of the Platonic Corpus Between the First Century B.C. and the Second Century A.D.'. PhD diss., Yale University, 1974.
Dunning, B. H. 'Strangers and Aliens No Longer: Negotiating Identity and Difference in Ephesians 2'. *Harvard Theological Review* 99 (2006): 1-16.
Eadie, J. A. *A Commentary on the Greek Text of the Epistle of Paul to the Ephesians*. 3rd ed. Edinburgh: T. & T. Clark, 1883.
Eden, G. R. and F. C. Macdonald, eds. *Lightfoot of Durham: Memories and Appreciations*. Cambridge: Cambridge University Press, 1932.
Ehrman, B. D. *Forgery and Counterforgery: The Use of Literary Deceit in Early Christian Polemics*. New York: Oxford University Press, 2013.
Ehrman, B. D. *The New Testament: A Historical Introduction to the Early Christian Writings*. 6th ed. Oxford: Oxford University Press, 2015 [1997].
Eichhorn, J. G. *Einleitung in das neue Testament*. 5 vols. Leipzig: Weidmann, 1804-27.
Eisenbaum, P. *Paul Was Not a Christian: The Real Message of a Misunderstood Apostle*. New York: HarperOne, 2009.
Ellicott, C. J. *St. Paul's Epistle to the Ephesians: with a Critical and Grammatical Commentary, and a Revised Translation*. 5th ed. London: Longmans, Green, 1884.
Elm, S. 'The Letter Collection of the Emperor Julian'. Pages 54-68 in *Late Antique Letter Collections: A Critical Introduction and Reference Guide*. Edited by C. Sogno, B. K. Storin, and E. J. Watts. Oakland, CA: University of California Press, 2017.
Engberg-Pedersen, T. *Paul and the Stoics*. Louisville: Westminster John Knox, 2000.
Ernst, J. *Die Briefe an die Philipper, an Philemon, an die Kolosser, an die Epheser*. Regensburger Neues Testament. Regensburg: Friedrich Pustet, 1974.
Esler, P. '"Remember my Fetters": Memorialisation of Paul's Imprisonment'. Pages 231-58 in *Explaining Christian Origins and Early Judaism: Contributions from Cognitive and Social Science*. Edited by P. Luomanen, I. Pyysiäinen, and R. Uro. Leiden: Brill, 2007.

Evans, R. *Reception History, Tradition, and Biblical Interpretation: Gadamer and Jauss in Current Practice*. The Library of New Testament Studies 510. London: Bloomsbury, 2014.

Eyl, J. 'Semantic Voids, New Testament Translation, and Anachronism: The Case of Paul's Use of Ekklēsia'. *Method and Theory in the Study of Religion* 26 (2014): 315–39.

Faust, E. *Pax Christi et Pax Caesaris: Religionsgeschichtliche, traditionsgeschichtliche und sozialgeschichtliche Studien zum Epheserbrief*. Novum Testamentum et Orbis Antiquus 24. Göttingen: Vandenhoeck & Ruprecht, 1993.

Fee, G. D. *The First Epistle to the Corinthians*. New International Commentary on the New Testament. Grand Rapids: Eerdmans, 1987.

Fischer, K. M. *Tendenz und Absicht des Epheserbriefes*. Forschungen zur Religion und Literatur des Alten und Neuen Testaments 111. Göttingen: Vandenhoeck & Ruprecht, 1973.

Fitzgerald, J. T. *Cracks in an Earthen Vessel: An Examination of the Catalogues of Hardships in the Corinthian Correspondence*. Society of Biblical Literature Dissertation Series 99. Atlanta: Scholars, 1988.

Foster, P. 'The First Contribution to the πίστις Χριστοῦ Debate: A Study of Ephesians 3.12'. *Journal for the Study of the New Testament* 85 (2002): 75–96.

Foster, P. 'Who Wrote 2 Thessalonians? A Fresh Look at an Old Problem'. *Journal for the Study of the New Testament* 35 (2012): 150–75.

Fowl, S. E. *Ephesians: A Commentary*. Louisville: Westminster John Knox, 2012.

Frede, H. J. 'Die Ordnung der Paulusbriefe und der Platz des Kolosserbriefs im Corpus Paulinum'. Pages 290–303 in *Epistulae Ad Philippenses Et Ad Colossenses*. Vol. 24/2 of *Vetus Latina: Die Reste der Altlateinischen Bibel*. Freiburg: Herder, 1969.

Fredriksen, P. 'Mandatory Retirement: Ideas in the Study of Christian Origins Whose Time Has Come to Go'. Pages 25–38 in *Israel's God and Rebecca's Children: Christology and Community in Early Judaism and Christianity. Essays in Honour of Larry W. Hurtado and Alan F. Segal*. Edited by D. B. Capes, A. D. DeConick, H. K. Bond, and T. A. Miller. Waco, TX: Baylor University Press, 2007.

Fredriksen, P. *Paul: The Pagans' Apostle*. New Haven: Yale University Press, 2017.

Frey, J., J. Herzer, M. Janssen, and C. K. Rothschild, eds. *Pseudepigraphie und Verfasserfiktion in Frühchristlichen Briefen*. Wissenschaftliche Untersuchungen zum Neuen Testament 246. Tübingen: Mohr Siebeck, 2009.

Froehlich, K., trans. and ed. *Biblical Interpretation in the Early Church*. Philadelphia: Fortress, 1984.

Furnish, V. P. 'Development in Paul's Thought'. *Journal of the American Academy of Religion* 38 (1970): 289–303.

Furnish, V. P. 'On Putting Paul in His Place'. *Journal of Biblical Literature* 113 (1994): 3–17.

Gadamer, H.-G. *Truth and Method*. Translated by J. Weinsheimer and D. G. Marshall. 2nd rev. ed. New York: Crossroad, 1991.

Gager, J. G. *Reinventing Paul*. Oxford: Oxford University Press, 2000.

Gamble, H. Y. *Books and Readers in the Early Church: A History of Early Christian Texts*. New Haven; London: Yale University Press, 1995.

Garlington, D. B. *The Obedience of Faith: A Pauline Phrase in Historical Context*. Wissenschaftliche Untersuchungen zum Neuen Testament 2/38. Tübingen: Mohr Siebeck, 1991.

Gaston, L. *Paul and the Torah*. Vancouver: University of British Columbia Press, 1987.

Gaventa, B. R. *Our Mother Saint Paul*. Louisville: Westminster John Knox, 2007.

Gese, M. *Das Vermächtnis des Apostels: Die Rezeption der Paulinischen Theologie im Epheserbrief.* Wissenschaftliche Untersuchungen zum Neuen Testament 2/99. Tübingen: Mohr, 1997.

Gibson, C. A. 'The Agenda of Libanius' Hypotheses to Demosthenes'. *Greek, Roman, and Byzantine Studies* 40 (1999): 171–202.

Gibson, R. 'Letters into Autobiography: The Generic Mobility of the Ancient Letter Collection'. Pages 387–416 in *Generic Interfaces in Latin Literature: Encounters, Interactions and Transformations.* Edited by Theodore D. Papanghelis, Stephen J. Harrison, and Stavros Frangoulidis. Trends in Classics—Supplementary Volumes 20. Berlin: de Gruyter, 2013.

Gibson, R. 'On the Nature of Ancient Letter Collections'. *Journal of Roman Studies* 102 (2012): 56–78.

Gibson, R. 'Reading the Letters of Sidonius by the Book'. Pages 195–219 in *New Approaches to Sidonius Appolinaris.* Edited by J. A. van Waarden and G. Kelly. Leuven: Peeters, 2013.

Gibson, R. K. and R. Morello. *Reading the Letters of Pliny the Younger: An Introduction.* Cambridge: Cambridge University Press, 2012.

Gnilka, J. *Der Epheserbrief.* 2nd ed. Herders Theologische Kommentar zum Neuen Testament 10. Freiburg: Herder, 1982.

Gnilka, J. 'Das Paulusbild im Kolosser- und Epheserbrief'. Pages 179–93 in *Kontinuität Und Einheit: Festschrift Franz Mussner.* Edited by P.-G. Müller and W. Stenger. Freiburg: Herder, 1981.

Godet, F. *Introduction au Nouveau Testament.* 2 vols. Paris: Librairie Fischbacher, 1894–99.

Goguel, M. *Introduction au Nouveau Testament.* 4 vols. Paris: Ernest Leroux, 1922–26.

Gombis, T. G. 'The Triumph of God in Christ: Divine Warfare in the Argument of Ephesians'. PhD diss., St. Andrews University, 2005.

Goodrich, J. *Paul as an Administrator of God in 1 Corinthians.* Society for New Testament Studies Monograph Series 152. Cambridge: Cambridge University Press, 2012.

Goodspeed, E. J. 'Editio Princeps of Paul'. *Journal of Biblical Literature* 64 (1945): 193–204.

Goodspeed, E. J. 'Ephesians and the First Edition of Paul'. *Journal of Biblical Literature* 70 (1951): 285–91.

Goodspeed, E. J. *An Introduction to the New Testament.* Chicago: University of Chicago Press, 1937.

Goodspeed, E. J. *The Key to Ephesians.* Chicago: University of Chicago Press, 1956.

Goodspeed, E. J. *The Meaning of Ephesians.* Chicago: University of Chicago Press, 1933.

Goodspeed, E. J. 'A New Organization of New Testament Introduction'. Pages 50–74 in *New Chapters in New Testament Study.* New York: Macmillan, 1937.

Goodspeed, E. J. *New Solutions of New Testament Problems.* Chicago: University of Chicago Press, 1927.

Goodspeed, E. J. 'The Place of Ephesians in the First Pauline Collection'. *Anglican Theological Review* 12 (1930): 189–212.

Goulet-Cazé, M.-O. 'L'arrière-plan scolaire de la *Vie de Plotin*'. Pages 229–328 in *Travaux préliminaires et index grec complet.* Edited by L. Brisson, M.-O. Goulet-Cazé, R. Goulet, and D. O'Brien. Vol. 1 of *Porphyre: La Vie de Plotin.* Histoire des doctrines de l'Antiquité classique 6. Paris: J. Vrin, 1982.

Grafton, A., and M. Williams. *Christianity and the Transformation of the Book.* Cambridge: Harvard University Press, 2006.

Gregory, C. R. Review of *History of Early Christian Literature*, by Adolf Harnack. *American Journal of Theology* 2 (1898): 574–97.

Griffiths, P. J. *Religious Reading: The Place of Reading in the Practice of Religion*. Oxford: Oxford University Press, 1999.

Grindheim, S. 'A Deutero-Pauline Mystery? Ecclesiology in Colossians and Ephesians'. Pages 173–95 in *Paul and Pseudepigraphy*. Edited by S. E. Porter and G. P. Fewster. Pauline Studies 8. Leiden: Brill, 2013.

Guthrie, D. 'The Development of the Idea of Canonical Pseudepigrapha in New Testament Criticism'. Pages 43–59 in *Vox Evangelica: Biblical and Historical Essays*. Edited by R. P. Martin. London: Epworth, 1962.

Hadot, P. *Marius Victorinus: Recherches sur sa vie et ses œuvres*. Paris: Études augustiniennes, 1971.

Hafemann, S. J. *Suffering and the Spirit: An Exegetical Study of 2 Cor. 2:14–3:3 within the Context of the Corinthian Correspondence*. Wissenschaftliche Untersuchungen zum Neuen Testament 2/19. Tübingen: Mohr Siebeck, 1986.

Hahneman, G. M. *The Muratorian Fragment and the Development of the Canon*. Oxford: Clarendon, 1992.

Hanges, J. C. *Paul, Founder of Churches: A Study in Light of the Evidence for the Role of 'Founder-Figures' in the Hellenistic-Roman Period*. Wissenschaftliche Untersuchungen zum Neuen Testament 292. Tübingen: Mohr Siebeck, 2012.

Hanson, A. T. 'The Domestication of Paul: A Study in the Development of Early Christian Theology'. *Bulletin of the John Rylands University Library of Manchester* 63 (1981): 402–18.

Harding, M. 'Disputed and Undisputed Letters of Paul'. Pages 129–68 in *The Pauline Canon*. Edited by S. E. Porter. Pauline Studies 1. Leiden: Brill, 2004.

Harless, G. C. A. *Commentar über den Brief Pauli an die Ephesier*. 2nd ed. Stuttgart: Liesching, 1858.

Harnack, A. *Geschichte der altchristlichen Litteratur bis Eusebius*. 4 vols. Leipzig: J. C. Hinrichs, 1893–1904.

Harrill, J. A. 'Ethnic Fluidity in Ephesians'. *New Testament Studies* 60 (2014): 379–402.

Harrill, J. A. *Paul the Apostle: His Life and Legacy in Their Roman Context*. Cambridge: Cambridge University Press, 2012.

Harris, H. *The Tübingen School: A Historical and Theological Investigation of the School of F. C. Baur*. Leicester: Apollos, 1990.

Harrison, J. R. *Paul's Language of Grace in its Graeco-Roman Context*. Wissenschaftliche Untersuchungen zum Neuen Testament 2/172. Tübingen: Mohr Siebeck, 2003.

Hay, D. M. 'Pauline Theology After Paul'. Pages 181–95 in *Looking Back, Pressing on*. Edited by E. E. Johnson and D. M. Hay. Vol. 4 of *Pauline Theology*. Edited by J. M. Bassler, D. M. Hay, and E. E. Johnson. Minneapolis: Fortress, 1997.

Hays, R. B. *Echoes of Scripture in the Letters of Paul*. New Haven: Yale University Press, 1989.

Hefner, P. 'Baur Versus Ritschl on Early Christianity'. *Church History* 31 (1962): 259–78.

Heil, J. P. *Ephesians: Empowerment to Walk in Love for the Unity of All in Christ*. Studies in Biblical Literature 13. Atlanta: Society of Biblical Literature, 2007.

Hendrix, H. 'On the Form and Ethos of Ephesians'. *Union Seminary Quarterly Review* 42 (1988): 3–15.

Hentschel, A. *Diakonia im Neuen Testament: Studien zur Semantik unter besonderer Berücksichtigung der Rolle von Frauen*. Wissenschaftliche Untersuchungen zum Neuen Testament 2/226. Tübingen: Mohr Siebeck, 2007.

Hilgenfeld, A. *Historisch-Kritische Einleitung in das Neue Testament*. Leipzig: Fues's Verlag, 1875.

Hilgenfeld, A. *Das Urchristenthum in den Hauptwendepuncten seines Entwickelungsganges*. Jena: Friedrich Mauke, 1855.
Hinkle, M. E. 'Proclaiming Peace: The Use of Scripture in Ephesians'. PhD diss., Duke University, 1997.
Hodge, C. Johnson *If Sons, then Heirs: A Study of Kinship and Ethnicity in the Letters of Paul*. New York: Oxford University Press, 2007.
Hodgson, P. C. *The Formation of Historical Theology: A Study of Ferdinand Christian Baur*. Makers of Modern Theology. New York: Harper & Row, 1966.
Hodgson, P. C. 'The Rediscovery of Ferdinand Christian Baur: A Review of the First Two Volumes of His *Ausgewählte Werke*'. *Church History* 33 (1964): 206–14.
Hoehner, H. W. *Ephesians: An Exegetical Commentary*. Grand Rapids: Baker Academic, 2002.
Hoffmann, R. J. *Marcion, On the Restitution of Christianity: An Essay on the Development of Radical Paulinist Theology in the Second Century*. Chico, CA: Scholars Press, 1984.
Holtzmann, H. *Kritik der Epheser- und Kolosserbriefe: Auf Grund einer Analyse ihres Verwandschaftsverhältnisses*. Leipzig: Wilhelm Engelmann, 1872.
Holtzmann, H. *Lehrbuch der historisch-kritischen Einleitung in das Neue Testament*. Freiburg: Mohr, 1886.
Hooker, M. D. and S. G. Wilson, eds. *Paul and Paulinism: Essays in Honour of C. K. Barrett*. London: SPCK, 1982.
Horsley, R. A. *Paul and Politics: Ekklesia, Israel, Imperium, Interpretation. Essays in Honor of Krister Stendahl*. Harrisburg, PA: Trinity Press International, 2000.
Hort, F. A. J. *Prolegomena to St Paul's Epistles to the Romans and the Ephesians*. London: Macmillan, 1895.
Houghton, H. A. G. *The Latin New Testament: A Guide to its Early History, Texts, and Manuscripts*. Oxford: Oxford University Press, 2016.
Hug, J. L. *Einleitung in die Schriften des neuen Testaments*. 3rd ed. 2 vols. Tübingen: Gotta, 1826.
Hultgren, A. J. *The Rise of Normative Christianity*. Minneapolis: Fortress, 1994.
Hüneburg, M. 'Paulus Versus Paulus: Der Epheserbrief als Korrektur des Colosserbriefes'. Pages 387–409 in *Pseudepigraphie und Verfasserfiktion in Frühchristlichen Briefen*. Edited by J. Frey, J. Herzer, M. Janssen, and C. K. Rothschild. Wissenschaftliche Untersuchungen zum Neuen Testament 246. Mohr Siebeck: Tübingen, 2009.
Hupfeld, H. Über *Begriff und Methode der sogennanten biblischen Einleitung*. Marburg: Elwert, 1844.
Hurel, D.-O. 'The Benedictines of the Congregation of St. Maur and the Church Fathers'. Pages 1009–38 in vol. 2 of *The Reception of the Church Fathers in the West: From the Carolingians to the Maurists*. Edited by Irena Backus. Leiden: Brill, 1997.
Hurtado, L. W. *The Earliest Christian Artifacts: Manuscripts and Christian Origins*. Grand Rapids: Eerdmans, 2006.
Hurtado, L. W. 'Interactive Diversity: A Proposed Model of Christian Origins'. *Journal of Theological Studies* 64 (2013): 445–62.
Hyldahl, N. *Die paulinische Chronologie*, Acta Theologica Danica 19. Leiden: Brill, 1986.
Jewett, R. *A Chronology of Paul's Life*. Philadelphia: Fortress, 1979.
Jewett, R. *Romans: A Commentary*. Hermeneia. Minneapolis: Fortress, 2007.
Johnson, W. *Readers and Reading Culture in the High Roman Empire: A Study of Elite Communities*. Classical Culture and Society. Oxford: Oxford University Press, 2010.
Johnson, W. 'Toward a Sociology of Reading in Classical Antiquity'. *American Journal of Philology* 121 (2000): 593–627.

Joubert, S. *Paul as Benefactor: Reciprocity, Strategy and Theological Reflection in Paul's Collection*. Wissenschaftliche Untersuchungen zum Neuen Testament 2/124. Tübingen: Mohr Siebeck, 2000.

Jowett, B. *The Epistles of St. Paul to the Thessalonians, Galatians, Romans, with Critical Notes and Dissertations*. 2 vols. 2nd ed. London: John Murray, 1859.

Jowett, B. 'On the Chronology of St. Paul's Life and Writings'. Pages 151–63 in *The Interpretation of Scripture, and Other Essays*. London: Routledge, 1907.

Jülicher, A. *Einleitung in das Neue Testament*. 7th ed. Tübingen: Mohr Siebeck, 1931 [1894].

Kannengieser, C. *Handbook of Patristic Exegesis*. 2 vols. Bible in Ancient Christianity 1. Leiden: Brill, 2004.

Käsemann, E. 'An Apologia for Primitive Christian Eschatology'. Pages 169–95 in *Essays on New Testament Themes*. London: SCM, 1964 (1952).

Käsemann, E. 'The Beginnings of Christian Theology'. Pages 82–107 in *New Testament Questions of Today*. New Testament Library. London: SCM, 1969.

Käsemann, E. 'Einführung'. Pages viii–xxv to vol. 1 of Ferdinand Christian Baur, *Ausgewählte Werke in Einzelausgaben*. Edited by Klaus Scholder. 5 vols. Stuttgart: Frommann, 1963.

Käsemann, E. 'Epheserbrief'. Pages 517–20 in vol. 2 of *Religion in Geschichte und Gegenwart* 3. Edited by K. Galling. Tübingen: Mohr Siebeck, 1958.

Käsemann, E. 'Ephesians and Acts'. Pages 288–97 in *Studies in Luke-Acts: Essays Presented in Honor of Paul Schubert*. Edited by L. E. Keck and J. L. Martyn. Nashville: Abingdon, 1966.

Käsemann, E. 'Das Interpretationsproblem des Epheserbriefes'. Pages 253–61 in *Exegetische Versuche und Besinnungen* 2. 3rd ed. Göttingen: Vandenhoeck & Ruprecht, 1970 [1961].

Käsemann, E. *Leib und Leib Christi: Eine Untersuchung zur paulinischen Begrifflichkeit*. Tübingen: Mohr, 1933.

Käsemann, E. 'On the Subject of Primitive Christian Apocalyptic'. Pages 108–37 in *New Testament Questions of Today*. New Testament Library. London: SCM, 1969.

Käsemann, E. 'Paul and Early Catholicism'. Pages 236–51 in *New Testament Questions of Today*. New Testament Library. London: SCM, 1969.

Käsemann, E. 'The Theological Problem Presented By the Motif of the Body of Christ'. Pages 102–21 in *Perspectives on Paul*. London: SCM, 1971.

Käsemann, E. 'Unity and Diversity in New Testament Ecclesiology'. *Novum Testamentum* 6 (1963): 290–97.

Keck, L. E. 'Images of Paul in the New Testament'. *Interpretation* 43 (1989): 341–51.

Keck, L. E. *Paul and His Letters*. 2nd rev. and enl. ed. Philadelphia: Fortress, 1988.

Keck, L. E. 'What to Do with Paul?' Pages 259–71 in *Christ's First Theologian: The Shape of Paul's Thought*. Waco, TX: Baylor University Press, 2015.

Kelhoffer, J. A. *Persecution, Persuasion, and Power: Readiness to Withstand Hardship as a Corroboration of Legitimacy in the New Testament*. Wissenschaftliche Untersuchungen zum Neuen Testament 270. Tübingen: Mohr Siebeck, 2010.

Kelly, J. N. D. *Early Christian Doctrines*. Rev. ed. San Francisco: Harper & Row, 1978.

Kemp, A. 'The *TEKHNĒ GRAMMATIKĒ* of Dionysius Thrax: English Translation with Introduction and Notes'. Pages 169–89 in *The History of Linguistics in the Classical Period*. Edited by D. J. Taylor. Studies in the History of the Language Sciences 46. Amsterdam: Benjamins, 1987.

Kenney, E. J. 'Books and Readers in the Roman World'. Pages 3–32 in *Latin Literature*. Edited by W. V. Clausen and E. J. Kenney. Vol. 2 of *The Cambridge History of Classical Literature*. Edited by P. E. Easterling, E. J. Kenney, B. M. W. Knox, and W. V. Clausen. Cambridge: Cambridge University Press, 2008.

Kenny, A. *A Stylometric Study of the New Testament.* Oxford: Clarendon, 1986.
King, K. L. *What is Gnosticism.* Cambridge, MA: Belknap, 2003.
Kirby, J. C. *Ephesians, Baptism and Pentecost: An Inquiry into the Structure and Purpose of the Epistle to the Ephesians.* London: SPCK, 1968.
Kitchen, M. *Ephesians.* New York: Routledge, 1994.
Klöpper, A. *Der Brief an die Epheser.* Göttingen: Vandenhoeck & Ruprecht, 1891.
Knopf, R. *Einführung in das Neue Testament.* Giessen: Töpelmann, 1919.
Knox, B. M. W. and P. E. Easterling. 'Books and Readers in the Greek World'. Pages 1–41 in *Greek Literature.* Edited by P. E. Easterling and B. M. W. Knox. Vol. 1 of *The Cambridge History of Classical Literature.* Edited by P. E. Easterling, E. J. Kenney, B. M. W. Knox, and W. V. Clausen. Cambridge: Cambridge University Press, 2008.
Knox, J. *Chapters in a Life of Paul.* Rev. ed. Edited with introduction by D. A. Hare. London: SCM, 1987.
Koester, H. *Introduction to the New Testament.* 2nd ed. 2 vols. Berlin: de Gruyter, 1995. Translation of *Einführung in das Neue Testament, im Rahmen der Religionsgeschichte und Kulturgeschichte der hellenistischen und römischen Zeit* (Berlin: de Gruyter, 1980).
Koester, H. 'New Testament Introduction: A Critique of a Discipline'. Pages 1–20 in vol. 1 of *Christianity, Judaism and Other Greco-Roman Cults: Studies for Morton Smith at Sixty.* Edited by J. Neusner. 4 vols. Studies in Judaism in Late Antiquity 12. Leiden: Brill, 1975.
König, J., and T. Whitmarsh. 'Ordering Knowledge'. Pages 3–40 in *Ordering Knowledge in the Roman Empire.* Edited by J. König and T. Whitmarsh. Cambridge: Cambridge University Press, 2007.
Köstlin, K. R. 'Zur Geschichte des Urchristenthums'. *Theologische Jahrbücher* 9 (1850): 1–62; 235–302.
Kreitzer, L. J. *Hierapolis in the Heavens: Studies in the Letter to the Ephesians.* The Library of New Testament Studies 368. New York: T&T Clark, 2008.
Kuhn, K. G. 'The Epistle to the Ephesians in the Light of the Qumran Texts'. Pages 115–31 in *Paul and Qumran.* Edited by J. Murphy-O'Connor OP. London: Geoffrey Chapman, 1968.
Kümmel, W. G. *Introduction to the New Testament.* Rev. ed. Translated by H. C. Kee. London: SCM, 1975.
Kümmel, W. G. *Das Neue Testament im 20. Jahrhundert: Ein Forschungsbericht.* Stuttgarter Bibelstudien 50. Stuttgart: Verlag Katholisches Bibelwerk, 1970.
Kümmel, W. G. *The New Testament: The History of the Investigation of its Problems.* Translated by S. McLean Gilmour and H. C. Kee. London: SCM, 1973.
Küng, H. *Structures of the Church.* Translated by Salvator Attanasio. New York: Thomas Nelson, 1964.
Lafer-Sousa, R., K. L. Hermann, and B. R. Conway. 'Striking Individual Differences in Color Perception Uncovered by "The Dress" Photograph'. *Current Biology* 25:13 (May 2015). https://doi.org/10.1016/j.cub.2015.04.053.
Lamm, J. A. 'Schleiermacher as Plato Scholar'. *Journal of Religion* 80 (2000): 206–39.
Lang, T. J. 'Disbursing the Account of God: Fiscal Terminology and the Economy of God in Colossians 1,24–25'. *Zeitschrift für die neutestamentliche Wissenschaft* 107 (2016): 116–36.
Lang, T. J. *Mystery and the Making of a Christian Historical Consciousness: From Paul to the Second Century.* Beihefte zur Zeitschrift für die neutestamentliche Wissenschaft und die Kunde der älteren Kirche 219. Berlin: de Gruyter, 2015.

Lang, T. J., and M. R. Crawford. 'The Origins of Pauline Theology: Paratexts and Priscillian of Avila's *Canons on the Letters of the Apostle Paul*'. *New Testament Studies* 63 (2017): 125–45.
Layton, R. A. 'Origen as a Reader of Paul: A Study of the *Commentary on Ephesians*'. PhD diss., University of Virginia, 1996.
Ledger, G. 'An Exploration of Differences in the Pauline Epistles Using Multivariate Statistical Analysis'. *Literary and Linguistic Computing* 10 (1995): 85–97.
Lightfoot, J. B. 'The Chronology of St. Paul's Life and Epistles'. Pages 215–33 in *Biblical Essays*. 2nd ed. London: Macmillan, 1904 (1863).
Lightfoot, J. B. 'The Destination of the Epistle to the Ephesians'. Pages 375–96 in *Biblical Essays*. 2nd ed. London: Macmillan, 1904 (1873).
Lightfoot, J. B. *Saint Paul's Epistle to the Galatians: A Revised Text with Introduction, Notes, and Dissertations*. 9th ed. London: Macmillan, 1887.
Lincicum, D. 'Ferdinand Christian Baur and the Theological Task of New Testament Introduction'. Pages 91–105 in *Ferdinand Christian Baur und die Geschichte des frühen Christentums*. Edited by M. Bauspiess, C. Landmesser, and D. Lincicum. Wissenschaftliche Untersuchungen zum Neuen Testament 333. Tübingen: Mohr Siebeck, 2014.
Lincicum, D. 'Learning Scripture in the School of Paul: From Ephesians to Justin'. Pages 148–70 in *The Early Reception of Paul*. Edited by K. Liljestrom. Publications of the Finnish Exegetical Society 99. Helsinki: Finnish Exegetical Society, 2011.
Lincicum, D. 'Mirror-Reading a Pseudepigraphal Letter'. *Novum Testamentum* 59 (2017): 171–93.
Lincoln, A. T. *Ephesians*. Word Biblical Commentary 42. Dallas: Word, 1990.
Lincoln, A. T. *Paradise Now and Not Yet: Studies in the Role of the Heavenly Dimension in Paul's Thought with Special Reference to his Eschatology*. Society for New Testament Studies Monograph Series 43. Cambridge: Cambridge University Press, 1981.
Lincoln, A. T. 'The Use of the OT in Ephesians'. *Journal for the Study of the New Testament* 14 (1982): 16–57.
Lindemann, A. *Die Aufhebung der Zeit: Geschichtsverständnis und Eschatologie im Epheserbrief*. Gütersloh: Gerd Mohn, 1975.
Lindemann, A. 'Bemerkungen zu den Adressaten und zum Anlaß des Epheserbriefes'. *Zeitschrift für die neutestamentliche Wissenschaft und die Kunde der älteren Kirche* 67 (1976): 235–51.
Lindemann, A. *Paulus im ältesten Christentum: das Bild des Apostels und die Rezeption der Paulinischen Theologie in der frühchristlichen Literatur bis Marcion*. Beiträge zur historischen Theologie 58. Tübingen: Mohr, 1979.
Lohse, B. 'Beobachtungen zum Paulus-Kommentar des Marius Victorinus und zur Wiederentdeckung des Paulus in der lateinischen Theologie des vierten Jahrhunderts'. Pages 351–66 in *Kerygma und Logos: Beiträge zu den geistesgeschichtlichen Beziehungen zwischen Antike und Christentum*. Edited by A. M. Ritter. Göttingen: Vandenhoeck & Ruprecht, 1979, 351–66.
Lovering, E. H. 'The Collection, Redaction, and Early Circulation of the Corpus Paulinum'. PhD diss., Southern Methodist University, 1988.
Lüdemann, G. *Paul, Apostle to the Gentiles: Studies in Chronology*. Translated by F. S. Jones. Philadelphia: Fortress, 1984.
MacDonald, M. Y. *Colossians and Ephesians*. Sacra Pagina 17. Collegeville, MN: Liturgical Press, 2000.

MacDonald, M. Y. *The Pauline Churches: A Socio-Historical Study of Institutionalization in the Pauline and Deutero-Pauline Writings.* Society for New Testament Studies Monograph Series 60. Cambridge: Cambridge University Press, 2004.

MacDonald, M. Y. 'The Politics of Identity in Ephesians'. *Journal for the Study of the New Testament* 26 (2004): 419–44.

MacDonald, M. Y. 'The Problem of Christian Identities in Ephesians'. *Studia Theologica* 70 (2016): 97–115.

Malherbe, A. J. *Social Aspects of Early Christianity.* 2nd enl. ed. Minneapolis: Fortress, 1983.

Malina, B. J. and J. H. Neyrey. *Portraits of Paul: An Archaeology of Ancient Personality.* Louisville: Westminster John Knox, 1996.

Malkani, G. *Londonstani.* London: Fourth Estate, 2006.

Mansfeld, J. *Prolegomena: Questions to Be Settled before the Study of an Author, or a Text.* Philosophia Antiqua 61. Leiden: Brill, 1994.

Marchesi, I. *The Art of Pliny's Letters: A Poetics of Allusion in the Private Correspondence.* Cambridge: Cambridge University Press, 2008.

Marguerat, D. 'Paul Après Paul: Une Histoire de Réception'. *New Testament Studies* 54 (2008): 317–37.

Marrou, H. I. *A History of Education in Antiquity.* Translated by George Lamb. London: Sheed & Ward, 1956.

Marshall, J. W. 'Misunderstanding the New Paul: Marcion's Transformation of the *Sonderzeit* Paul'. *Journal of Early Christian Studies* 20 (2012): 1–29.

Martens, P. W. *Origen and Scripture: The Contours of the Exegetical Life.* Oxford: Oxford University Press, 2012.

Martin, R. P. *Ephesians, Colossians, Philemon.* Interpretation. Atlanta: John Knox, 1991.

Martin, R. P. 'An Epistle in Search of a Life-Setting'. *Expository Times* 79 (1968): 296–302.

Martyn, J. L. *Galatians: A New Translation, with Introduction and Commentary.* Anchor Bible 33A. New York: Doubleday, 1997.

Mayerhoff, E. T. *Der Brief an die Kolosser, mit vornehmlicher Berücksichtigung der drei Pastoralbriefe.* Berlin: Schultze, 1838.

Mealand, D. L. 'The Extent of the Pauline Corpus: A Multivariate Approach'. *Journal for the Study of the New Testament* 59 (1995): 61–92.

Mealand, D. L. 'Positional Stylometry Reassessed: Testing a Seven Epistle Theory of Pauline Authorship'. *New Testament Studies* 35 (1989): 266–86.

Meeks, W. A. 'Epilogue: The Christian Proteus'. Pages 689–94 in *The Writings of St. Paul: Annotated Text, Reception and Criticism.* Edited by W. A. Meeks and J. T. Fitzgerald. Norton Critical Edition. London: Norton, 2007.

Meeks, W. A. *The First Urban Christians: The Social World of the Apostle Paul.* 2nd ed. New Haven: Yale University Press, 2003.

Merkel, H. 'Der Epheserbrief in der neuren exegetischen Diskussion'. *ANRW* 25.4:3156–3246. Part 2, *Principat*, 25.4. Edited by H. Temporini and W. Haase. New York: de Gruyter, 1987.

Merklein, H. *Das Kirchliche Amt nach dem Epheserbrief.* Studien zum Alten und Neuen Testament 33. Munich: Kösel, 1973.

Merklein, H. 'Paulinische Theologie in der Rezeption des Kolosser- und Epheserbriefes'. Pages 25–69 in *Paulus in Den Neutestamentlichen Spätschriften.* Edited by K. Kertelge. Quaestiones disputatae 89. Freiburg: Herder, 1981.

Metzger, B. M. *The Canon of the New Testament: Its Origin, Development, and Significance.* New York: Oxford University Press, 1987.

Metzger, B. M. *The Text of the New Testament: Its Transmission, Corruption, and Restoration.* 2nd ed. Oxford: Clarendon, 1968.
Meyer, H. A. W. *Kritisch-exegetisches Handbuch über den Brief an die Epheser.* 5th ed. Kritisch- exegetischer Kommentar über das Neue Testament. Göttingen: Vandenhoeck & Ruprecht, 1878.
Meyer, P. W. 'Pauline Theology: A Proposal for a Pause in Its Pursuit'. Pages 140–60 in *Looking Back, Pressing on.* Edited by E. E. Johnson and D. M. Hay. Vol. 4 of *Pauline Theology.* Edited by J. M. Bassler, D. M. Hay, and E. E. Johnson. Minneapolis: Fortress, 1997.
Michaelis, J. D. *Introduction to the New Testament.* Translated by Herbert Marsh. London: Rivington, 1823. Translation of *Einleitung in die göttlichen Schriften des neuen Bundes.* 4th ed. 4 vols. Göttingen: Vandenhoeck & Ruprecht, 1788.
Mills, I. N. 'Pagan Readers of Christian Scripture: The Role of Books in Early Autobiographical Conversion Narratives'. *Vigiliae Christianae* 73 (2019): 481–506.
Mitchell, M. M. *The Heavenly Trumpet: John Chrysostom and the Art of Pauline Interpretation.* Louisville: Westminster John Knox, 2002.
Mitchell, M. M. '"A Variable and Many-sorted Man": John Chrysostom's Treatment of Pauline Inconsistency'. *Journal of Early Christian Studies* 6 (1998): 93–111.
Mitton, C. L. *The Epistle to the Ephesians: Its Authorship, Origin, and Purpose.* Oxford: Clarendon, 1951.
Mitton, C. L. 'Important Hypotheses Reconsidered: VII. The Authorship of the Epistle to the Ephesians'. *Expository Times* 67 (1956): 195–98.
Moffatt, J. *An Introduction to the Literature of the New Testament.* 3rd ed. Edinburgh: T. & T. Clark, 1918.
Mommsen, T. 'Zur Lebensgeschichte des jüngeren Plinius'. *Hermes* 3 (1869): 31–136.
Morello, R. 'Pliny Book 8: Two Viewpoints and the Pedestrian Reader'. Pages 146–86 in *Pliny the Book-Maker.* Edited by I. Marchesi. Oxford: Oxford University Press, 2015.
Morgan, R. 'Biblical Classics II. F. C. Baur: Paul'. *Expository Times* 90 (1978): 4–10.
Morgan, R. 'Paul's Enduring Legacy'. Pages 242–55 in *The Cambridge Companion to St. Paul.* Edited by J. D. G. Dunn. Cambridge: Cambridge University Press, 2003.
Morgan, R. 'The Significance of Paulinism'. Pages 320–38 in *Paul and Paulinism: Essays in Honour of C. K. Barrett.* Edited by M. D. Hooker and S. G. Wilson. London: SPCK, 1982.
Moritz, T. *A Profound Mystery: The Use of the Old Testament in Ephesians.* Supplements to Novum Testamentum 85. Leiden: Brill, 1996.
Morrison, A. D. 'Narrativity and Epistolarity in the "Platonic" Epistles'. Pages 107–31 in *Epistolary Narratives in Ancient Greek Literature.* Edited by O. Hodkinson, P. A. Rosenmeyer, and E. Bracke. Mnemosyne Supplements 359. Leiden: Brill, 2013.
Mouton, E. 'Memory in Search of Dignity? Construction of Early Christian Identity Through Redescribed Traditional Material in the Letter to the Ephesians'. *Annali di Storia dell'Esegesi* 29 (2012): 133–53.
Mratschek, S. 'The Letter Collection of Sidonius Apollinaris'. Pages 309–36 in *Late Antique Letter Collections: A Critical Introduction and Reference Guide.* Edited by C. Sogno, B. K. Storin, and E. J. Watts. Oakland, CA: University of California Press, 2017.
Muddiman, J. *The Epistle to the Ephesians.* Black's New Testament Commentary. London: Continuum, 2001.
Munro, W. 'Col.iii.18–iv.1 and Eph.v.21–vi.9: Evidence of a Late Literary Stratum?' *New Testament Studies* 18 (1972): 434–47.

Murgia, C. E. 'Pliny's Letters and the *Dialogus*'. *Harvard Studies in Classical Philology* 89 (1985): 171–206.
Murphy-O'Connor OP, J. *Paul: A Critical Life*. Oxford: Oxford University Press, 1997.
Murphy-O'Connor OP, J., ed. *Paul and Qumran*. London: Geoffrey Chapman, 1968.
Mussner, F. *Der Brief an die Epheser*. Ökumenischer Taschenbuch-Kommentar 10. Gütersloh: Gütersloh Verlagshaus, 1982.
Mussner, F. 'Contributions Made By Qumran to the Understanding of the Epistle to the Ephesians'. Pages 159–78 in *Paul and Qumran*. Edited by J. Murphy-O'Connor OP. London: Geoffrey Chapman, 1968.
Nanos, M. D. and M. Zetterholm, eds. *Paul within Judaism: Restoring the First-Century Context to the Apostle*. Minneapolis: Fortress, 2015.
Nauroy, G. 'The Letter Collection of Ambrose of Milan'. Translated by C. Sogno. Pages 146–60 in *Late Antique Letter Collections: A Critical Introduction and Reference Guide*. Edited by C. Sogno, B. K. Storin, and E. J. Watts. Oakland, CA: University of California Press, 2017.
Neill, S. and T. Wright. *The Interpretation of the New Testament, 1861–1986*. 2nd ed. Oxford: Oxford University Press, 1988.
Neumann, K. J. *The Authenticity of the Pauline Epistles in the Light of Stylostatistical Analysis*. Society of Biblical Literature Dissertation Series 120. Atlanta: Scholars Press, 1990.
Neuschäfer, B. *Origenes als Philologe*. 2 vols. Schweizerische Beiträge zur Altertumswissenschaft 18. Basel: Reinhardt Verlag, 1987.
Nineham, D. 'The Case Against the Pauline Authorship'. Pages 21–35 in *Studies in Ephesians*. Edited by F. L. Cross. London: Mowbray, 1956.
Nogalski, J. D. 'One Book and Twelve Books: The Nature of the Redactional Work and the Implications of Cultic Source Material in the Book of the Twelve'. Pages 83–114 in *The Book of the Twelve and Beyond: Collected Essays of James D. Nogalski*. Ancient Israel and its Literature 29. Atlanta: SBL Press, 2017.
O'Brien, P. T. *The Letter to the Ephesians*. Pillar New Testament Commentary. Grand Rapids: Eerdmans, 1999.
O'Loughlin, T. 'De Bruyne's *Sommaires* on its Centenary: Has its Value for Biblical Scholarship Increased?' Introduction to *Summaries, Divisions and Rubrics of the Latin Bible*, by D. de Bruyne. Studia Traditionis Theologiae 18. Turnhout: Brepols, 2015.
Olshausen, H. *Biblical Commentary on St Paul's Epistles to the Galatians, Ephesians, Colossians, and Thessalonians*. Translated by A Clergyman of the Church of England. Edinburgh: T. & T. Clark, 1851.
Ong, W. J. *Orality and Literacy: The Technologizing of the Word*. 2nd 30th Anniversary Edition. New York: Routledge, 2012.
Paget, J. C. 'The Reception of Baur in Britain'. Pages 335–86 in *Ferdinand Christian Baur und die Geschichte des frühen Christentums*. Edited by M. Bauspiess, C. Landmesser, and D. Lincicum. Wissenschaftliche Untersuchungen zum Neuen Testament 333. Tübingen: Mohr Siebeck, 2014.
Paley, W. *Horae Paulinae; or the Truth of the Scripture History of St. Paul Evinced, by a Comparison of the Epistles Which Bear His Name, with the Acts of the Apostles, and with One Another*. London: SPCK, 1855 [1790].
Penny, D. N. 'The Pseudo-Pauline Letters of the First Two Centuries'. PhD diss., Emory University, 1979.
Percy, E. *Die Probleme der Kolosser- und Epheserbriefe*. Lund: Gleerup, 1946.

Perkins, P. *Ephesians*. Abingdon New Testament Commentaries. Nashville: Abingdon, 1997.
Pervo, R. I. *The Making of Paul: Constructions of the Apostle in Early Christianity*. Minneapolis: Fortress, 2010.
Peterman, G. W. *Paul's Gift from Philippi: Conventions of Gift-Exchange and Christian Giving*. Society for New Testament Studies Monograph Series 92. Cambridge: Cambridge University Press, 1997.
Pfleiderer, O. *Paulinism: A Contribution to the History of Primitive Christian Theology*. Translated by E. Peters. 2 vols. London: Williams & Norgate, 1877. Translation of *Der Paulinismus: ein Beitrag zur Geschichte der urchristlichen Theologie*. 2nd ed. Leipzig: Riesland, 1890 [1873].
Pfleiderer, O. *Das Urchristentum: seine Schriften und Lehren in geschichtlichen Zusammenhang*. 2nd ed. Berlin: Reimer, 1902.
Pfeiffer, R. *History of Classical Scholarship*. 2 vols. Oxford: Clarendon, 1968–76.
Planck, K. C. 'Judenthum und Urchristenthum'. *Theologische Jahrbücher* 6 (1847): 258–93; 409–34; 448–506.
Pokorný, P. *Der Brief des Paulus an die Epheser*. Theologischer Handkommentar zum Neuen Testament 10/2. Leipzig: Evangelische Verlagsanstalt, 1992.
Pokorný, P. *Der Epheserbrief und die Gnosis: Die Bedeutung des Haupt-Glieder-Gedankens in der entstehenden Kirche*. Berlin: Evangelische Verlagsanstalt, 1965.
Porter, S. E., ed. *The Pauline Canon*. Pauline Studies 1. Leiden: Brill, 2004.
Porter, S. E., ed. 'When and How Was the Pauline Canon Compiled? An Assessment of Theories'. Pages 95–128 in *The Pauline Canon*. Edited by S. E. Porter. Pauline Studies 1. Leiden: Brill, 2004.
Porter, S. E. and G. P. Fewster, eds. *Paul and Pseudepigraphy*. Pauline Studies 8. Leiden: Brill, 2013.
Price, Robert M. 'The Evolution of the Pauline Canon'. *Hervormde Teologiese Studies (HTS Teologiese Studies/HTS Theological Studies)* 53 (1997): 36–67.
Radde-Gallwitz, A. 'The Letter Collection of Basil of Caesarea'. Pages 69–80 in *Late Antique Letter Collections: A Critical Introduction and Reference Guide*. Edited by C. Sogno, B. K. Storin, and E. J. Watts. Oakland, CA: University of California Press, 2017.
Ramelli, I. L. E. 'The Pseudepigraphical Correspondence Between Seneca and Paul: A Reassessment'. Pages 319–36 in *Paul and Pseudepigraphy*. Edited by S. E. Porter and G. P. Fewster. Pauline Studies 8. Leiden: Brill, 2013.
Reed, A. Y. 'Christian Origins and Religious Studies'. *Studies in Religion* 44 (2015): 307–19.
Reicke, B. *Re-examining Paul's Letters: The History of the Pauline Correspondence*. Edited by D. P. Moessner and I. Reicke. Harrisburg, PA: Trinity Press International, 2001.
Renan, E. *Histoire des origins du christianisme*. 7 vols. Paris: Michel Lévy, 1863–83.
Rensberger, D. K. 'As the Apostle Teaches: The Development of the Use of Paul's Letters in Second Century Christianity'. PhD diss., Yale University, 1981.
Reumann, J. 'Oikonomia-Terms in Paul in Comparison with Lucan *Heilsgeschichte*'. *New Testament Studies* 13 (1967): 147–67.
Reuss, E. *History of the Sacred Scriptures of the New Testament*. Translated by E. L. Houghton. Boston: Houghton, Mifflin, 1884 [1842].
Richards, E. R. *Paul and First-Century Letter Writing: Secretaries, Composition and Collection*. Downers Grove, IL: InterVarsity, 2004.
Ridderbos, H. N. *Paul, An Outline of His Theology*. Translated J. R. de Witt. London: SPCK, 1977.

Riesner, R. *Paul's Early Period: Chronology, Mission Strategy, Theology*. Translated by Doug Stott. Grand Rapids: Eerdmans, 1998.
Ritschl, A. *Die Entstehung der altkatholischen Kirche*. Bonn: Marcus, 1857.
Roberts, C. H. and T. C. Skeat. *The Birth of the Codex*. London: Oxford University Press, 1983.
Robinson, J. A. *Euthaliana: Studies of Euthalius, Codex H of the Pauline Epistles, and the Armenian Version*. Cambridge: Cambridge University Press, 1895.
Robinson, J. A. *St. Paul's Epistle to the Ephesians: A Revised Text and Translation with Exposition and Notes*. London: Macmillan, 1903.
Robinson, J. A. T. *Redating the New Testament*. London: SCM, 1976.
Robinson, J. M. and H. Koester. *Trajectories through Early Christianity*. Philadelphia: Fortress, 1971.
Roetzel, C. J. *The Letters of Paul: Conversations in Context*. 4th ed. Louisville: Westminster John Knox, 1998.
Roitto, R. *Behaving as a Christ-Believer: A Cognitive Perspective on Identity and Behavior Norms in Ephesians*. Coniectanea Biblica: New Testament Series 46. Winona Lake, IN: Eisenbrauns, 2011.
Rollens, S. E. 'The God Came to Me in a Dream: Epiphanies in Voluntary Associations as a Context for Paul's Vision of Christ'. *Harvard Theological Review* 111 (2018): 41–65.
Rollman, H. 'From Baur to Wrede: The Quest for a Historical Method'. *Studies in Religion* 17 (1988): 443–54.
Runesson, A. 'The Question of Terminology: The Architecture of Contemporary Discussions of Paul'. Pages 53–78 in *Paul within Judaism: Restoring the First-Century Context to the Apostle*. Edited by M. D. Nanos and M. Zetterholm. Minneapolis: Fortress, 2015.
Russell, D. A. *Criticism in Antiquity*. Berkeley: University of California Press, 1981.
Salzman, M. R. 'Latin Letter Collections Before Late Antiquity'. Pages 13–37 in *Late Antique Letter Collections: A Critical Introduction and Reference Guide*. Edited by C. Sogno, B. K. Storin, and E. J. Watts. Oakland, CA: University of California Press, 2017.
Sampley, J. P. *'And the Two Shall Become One Flesh': A Study of Traditions in Ephesians 5:21–33*. Society for New Testament Studies Monograph Series 16. Cambridge: Cambridge University Press, 1971.
Sanders, E. P. *Paul: The Apostle's Life, Letters, and Thought*. Minneapolis: Fortress, 2016.
Sanders, E. P. *Paul and Palestinian Judaism: A Comparison of Patterns of Religion*. London: SCM, 1977.
Sanders, E. P. *Paul, the Law and the Jewish People*. Philadelphia: Fortress, 1983.
Sanders, J. N. 'The Case for the Pauline Authorship'. Pages 9–20 in *Studies in Ephesians*. Edited by F. L. Cross. London: Mowbray, 1956.
Sanders, J. T. 'Hymnic Elements in Ephesians 1–3'. *Zeitschrift für die neutestamentliche Wissenschaft und die Kunde der älteren Kirche* 56 (1965): 214–32.
Sandmel, S. *The First Christian Century in Judaism and Christianity: Certainties and Uncertainties*. Oxford: Oxford University Press, 1969.
Schäfer, K. 'Marius Victorinus und die marcionitischen Prologe zu den Paulusbriefen'. *Revue bénédictine* 80 (1970): 7–16.
Schäublin, C. 'Homerum ex Homero'. *Museum Helveticum* 34 (1977): 221–27.
Schenke, H.-M. 'Das Weiterwirken des Paulus und die Pflege seines Erbes durch die Paulus-Schule'. *New Testament Studies* 21 (1975): 505–18.
Scherbenske, E. W. *Canonizing Paul: Ancient Editorial Practice and the Corpus Paulinum*. New York: Oxford University Press, 2013.

Schleiermacher, F. D. E. *Einleitung ins neue Testament*. Pt. 1 Vol. 8 of *Friedrich Schleiermacher's sämmtliche Werke*. Edited by G. Wolde. Berlin: Reimer, 1845.
Schleiermacher, F. D. E. 'General Introduction'. Pages 1-47 in *Introductions to the Dialogues of Plato*. Translated by William Dobson. London: J. W. Parker, 1836.
Schleiermacher, F. D. E. *Über den sogenannten ersten Brief des Paulos an den Timotheos: Ein kritisches Sendschreiben an J. C. Gass*. Berlin: Realschulbuchhandlung, 1807.
Schlier, H. *Der Brief an die Epheser: Ein Kommentar*. Düsseldorf: Patmos, 1971.
Schlier, H. *Christus und die Kirche im Epheserbrief*. Beiträge zur historischen Theologie 6. Tübingen: Mohr Siebeck, 1930.
Schmid, J. *Der Epheserbrief des Apostels Paulus: Seine Adresse, Sprache und literarischen Beziehungen*. Freiburg: Herder, 1928.
Schnackenburg, R. *Ephesians: A Commentary*. Translated by Helen Heron. Edinburgh: T. & T. Clark, 1991. Translation of *Der Brief an die Epheser*. Evangelisch-katholischer Kommentar zum Neuen Testament 10. Zurich: Benziger, 1982.
Schnelle, U. *Apostle Paul: His Life and Theology*. Translated by M. E. Boring. Grand Rapids: Baker Academic, 2005.
Schnelle, U. *Einleitung in das Neue Testament*. 8th ed. Göttingen: Vandenhoeck & Ruprecht, 2013 [1994].
Schreiner, T. R. *Paul, Apostle of God's Glory in Christ: A Pauline Theology*. Downers Grove, IL: InterVarsity, 2001.
Schütz, C. G. M. T. *Ciceronis Epistolae ad Atticum ad Quintum Fratrem et quae vulgo ad Familiares dicuntur temporis ordine dispositae*. Halae: Hemmerdeana, 1809-11.
Schwegler, A. *Das nachapostolische Zeitalter in den Hauptmomenten seiner Entwicklung*. Tübingen: Fues, 1846.
Schweitzer, A. *The Mysticism of Paul the Apostle*. London: A. & C. Black, 1953 [1931].
Schweitzer, A. *Paul and His Interpreters: A Critical History*. Translated by W. Montgomery. London: A. & C. Black, 1912.
Schwindt, R. *Das Weltbild des Epheserbriefes: Eine religionsgeschichtlich-exegetische Studie*. Wissenschaftliche Untersuchungen zum Neuen Testament 148. Tübingen: Mohr Siebeck, 2002.
Scott, E. F. *The Literature of the New Testament*. New York: Columbia University Press, 1932.
Sellin, G. *Der Brief an die Epheser*. Kritisch-exegetischer Kommentar über das Neue Testament 8. Göttingen: Vandenhoeck & Ruprecht, 2008.
Semler, J. S. *Abhandlung von freier Untersuchung des Canon*. 4 vols. Halle: Hemmerde, 1771-75.
Shackleton Bailey, D. R. *Cicero: Epistulae ad Familiares*. 2 vols. Cambridge Classical Texts and Commentaries. Cambridge: Cambridge University Press, 1977.
Shackleton Bailey, D. R. *Cicero: Epistulae ad Quintum Fratrem et M. Brutum*. Cambridge Classical Texts and Commentaries. Cambridge: Cambridge University Press, 1980.
Shackleton Bailey, D. R. *Cicero: Letters to Atticus*. 5 vols. Cambridge Classical Texts and Commentaries. Cambridge: Cambridge University Press, 1965-66.
Sherwin-White, A. N. *The Letters of Pliny: A Historical and Social Commentary*. Oxford: Clarendon, 1966.
Shkul, M. *Reading Ephesians: Exploring Social Entrepreneurship in the Text*. The Library of New Testament Studies 408. London: T&T Clark, 2009.
Simonetti, M. *Biblical Interpretation in the Early Church: An Historical Introduction to Patristic Exegesis*. Edinburgh: T. & T. Clark, 1993.

Soden, H. *Die Briefe an die Kolosser, Epheser, Philemon; die Pastoral Briefe*. 2nd ed. Handkommentar zum Neuen Testament 3. Freiburg: Mohr, 1893.
Sogno, C. 'The Letter Collection of Quintus Aurelius Symmachus'. Pages 175–89 in *Late Antique Letter Collections: A Critical Introduction and Reference Guide*. Edited by C. Sogno, B. K. Storin, and E. J. Watts. Oakland, CA: University of California Press, 2017.
Sogno, C., B. K. Storin, and E. J. Watts, eds. *Late Antique Letter Collections: A Critical Introduction and Reference Guide*. Oakland, CA: University of California Press, 2017.
Sogno, C., B. K. Storin, and E. J. Watts. 'Introduction: Greek and Latin Epistolography and Epistolary Collections in Late Antiquity'. Pages 1–10 in *Late Antique Letter Collections: A Critical Introduction and Reference Guide*. Edited by C. Sogno, B. K. Storin, and E. J. Watts. Oakland, CA: University of California Press, 2017.
Souter, A. *The Earliest Latin Commentaries on the Epistles of St. Paul*. Oxford: Clarendon, 1927.
Souter, A. *The Text and Canon of the New Testament*. New York: Scribner's, 1913.
Speyer, W. *Die Literarische Fälschung im Hiednischen und Christlichen Altertum*. Handbuch der Altertumswissenschaft 1/2. München: C. H. Beck, 1971.
Stanley, A. P. *The Epistles of St. Paul to the Corinthians*. 2 vols. London: John Murray, 1855.
Stendahl, K. *Paul among Jews and Gentiles, and Other Essays*. London: SCM, 1976.
Sterling, G. E. 'From Apostle to the Gentiles to Apostle of the Church: Images of Paul at the End of the First Century'. *Zeitschrift für die neutestamentliche Wissenschaft und die Kunde der älteren Kirche* 99 (2008): 74–98.
Still, T. D. and D. E. Wilhite, eds. *The Apostolic Fathers and Paul*. Pauline and Patristic Scholars in Debate 2. London: Bloomsbury T&T Clark, 2017.
Still, T. D. and D. E. Wilhite, eds. *Irenaeus and Paul*. Pauline and Patristic Scholars in Debate 3. London: Bloomsbury T&T Clark, 2020.
Still, T. D. and D. E. Wilhite, eds. *Tertullian and Paul*. Pauline and Patristic Scholars in Debate 1. New York: Bloomsbury T&T Clark, 2013.
Stirling, A. M. 'Transformation and Growth: The Davidic Temple Builder in Ephesians'. PhD diss., St. Andrews University, 2012.
Stowers, S. K. 'Text as Interpretation: Paul and Ancient Readings of Paul'. Pages 17–27 in *Judaic and Christian Interpretation of Texts: Contents and Contexts*. Edited by J. Neusner and E. S. Frerichs. New Perspectives on Ancient Judaism. Lanham, MD: University Press of America, 1987.
Strawbridge, J. R. *The Pauline Effect: The Use of the Pauline Epistles by Early Christian Writers*. Studies of the Bible and Its Reception 5. Berlin: de Gruyter, 2015.
Suhl, A. *Paulus und seine Briefe: Ein Beitrag zur paulinischen Chronologie*, SNT 11. Gütersloh: Mohn, 1975.
Tarrant, H. *Thrasyllan Platonism*. Ithaca, NY: Cornell University Press, 1993.
Tate, J. *The Horae Paulinae of William Paley, D.D., Carried out and Illustrated in a Continuous History of the Apostolic Labours and Writings of St. Paul, on the Basis of the Acts, with Intercalary Matter of Sacred Narrative Supplied from the Epistles*. London: Longman, Orme, Brown, Green, & Longmans, 1840.
Tatum, G. *New Chapters in the Life of Paul: The Relative Chronology of His Career*. Catholic Biblical Quarterly Monograph Series 41. Washington, DC: Catholic Biblical Association of America, 2006.
Temporini, H., and W. Haase, eds. *Aufstieg und Niedergang der römischen Welt: Geschichte und Kultur Roms im Spiegel der neuren Forschung*. Part 2, *Principat*. Berlin: de Gruyter, 1972.

Tennemann, W. G. *System der platonischen Philosophie*. Leipzig: J. A. Barth, 1792.
Theissen, G. *The Social Setting of Pauline Christianity: Essays on Corinth*. Edited and translated by John H. Schütz. Edinburgh: T. & T. Clark, 1982.
Thielman, F. *Ephesians*. Baker Exegetical Commentary on the New Testament. Grand Rapids: Baker Academic, 2010.
Thiessen, M. 'The Construction of Gentiles in the Letter to the Ephesians'. Pages 13–25 in *The Early Reception of Paul the Second Temple Jew: Text, Narrative and Reception History*. Edited by I. W. Oliver, G. Boccaccini, and J. Scott. The Library of Second Temple Studies 92. London: T&T Clark, 2018.
Thiessen, M. *Paul and the Gentile Problem*. New York: Oxford University Press, 2015.
Thiselton, A. C. *The First Epistle to the Corinthians*. The New International Greek Testament Commentary. Grand Rapids: Eerdmans, 2000.
Thompson, D. M. *Cambridge Theology in the Nineteenth Century: Enquiry, Controversy and Truth*. New York: Routledge, 2016.
Treloar, G. R. *Lightfoot the Historian: The Nature and Role of History in the Life and Thought of J. B. Lightfoot (1828–1889) as Churchman and Scholar*. Wissenschaftliche Untersuchungen zum Neuen Testament 2/103. Tübingen: Mohr Siebeck, 1998.
Trobisch, D. *Die Entstehung der Paulusbriefsammlung: Studien zu den Anfängen Christlicher Publizistik*. Novum Testamentum et Orbis Antiquus 10. Freiburg; Göttingen: Universitätsverlag; Vandenhoeck & Ruprecht, 1989.
Trobisch, D. *Paul's Letter Collection: Tracing the Origin*. Minneapolis: Fortress, 1994.
Turner, C. H. 'Greek Patristic Commentaries on the Pauline Letters'. Pages 484–531 in vol. 5 of *Dictionary of the Bible*. Edited by James Hastings. 5 vols. New York: Scribner's, 1904.
Tyrrell, R. Y., and L. C. Purser, eds. *The Correspondence of M. Tullius Cicero, Arranged According to its Chronological Order*. 2nd ed. 7 vols. London: Longmans, Green, & Co., 1879–33.
Usteri, L. *Entwickelung des paulinischen Lehrbegriffes mit Hinsicht auf die* übrigen *Schriften des Neuen Testament*. Zurich: Orill, Füssli, 1824.
van Kooten, G. H. *Cosmic Christology in Paul and the Pauline School: Colossians and Ephesians in the Context of Graeco-Roman Cosmology, with a New Synopsis of the Greek Texts*. Wissenschaftliche Untersuchungen zum Neuen Testament 2/171. Tübingen: Mohr Siebeck, 2003.
van Roon, A. *The Authenticity of Ephesians*. Supplements to Novum Testamentum 39. Leiden: Brill, 1974.
Vielhauer, P. *Geschichte der urchristlichen Literatur: Einleitung in das Neue Testament, die Apokryphen und die apostolischen Väter*. Berlin: de Gruyter, 1975.
Watson, F. 'Does Historical Criticism Exist? A Contribution to Debate on the Theological Interpretation of Scripture'. Pages 307–18 in *Theological Theology: Essays in Honour of John B. Webster*. Edited by R. D. Nelson, D. Sarisky, and J. Stratis. London: Bloomsbury T&T Clark, 2015.
Watson, F. *Paul and the Hermeneutics of Faith*. London: T&T Clark International, 2004.
Watson, F. *Paul, Judaism, and the Gentiles: Beyond the New Perspective*. Rev. and exp. ed. Grand Rapids: Eerdmans, 2007.
Way, D. V. *The Lordship of Christ: Ernst Käsemann's Interpretation of Paul's Theology*. Oxford: Clarendon, 1991.
Weiss, J. *The History of Primitive Christianity*. Edited by Frederick C. Grant. Translated by Four Friends. 2 vols. London: Macmillan, 1937. Translation of *Das Urchristentum*. Göttingen: Vandenhoeck & Ruprecht, 1917.

Weizsäcker, K. *Das apostolische Zeitalter der christlichen Kirche*. 2nd ed. Tübingen: Mohr Siebeck, 1892.
Wendt, H. *At the Temple Gates: The Religion of Freelance Experts in the Roman Empire*. New York: Oxford University Press, 2016.
Wendt, H. 'James C. Hanges, *Paul, Founder of Churches: A Study in Light of the Evidence for the Role of "Founder-Figures" in the Hellenistic-Roman Period*. A Review Essay'. *Religion and Theology* 20 (2013): 292–302.
Westcott, B. F. *St. Paul's Epistle to the Ephesians*. London: Macmillan, 1906.
White, B. L. *Remembering Paul: Ancient and Modern Contests over the Image of the Apostle*. New York: Oxford University Press, 2014.
Whiteley, D. E. H. *The Theology of St. Paul*. 2nd ed. Oxford: Blackwell, 1974.
Wieland, C. M. *M. Tullius Cicero's sämmtliche Briefe*. Zurich: Gessner, 1808–21.
Wieseler, K. G. *Chronologie des apostolischen Zeitalters, bis zum Tode der Apostel Paulus und Petrus: ein Versuch über die Chronologie und Abfassungszeit der Apostelgeschichte und der paulinischen Briefe*. Göttingen: Vandenhoeck & Ruprecht, 1848.
Wild, S.J., R. A. 'The Warrior and the Prisoner: Some Reflections on Ephesians 6:10–20'. *Catholic Biblical Quarterly* 46 (1984): 284–98.
Wiles, M. F. *The Divine Apostle: The Interpretation of St. Paul's Epistles in the Early Church*. London: Cambridge University Press, 1967.
Willard, L. C. *A Critical Study of the Euthalian Apparatus*. Arbeiten zur neutestamentlichen Textforschung 41. Berlin: de Gruyter, 2009 (1970).
Williams, M. *Rethinking Gnosticism*. Princeton: Princeton University Press, 1996.
Wilson, A. N. *Paul: The Mind of the Apostle*. London: Sinclair-Stevenson, 1997.
Wischmeyer, O., ed. *Paul: Life, Setting, Work, Letters*. Translated by Helen S. Heron. Revised by Dieter T. Roth. London: T&T Clark, 2012.
Wolter, M. *Paul: An Outline of His Theology*. Translated by Robert L. Brawley. Waco, TX: Baylor University Press, 2015.
Wrede, W. *Paul*. Translated by E. Lummis. London: Green, 1907.
Wright, Tom. *Paul: A Biography*. London: SPCK, 2018.
Wright, N. T. *The Climax of the Covenant: Christ and the Law in Pauline Theology*. Edinburgh: T. & T. Clark, 1991.
Wright, N. T. *Paul and the Faithfulness of God*. 2 vols. Christian Origins and the Question of God 4. Minneapolis: Fortress, 2013.
Wright, N. T. *Paul and His Recent Interpreters: Some Contemporary Debates*. Minneapolis: Fortress, 2015.
Yee, T.-L. N. *Jews, Gentiles and Ethnic Reconciliation: Paul's Jewish Identity and Ephesians*. Society for New Testament Studies Monograph Series 130. Cambridge: Cambridge University Press, 2005.
Yoder Neufeld, T. R. *'Put on the Armour of God': The Divine Warrior from Isaiah to Ephesians*. Journal for the Study of the New Testament Supplement Series 140. Sheffield: Sheffield Academic Press, 1997.
Young, F. *Biblical Exegesis and the Formation of Christian Culture*. Cambridge: Cambridge University Press, 1997.
Young, F. 'The Rhetorical Schools and Their Influence on Patristic Exegesis'. Pages 182–99 in *The Making of Orthodoxy: Essays in Honour of Henry Chadwick*. Edited by R. Williams. Cambridge: Cambridge University Press, 1989.

Zachhuber, J. 'The Absoluteness of Christianity and the Relativity of All History: Two Strands in Ferdinand Christian Baur's Thought'. Pages 313–31 in *Ferdinand Christian Baur und die Geschichte des frühen Christentums*. Edited by M. Bauspiess, C. Landmesser, and D. Lincicum. Wissenschaftliche Untersuchungen zum Neuen Testament 333. Tübingen: Mohr Siebeck, 2014.

Zachhuber, J. *Theology as Science in Nineteenth Century Germany: From F. C. Baur to Ernst Troeltsch*. Changing Paradigms in Historical and Systematic Theology. Oxford: Oxford University Press, 2013.

Zahn, T. *Einleitung in das Neue Testament*. 3 vols. Leipzig: A. Deichert, 1897–99.

Zuntz, G. *The Ancestry of the Harklean New Testament*. The British Academy Supplemental Papers 7. London: Oxford University Press, 1945.

Zuntz, G. *The Text of the Epistles: A Disquisition upon the Corpus Paulinum*. Oxford: Oxford University Press, 1953.

INDEX OF REFERENCES

HEBREW BIBLE/ OLD TESTAMENT		APOCRYPHA/DEUTERO- CANONICAL WORKS		1.13	157
				1.15	152, 153, 157, 167
Exodus		*1 Maccabees*			
3.14	105	11.58	139	1.18–32	40, 63, 167
Judges		NEW TESTAMENT		1.20	112
13.8 LXX	155	*Matthew*		1.24–27	110
		6.20–21	127	1.25	115
Esther		26.25	124	1.26	115, 119, 120
1.10	139				
2.2	139	*John*		3.20	125
6.3	139	15.19	127	3.24–26	167
6.5	139	16.24	124	3.27–28	125
		17.24	124	3.29–30	168
Psalms				4.16–18	167
68.19	115	*Acts*		4.23–5.2	110, 111
85.11	124	8	148	5–8	111
		10	148	5–7	112
Proverbs		14.4	150	5.12–15	112
10.4	139	14.14	150	5.16–19	110
		15	105, 166, 170	5.20–6.2	110, 112
Daniel				6.3–11	167
2.1	145	15.22–29	170	6.3–5	110
2.18	145	19–20	128	6.5	127
2.19	145	19	105	6.6–7.25	112
2.27	145			6.13	114
2.28–30	145	*Romans*		6.23	110
2.28	145	1–11	153	8.2–10	112
2.47	145	1.1	153	8.5–9	110, 111
		1.3–4	40	8.9–11	167
Hosea		1.5	58, 156, 157, 166	8.9	127
1.10	154			8.11–13	112
2.23	154	1.9	153	8.15–17	110
		1.11	157	8.17–18	159
		1.13–15	166	8.17	126
		1.13–14	58	8.19–27	112

8.19	119	15	157	3.5–4.5	143, 166
8.22	119	15.7–13	157	3.5	143
8.23	63, 118, 167	15.8–12	40	3.6–9	143
		15.14–21	166	3.6	143
8.28–30	114	15.15–21	58	3.9–14	143
8.29	123	15.15–16	157	3.10	143, 156, 157, 162, 166
8.32	124	15.15	156, 166		
8.34–39	110	15.16	153, 157, 162		
8.35–39	130			3.16	143
8.35–37	130	15.19	153	3.17	143
8.38–39	130	15.20	153	3.19–23	112
9–11	113	15.25–29	157	3.21–22	143
9	168	15.25–27	157	3.22	147
9.4–5	40	16.5–16	112	4.1	143, 144, 146, 147, 166
9.4	119	16.7	150		
9.16–29	112	16.19–20	112		
9.22–24	168	16.22	76	4.6	147
9.23–24	154	16.25–27	108, 146	4.9	147
9.23	159	16.25	146	4.15	143
9.24–26	167, 168			5–6	168
9.24	123, 154	*1 Corinthians*		5.1–2	129
9.25–26	154	1.10–4.21	143	5.9–10	168, 169
10.12	168	1.10–17	151	5.9	76, 168, 169
11	63, 115, 155	1.11	129		
		1.12	48, 52	5.10	169
11.7–32	108, 155	1.17	153	5.11	168, 169
11.7	113	1.28	128	6.9–10	168, 169
11.12	154, 155	1.29	128	6.13–14	110
11.13–14	144, 156, 157, 166	2.1–7	91, 113	7	170
		2.1	92, 146, 147, 151, 166	7.5	129
11.13	58			7.7–8	110
11.14	156			7.19	63
11.17–24	168	2.4	128	7.28–35	110–12
11.17	54, 167, 168	2.6–16	147	9.5–6	150
		2.6–10	147, 166	9.5	147
11.24	168	2.7–8	92	9.15–18	144, 166
11.25–26	40, 146, 166	2.7	92, 112, 146, 147, 166	9.16	153
				9.17	143, 144
11.25	113, 146, 166			9.18	153
		2.8–9	91	9.19–23	3
11.33	155	2.8	92	10.13	129
12.1–12	112	2.10	147	10.32	168
12.3	156	3–4	152	11.1	129
12.9	119	3	157	11.2	152, 162
13.13–14	100	3.2	130	11.31–32	112
13.14	126	3.3	129	12	114
14.1–2	96	3.4–4.5	151	12.13	118

Index of References

1 Corinthians (cont.)		3.6	143, 144	11.23–29	159, 160, 166, 167		
12.28	124	3.7–21	144				
12.29	147	3.18	161	11.23	9, 69, 143		
13.2	146–8	4.1	144, 160, 161, 166	11.28	167		
13.9	127			12.1–7	160		
13.12	127	4.2–3	110, 112	12.4	128, 130		
13.21	119	4.4	153	12.7–10	160		
15	40, 120, 124, 152	4.5	153	12.7–8	112		
		4.8–12	159, 160, 166, 167	12.11	150, 160		
15.1–11	151–3, 166			12.15	159, 160		
		4.13–15	161	13.1–4	110		
15.1–3	151	4.13	161				
15.1–2	151, 152	4.15	161	*Galatians*			
15.1	151, 153	4.16–17	161, 166	1–2	148, 152		
15.2	153	4.16	160, 161	1	148		
15.3–8	151	4.17	159	1.2–5	112		
15.3	151, 162	4.18–5.9	110, 112	1.4	114, 126, 127		
15.5–8	147	5.1–5	167				
15.9	151	5.5	63	1.6–9	150		
15.10	151, 156	5.7	119	1.7	153		
15.11	151	5.15–6.1	110	1.8–9	153		
15.24–30	112	5.16	30	1.8	153		
15.25	127	5.18	144	1.10–17	151		
15.26–28	120	5.20	144	1.11–2.10	166		
15.36–45	112	6.4–5	159, 160, 166	1.11–12	146, 147, 149, 151		
15.42–44	118						
15.49	127	6.4	143, 160	1.11	153		
15.50–16.7	112	6.5	9	1.12	146, 166		
15.51	146	6.6	119	1.13–14	40		
		6.7	160	1.13	142		
2 Corinthians		7.8–12	112	1.15–19	151		
1.1–11	166	9.13	153	1.15–17	151		
1.3–11	159, 160, 166	10	153	1.15–16	63, 147, 153, 156		
		10.2–7	110, 111				
1.6	160, 166	10.10	135, 162	1.16–17	149, 150		
1.8–11	167	10.13–18	166	1.16	146, 153, 154, 166		
1.8	159, 160	10.14	152, 153				
1.20	63, 167	10.16–11.1	112	1.17	149		
1.22	63, 167	10.16	152, 153	1.18–19	147		
2.1	146	11–12	150, 160	1.23	142		
2.7	146	11.4–5	150	2	149, 150		
2.10	112, 146	11.5	150	2.1–14	151		
2.12	153	11.6	126	2.1–10	149, 151, 166, 170		
2.14–17	160	11.7	153				
3.3	143	11.12–13	150	2.1	149		
3.4–18	160	11.13	150, 160	2.2	146, 149, 170		
3.4	160						

2.3	149	*Ephesians*		1.22–23	118, 120
2.4–10	150	1–3	10, 111,	1.22	127, 154
2.4–5	149		117, 164	2.1–5	126
2.5	149	1–2	69, 125,	2.1–3	63, 64,
2.6	149		128, 129,		110–12,
2.7–9	149		167, 168,		167
2.7–8	63		170	2.1	126
2.7	149	1	122	2.4–10	110–12
2.8	147	1.1–14	166	2.4–9	167
2.9	17, 58,	1.1–2	11	2.4–8	140
	149, 150,	1.1	64, 104,	2.4–7	153
	154, 156,		105, 114,	2.4	153
	157, 166,		128	2.5	125
	170	1.3–14	69, 108,	2.6	53, 115,
2.15–3.7	110		140, 153		118, 127,
2.15	40, 167	1.3–10	91, 93,		145
2.16	125		110–13	2.7	119
2.17–21	167	1.3–6	118	2.8–10	49, 157
3.1–5	63, 167	1.3–4	113	2.11–3.13	58, 115
3.2	125	1.3	118, 126,	2.11–22	49, 53,
3.5–4.5	151		127, 153		62, 63,
3.5	125	1.4–23	122		66, 70,
3.7–9	167	1.4–5	126		108, 125,
3.10	125	1.4	112, 113,		140, 154,
3.13–14	167		123		167
3.14	63, 167	1.6–7	113	2.11–16	49, 62
3.25–29	167	1.7–9	113	2.11–13	140, 167,
3.27–29	167	1.7	12, 153		168
3.28	167	1.8–9	126, 127	2.11–12	138
3.29	167	1.9–10	108	2.11	63, 64,
4.4	119	1.9	92, 148		125
4.6	63	1.10	119, 141	2.12	126, 138,
4.8–9	168	1.11–12	125		167
4.13	153	1.11	145	2.13–18	153
4.23–24	167	1.13–14	63, 118,	2.13	138
4.26–31	167		167, 169	2.14–18	126, 140,
4.28–31	168	1.13	125, 126,		167
4.31	167		128	2.14–16	167
5–6	150	1.14	118, 145	2.14–15	115, 125
5.11	40	1.15–18	126	2.15	115, 125,
5.16–21	110–12	1.15	64, 69,		167
5.19–21	129, 167		106, 125,	2.17	167
5.22	126		138, 167	2.18	167
6.2	126	1.18–19	153	2.19–3.8	166
6.7–10	112	1.18	145	2.19–22	140, 142,
6.12–13	150	1.19–23	112		143, 157,
		1.19–21	124		168

Ephesians (cont.)		3.3–6	63, 150, 151	3.9–10	145
2.19	138, 167		151	3.9	92, 115,
2.20	50, 53, 70, 124	3.3–5	144–8, 150–2		126, 128, 141,
3	136, 144, 152, 154, 157, 158, 161	3.3–4	108, 128, 147, 151, 166	3.10	154–8 58, 115, 154, 158
		3.3	70, 92, 108, 138,	3.12	160
3.1–13	5, 6, 8, 14, 60, 61, 72, 131,		144, 146, 150, 154, 155, 167	3.13	126, 138, 158–61, 166
	135–40, 144, 152,	3.4–5	108	3.14 3.15	138 138
	155, 156, 159, 161,	3.4 3.5–9	144 111, 162	3.16–19 3.16–17	126 63
	162, 164,	3.5–8	110	3.20	160
	166, 167,	3.5–7	70, 125	4–6	117, 129,
	170	3.5–6	50, 149, 150	4	164 115
3.1–12	160	3.5	53, 92,	4.1	64, 158,
3.1–9	111, 154		115,		160
3.1–5	91, 110, 111		144, 145, 147–51,	4.2 4.5–6	126 50
3.1–3	126		154, 155	4.5	53
3.1	64, 106, 125, 138, 154,	3.6–7	138, 140, 143, 144, 151	4.7 4.9–10 4.11–13	114, 115 115 53
	158–60, 167	3.6	108, 126, 138, 140,	4.11–12 4.14–15	124 53
3.2–13	70, 145, 146, 152, 157, 158	3.7–8	146–51, 154, 155 166	4.14 4.15 4.17–5.14	70 53, 119 168–70
3.2–12	160	3.7	119, 139,	4.17–19	63, 64,
3.2–9	158		140, 143,		110, 167,
3.2–7	138, 142, 152, 154, 156	3.8–12	152, 156, 157, 160 158	4.19	169 115, 119, 120, 127,
3.2–6	146	3.8–11	115		130
3.2–3	138, 140, 144, 151	3.8–10 3.8–9	155 138, 141,	4.20–22 4.20–21	58 151
3.2	64, 69, 138,		142, 152, 155–8	4.21	64, 69, 106, 167
	140–4, 146, 152, 154–7,	3.8	111, 138, 142, 144, 152–7	4.22 4.23–24 4.25–31	169 169 169
	166, 167	3.9–13 3.9–12	91, 110 158	4.32 5.1	129 129

5.2	124	1.24–25	154, 161	*2 Thessalonians*	
5.3–4	169	1.24	161	1.1–10	112
5.3	127	1.25–27	161	1.1–6	111
5.5–11	168, 169	1.25–26	146, 166	1.8	153
5.5	127, 169	1.25	92, 141, 142	2.12–17	111, 112
5.7	168, 169			2.15	152, 162
5.8–10	169	1.26–27	91, 92, 110, 147	3.6	152, 162
5.11	126, 169				
5.12	126	1.26	92, 148	*1 Timothy*	
5.16	126	1.27	92, 155	1.5–7	111
5.23	53	1.28	155	1.11	153
5.24	129	1.29	161	2.7	153
5.27	129	2.2–3	91, 92	2.11–15	112
6.10–17	108	2.8–23	167	4.1–2	111
6.10–11	112	2.9–10	110	5.4–15	111
6.11	126	2.11–12	110	6.13–16	112
6.12	40, 129, 130	2.13	112		
		2.20–23	96	*2 Timothy*	
6.19–20	167	4.3	146, 166	1.8–14	111, 112
6.19	151, 158–60	4.7–8	11	1.8	111
		4.7	11	2.8	153
6.20	64	4.12–13	69	2.11–12	119
6.21–22	11, 64, 69, 105, 120, 146	4.13	69	2.20–26	112
		4.14	12	2.23–26	111
		4.15–16	69	3.1–9	111
6.21	11	4.16	9, 11, 55, 76, 164, 170	4.6–7	106
				4.12	105, 120
Philippians				4.17	153
1.27	153	4.20	12		
2	115			*Titus*	
2.5–8	115	*1 Thessalonians*		2.11–12	112
2.25–30	150	1.1	150	3.3–7	111, 112
3.2–11	135	1.5	150		
3.5–6	40	1.7	150	*Philemon*	
3.17–4.2	110	2.1	150	22	69
3.20	127	2.2	153		
4.18	150	2.4	150	*Hebrews*	
		2.7	150	2.8	127
Colossians		2.8–9	153	2.19	119
1	161	2.9	150	3.13	113
1.1–2	11	2.13–3.5	112	6.4–7.28	112
1.7	69	2.13	150	6.5	126
1.9	160	2.16	153	10.35–11.34	112
1.15–16	110	3.2	153		
1.23–28	161	4.3–8	127	*1 Peter*	
1.24–2.5	167	4.6	127	5.22–23	170
1.24–29	60, 161	4.13–18	40		

Revelation
2–3 98

PSEUDEPIGRAPHA
1 Enoch
103.2 145

4 Baruch
7.2 141
9.23 145
9.29 141, 145
9.31 141

4 Ezra
12.36–38 145

4 Maccabees
9.17 139

Jubilees
4.18 145

Testament of Abraham
9.24 139

Testament of Joseph
12.3 141

Testament of Levi
2.10 145

QUMRAN
1QHa
9.21 145
10.13–14 145
12.27–28 145

1QS
11.5 145
11.6 145
11.7–8 145

1QpHab
7 145

PHILO
De cherubim
48–49 145

De decalogo
53 141

De Josepho
167 139
241–42 139

De vita Mosis
1.82–84 139

JOSEPHUS
Antiquities of the Jews
2.57 141
2.87–90 141
2.93–94 141
10.177 139
18.262 139
18.265 139
18.278 139
18.283 139
19.166.5 87
3.p.11 87
7.391 141

The Jewish War
3.352–54 139
3.352–53 140
4.622–29 139, 140
4.626 139, 140

CHRISTIAN AUTHORS
Didache
11.11 148

Diognetus
4.6 148
7.1–2 148
8.10 148
10.7 148
11.2 148
11.5 148

Epistles of Paul and Seneca
1 1, 100
3 1, 100
5 1

Ignatius
To the Ephesians
19.1 148

To the Magnesians
9.2 148

To the Trallians
2.3 148

Pseudo-Clementines
4.15 87

CLASSICAL SOURCES
Aeschylus
Prometheus Vinctus
941–43 139

Albinus
Prologus
4 77
4.16–17 77
5–6 77
6 77

Ambrose
Epistulae
32 80
37 100
37, 6 100

Ambrosiaster
Commentarius in Epistulam ad Romanos
Arg. 1 123
Arg. 2–3 123

Anonymous Prolegomena to Platonic Philosophy
24 77
24–26 77

Index of References

Apollinaris
Epistulae
1.1	82
8.16	82
9.1	82
9.16	82
9.16.3	82

Aristotle
Politica
1253b	141

Augustine
Confessions
8.12.29	100
8.12.30	100
8.2.3–4	121
8.6.14	100
8.8.19–8.12.30	100

Aulus Gellius
Noctes Atticae
13.31.5	84

Basil of Caesarea
Adversus Eunomium
2.19	105

Cicero
Epistulae ad Atticum
16.5.5	81, 82

De inventione rhetorica
2.117	121

Cornelius Atticus
16.3–4	80

Cyprian
Ad Quirinum testimonia adversus Judaeos
1 Pref 3	93
2 Pref 73	93

Demosthenes
Oratio
18.26	87
18.30	87

Dio Cassius
41.57.3	87

Diogenes Laertius
3.1	76
3.47	76
3.56–61	77
3.57–61	76
3.57	77
3.62	77
3.65	79
3.1–47a	76

Eusebius
Historia ecclesiastica
3.25	25

Fronto
Epistulae
2.2	82

Galen
De Indolentia
14	84

Gregory Nazianus
Carmina moralia
8	87

Jerome
Commentariorum in Epistulam ad Ephesios libri III
1.Prol	107, 125, 126
3.Prol	125, 128

Commentariorum in Epistulam ad Galatas libri III
1.Prol	121, 125

De viris illustribus
90	98
101	121

John Chrysostom
Homiliae in epistulam ad Romanos
Arg 2	94

Homiliae in epistulam ii ad Corinthios
21.4	114

Homiliae in epistulam ad Ephesios
1.1	114
2.1	114
5	115
5.2–3	115
5.3	115
6	115
6.1	115
7	115
7.1	115
11.1	115
11.2	115
13	115
13.1	115
18.3	115
22.3	114

Libanius
Declamationes
24.2.25	87
Pref 2–13	94
Pref 14–21	94

Lucian
Charon
1	139

Dialogi deorum
7.3	139
24.1–2	139

Origen
Commentarii in Romanos
5.9   127

Ovid
Epistulae ex Ponto
3.9.51–54   81

Plato
Politicus
290c–e   139
299d–3   139

Respublica
2.370e   139
2.371a–e   139

Pliny the Younger
Epistulae
1.1   81
1.1.1   81
9.40   81

Plutarch
Vitae Parallelae
26.6   87

Polybius
3.62.2   87
15.11.1   87

Porphyry
Vita Plotini
1–23   78
4–6   78, 79
8.1–4   78
8.4–6   78
24–26   78, 79
24.2–7   75, 79
24.5–7   79

24.6–11   79
24.12   79
24.13–14   79
26.1–7   79
26.32–40   78
26.32–35   78

Priscillian
Canones Epistularum Pauli Apostoli
5   112
6   112
8   93, 112, 113
9   93, 112, 113
10   93, 112, 113
15   91–3, 112, 113
15   93
22   112
24   93, 112, 113
25   93, 113
26   112
28   112
29   112
41   111
71   111
72   111
73   111
74   111
75   111
76   111
78   93, 111, 112
79   112
89   112
90   112

Pseudo-Plutarch
De liberis educandis
8B   75

Quintilian
Institutio oratoria
1.8.1–2   84
2.5.1–9   84
10.1.76   94

Rufinus
De adulteratione librorum Origenis
41–43   80

Socrates
Historia ecclesiastica
4.23.11   101

Suetonius
De grammaticis
24   90

Sulpicius Severus
Chronicles
2.46.51   89

Tertullian
Adversus Marcionem
5   101
5.11   105, 170
5.17   105, 170

Thucydides
2.88.1   87
8.76.3   87

Xenophon
Oeconomicus
1.1–4   141

INDEX OF AUTHORS

Aageson, J. W. 42
Abbott, T. K. 45, 55, 56, 64, 155, 158
Agamben, G. 141, 142, 154
Alkier, S. 34
Altman, J. G. 23
Arnal, W. 65
Arnold, C. E. 47, 59, 61, 64
Aune, D. E. 47

Babcock, W. S. 113
Bacon, B. 33
Baird, W. 31
Barchiesi, A. 81, 82
Barclay, J. M. G. 40, 62-4, 156
Barlow, C. W. 1
Barrett, C. K. 35, 36, 41-3, 46, 47, 57, 58, 136, 143, 162
Barth, M. 6, 46, 59, 67, 72, 157, 168
Bassler, J. M. 39
Bauer, B. 18, 64
Baum, A. D. 47
Baur, F. C. 4, 13, 18, 19, 24-7, 30-6, 38, 41-5, 47-56, 60-6, 70, 72, 75, 88, 120, 136, 140, 148
Bauspiess, M. 24
Beard, M. 5, 6, 20, 21, 72, 75, 80-2
Beare, F. W. 46
Beker, J. C. 39-41, 57, 136, 153, 162
Bessiéres, M. 23
Best, E. A. 11-14, 47, 61, 64, 72, 137, 139, 142, 144, 148, 153
Beyer, H. W. 139
Bidez, J. 22
Bird, M. F. 113
Birks, T. R. 28
Blasi, A. J. 42
Blomkvist, V. 3, 83, 86-8, 94, 96, 97, 99, 108

Bockmuehl, M. N. A. 145, 146
Bodel, J. 80
Bornkamm, G. 33-6
Boyarin, D. 9, 40, 68, 171
Bray, G. 123
Brown, R. E. 33, 46, 47, 136
Brox, N. 47
Bruce, F. F. 10, 35, 36, 54, 56, 171
Buck, C. H. 36-8
Bultmann, R. 39, 51, 53
Butler, S. 90

Cadbury, H. J. 4, 46, 47
Caird, G. B. 56, 171
Campbell, D. A. 9-13, 37, 40, 64, 68-71, 107, 146, 151, 165, 170, 171
Cavadini, J. C. 102, 165
Chadwick, H. 46, 67, 89, 100, 164
Childs, B. S. 6, 39
Chin, C. M. 84, 93
Choat, M. 80
Cohick, L. H. 47, 64
Collins, J. N. 139, 140
Colpe, C. 59
Conti, M. 89, 91, 111
Conway, B. R. 163
Conybeare, W. J. 28, 29, 36
Conzelmann, H. 41
Cooper, S. 94, 98, 121-5
Cousar, C. B. 35, 36
Coutts, J. 11
Crawford, M. R. 89-91, 109
Credner, K. A. 33, 47
Cribiore, R. 84
Cullmann, O. 141, 142
Cumont, F. 22

Dahl, N. A. 3, 18, 54, 59, 64, 68, 70, 71, 82, 83, 85, 86, 88, 94, 96, 105, 107, 108, 117, 118, 140, 154, 168, 171
Darko, D. K. 59, 61
Dassmann, E. 41, 159
Davidson, S. 32–4, 45
Dawes, G. W. 62
de Boer, M. C. 39–42, 47, 57, 58, 137
de Bruyne, D. 89, 90, 94, 96, 105, 109, 125, 170
de Wette, W. M. L. 32, 33, 45, 47
Deissmann, A. 24, 39, 64
Detering, H. 64
Dibelius, M. 45
Dodd, C. H. 55, 56, 171
Dodson, J. R. 113
Dover, K. J. 8, 18, 27, 43, 75, 165
Dunn, J. D. G. 38–40, 56–8
Dunn, M. R. 77
Dunning, B. H. 59

Eadie, J. A. 45
Easterling, P. E. 79
Eden, G. R. 31
Ehrman, B. D. 32, 33, 47
Eichhorn, J. G. 33, 47
Eisenbaum, P. 166
Ellicott, C. J. 45
Ellis, E. 150
Elm, S. 22
Engberg-Pedersen, T. 40, 62
Ernst, J. 137
Esler, P. 61, 159
Evans, R. 7
Eyl, J. 140

Faust, E. 59
Fee, G. D. 144
Field, F. 114
Fischer, K. M. 137, 159
Fitzgerald, J. T. 3, 24, 159
Foerster, R. 94
Foster, P. 9
Fowl, S. E. 47, 59, 60
Frede, H. J. 91, 92, 94, 95, 97, 98, 106
Fredriksen, P. 39–41, 62, 63, 149, 166, 168
Froehlich, K. 113
Furnish, V. P. 38, 43, 136

Gadamer, H.-G. 7
Gager, J. G. 40, 62, 166
Gamble, H. Y. 17, 18, 79
Garlington, D. B. 156
Gaston, L. 9, 40, 62, 63, 171
Gaventa, B. R. 39, 40
Gese, M. 137
Gibson, C. 94, 96
Gibson, R. 5, 6, 20–3, 75, 80–2
Gnilka, J. 45, 64, 71, 72, 118, 137, 159
Godet, F. 33
Goguel, M. 33
Gombis, T. G. 59, 61, 158
Goodrich, J. 141, 142
Goodspeed, E. J. 4, 5, 11, 18, 32, 46, 67–71, 107, 113, 122, 165, 170–1
Gori, F. 121, 122
Goulet-Cazé, M.-O. 78
Grafton, A. 102
Greer, R. A. 94, 117
Gregg, J. A. F. 105, 126–8
Griffiths, P. J. 90, 93

Hafemann, S. J. 159
Halkin, F. 80
Hanges, J. C. 145
Harless, G. C. A. 45
Harnack, A. 18, 34, 171
Harrill, J. A. 35, 36, 59
Harris, H. 24
Harrison, J. R. 156
Hay, D. M. 39
Hays, R. B. 40, 62
Hederich, B. 89
Hefner, P. 34, 48, 65
Heil, J. P. 59
Heine, R. E. 95, 98, 103, 105, 107, 120, 125–30
Hendrix, H. 64
Hentschel, A. 139
Hermann, K. L. 163
Hilgenfeld, A. 32–4, 45, 50, 51, 65, 70, 72
Hill, R. C. 95, 119, 120
Hinkle, M. E. 59
Hodge, C. J. 166
Hodgson, P. C. 24, 25, 52
Hoehner, H. W. 46, 47, 64, 72, 140, 142
Hoffmann, R. J. 64
Holtzmann, H. 11, 31–3, 45, 50

Horsley, R. A. 62, 63
Hort, F. A. J. 31, 55, 64
Houghton, H. A. G. 90, 100, 130
Howson, J. S. 28, 29, 36
Hüneburg, M. 47, 60
Hug, J. L. 33, 47
Hultgren, A. J. 56, 57
Hunter, D. G. 94, 123, 125
Hupfeld, H. 31, 32
Hurel, D.-O. 23
Hurtado, L. W. 4, 17
Hyldahl, N. 36, 37

Jewett, R. 36, 37, 146
Johnson, E. E. 7, 39, 165
Johnson, W. 6, 7, 84, 93, 165
Joubert, S. 156
Jowett, B. 29–31, 164
Jülicher, A. 2, 3, 32, 33, 65, 68

Käsemann, E. 4, 13, 43, 44, 48, 50–4, 56–8, 61–6, 70–2, 124, 136
Kannengieser, C. 114
Keck, L. E. 13, 35, 36, 43, 57
Kelhoffer, J. A. 159
Kelly, J. N. D. 124
Kemp, A. 84
Kenney, E. J. 79, 89, 90
Kenny, A. 10
King, K. I. 49
Kirby, J. C. 46, 59, 64
Kitchen, M. 47
Klöpper, A. 45
Knopf, R. 33, 34
Knox, B. M. W. 79
Knox, J. 36, 37
König, J. 86, 104
Köstlin, K. R. 34
Koester, H. 32–4, 56, 57, 67
Kreitzer, L. J. 59
Kümmel, W. G. 24, 31–3, 65
Küng, H. 52
Kuhn, K. G. 59

Lafer-Sousa, R. 163
Lamm, J. A. 19, 20
Landmesser, C. 24
Lang, T. J. 89–91, 109, 142, 146, 147, 156, 158, 161

Layton, R. A. 98, 126, 128, 129
Ledger, G. 10
Lewis, C. T. 1, 79, 89, 100
Lightfoot, J. B. 10, 29–31, 54, 55, 64, 105
Lincicum, D. 24, 27, 32, 33, 64
Lincoln, A. T. 47, 59, 61, 64, 118, 137, 139, 140, 142, 144, 146, 148, 151, 154, 155, 157–60
Lindemann, A. 41, 42, 59, 64, 113, 118, 137
Lohse, B. 120
Louw, J. P. 139
Lovering, E. H. 18
Lüdemann, G. 36, 37

MacDonald, M. Y. 42, 47, 52, 53, 59–61, 137
Macdonald, F. C. 31
Mai, A. 89
Malherbe, A. J. 39, 86, 87
Mansfeld, J. 76, 77, 79
Marchesi, I. 80, 82
Marguerat, D. 41, 42, 57, 58, 136
Marrou, H. I. 84, 85
Marshall, J. W. 57, 140
Martens, P. W. 126
Martin, R. P. 46
Martyn, J. L. 13, 39, 40
Mayerhoff, E. T. 11
Mealand, D. L. 10
Meeks, W. A. 3, 24, 39, 40, 62
Merkel, H. 45, 50, 51, 54, 65
Merklein, H. 137
Metzger, B. M. 17, 31, 99, 155
Meyer, H. A. W. 45
Meyer, P. W. 39
Michaelis, J. D. 32, 33, 47, 102
Migne, J. P. 22, 23, 83, 88, 119
Mills, I. N. 100
Mitchell, M. M. 3, 95, 96, 104, 113–15, 130, 135, 166
Mitton, C. L. 2, 11–13, 46, 55, 141
Moffatt, J. 31–4, 45, 46, 124
Mommsen, T. 81
Morello, R. 80, 81
Morgan, R. 3, 25, 42, 43, 48, 50, 72
Moritz, T. 59, 62
Morrison, A. D. 77
Mouton, E. 59

Mratschek, S. 80, 82
Muddiman, J. 47, 118, 137, 139, 142, 154, 155
Munro, W. 11
Murgia, C. E. 80
Murphy-O'Connor, J. 36, 37, 59
Mussner, F. 45, 59, 72

Nanos, M. D. 40, 166
Nauroy, G. 79, 80, 100
Neill, S. 31
Neumann, K. J. 10
Neuschäfer, B. 126
Nida, E. A. 139
Nogalski, J. D. 69
Nüsser, O. 77

O'Brien, P. T. 47, 64, 139, 155, 158
O'Loughlin, T. 90
Olshausen, H. 45
Ong, W. J. 12

Paget, J. C. 30, 31
Paley, W. 27, 28
Penny, D. N. 47, 57, 137, 144
Percy, E. 2
Perkins, P. 47
Pervo, R. I. 41, 42, 57, 113, 137, 145, 152, 162
Peterman, G. W. 156
Pfeiffer, R. 76
Pfleiderer, O. 34, 35, 45, 50, 51, 63, 65, 66
Piere, F. 125
Planck, K. C. 34
Pokorný, P. 45, 59
Porter, S. E. 1, 18, 47
Price, R. M. 18
Purser, L. C. 21, 22, 31

Radde-Gallwitz, A. 23
Ramelli, I. L. E. 1
Reed, A. Y. 65
Reicke, B. 64
Renan, E. 34
Reumann, J. 142
Reuss, E. 33, 34
Richards, E. R. 13
Ridderbos, H. N. 38, 39
Riesner, R. 36, 37

Römer, C. 1
Robinson, J. A. 45, 55, 56, 64, 67, 83, 86, 101, 142, 155, 171
Robinson, J. M. 57
Roitto, R. 59
Rollens, S. E. 145
Rollman, H. 24, 48
Runesson, A. 140
Russell, D. A. 77

Salzman, M. R. 80
Sample, I. 163
Sampley, J. P. 59, 61, 62
Sanders, E. P. 9, 35, 36, 40, 57, 62, 63
Sanders, J. N. 46
Sanders, J. T. 64
Sandmel, S. 4, 67, 68, 165
Schäfer, K. 105
Schäublin, C. 76
Schenke, H.-M. 41
Schenkl, K. 100
Schepss, G. 89–91, 109–11
Scherbenske, E. W. 76, 83, 85, 86, 88, 94, 95, 97, 101, 130
Schleiermacher, F. D. E. 19–21, 29, 33, 47, 75, 76
Schlier, H. 45, 50, 51, 64
Schmid, J. 2
Schnackenburg, R. 45, 61, 64, 137, 139, 142, 154, 159, 160
Schnelle, U. 32, 33, 38, 39
Schreiner, T. R. 38, 39
Schütz, C. G. 20–2, 31, 39
Schulhof, J. M. 55
Schwegler, A. 34, 45
Schweitzer, A. 38, 66
Schwyzer, H.-R. 78
Scott, E. F. 33, 56
Sellin, G. 45, 64, 137, 159
Semler, J. S. 31
Shackleton Bailey, D. R. 21
Sherwin-White, A. N. 81
Shkul, M. 59, 61, 136
Short, C. 1, 79, 89, 100
Simonetti, M. 113, 114, 117
Soden, H. 45
Sogno, C. 20, 21, 23, 28, 80, 82
Souter, A. 94, 95, 97, 98, 106, 120, 121, 123, 125

Speyer, W. 47
Staab, K. 105, 106
Stanley, A. P. 29
Stendahl, K. 40, 56, 62
Sterling, G. E. 41, 57, 60, 136, 144, 147, 161
Still, T. D. 113
Stirling, A. M. 59, 61
Storin, B. K. 20–3, 28, 82
Stowers, S. K. 18
Strawbridge, J. R. 129
Suhl, A. 36, 37
Swete, H. B. 116, 117, 119

Tarrant, H. 77
Tate, J. 28
Tatum, G. 36, 37
Taylor, G. 36–8
Tennemann, W. G. 19, 20
Theissen, G. 39
Thielman, F. 47, 64, 142, 146, 154, 155, 158–60
Thiessen, M. 9, 63, 166
Thiselton, A. C. 151
Thompson, D. M. 27
Treloar, G. R. 29, 30
Trobisch, D. 6, 17, 18, 83
Turner, C. H. 102, 114
Tyrrell, R. Y. 21, 22, 31

Usteri, L. 38

van Kooten, G. H. 11–14, 12, 47, 59, 60
van Roon, A. 2, 46
Vielhauer, P. 34

Watson, F. 40, 62, 102, 144, 149
Watts, E. J. 20, 21, 23, 28, 82
Way, D. V. 51
Weiss, J. 34, 35
Weizsäcker, K. 34, 35, 45, 50, 65
Wendt, H. 145, 146
Westcott, B. F. 30, 31, 45, 55
White, B. L. 2, 6, 41, 46, 62, 135
White, H. J. 89, 91, 95, 106
Whiteley, D. E. H. 39
Whitmarsh, T. 86, 104
Wieland, C. M. 20–2, 31
Wieseler, K. G. 33
Wild, R. A. 137, 161
Wiles, M. F. 113
Wilhite, D. E. 113
Willard, L. C. 83, 85, 94
Williams, Me. 102
Williams, Mi. 49
Wilson, A. N. 36
Wischmeyer, O. 36
Wolter, M. 39
Wordsworth, J. 89, 91, 95, 106
Wrede, W. 24
Wright, N. T. 31, 37, 39, 40, 56, 171

Yee, T.-L. N. 61, 62
Yoder Neufeld, T. R. 59
Young, F. 114, 117

Zacagni, L. 83, 88, 94
Zachhuber, J. 24
Zahn, T. 18, 33
Zetterholm, M. 40, 166
Zuntz, G. 18, 83–5

www.ingramcontent.com/pod-product-compliance
Lightning Source LLC
Chambersburg PA
CBHW062223300426
44115CB00012BA/2189